BJU
and Me

BJU
and Me

QUEER VOICES *from the*
WORLD'S MOST CHRISTIAN
UNIVERSITY

EDITED *by* LANCE WELDY

THE UNIVERSITY OF
GEORGIA PRESS
Athens

Most University of Georgia Press titles are available from
popular e-book vendors.

Printed in the United States of America
26 25 24 23 22 P 5 4 3 2 1

Library of Congress Cataloging-in-Publication Data

Names: Weldy, Lance, editor.
Title: BJU and me : queer voices from the world's most
    Christian university / edited by Lance Weldy.
Description: Athens : University of Georgia Press, [2022] |
    Includes bibliographical references.
Identifiers: LCCN 2021061574 (print) | LCCN 2021061575
    (ebook) | ISBN 9780820361604 (hardback) |
    ISBN 9780820361598 (paperback) |
    ISBN 9780820361581 (ebook)
Subjects: LCSH: Bob Jones University—Students—Biography.
    | Bob Jones University—Alumni and alumnae—
    Biography. | Sexual minority college students—South
    Carolina—Greenville—Biography. | Sexual minority
    college students—South Carolina—Greenville—Social
    conditions. | Homophobia in higher education—South
    Carolina—Greenville. | Homosexuality and education—
    South Carolina—Greenville. | Christian universities and
    colleges—United States. | Fundamentalism—United States.
Classification: LCC LD457 .B58 2022 (print) | LCC LD457
    (ebook) | DDC 378.1/982660975727—dc23/eng/20220223
LC record available at https://lccn.loc.gov/2021061574
LC ebook record available at https://lccn.loc.gov/2021061575

To my immediate family,

To my extended family,

To my BJU family,

To my chosen family,

Petimus Credimus.

contents

acknowledgments

Earlier versions of stories from the following contributors were first published on the BJUnity.org website: Curt Allison, Bill Ballantyne, Andrew Bolden, David Diachenko, Blair Durkee, Elena Kelly, Rachel Oblak, Steve Shamblin, and Lance Weldy.

This project is the product of many voices, and I first need to thank all the contributors who willingly shared their stories for this collection. Your stories are important, powerful, and moving, and without you, there would be no book. Thanks so much for all your hard work and patience during the writing and revision process.

I also need to thank so many others who worked behind the scenes or provided encouragement, suggestions, opportunities, or venues to make this passion project come to fruition. Let me begin with my Francis Marion University family. The campus environment, especially my own English department, has always been friendly and collegial to me. When I came out at work, my then–department chair, Christopher Johnson, shook my hand and congratulated me. Chris, you will never know how much your act of kindness meant to me.

I need to thank a few more FMU colleagues in my department too. Beckie Flannagan, my current chair, thank you for your endless support and enthusiasm. To misquote the line from Katharine Hepburn to John Wayne in the movie *Rooster Cogburn*, "You're a credit to your sex, and I'm proud to call you my friend." Meredith Love, you're a valuable member of our team. Thank you for your constant encouragement. Jo Angela Edwins, can we just take a step back for a minute and say how precious it is when you remind me we're having a meeting? Thank you for keeping me on track during this whole process. Adam and Landon Houle, if you ever get the urge to change, please don't. Many thanks also to J. Mark Blackwell and Peter Whelan for helping me with my religious history and Latin questions.

I'd also like to thank the FMU English Department for help in securing partial funding to travel to the Center for LGBTQ Studies (CLAGS) at the CUNY Graduate Center, where I presented this book project in its early stages. FMU also supported this book project by awarding me a sabbatical and a summer research stipend. I'm grateful to be part of a university that values diversity. Special thanks to the amazing staff at the FMU James A. Rogers Library, including those in circulation, interlibrary loan, and acquisitions, and especially Cynthia N. Allen, Steven L. Jackson, and Steven Sims. Librarians rock.

Next, I'd like to thank my BJU family. That may sound weird, given the issues addressed in this book about BJU's fundamentalism. But I specifically mean people who are now part of the queer BJU community. Dan Marvin, thank you so much for reaching out to me and inviting me to join this community. It was extremely uncomfortable in the very beginning, but I needed that nudge to begin this journey to find myself. Thanks for your willingness to chat, listen, and provide advice. Colin Gray and Steve Shamblin, both of you were great sounding boards when I started the process of coming out. Thank you so much for all your help. Rich Merritt, thanks for being the catalyst for this writing project. Elijah T. Jones, you've been there for me at my lowest times and have seen me when I was tired and at my worst. We've known each other while being both inside and outside of fundamentalism, and I am so grateful for your friendship. Scott Olsen, thanks for always listening. There are too many others in this queer BJU community to mention right now, but I am thankful for all of you.

So many other friends and allies offered encouragement during the development of this book. I want to especially thank Carrie Hintz for her feedback and suggestions during the early stages of this book. With her help, I presented my ideas about this project at CLAGS. Jason Tougaw, Cynthia Burack, and Jeff Mann were all gracious with their time, suggestions, and encouragement. Sarah Einstein provided valuable input on where to find a home for the book. G. Elijah Dann, who has edited his own amazing anthology about leaving fundamentalism, provided helpful feedback when this book was in its early proposal stages. Thanks also to the anonymous reviewers for the encouragement at the proposal and manuscript revision stages.

To RT, TC, and AC: you each have left an indelible mark on my life, have given me wonderful memories, and have taught me the value of queer fellowship. Thank you so much. Also, much thanks to Lisa Bayer and the rest of the staff at UGA Press for their support and patience during this publishing process. Finally, I want to tell my immediate and extended family how much I love them. I assumed most of them would not be thrilled with this book, so I refrained from mentioning them whenever possible out of respect, including in this section. But we lost two beloved family members in a devastating manner during this pandemic, so I need to take this opportunity to say how precious you are to me. I hope you understand.

BJU
and Me

introduction   What Is BJU?

> Wherefore come out from among them, and be ye
> separate, saith the Lord, and touch not the unclean
> thing; and I will receive you.
>
> II CORINTHIANS 6:17

The Title

Bob Jones University (BJU) is a Christian, fundamentalist, nondenominational school founded as Bob Jones College in 1927 in Panama City, Florida, by evangelist Bob Jones Sr. In 1933 it relocated to Cleveland, Tennessee, before finally settling in Greenville, South Carolina, in 1947. Until recently, the ruling administration of BJU was dynastic: Bob Jones Sr., Jr., III, and finally Stephen Jones each served as his generation's university president. But when Stephen stepped down prematurely at the end of 2013 because of health issues, the university community was forced to choose someone outside the immediate family and elected Steve Pettit in 2014.

BJU might seem too obscure a subject for a book-length analysis, but it has been nationally recognized for decades. *TIME* magazine showcased BJU in a brief article for the school's twenty-fifth anniversary in 1952, and the *New York Times* reported on the death of Bob Jones Jr. in 1997.[1] Of course, the school has made national news in other ways that I will refer to shortly, but no matter the decade, BJU has brand recognition as a bastion of fundamentalism. Liberty University might be the current national face of evangelical colleges, but BJU has equal footing as the United States' premier fundamentalist institution of higher education.

For the record, we the contributors to this book recognize the double entendre in the school's name, BJU. Since we have spent time away from Bob Jones University and identify as queer, we can openly smirk about that awareness. These days, when some of us march in Pride parades under the auspices of BJUnity—a not-for-profit group of queer and affirming former BJU students *not* affiliated with BJU—we notice our name signs always provoke a delighted, bawdy response from the crowds. But most of us who contributed to this book grew up in a Christian fundamentalist community with very limited sex education, so during our time at the school, we were likely unaware of the worldly connotation of "BJ." Or, if we were aware, we probably would not have openly admitted it. After all, as the Bible says, we ought to think about edifying things, not about oral sex.[2]

The first part of this book's title, *BJU and Me*, works on several levels. I'm assuming that readers outside of fundamentalism, like those crowds at Pride parades, will instantly grin because of its inherent salacious connotation, but this phrase also resonates with former BJU students who recognize 1-800-BJ-AND-ME as the long-standing number for the school's admissions department, a number that establishes the desired personal relationship between student and university.[3] Yet this phrase connects well to the second part of the title, *Queer Voices*, because it specifically recognizes the book's focus on the LGBT+ student experience and relationship with the university. Collectively, we are the *Queer Voices* giving our stories about *BJU and Me*, focusing on how the school has affected our individual lives.

The last part of the title, *The World's Most Christian University*, is a bit cheeky, but by describing BJU this way it invites scrutiny in at least two ways. First, it questions how BJU sees itself as a Christian institution on a global scale. Clearly, the label "most Christian" absurdly defies quantifiability and contradicts one of the basic tenets of Christianity—humility.[4] And even though BJU has never explicitly described itself as the "most Christian university," some of its own descriptors verge on this sentiment: the Fortress of Faith,[5] God's Special Place for You,[6] the World's Most Unusual University.[7] Additionally, the university pledge insists that it has long "determined that no school shall excel it in the thoroughness of its scholastic work; and, God helping it, it endeavors to excel all other schools in the thoroughness of its Christian training."[8] While it is possible that any university pledge would announce its own exceptionalism as a means of marketing, a declaration such as this one further suggests BJU's aim at being the world's best Christian school.[9] Undoubtedly, BJU takes its Christianity seriously, and the *Queer Voices* in this book question BJU's fundamentalist policies and the disciplinary methods enforced there in the name of Christian love.

Second, besides scrutinizing BJU's reputation and institutional practices, this part of the book's title also focuses on the unexpected presence of queer students at a strictly religious place such as BJU. Given that most BJU students come from fundamentalist communities that are well aware of BJU's rules and conservative lifestyle, the reader might legitimately wonder: Why would queer students attend 'the most Christian university' like BJU in the first place?[10] What's more, is there—or could there ever be—a welcoming place for queer students at BJU? As a whole, the book's title takes the first step in addressing these questions. *BJU and Me: Queer Voices from the World's Most Christian University* provides behind-the-scenes experiences and explanations from nineteen former BJU students from the past few decades who now identify as LGBT+.

Defining Fundamentalism

When the contributors to this book discuss the influence of Christian fundamentalism on their lives, we are referring to BJU's specific brand of United States Protestant fundamentalism. Scholars describe this fundamentalism as a reactionary movement beginning in the late nineteenth century and early twentieth century against modernism—a "theological position" defined by BJU faculty member David O. Beale that, among other things, "rejects any or all of the Bible as the absolute, infallible, and authoritative Word of God."[11] Becoming more solidified in the 1920s after a series of pamphlets called *The Fundamentals: A Testimony to the Truth* was published to identify and preserve crucial fundamentalist doctrines, fundamentalists as a group began to take a different approach to protecting their belief system, especially after the disaster of the 1925 Scopes Monkey Trial.[12] This trial of a high school teacher being charged with illegally teaching evolution as part of a high school curriculum was supposed to champion the biblical creation account and reinforce fundamentalist doctrine; instead, it effectively painted fundamentalists as anti-intellectual. With their public image ruined, fundamentalists withdrew from the world and took it upon themselves to perpetuate their beliefs by constructing their own educational system, where, among other things, evolution would not be taught as a fact.[13] Scholars specifically list BJU as an example of fundamentalist separatism from this time period.[14]

But what were the crucial doctrines of fundamentalism? Various scholars have synthesized them down to five, six, or even seven basic tenets,[15]
but because this book specifically looks at BJU's fundamentalism, I include below the university creed—which composes much of the university charter—in its entirety, as it encapsulates many of the basic tenets of
fundamentalism listed by these scholars:

> [I believe in] the inspiration of the Bible (both the Old and the New Tes-
> taments); the creation of man by the direct act of God; the incarnation
> and virgin birth of our Lord and Saviour, Jesus Christ; His identification
> as the Son of God; His vicarious atonement for the sins of mankind by the
> shedding of His blood on the cross; the resurrection of His body from the
> tomb; His power to save men from sin; the new birth through the regen-
> eration by the Holy Spirit; and the gift of eternal life by the grace of God.[16]

BJU's fundamentalist creed emphasizes the need for an individual's biblical literacy and personal relationship with Jesus Christ.[17] In fact, a student must submit a written conversion narrative to enroll at BJU.[18] In
other words, BJU students must describe how they personally asked Jesus to be their personal Savior as part of their application.

Posting this creed here in its entirety also reveals the individual's articulated connection to BJU. We as BJU students were required to memorize this creed word perfect as part of our freshman orientation class,
and the entire student body recited this creed at the beginning of every
chapel session. That's at least four times a week each semester that we as
students both verbalized and internalized the regular chant of this fundamentalist belief system, and that's not counting the times we recited
it at other religious and special services throughout the semester. Mass
group recitation rarely sounds engaging, but no matter how unenthusias-
tically the student body may have chanted that creed on a daily basis, our
physical utterance of it established a consistent connection with BJU's
fundamentalism.

Separation from Evangelicals and Pentecostals/Charismatics

But these tenets only serve as one part of BJU's fundamentalism. The
other crucial part of this belief system is the doctrine of separation both
from the world—that is, mainstream popular culture—and from those
who affiliate with the world.[19] In his concise definition, Beale notes that

a "fundamentalist is one who defends the whole Bible as the absolute, inerrant, and authoritative Word of God and is committed to the biblical doctrine of holiness or separation from all apostasy and willful practices of disobediences to the Scriptures."[20] As the chapters in this book reveal, BJU students are heavily motivated to refrain from participating in contemporary popular culture activities including smoking, drinking, and dancing, as are many conservative evangelicals. But BJU students also refrain from other activities that may not be forbidden by many evangelicals, such as attending movie theaters or listening to (or even singing) secular music or Christian music that resembles the secular style.

As the twentieth century progressed, this vehement separation became a hallmark of BJU's practices, both as it disciplined its community from within and also as it distanced itself from the broader Christian community of evangelicals outside its campus.[21] By the 1950s, a growing demarcation developed between fundamentalists and evangelicals because of a difference in opinion on how to interact with mainstream society. Fundamentalists were resistant to what they saw as evangelicals' worldly compromise and alliances in areas ranging from theology to music standards. As a result, by the 1970s, fundamentalists at BJU had separated from mainstream religious figures like Billy Graham, Jerry Falwell, and Pat Robertson.[22]

Nevertheless, fundamentalists believed the same as religious conservatives and evangelicals about major political topics, such as homosexuality, but the problem for fundamentalists lay with any kind of ecumenical coalitions made in the process.[23] The same hesitancy can be said for the fundamentalist's political relationship with Pentecostals and Charismatics, denominations that hold similar religiously conservative ideas as fundamentalists.[24] Scholars list key figures in this camp such as Jim Bakker and Tammy Faye Bakker Messner, Oral Roberts, Pat Robertson, and Jimmy Swaggart, people who "share the biblical literalism and moralism associated with fundamentalism" but who diverge from fundamentalism's placement of the Bible as the sole religious authority.[25] Martin Marty and R. Scott Appleby note that "pentecostals give a far greater weight to prophecy, speaking in tongues, faith healing, and other 'spiritual gifts' than do fundamentalists," and George M. Marsden points out that the Pentecostal and Charismatic movements "tended to set the tone much more widely for evangelical worship, which became more oriented toward expressive spirituality, especially in contemporary praise music, and increasingly emphasized the immediate benefits of faith."[26] Fundamentalists object to the extent Pentecostals and Charismatics emphasize the workings of the Holy Spirit and also to the style of worship that allows for "expressive spirituality" and a genre of music that does not reflect a separation from the world.[27]

BJU's Institutional Separation: Race and Accreditation

Historically speaking, BJU's separatist fundamentalism has extended beyond the religious sphere and into the secular: it has clashed with federal law as well as governing bodies of higher education, actions which have affected generations of students. It is possible that BJU cemented its reputation as both old-fashioned and racist by the end of the twentieth century because of its interracial dating policy, but let us also consider the importance of the early twentieth-century, when BJU was founded as a religious predominantly White institution (PWI) in the southern United States.[28]

We could begin this discussion about BJU's policies on race and separation by first considering Martin and Appleby's observation that "the American fundamentalisms of the 1920s were composed of white citizens" and that African Americans "were not attracted to hardline fundamentalism, with its European philosophical background." In his section on "African American Evangelicalism," Marsden contextualizes this White fundamentalism phenomenon by showing how Jim Crow–era segregation was reflected in the church community: "Southern white church members, firmly convinced of the inferiority of the black race and reinforced in these views by growing racial prejudices in both North and South, often lent theological support to such separation and discrimination."[29] That historical backdrop of using the Bible to rationalize segregation leads us to focus on the titular question of the radio address transcribed in a 1960 pamphlet by Bob Jones Sr., called *Is Segregation Scriptural?*[30] Since no African Americans were allowed to be students at this time, we can already surmise Jones's answer to his own question. His anti-miscegenation views are clear in this radio address and in his refusal to "sign an act of compliance with the 1964 Civil Rights Act."[31]

Dennis Ronald MacDonald, a 1968 BJU graduate, recalls being in the audience during the 1968 Bible Conference service when Bob Jones Jr. announced that Martin Luther King Jr. had been assassinated and also declared his refusal to fly the school's flag at half-mast for an "apostate." According to MacDonald, the audience cheered Jr.'s response, which sounds consistent with a student body trained to absorb anti–civil rights rhetoric through messages from Jones Sr. and the biblical verses later cited by the administration to ban interracial dating.[32] MacDonald reflected, "Never in my life had I seen, never in my mind had I imagined, such an outpouring of racist hatred." He received 125 demerits for sharing his outrage to his dormitory prayer group and spent his last ten weeks before graduating under severe restrictions, including being campused, which meant losing the privilege of leaving campus.[33] His punishment serves as another example in a long tradition of BJU disciplining its community from within for questioning the administration.

Two years later, in 1970, BJU's racial separatism caught the attention of the IRS, sparking a lengthy legal battle about BJU's ban on interracial dating. Through the first half of this decade, BJU slowly began to allow Black students to enroll but kept the dating ban in place. BJU's fight for its tax-exempt status went all the way to the Supreme Court, where it lost its case in 1983.[34] In 1992, less than a decade after the Supreme Court decision, Bob Jones Jr. recounted the situation on a PBS documentary about fundamentalism, arguing that the issue didn't promote White supremacy because the dating ban was applied equally to all races on campus.[35] What he failed to acknowledge was how this ban disadvantaged and endangered minority student life in this artificial PWI campus environment: any time a man and a woman are in proximity or "alone" together, no matter how public the situation, it is considered dating.[36]

Quincy Thomas, a 1998 graduate, wrote about his experiences on campus as an African American student, chronicling the resulting clash between his faith and his status as a racial minority at a place he considered a "sanctuary for young Christians."[37] Unaware as a student of the school's racist history, Thomas maps the trajectory of his disillusionment and inability to ignore the presence of racism on campus, including a "The South Will Rise Again" poster on a dormitory door, student microaggression comments about the texture of his hair, and an overtly racist, anonymous note sent to his campus PO box.[38] Racial tensions heightened when he was physically accosted by several students "for looking at one of their girlfriends" and also accused by a staff member of interracial dating, an expellable offense.[39]

He explains the statistical predicament racial minority students faced daily: a platonic activity like eating dinner with a coworker in the dining common could be construed as a date. While BJU claims not to have kept racial statistics of its students in the twentieth century, Thomas asserts that "the number of African Americans on campus was demonstratively and obviously low," making it impossible to appease administrative guidelines by dating those of his own race and also to avoid the dangers of accidentally socializing too much with White women.[40] Approximately two years after Thomas graduated, in February 2000, George W. Bush spoke at BJU and caused BJU's interracial dating policy to become nationally scrutinized, which prompted Bob Jones III to appear on *Larry King Live* in March to make a surprise announcement that the ban, which he called "insignificant," had been lifted.[41] In 2008 BJU posted an apology about its racist past, which many saw as a step in the right direction, but student experiences like Thomas's reveal that this ban was anything but casual, invisible, equitable, or easily swept under the rug.[42]

BJU's stance on race influenced generations, championing theological separatism from the chapel podium and administrative separatism by denying enrollment based on race. However, in his Larry King interview, Bob Jones III tried to downplay the scandal of the Supreme Court case as being less about race and more about religious freedom. This same tune about diminishing the severity of BJU's separatist policy also applies to accreditation, which had affected all its enrolled students since its first year as a school.

Bob Jones III authored an undated pamphlet, *Taking the Higher Ground: The Accreditation Issue from the Bible Point of View*, in which he used separation from the world for the sake of religious integrity as the main reason BJU has always been against regional accreditation. In this pamphlet, Jones notes that "in the 1960s, Congress linked federal funding eligibility to membership in a regional accrediting association, thus making the accreditation process quasi-governmental."[43] Because of this lack of accreditation, any student who attended BJU before 2006 knows that few outlets existed for monetary support to pay for college besides taking loans directly through BJU.[44] But in 2006 BJU became part of the Transnational Association of Christian Colleges and Schools, a national accrediting association, allowing its students to apply for federal student aid. And then in June 2017, ninety years after its founding, BJU received regional accreditation through the Southern Association of Colleges and Schools Commission on Colleges.

BJU's regional accreditation is a revolutionary turning point in the eyes of many former BJU students who had long believed the administration's words about the religious dangers of being accredited by an outside organization. In his 1996 book chapter that covers BJU's treatment of accreditation and student life, Mark Taylor Dalhouse remarks about the ways BJU is "selectively separatist," such as boasting about its superior academic curriculum without verifying that claim through secular accreditation.[45] However, given the evolution of BJU's position on race and accreditation in the twenty-first century, we could tweak Dalhouse's phrase to consider how BJU is "conveniently separatist" as it alters certain religious convictions for the sake of financial survival in the current landscape of conservative Christian colleges.

As radical as a regionally accredited BJU sounds to older alumni like me, and as startling as it was to watch Bob Jones III announce on TV that BJU's long-standing rule separating race was gone in an instant, I have to consider these changes as a sign that perhaps other modes of separation may also be altered in the future toward other groups of people, such as queer students. But until that day, we can at least be encouraged that this new accreditation status will allow present and future queer BJU students to transfer to a more affirming school without the risk of losing money, time, and transfer credits that many of the contributors to this collection faced.

BJU's Separation from Sinners: Student Turmoil with Clobber Passages

A little earlier, I mentioned that BJU practices separation within its own community as a form of fundamentalist punishment. This punishment is predominately used against students who have committed spiritually egregious offenses. One kind of student susceptible to extreme discipline—expulsion—is one who secretly identifies or unintentionally presents as LGBT+.

Most BJU students have grown up in fundamentalist (or religiously conservative) communities with churches that emphasize what have been colloquially called the Clobber Passages: six specific verses or passages from the Bible (three from the Old Testament, three from the New Testament) that have been traditionally used to prove that homosexuality is a sin. Because most fundamentalist churches use the King James Version to literally interpret these specific passages, my discussion about these passages will use the KJV as well. In this book's concluding chapter, I offer a brief refutation to these passages using arguments published by BJU graduates that question the reliance on the KJV translation as part of a legitimate interpretation. But for now, I briefly list how these passages are used by fundamentalists.

GENESIS 19: SODOM

First, and probably most well known, is the Genesis chapter 19 story of Abraham's nephew Lot in the city of Sodom, where a mob of men intends to rape two male (angel) visitors. Because the word "sodomy" is still in our vocabulary today, it is easy to see why this story has become so difficult to defuse.

LEVITICUS 18:22 AND 20:13: ABOMINATION

The next verses come collectively from Leviticus 18:22 and 20:13 and are likely the second-most commonly cited verses to denounce homosexuality: each verse specifically condemns a man lying with another man and calls the act an abomination.

ROMANS 1:26–27: UNNATURAL

The third passage, Romans 1:26–27, is another of the more popularly used verses to censure homosexuality: the verses state that it is unnatural for men to have sex with men.

I CORINTHIANS 6:9–10: *MALAKOI*

I Corinthians 6:9–10 is the fourth passage, and it lists people who will not go to heaven, which includes the "effeminate" (malakoi) *and "abusers of themselves with mankind," both of which have been interpreted to connote homosexuality.*

I CORINTHIANS 6:9–10 AND I TIMOTHY 1:10: *ARSENOKOITAI*

Similarly, the fifth passage in I Timothy 1:9–10 lists the same phrase as the fourth passage—"them that defile themselves with mankind" (arsenokoitai)*—to suggest homosexuality is a sinful act.*

JUDE 7: STRANGE FLESH

Finally, Jude 7 rounds out the sixth passage by stating the reason for Sodom's destruction in the Old Testament was for "going after strange flesh," again, with the connotation referring to homosexual acts.

BJU reinforces its separatist practices by incorporating the Clobber Passages into its standards. The *BJU 2020–2021 Student Handbook* lists the school's beliefs about sexuality in appendix B and uses three of the six Clobber Passages as part of its rationale against homosexuality.[46] But the Clobber Passages don't really address gender identity, which is why BJU's appendix B uses three other passages to refute transgender identities.

First, it cites Genesis 1:26–27—about God creating male and female— as the establishment of "two distinct but equal genders" as a binary that must not be crossed. Second, the appendix uses Psalm 139:13–16, which discusses how God recognized us in our mother's womb, to argue that "individual gender is assigned by God and determined at conception." The final passage used against transgender individuals in appendix B is I Corinthians 10:31, which states that we are supposed to do everything "to the glory of God." This is intended to connect to the previous passage from Psalms because, according to BJU, "to intentionally alter or change one's physical gender or to live as a gender other than the one assigned at conception is . . . a personal rejection of His plan to glorify Himself through the original gender He assigned that individual."[47]

Through these passages, BJU argues that the Bible condemns homosexual and transgender identities. Remember, every week the entire student body articulates the university creed, part of which explicitly states a devout belief in the whole Bible, including biblical passages referenced in the student handbook appendix about homosexuality and gender identity. For an LGBT+ BJU student from any decade, this repeated statement of believing in a text that condemns who they are is a recipe for religious and psychological crisis. All the contributors to this collection have been at least indirectly affected by these passages, even if they do not address these specific verses in their stories.

Meanings of Queer

Just as the word "fundamentalism" suggests different meanings that need to be clarified within the context of this book, so does the word "queer." I want to mention four meanings of "queer" used in this book, consider the limitations of this word, and rationalize my use of it.

To establish definitions of this word, many scholars, such as Patrick Cheng, Kerry Mallan, and Siobhan B. Somerville, begin with the *Oxford English Dictionary*, which catalogs the origins and changes in meanings of words.[48] According to the *OED Online*, the first meaning of the adjectival form of the word "queer" in the early sixteenth century meant "strange, odd, peculiar, [and] eccentric."[49] Although the *OED Online* asserts that this meaning is rarely used after the early twentieth century, we could connect this older meaning to BJU as an institution because of its fundamentalist doctrine of separation from mainstream society, which would make its practices, beliefs, and university policies seem very strange to the general reader. Since its inception as a reaction against modernism and the teaching of evolution as a fact, BJU has marketed itself as that educational alternative from secular, mainstream schools, and the ways BJU has continued to operate can still be described as queer in this sense of the word.

But BJU would not have used the word "queer" in its promotional materials because of its second definition. As Somerville notes, "By the first two decades of the twentieth century, 'queer' became linked to sexual practice and identity" and was recognized as an offensive term.[50] Since its founding in 1927, BJU has well documented its traditionalist, heterosexual, gender-conforming values, so BJU would have branded itself as "unusual" rather than "queer," which would have been a derogatory reference to sexuality outside the confines of heteronormative traditions. To expound upon this second definition of "queer," we can explore two more non-derogatory ways this book implements this word.

Many scholars including Cheng and Meg-John Barker and Julia Scheele have noted a third definition: by the early twenty-first century, "queer" had come to be used as a positive, all-encompassing adjectival term to describe anyone with "non-normative sexualities and/or gender identities," so when I reference queer BJU students for this book, I mean they identify somewhere under the acronym umbrella of LGBT+ as lesbian, gay, bisexual, transgender, and other non-normative identities, such as pansexual and gender nonbinary.[51] Whenever possible, I have allowed contributors to use their own variations of this acronym with the understanding that they are referencing the larger non-normative community.

For our fourth definition, consider how the word "queer" can be used as a verb to mean a questioning or changing of specific practices. For example, by using the word "queer" in my book title to refer to LGBT+ BJU students in a positive light, I am reclaiming the word from its negative past. As Cheng notes, "to queer" in this sense is "about seeing things in a different light and reclaiming voices and sources that previously had been ignored, silenced, or discarded," and Michael Warner uses the verb to refuse the "minoritizing logic of toleration . . . in favor of a more thorough resistance to regimes of the normal."[52] Both of these verbs inform my intent for this book: letting the contributors tell their stories as a way of reclaiming their voices, helping people inside and outside religiously conservative communities understand why BJU was a part of our lives, and rejecting a religious regime that does not tolerate our existence on campus.

To recap, the word "queer" takes four meanings in this introduction: 1) it suggests how BJU looks strange to outsiders; 2) it describes the derogatory way BJU perceives those outside of the sexual and gender-identity norms, e.g., through the Clobber Passages; 3) it positively refers to LGBT+ BJU students collectively; and 4) it questions the negative image applied to former LGBT+ BJU students through BJU's fundamentalism. While I periodically suggest in this chapter that BJU's practices and public image appear "queer," meaning strange, I mostly use "queer" in this chapter and throughout the book to denote the third meaning—positively referencing LGBT+ students or the larger non-normative community.

But as much as "queer" seems to serve as the mainstream, all-encompassing word to positively describe a non-normative community, the word itself, like all language, has limitations. For example, it has been contested as a proper representative of identity from people of color. In 2001, Patrick E. Johnson suggested using the word "quare" instead to better represent the plight of LGBT+ people of color "against all forms of oppression—racial, sexual, gender, class, religious, etc." Sharon P. Holland argued in 2005 that the word "queer" along with queer studies and queer theory have been whitewashed to be more palatable to a mainstream audience, and BJU graduate Myron M. Beasley discussed in 2008 how similar words, like "gay," are contested in the Black community because they suggest a default connotation of whiteness. As an alternate word for "gay," he provides "affirming phrases such as 'same-gender-loving,' 'Adodi,' and 'same-gender-loving men of African descent.'"[53] This book project features voices from a PWI campus that was forced to admit Black students in the seventies and strongarmed into canceling its interracial dating ban in 2000. We should be mindful when identity terms are not fully embraced by racial minorities, no matter how mainstream those terms may have become. Language truly is dynamic, limited, and limiting.

Obviously, "queer" still has its flaws, but I am not using it as an umbrella term just for a convenient shorthand; I am purposefully using it as other scholars have done "to avoid dynamics of inclusion and exclusion" that can be found in well-meaning acronyms like LGBTQIA.[54] In other words, while LGBT+ might accurately describe the group of contributors to this particular book, I will be predominately using the word "queer" as a way of underscoring the point that queerness comes in many forms that are not always included in abbreviations. But beyond this argument, I believe that the word "queer" best suits this book's unique emphasis because of its intertwining relationship between the exceptionalism of BJU's fundamentalism and the special qualities of non-normative identities. We can appreciate the queer voices in this collection because of their multivalent lived experiences that combine the first definition (being called out as a separate religious "peculiar people"[55]), second definition (internalized discomfort from the Clobber Passages and other anti-LGBT+ rhetoric), and the third definition of "queer" (navigating a non-normative psychological or physical path at BJU and beyond campus).

Our stories show that we are no longer part of the BJU fundamentalist network. One of the ways our dissenting voices have been galvanized recently is under the auspices of BJUnity. To be clear, BJUnity is in no way affiliated with or sponsored by Bob Jones University. Rather, it is a charitable organization composed of former BJU students who identify as queer or allies to help queer and queer-affirming people "affected by fundamentalist Christianity."[56] Initially founded in 2012 as a means of combating homophobic statements made by Bob Jones III in the eighties, BJUnity stimulated interest through social networking and personal experience blog posts and made its first formal appearance marching in the 2012 New York City Pride parade. Since then, BJUnity has marched in parades around the Midwest and eastern United States and has actively provided individuals with resources for access to counseling, temporary housing, and other physical needs.

Purpose of the Book

The reader should take away several important ideas from this book. First, this collection of voices showcases a queer community from an unexpected place—fundamentalist circles. The concluding chapter reveals that queer students still currently attend conservative Christian colleges and need support. This book offers that support through the powerful message that "you are not alone," which can make a difference to any queer student feeling isolated at a tightly controlled conservative Christian campus. Beyond that, this message can aid queer non-students, allies, and their respective loved ones of any age around the world.[57]

Second, these stories reveal how the psychological frustrations between religious teachings and experiential feelings affect queer individuals. Somewhere along the way, we discovered that the prescriptive, fundamentalist life did not align with our experiential selves, and we want to explain how we arrived at the epiphany that a community where one's mobility, speech, and wardrobe were all tightly controlled was not worth participating in anymore. By giving names to a community erroneously stereotyped by conservative religious leaders, this book provides humanized examples for the queer community in the twenty-first century. Readers will journey beyond the caricatured coverage of BJU from a national news perspective to discover the real struggles of repression and survival that we writers faced on campus as we sought to understand our own sexuality and gender identities.

But this book is more than just a professional project. It holds significant personal meaning for me too. I am the product of BJU's specific brand of fundamentalism. In the mid- to late nineties, I willingly attended BJU, hoping to retrace my parents' footsteps and meet my future spouse on campus, as they had. Each dorm room was smaller than four hundred square feet and designed to house five people. The dorms' rising bells rang at 6:55 a.m., lights-out was at 11:00 p.m., room chores were checked daily, residence doors had no locks, gender-conforming dress codes were highly enforced, and leaving campus required a written signature.[58] Despite this description of a rigid dorm life, I must reiterate that I willingly attended and enjoyed my time there. However, keeping with the spirit of Johnson's use of "quare studies" that insists on the critic disclosing their position of racial privilege within an "oppressive system" such as BJU's campus, I recognize that as a second-generation White BJU student who grew up in BJU's system of networks and thus was well versed in fundamentalist cultures, rituals, and vocabularies, I didn't have to worry about BJU's history of segregation on a daily basis like Quincy Thomas did.[59]

Still, that privilege did not provide me with complete immunity: by the time I was twenty-two, I had been expelled. Like many of the contributors to this book, I spent years trying to psychologically compartmentalize my identity as a means of functioning in the spiritual, fundamentalist community while simultaneously exploring the carnal gay network.[60] And just like everyone in this book, I experienced a breaking point when I could no longer stay in the closet. I present my story more fully in the next chapter.

But *BJU and Me: Queer Voices from the World's Most Christian Uni-*

versity is not the first published account of experiences at BJU by a queer person. In his memoir, *Secrets of a Gay Marine Porn Star*, Rich Merritt thoroughly discusses his time at Bob Jones Elementary School, Academy, and University, including how he was expelled from the university, not for being gay, but for breaking other rules.[61] However, *BJU and Me* offers a first-ever behind-the-scenes look at BJU from queer perspectives over the past few decades: some from students who graduated under the radar; others who transferred but faced reparative therapy elsewhere; some who endured mandatory counseling sessions on campus; and still others who faced incredible obstacles after being outed to the BJU administration. Though all of these voices faced internal or external trauma, we all have found our own path out of fundamentalism.

Selection Process and Challenges

Compiling these stories proved to be challenging in several ways. First, all of us contributors found this specific genre of writing demanding. Some had been out of the practice of writing; others had moved on psychologically and were hesitant to revisit this time period of their lives; still others found it mentally challenging to remember enough specific events to provide a story. Any of these reasons may have prevented the participation of several other potential contributors I queried about taking part in this project.

Second, when finalizing the list of contributors for this book, I made the best effort to provide a balanced representation from both the LGBT+ and age spectrums while negotiating word-count constraints. I am extremely grateful for all the writers and am proud to have sampled an almost-continuous coverage of stories from the late seventies to the past decade. Others could have contributed to this book but would not have provided the LGBT+ balance I was looking for; because of my space limit, I had to forgo other additions for this project. That being said, those included in this collection do not represent an exhaustive sampling of the diverse experiences of queer students at BJU. Queer life at BJU is not monolithic: many of the contributors might have come from similar backgrounds, but their experiences vary as widely as their views on topics such as politics and religion.

Third, just as I earlier explained the limitations of the word "queer," so must I acknowledge the limited representations in this book. I just noted how proud I am about the healthy distribution of the age spectrum in this book, but I would have liked a better balance with representation from the bisexual and transgender communities. Furthermore, this book lacks more stories from people of color. BJU's reputation as a PWI with its unique history of racism is deeply tied to the limited racial diversity of its student body. Regardless, the population of BIPOC (Black, indigenous, and people of color) students who have attended BJU must undoubtedly include a substantial amount of LGBT+ individuals with important perspectives to share.

While this project is not sponsored by BJUnity, it has been shaped largely in part by the BJUnity connections I have made over the past ten years through networking with former BJU students via social media and at Pride parades. But these connections primarily consist of White people, perhaps for reasons akin to what Beasley, Holland, and Johnson have noted about whiteness being the default connotation for "queer" and a hesitancy for LGBT+ BIPOC participation in White queer organizations. As such, this collection of narratives includes only one BIPOC voice. Again, this project is not a definitive collection of voices of any kind from BJU. Instead, it's a sampling of a specific subculture, a project that materialized through social outreach rather than through academic channels, which might have attracted more diverse attention.[62] That said, I know that I and those at BJUnity would greatly benefit from meeting any interested BIPOC individuals. My hope is that this book will inspire enthusiasm for a second volume, a revised edition that will include better racial diversity, or an adaptation in another medium; or perhaps this book will encourage others to assemble their own collections of underrepresented voices.[63]

Finally, I worried about verifying when certain policies or terminologies changed in BJU's history, which would have required access to a wealth of archives. Fortunately, that kind of historical scholarship is outside the scope of this book. Instead, I refer generally to university rules unless specifically citing dates or student stories.

BJU's Cultural Climate: The Privilege of Being a Student

I have already described how queer students on the BJU campus have been burdened by the Clobber Passages and BJU's disciplinary practices of separation. To further establish the cultural climate experienced by all the former students in this collection, specifically in their relationship with the university, I provide the following university declaration, which can be found on numerous documents for students as far back as the undergraduate catalog from 1947.[64] I quote it in its entirety because it encapsulates the mindset of the university and provides a rationale for any actions it may take toward students:

> It is understood that attendance at Bob Jones University is a privilege and not a right, which privilege may be forfeited by any student who does not conform to the standards and regulations of the institution, and that the University may request the withdrawal of any student at any time, who, in the opinion of the University, does not fit into the spirit of the institution, regardless of whether or not he conforms to the specific rules and regulations of the University.[65]

This decree, still found on BJU materials in 2021, establishes several important ideas about the nature of BJU and its relationship with students. First, it requires students to be grateful for simply being a BJU student. Second, it suppresses any spirit of administrative scrutiny. Third, it situates the student's status as continually tenuous. Fourth, it informs students that simply following the rules is not enough to maintain student status. Finally, it reinforces the university's position of power as simultaneously authoritarian and subjective because "the opinion of the University" is all that is required to withdraw any student. The message is clear: BJU values the cheerfully compliant student and can expel anyone at any time. In fact, expulsion has been a tradition since the school's founding.[66] Despite BJU's reputation for military-like strictness, or perhaps because of it, the school still attracts students who desire a high-quality Christian education in a strict environment that demands structure, submission to authority, appreciation of the arts, conscientious self-evaluation, and utmost professionalism.

Perhaps this brand of spiritual elitism is one of the reasons BJU has been labeled "the West Point of Fundamentalism."[67] Student status itself is a privilege because it requires enduring a rigorous structure and it can be revoked at any time. Psychologist Angela Duckworth investigated why certain West Point Military Academy cadets completed the rigorous program and others did not, concluding that it was a "combination of passion and perseverance" or what she labeled "grit." While some have questioned her argument, and some academics may be fatigued from this overused buzzword, we can generally apply her concept to the motivation of BJU students.[68] BJU is a place where academic excellence, financial hardships, and campus restrictions have been spiritualized as character-building obstacles. As such, many students have been trained to find "God's will" for their life at this spiritually elite campus through an equivalent "spiritual grit"—a righteous fervor and determination to finish their spiritual race.[69] When the chapel speaker says, "For many are called, but few are chosen," it's both a spiritual and a student-retention challenge.[70] But spiritual grit is not always enough to predict success when student status is a privilege.

The contributors to this book did not enroll with the intent to rebel against BJU rules or to make waves within Christian fundamentalism. To the contrary, this sample of voices reveals the successful marketing strategies of primary and secondary school and church personnel, traveling ministry teams, and promotional materials that stoked their student enthusiasm and religious zeal for BJU. These voices include stellar students who consistently received few or no demerits; who developed friendships with the university president; who passed extra screening from the administration to remain as graduate assistants, faculty, and staff; and who earnestly wanted to remain in BJU's Christian fellowship after leaving campus, both on good terms and dishonorable terms.

True, a healthy portion of these contributors attended BJU because of church and parental influence, lack of options for Christian higher education, or maybe as the path of least resistance, but those reasons alone do not inspire any abject resistance to the campus. If anything, their attitudes convey their determination to overcome physical, psychological, financial, or interpersonal challenges by enduring the rigorous structure of fundamentalist training at BJU. But not all contributors held on to their spiritual grit at BJU for the same amount of time. Some lost their determination because of outside forces or internal disillusionment.

Contributor Descriptions

Readers will notice a glossary of BJU terms at the back of the book. This glossary serves as a primer for readers about the terminology used within the chapters. Because the chapters are designed to stand alone, I have made my best effort to define any jargon in each one.

Overall, the contributors address three questions they are most often asked:

1) Why would you go to such a controlling place, especially if you knew you were queer?

2) If you didn't like it there, why didn't you just leave?

3) Why and how did you get away from BJU and fundamentalism?

To better emphasize the different experiences, I have grouped the chapters into themed parts. This is not to say that the chapters are limited to contributing insight only to their respective highlighted theme. For example, Curt Allison's story is included in the part about student experiences at other institutions, but he also still identifies as religious, which could also place him in the part about religion and spirituality. The grouping serves only as a starting point for readers to notice and appreciate how each narrative highlights a specific facet of the queer fundamentalist life before branching out beyond its assigned categories into a broader mosaic of experiences.

PART ONE: SURVEILLANCE, CONTROL, AND RUMORS

The first part, "Surveillance, Control, and Rumors," highlights what BJU might be most famous for: its need and ability to keep track of its students. Lance Weldy's story in the mid- to late nineties examines how BJU functions as a site of strict surveillance and describes how he was expelled for being gay. Next, Bill Ballantyne describes enrolling at BJU at the age of sixteen in the early eighties and learning to keep his mouth shut to avoid negative attention on campus. Andrew Bolden's story shows what it was like to be constantly in trouble with the administration during the mid- to late nineties, which required many semesters of meetings and counseling sessions with spiritual leaders, all on a mission to make Andrew more masculine and less homosexual. Fawn Mullinix explains how her same-sex relationship with another BJU student caught the attention of the administration and got her expelled from BJU in the late nineties. Finally, Megan Milliken's story, set in the early to mid-2000s, reveals her love for her girlfriend, another BJU student, and her desire to protect her girlfriend from their "concerned" friends and administrators.

PART TWO: OTHER INSTITUTIONS

The next part, "Other Institutions," helps readers compare and contrast student experiences at BJU by describing life at similar Christian colleges after leaving BJU. Curt Allison attended BJU for a few semesters in the early eighties before transferring to a state school. He then completed a graduate degree in church music at Oral Roberts University, a Charismatic evangelical school. He is also the only contributor to this book who participated in the ex-gay ministry Exodus International. Next, Micah J. Smith attended BJU as a third-generation student in the early 2000s. Micah's time at BJU was short-lived because of his father's intervention, but he was allowed to transfer to Pensacola Christian College, a like-minded fundamentalist school. His time was cut short there, too, because of rumors that he was gay.

PART THREE: INTERSECTIONS

The third part, "Intersections," takes a nod from Kimberlé Crenshaw's notion of intersectionality and "highlights the complex interaction between identities and unequal power relations that structure our experience in diverse—often contradictory—ways."[71] This part looks at how the contributors negotiated different identities within a rigorous religious campus environment. Marshall, who attended in the mid- to late eighties, faced many financial obstacles in their attempt to maintain student status and to fit in to BJU's expectations about gender performance. They took time after BJU to understand their gender identity as a transman. Second, Sandra Merzib eloquently describes life at BJU as an international student in the late nineties and early 2000s. As a Canadian with no real connections to the university other than attending a BJU-oriented church at home, Sandra tried to adjust to the campus culture and learned that being honest with the administration is not always the best move. Next, Reid is our only non-White voice in this book, and his story about growing up as an Asian American in Hawaii provides a thought-provoking perspective about feeling culturally and socially isolated because of his fundamentalist upbringing. A student from the mid- to late 2000s, Reid recounts the chapel services about homosexuality and how he learned to identify fundamentalism's tactic of stigmatizing homosexuals to keep them isolated. The fourth story comes from Rachel Oblak, who articulates the linguistic, psychological, and physical complexities unique to her situation as a young fundamentalist woman who is attracted to men and women. A BJU student in the mid- to late 2000s, Rachel explains how she eventually learned about bisexuality, which helped her develop a better understanding of herself. The final story in this part comes from Blair Durkee, who explains the tension between her gender identity and the religious indoctrination at BJU in the mid- to late 2000s. After she graduated and left the BJU community, she found her authenticity as a transwoman.

PART FOUR: FAMILY, GUILT, AND SHAME

The fourth part focuses on the theme of family, both how queer individuals deal with personal feelings of guilt or shame when navigating their sexuality, and also what kind of acceptance family members do or do not provide. David Diachenko notes his long-standing cycle of same-sex activity and extreme guilt. Attending during the mid- to late nineties, David remained as music faculty after graduation until around the mid-2000s. Knowing that he could not be openly gay and a member of the BJU community, David describes how he left his job, his church, and his family on his own terms. Next, during his time as a student in the early to mid-2000s, Peter Crane describes dealing with his long-standing shame of being gay. After graduating, he worked on staff at the BJU Press in the graphic design department until 2012. With the support of his gay uncle, Peter began to love himself as a gay man.

PART FIVE: IDENTIFYING AS RELIGIOUS AND SPIRITUAL

The final part, "Identifying as Religious and Spiritual," showcases students who currently identify as religious or spiritual in some capacity and proves that queer former students can still find a relationship with religion and spirituality after their time at BJU. Jeff Mullinix (the uncle of Fawn Mullinix) describes his short time at BJU in the late seventies, when he faced several same-sex situations without the proper mechanisms to effectively process his feelings. After his time at BJU, Jeff faced a series of obstacles before becoming a minister in the United Methodist church. Next, Elena Kelly attended BJU in the early eighties and was strongly connected to the Bob Jones family and upper administration. After graduating and moving back west to pastor a church, Elena became aware of both her gender identity as a transwoman and also her spiritual beliefs. The third story, from Steve Shamblin, tells how he began at BJU in the early eighties and spent almost twenty years at BJU, first as a student and then as a staff member. After a long time away from BJU and church, he married Jeff Mullinix and found himself closer to God in his church ministry. Fourth is Christy Haussler, who tells how she attended BJU in the late eighties and early nineties. Her journey of self-acceptance began when discovering the Metropolitan Community Church as a safe space, a place where she and her wife still worship. The final contributor in this part, Avery Wrenne, was born in the hospital on campus. They recount their time on campus up to the early to mid-2010s. After leaving BJU, they spent time in theology school before finding their own spirituality outside of the classroom.

Making Meaning: Autoethnography, Vulnerability Narratives, and Religious Trauma

With these chapter summaries in mind, the reader might wonder, "How do we process these stories?" The answer comes by recognizing these experiences as representative of three interrelated kinds of writing: autoethnography, vulnerability narratives, and religious trauma writing. As Tony E. Adams, Stacy Holman Jones, and Carolyn Ellis describe it, "The term autoethnography invokes the *self* (auto), *culture* (ethno), and *writing* (graphy). When we do autoethnography, we study and write culture from the perspective of the self. When we do autoethnography, we look *inward*—into our identities, thoughts, feelings and experiences—and *outward*—into our relationships, communities, and cultures."[72]

The contributors to this book are not simply writing their coming-out stories, as inspiring as that endeavor may be; rather, they are dissecting and exposing the fundamentalist movement through their experiential responses as students at "the World's Most Unusual University." Moreover, Sally Denshire notes that the phenomenon of autoethnography can occur when "writers critique the depersonalizing tendencies that can come into play in social and cultural spaces that have asymmetrical relations of power," spaces that can include schools.[73] If we recall the BJU decree about a student's status being a privilege and not a right, we can certainly see how BJU represents this kind of writing both in how the administration controls all the power and also in how fundamentalism depersonalizes queer students by reducing their identities to biblical abominations.

Next, the stories in *BJU and Me* can be appreciated as vulnerability narratives if we follow Barbara A. Misztal's mindset that "human beings are vulnerable to many kinds of affliction."[74] Specifically, her book looks at three forms of vulnerabilities, all of which could be applied to the contributors of this collection and their relationship to fundamentalism and BJU: The first form, "our dependence on others," could connect to the absolute control that the Bible and BJU have over every student. The second form, "the unpredictability of human experience and action" and the "uncertainty and fear about the future," could refer to the student's status being perpetually tenuous and unsecure in light of BJU's subjective control. Finally, the third form, "that we cannot easily free ourselves from the consequences of past traumas or wrongdoing," could relate to any number of suggested or actual consequences meted out by the school, including forced counseling or expulsion.[75] In one way or another, the contributors grapple with one or all forms of these vulnerabilities in their narratives because fundamentalism taught us to have a healthy fear of God and authority figures. Misztal's last point about trauma segues into the third important way we can approach this book—through the lens of religious trauma.

The third kind of writing, religious trauma writing, stems from Marlene Winell, who has been credited with coining the term "religious trauma syndrome." She defines this as "the condition experienced by people who are struggling with leaving an authoritarian, dogmatic religion and coping with the damage of indoctrination." What's more, her original audience for this term is former fundamentalist Christians who "may be going through the shattering of a personally meaningful faith and/ or breaking away from a controlling community and lifestyle."[76] Just as we contributors have experienced vulnerability in one way or another, so also have we endured some form of religious trauma because of our time at BJU. Most of us attended BJU because of our "personally meaningful faith," so to be rejected by fundamentalism exacts a heavy psychological toll. Through *BJU and Me*, we incorporate elements of autoethnography, vulnerability narratives, and religious trauma as we write about our experiences, reflect on our relationship with a religious institution, and explain how vulnerable we were to a controlling regime that has left an indelible mark on us psychologically, emotionally, physically, and spiritually.

BJU's Denial of Skeletons in the Closet

To conclude this chapter, I refer to the preface of Daniel L. Turner's *Standing without Apology: The History of Bob Jones University*, which argues that there are no "skeletons in the institutional closet." "The closet is clean," he says, and he credits this cleanliness to "the administration's vigilance."[77] I began this chapter with a smirk about the double entendre of BJU, and I cannot resist smirking again at Turner's conclusion: his use of the closet metaphor is too fitting for *BJU and Me* to overlook. To the extent that the administration expels those it can locate who do not conform to its spiritual and behavioral expectations, Turner's statement is true.

However, *BJU and Me* reveals that the closet is not as clean as BJU would like. As a part of its institutional desire for control, BJU has always kept meticulous track of the whereabouts of most former students so it can send them promotional materials in the mail. Even in the past few years, it has spearheaded a campaign to request success stories from alumni to publish. Through the BJU Alumni Department, I received an email that asked for me to share my story with them.[78] I doubt BJU would want stories from me or any of the contributors in this book, but our stories have value and deserve to be heard. Though we are technically no longer accepted citizens of BJU's fundamentalist community, we are still representative voices of that institutional closet, telling our stories as a way of publicizing its existence, promoting our own self-worth, and queering the narrative.

BJU's closet is messier than the school would like to believe. Our stories are just some of the skeletons that BJU wants to keep hidden, and I have a feeling this book might inspire more skeletons to appear too. We have no doubt that some of BJU's current student body could be hiding in that closet for good reason. We hope our stories comfort them and keep them company.

Notes

1. "World's Most Unusual," 76; Honan, "Bob Jones Jr.," 86.
2. Philippians 4:8.
3. Further, those who attended BJU in the late nineties might recall a Bob Jones III impersonator singing a song called "BJU and Me"—a parody of Disney's "Beauty and the Beast"—which aired on WBJU, the student-run radio station.
4. Luke 14:11.
5. Wright, *Fortress of Faith*.
6. *Bob Jones University Undergraduate Bulletin, 1993–1994*, 3.
7. Turner, *Standing without Apology*, 143; Bob Jones University Brand Communications, "History of the BJU Brand." According to BJU's "History of the BJU Brand" page, when the school became a university in the late 1940s, "Advertising during this time talked about the unique product—so unique, in fact, that the tagline, *World's Most Unusual University*, would become a dominant branding element for six decades." BJU's long-running affiliation with this tagline further cements my intended connection to the "World's Most Christian University" part of this book's title.
8. *Bob Jones University Announcements, 1947–1948*, 3.

9. This scrutiny about BJU's specific brand of fundamentalist Christianity also nods to the work of comedian Deven Green's character Mrs. Betty Bowers, who satirically dubs herself "America's Best Christian" and whose videos expose inconsistencies in literal readings of the Bible. Green, "Betty Bowers Explains."

10. Paul Carlos Southwick addresses the flawed nature of this question as it relates to a current controversy with religious colleges. I comment on this in the conclusion. Avery, "LGBTQ Students at Christian Colleges."

11. Beale, *S.B.C. House on the Sand*, 209.

12. For a more in-depth, accessible distillation of the history of fundamentalism, see G. Elijah Dann, *Leaving Fundamentalism*, 2–12. For a more academic but just as equally enlightening history, see Mark Taylor Dalhouse, *Island in the Lake*, 10–19.

13. Jones, *Perils of America*, 31–33.

14. Marsden, *Fundamentalism and American Culture*, 238; Ruthven, *Fundamentalism*, 15.

15. Morris, *Revival of the Gnostic Heresy*, 80–86; Dann, *Leaving Fundamentalism*, 6; Ruthven, *Fundamentalism*, 7.

16. *Bob Jones University Undergraduate Catalog, 2018–2019*, 8.

17. Dann, *Leaving Fundamentalism*, 14–16.

18. Bob Jones University, "Undergraduate Admissions Process." Step 1 says to include "your personal profession of faith."

19. Dann, *Leaving Fundamentalism*, 8; Dalhouse, *Island in the Lake*, 3–4; Beale, *In Pursuit of Purity*, 6.

20. Beale, *S.B.C. House on the Sand*, 207.

21. Stephanie Firebaugh Rose and Michael W. Firmin note, "Evangelicalism is a broad category that includes Christian believers who adhere to the authority of Scripture, eternal salvation through faith in Jesus Christ, and the importance of sharing the 'evangel'— meaning the good news of Christ." They go on to say that "fundamentalism is a subgroup of evangelicalism . . . that shares similar basic doctrinal values with evangelicalism, yet is characterized by a commitment to separatism and uncompromising enforcements of the 'fundamental' beliefs, a strict belief in moral absolutes, and the application of biblical principles (e.g., sexual purity and virtue) to daily life." Rose and Firmin, "Racism in Interracial Dating," 146.

22. Dann, *Leaving Fundamentalism*, 8–10; Dalhouse, *Island in the Lake*, 88–116.

23. Turner, *Standing without Apology*, 246–47.

24. Marty and Appleby, *The Glory and the Power*, 68. Marty and Appleby note that fundamentalists and Pentecostals and Charismatics "could join in matters having to do with personal and familial values, or single issues in politics. . . . But the two groups, along with the evangelicals, often found validity in a common political front which became particularly strong in the 1960s and 1970s."

25. Marty and Appleby, *The Glory and the Power*, 43; Marsden, *Fundamentalism and American Culture*, 236; Marsden, *Understanding Fundamentalism and Evangelicalism*, 78.

26. Marty and Appleby, *The Glory and the Power*, 43; Marsden, *Fundamentalism and American Culture*, 236.

27. Dann, *Leaving Fundamentalism*, 11. According to G. Elijah Dann, Charismatics transcend denominations and differed with Pentecostals because they believed "their Pentecostal brethren overemphasized the ability to speak in tongues at the expense of all the other gifts of the Spirit." For a better summary of the similarities and differences, see Dann, *Leaving Fundamentalism*, 10–12.

28. Brown and Dancy, "Predominantly White Institutions," 523. The authors note this term is "used to describe institutions of higher learning in which Whites account for 50% or greater of the student enrollment. However, the majority of these institutions may also be understood as historically White institutions in recognition of the binarism and exclusion supported by the United States prior to 1964."

29. Martin and Appleby, *The Glory and the Power*, 65; Marsden, *Understanding Fundamentalism and Evangelicalism*, 47. Marsden says that "Black Protestants were one of the largest American religious groups who were shaped by the evangelical heritage and preserved it the longest; but because of racial segregation that isolated them from their white counterparts, they seldom used the term 'evangelical,' and their experience is usually regarded as a distinct type in itself" (46). See also the section "African American Evangelicalism," in Marsden, *Understanding Fundamentalism and Evangelicalism*, 46–50.

30. Lewis, "A Is for Archive," 15–18; Dalhouse, *Island in the Lake*, 155; Babinski, *Leaving the Fold*, 38–39; Jones, *Is Segregation Scriptural?*

31. Dalhouse, *Island in the Lake*, 156.

32. *Bob Jones University Student Handbook, 1970–71*, 8; *Religious Freedom Imperiled*, 41. The 1970–71 student handbook states, "Bob Jones University will not retain any student who is directly or indirectly involved in 'civil rights' or other demonstrations, riots, or acts of violence." *Religious Freedom Imperiled*, the pamphlet published in the eighties, articulates the school's long-standing view on this matter under the section "Bob Jones University's Position on Interracial Marriage," citing the following verses: Acts 17:26; Genesis 10:5, 32; Genesis 11:8, 9; Deuteronomy 32:8; Daniel 7:13, 14; Zechariah 14; Revelation 11:15; Revelation 21:24; Romans 9:19–24.

33. MacDonald, "Dennis Ronald MacDonald," 111; *The Glory and the Power*. MacDonald also speaks about this memory in *The Glory and the Power*.

34. Dalhouse, *Island in the Lake*, 155–58.

35. *The Glory and the Power*.

36. I say "alone" because technically a man and a woman would never be allowed to be completely alone without some kind of chaperone or public-surveillance component. The student handbook specifies times when co-ed students could socialize together in specific locations, such as front campus or sites of athletic games. But these rules also applied to men and women who might not even know each other. For example, the Periodicals Department in the BJU Mack Library had several massive tables where students could study together, but part of my job as a student worker was to make sure men and women were not sitting at the same table. A man could be sitting at one end of the table and a woman sitting eight to ten feet away at the opposite end, yet our job required us to ask one of them to move to another table. (Usually, we would ask the man.) It didn't matter that the two clearly didn't know each other. What mattered was that this was not a sanctioned public place for a man and a woman to be "dating," or in close proximity. See Dalhouse, *Island in the Lake*, 144 for more discussion about no dating in the library.

37. Thomas, "Performing White and Fine," 168.

38. Thomas, "Performing White and Fine," 169–72. To read more about how "Afro hair, particularly when it is allowed to do what it naturally does, is politicized," see Martin and Washington, "Kitchens and Edges," 87.

39. Thomas, "Performing White and Fine," 173; *Bob Jones University Student Handbook, 1997–1998*, 28. Thomas was informed by his dormitory supervisor about the serious accusation, but when he inquired about specifics, his supervisor backtracked and said a staff member commented that Thomas looked like he would date interracially. This administrative tactic of accusing students of expellable offenses without concrete evidence

is designed to trick or guilt confessions out of students. It is a strategy of surveillance and manipulation by the administration similar to ones described by contributors in this collection.

Thomas's fear of having his friendships mistaken for interracial innuendo and dating could be considered through the lens of W. E. B. Du Bois's concept of the double-consciousness: "It is a peculiar sensation, this double-consciousness, this sense of always looking at one's self through the eyes of others, of measuring one's soul by the tape of a world that looks on in amused contempt and pity." At BJU, Thomas had to constantly look at himself through the eyes of White fundamentalists who would see a Black man as a danger that must be separated from White women. Whom he could socialize with on campus was staggeringly limited because of his race. Du Bois, *The Souls of Black Folk*, 2.

40. Thomas, "Performing White and Fine," 174; "Good Luck!," 66. Thomas comments about the Black student population in the late nineties: "When I attended, I knew few black students who stayed for a prolonged period, and while some of them may have been in my general education classes, I was the only African American in any of the courses related to my major or my minor. Typically, black students would leave after a first semester or after their freshmen year. Personally, their departure posed a difficulty for me as I tried to build relationships and community." His statement is consistent with my experience in the PWP 414: Poetry Writing class we took together in the Spring 1997 semester. He was the only Black student in an upper-level class of eighteen.

41. Turner, *Standing without Apology*, 248–50; Jones III, "Dr. Bob Jones III Discusses."

42. Bob Jones University, "Statement about Race."

43. Jones III, *Taking the Higher Ground*, 4.

44. *Bob Jones University Undergraduate Bulletin, 1993–1994*, 32. For example, the section on financial aid in the 1993–94 undergraduate bulletin states: "Our students are denied aid through government-sponsored programs because of the University's religious convictions." Because of this, most financial aid available for students was limited to loans either from the school or outside companies.

45. Dalhouse, *Island in the Lake*, 118.

46. *Bob Jones University Student Handbook, 2020–2021*, 68.

47. *Bob Jones University Student Handbook, 2020–2021*, 68.

48. Cheng, *Radical Love*, 3; Mallan, "Queer," 161; Somerville, "Queer," 203.

49. *Oxford English Dictionary*, 3rd ed., "queer, adj. 1a."

50. Ibid., "queer, adj. 3"; Somerville, "Queer," 204.

51. Cheng, *Radical Love*, 3; Barker and Scheele, *Queer*, 11; University of Guelph, "LGBTQ2IA+ Students"; Henderson, *Queer Studies*, 18–29. Not everyone uses the same generalized acronym, which made it difficult for me to choose one just for this sentence alone. For example, the University of Guelph Student Experience page mentions "the term LGBTQ2IA+, which stands for Lesbian, Gay, Bisexual, Transgender, Queer, Questioning, Two-Spirit, Intersex, Asexual, and other identities that fall outside of cisgender and heterosexual paradigms." For an extended conversation about this topic, see Bruce Henderson's *Queer Studies* chapter 1, "Queering Language: Words and Worlds," specifically the section "LGBTQIA+: Alphabet Soup or Little Boxes?"

52. Cheng, *Radical Love*, 6; Warner, "Introduction," xxvi; Henderson, *Queer Studies*, 15. Henderson also notes that the verb "is often used to mean a process by which some phenomenon (a social event, an artistic text, a set of attitudes) is reevaluated and reread in ways that break down assumptions of what is 'normal.'"

53. Johnson, "'Quare' Studies," 97; Holland, "Foreword", ix; Beasley, "'Tribute to the Ancestors,'" 448. Special thanks to Myron M. Beasley for his crucial insights about this section.

54. Matos and Wargo, "Editors' Introduction," 1; Henderson, *Queer Studies*, 4. I would also echo Bruce Henderson's similar conversation about his choice to use "queer" over "LGBT" for his book title when he says that "LGBT" "has become somewhat outmoded, as various, more specific ways of describing sexual identity have come into existence."

55. I Peter 2:9.

56. BJUnity, "About."

57. REAP. Obviously, BJU citizens are not the only people who have ever struggled reconciling faith and sexuality. As the Religious Exemption Accountability Project (REAP) notes, "We're building a nationwide movement to show LGBTQ students facing discrimination on religious campuses that they are not alone."

58. See Dalhouse, *Island in the Lake*, 142 for more discussion of dorm life.

59. Johnson, "'Quare' Studies," 103.

60. Elsewhere, I have taken the beginning steps to articulate this phenomenon. I have written on the relationship between religious cognitive dissonance and fundamentalism, have published about being gay and fundamentalist (what I've termed "fundy-queer"), and plan to write more about this topic soon. Weldy, "Religious Cognitive Dissonance," 35–46; Weldy, "Graphically/Ubiquitously Separate," 263–77; Weldy, "Part 1: Wounded Children?"

61. Merritt, *Secrets of a Gay Marine*.

62. Weldy, "Queer Life at Bob Jones"; "The Call for Papers Website." I did, however, advertise my intentions through my presentation at CUNY CLAGS, which was about this topic in its early stages. Since this book is not a collection of scholarly essays and since the majority of the contributors to this collection are not working within academia, I knew I would need to query through other channels besides the usual route of the Call for Papers website, but perhaps I should have, and I take ownership of that mistake.

63. Special thanks to Myron M. Beasley for his important thoughts about this section.

64. *Bob Jones University Announcements, 1947–1948*, 2.

65. *Bob Jones University Announcements, 1947–1948*, 2.

66. As Turner notes, seventeen of the eighty-five students were expelled that first year "for violations of campus rules." Turner, *Standing without Apology*, 38.

67. For example, the narrator gives BJU this label in *The Glory and the Power*.

68. Duckworth, *Grit*, 8; Daniel Engber, "Is 'Grit' Really."

69. II Timothy 4:7.

70. Matthew 22:14.

71. Barker and Scheele, *Queer*, 47.

72. Adams et al., *Autoethnography*, 46.

73. Denshire, "Autoethnography," 2.

74. Misztal, *The Challenges of Vulnerability*, 2; "Dr. Todd Couch." Special thanks to Francis Marion University Sociology Professor Todd Couch for introducing me to this term.

75. Misztal, *The Challenges of Vulnerability*, 8.

76. Winell, "Understanding Religious Trauma Syndrome."

77. Turner, *Standing without Apology*, viii.

78. Bob Jones University, e-mail message to author.

PART ONE

Surveillance, Control,
and Rumors

Whither shall I go from thy spirit? or whither shall
I flee from thy presence? If I ascend up into heaven,
thou art there: if I make my bed in hell, behold, thou
art there. If I take the wings of the morning, and
dwell in the uttermost parts of the sea; Even there
shall thy hand lead me, and thy right hand shall
hold me.

PSALM 139:7–10

Most fundamentalist children are trained early about the attributes of
God, especially His three O's: omniscience, omnipotence, and omnipresence. The obvious aspect to highlight from this passage in Psalms would
be God's omnipresence, citing His ability to be everywhere at once. But I
can see God's omniscience factoring into this scenario from Psalms too. If
He is already everywhere, then He already *knows* where you are wherever
you go. Even His omnipotence is suggested near the end of the passage,
with His strength to lead and hold in the most extreme elemental envi-
ronments. With passages like this, fundamentalist youth are taught to enjoy the pleasant security of being cared for by an Almighty God.

This specific passage from Psalms was quite popular for students to
memorize at BJU too. I'm fairly sure it was used in several different required Bible classes, but the one I remember it from was BI 502: Bible
Doctrines, part of a two-semester course required for the majority of the
student body. These classes placed heavy emphasis on weekly King James
verse memorization to reinforce the respective thematic doctrine covered
in the curriculum. Just like the fundamentalist child, the earnest BJU
student would find comfort in a God who can protect them anywhere.
But the five stories in this section ask the reader to reconsider these verses
from Psalm 139 in the context of living on BJU's campus: What happens
when authoritarian, benevolent omnipresence sours into surveillance?
How do rumors perpetuate the culture of surveillance? And how does
surveillance reinforce BJU's control on campus?

Lance Weldy's story describes BJU as a site of strict surveillance disguised as a safe, spiritual space where parents can send their children. Set in the mid- to late nineties, my story describes my adjustments to dormitory life as I simultaneously explored my growing same-sex desires and worried about jeopardizing my status as a BJU student. I demonstrate how the campus operates on rumors and damning information, which pressured me to shun my good friend to escape the gay rumors about us. My expulsion was the direct result of the surveillance network. Second, Bill Ballantyne's story catalogs both how BJU factored into contemporary national news with its 1980s Supreme Court case about tax exemption and also how BJU manufactured a specific, caricatured representation of homosexuality to students during the beginnings of the AIDS epidemic. But he also mentions that having no privacy in the dorms elicited perplexing dormitory announcements banning back rubs. Through "purge" events, where students tattled to avoid serious punishment, Bill learned to keep his mouth shut.

Andrew Bolden's exposé of his time during the mid- to late nineties details how a complaint to the administration from a former friend leads the dean of men to ask him about his homosexual tendencies. For the rest of his college career there, Andrew faced being blacklisted from certain opportunities related to his major, being shunned by friends, and being forced to attend masculinity counseling sessions. He learned that being honest about spiritual matters was only rewarded with more administrative scrutiny. Attending BJU in the late nineties, Fawn Mullinix, the niece of Jeff Mullinix, whose story appears later in this collection, is a third-generation BJU student. Unable to accept her lesbian identity because of her fundamentalist faith, Fawn nevertheless developed a same-sex relationship with another BJU student that crescendoed into crisis mode when their privacy was violated under the surveillance culture. She and her girlfriend faced the tough decision of how to leave campus on their own terms and not under BJU's control.

In the 1992 PBS documentary about fundamentalism, the camera crew spends an extensive time on BJU's campus interviewing various people. One student, Jessica Lloyd, explains her rationale for attending BJU, noting that she was living on her own in Los Angeles: "I think one of the big reasons I was attracted to it is because there is so much order here. And when I got here, you know, I had a lot of disorder going on, and it was attractive to me."[1] BJU's system of order is also what attracted Megan Milliken to BJU during her time on campus in the early to mid-

2000s. Her story finishes this part by illustrating how disenchanted she became when the structured stability of campus devolved into rumors begun by students about her and her girlfriend, another BJU student. Megan's quick thinking saved her from trouble several times, including in a meeting with a school counselor. The essays in this part provoke the reader to consider how far a Christian campus will go to maintain control over its students.

Note

1. *The Glory and the Power.*

I don't remember if he was a former or current BJU student, but after a few minutes sitting next to me, he confronted me—as good BJU Christians do. He first asked me to step outside so he could speak more freely to me, which was very considerate. His line of questioning immediately indicated that he knew I was a BJU student. He asked about my actions in this disappointed, fatherly tone, and my heart sank. Then, he bluntly asked for my name.

A Father's Warning

"Remember, Lance," my father said, "there are unsaved people everywhere—even at Bob Jones University." It was the summer of 1994, and I was seventeen, a rising senior in high school. I was getting ready to fly from Illinois to South Carolina, where I would take six college credit hours at BJU as part of their Limited Early Admissions Program (LEAP). The previous year, my mother had noticed in BJU's *Voice of the Alumni* magazine that children of alumni could take college classes tuition-free through LEAP, as long as they stayed in the dorms. I qualified to participate because my parents were both alumni. In fact, they had met at BJU.

"Take the rules very seriously," my father continued. "People can do stupid stuff without realizing the consequences." He ought to know. As part of his duties in the early seventies as a hall monitor, BJU's version of a resident assistant, he had observed all kinds of student behavior. "Even when classes are officially over, don't get wild. One time, after exams were finished but before commencement, a guy threw water balloons out of his dorm window just to be stupid. They shipped him."

They shipped him. Expelled him.

I couldn't respond immediately because his words of caution were still sinking in. I slowly processed the image of a guy with water balloons and wondered how that expelling process worked. Growing up, we had been taught that God was omnipresent and therefore always watching us. God's omnipresence automatically prompted a series of questions for me about this balloon incident: Had somebody seen him do it? Did somebody report him to someone? Was somebody at BJU *always* watching? Then, I worked backward to the first thing my dad told me, which actually terrified me far worse than getting expelled: there were unsaved people at BJU. Could he be serious?

Up to that point, everything I had associated with BJU had been extremely positive. Technically speaking, if it weren't for BJU, I wouldn't have been born. BJU was the place where my mother and father had eventually begun their married, Christian lives together. As a child, I had enjoyed looking through their old college yearbooks, picturing the kind of wholesome fun they had enjoyed while on campus.

As a sophomore in public high school, I had visited the campus and thoroughly enjoyed the Christian environment there. During that visit, I had even met with an admissions counselor and filled out a college application. I knew it was a bit premature, with college still two years away, but I was determined to be a BJU student. My parents had often told me and my siblings that they would offer financial support for higher education as long as we attended a Christian college for at least one year. But never was my arm implicitly or explicitly twisted to attend BJU specifically. My sister eventually attended BJU, too, but my two brothers attended other fundamentalist colleges with my parents' full blessing. Somehow, though, BJU just felt like my destiny.

But my dad's words began to register a little bit more. BJU—my ideal Christian paradise for fellowship and academics—could have unsaved people there? How could that be? When I applied, I had to provide my personal testimony of how I became a Christian. As a pastor's son, I had earnestly accepted Christ as my personal Savior at the age of five and from an early age was well versed in how to publicly provide a personal testimony of that conversion experience. But could other students be lying on their application about their conversion experience? Or could they just somehow be mistaken about their identity? It was a sobering thought, and it felt like we were having a biblical father-son moment that reminded me of King Solomon's words in Proverbs 1:10: "My son, if sinners entice thee, consent thou not." My father's words unsettled me because this was the first warning I'd ever been given about a place I'd idealized since I was a child. I appreciated his advice, and I would be careful. But BJU was where I belonged.

College Aspirations

My first taste of college that summer of 1994 was extremely fulfilling. I couldn't wait for more the next year when I attended BJU for my first real semester in the fall of 1995. This was my chance to really begin my young adult life, to really enjoy the Christian peer interaction I had craved for so long while attending a very small, public, rural junior high and high school. But, more importantly, BJU was where I wanted to find a wife so that I could emulate my parents' footsteps and timeline. Practically every-thing I had ever witnessed firsthand about my parents, both as their child and also as a member of their church congregation, was overwhelmingly idyllic. I wanted their kind of romantic relationship in my young adult life, and BJU was going to help me get that.

But there was a problem: by the time I was ready for college, I'd already had quite a few experiences with guys, but none with any young ladies. Like most who'd grown up in the fundamentalist system, I was intensely aware that homosexuality was considered an abomination because of the Clobber Passages mentioned during church or covered during my own personal Bible reading time, but I had found creative ways of rationaliz-ing my interactions with men. For example, I knew that Leviticus states a man should not lie down with another man, so I played with the seman-tics and reasoned that I wasn't *technically* lying down with another man in a literal bed when hooking up: I was in other physical positions. Deep down, I knew this defense was flimsy, but it buttressed my ongoing denial and allowed me to maintain my devout Christian persona.

During that first year at BJU, I began to notice the level of surveillance and control from the administration. Yes, I had known about the strict rules in general before I enrolled, and had even experienced some of them while a summer school student the previous year, but the regular semes-ter is much more regulated. I had to make some serious adjustments from home, beginning with life in the dorms, where each room was less than 400 square feet and was equipped with 5 bunks, 1 sink, 2 desks with draw-ers, 2 dressers, 3 closets, and various overhead storage spaces. During my time at school, I was not aware of any men's dorm rooms filled to capac-ity with 5 students. Most only had 3 or 4 students per room, but those extra bunks would be utilized at various times throughout the semester for potential students or visitors spending the night while attending events held on campus.

BJU regulated our daily lives through the bells that rang throughout the weekday in the dorms, from rising bell at 6:55 a.m. to the lights-out bell at 11:00 p.m. And it wasn't just that we had to be in bed by 11:00 p.m.; we were required to stay up *until* 11:00 because we had to participate in prayer group activities in the dorm each night from 10:30 to 10:45. The ramifications of this requirement affected both my sleep patterns and my allotted time to complete work outside the classroom. As dedicated as I was to the BJU system, I remember having to train my body to stay up that late, in contrast to my going to bed much earlier while living at home. As a conscientious student, I knew that time was a limited, well-governed commodity that I needed to manage well if I wanted to keep up with the volume of required classroom reading.

Despite all the adjustment, I cannot overstate my excitement about finally finding steady, social interaction with Christian friends, both new ones (other energetic freshmen like me) and old ones (cousins and friends from my cousin's church). Though BJU's campus was relatively small, it wasn't unusual to meet strangers while eating next to them at the long tables of the dining common or at other such gathering places. I learned the art of "fellowshipping" on a friendship level, but I could never seem to make the transition to anything more than that with the ladies. I'd never had a girlfriend before, and I knew I wanted and was expected to have one. I just wondered how I would find her.

The Opportunity Place

Fortunately, BJU promoted itself as "the Opportunity Place." My mind went beyond the obvious academic implications of this motto. I interpreted the most important opportunity on campus to be the dating possibilities, as evidenced by the ways BJU manufactures social gatherings all semester long. My first exposure to this was during that first week of school before classes had officially started. Many of us freshmen hung out in the Social Parlor, informally known as the dating parlor, which was a public space on front campus located in the student mall area designated for couples to spend chaperoned time together. None of us in the large group were dating, but it was one of the few places where we could hang out in mixed groups and play games.

A second form of social gatherings for potential dating also presented itself during that first week. Every freshman is required to choose a Greek literary society—the BJU version of fraternities and sororities—during the rush ceremonies that opening weekend. We as new society members were told that each society held a dating outing once a year where we could invite a date.[1] Depending on the theme, the outing could be casual or formal, but I discovered that these events were one of the few approved occasions where couples could hold hands, as long as it was part of the activities, such as relay races. That was the extent of any kind of BJU-sanctioned physical contact between male and female students that I was aware of.

Throughout my time as an undergrad, I actively participated in my society. (I had purposefully chosen my father's society, Phi Kappa Pi.) I played in our pep band for soccer games and served as an officer for a semester or two. Plus, I attended each dating outing our society hosted and was also asked to the occasional dating outing from a female friend here and there, but these moments never led to anything serious.

But there were other dating venues besides the dating parlor and dating outings too. BJU combined on-campus cultural events with social ones and highly encouraged bringing a date to anything from Bible Conference church services (a week-long series of sermons in lieu of a spring break), intramural sporting events, student recitals and performances, and, most importantly, the Artist Series, which was a classic play, opera, or special concert production. These Artist Series were exclusively designed for male students to dress up and take a "special girl" out as if on a date, which began with the men walking over to the women's dorm, "picking her up," taking pictures in the dorm lobby, and then walking her to the concert venue on campus.

In the late nineties, my friends and I were cognizant that the dating environment on campus had transitioned from the serious one-on-one style of our parents' generation to more informal "group dating," where groups of men and women would attend events together. There was even less stigma attached to a group of ladies or a group of gentlemen attending these events alone. (Though no one ever really said it, some of these events felt more of a requirement to fulfill rather than an opportunity, especially when these events were scheduled at inconvenient times, like during the middle of the school week.) For the most part, I wanted to make the most of this "opportunity": I'd take dates, but I never felt a real physical or emotional connection. Perhaps my lack of dating experience in high school contributed to my failure, but more than likely, I wasn't more proactive because the physical drive just wasn't there.

Before I knew it, I was an upperclassman, and I heard a faint voice of disappointment in the back of my head. My parents had gotten married right after graduation, and with no serious prospects on my horizon, I was nowhere near their established schedule. (By this time, my older brother had already followed in my parents' footsteps and married soon after college; my younger brother would eventually do the same.)

In May 1997 the devout fundamentalist in me felt very proud to receive a glowing letter from the then-president, Bob Jones III, commending me for accruing no demerits for the entire year. I wouldn't admit it openly, but I thought it would be gratifying to hold a certain amount of spiritual leadership at BJU. After all, my father had been a hall leader in his time, and I was secretly proud of that legacy. But to embody the spiritual persona the administration wanted for that level of student leadership, I needed a girlfriend, a crucial component of that desired persona that I sorely lacked.

The highest spiritual position I ever held was an assistant prayer captain (APC), the spiritual leader in every dorm room that does not already have a higher-ranking prayer captain (PC). At the end of every academic year, all students are evaluated by their direct spiritual superior to see if they are "worthy" of being promoted to the next level of spiritual leadership. At the end of my second full year, I had just completed my first year of being an APC, and my PC seemed spiritually distraught whether to recommend me for PC the next year. After some time, he returned with his answer that he didn't feel spiritually moved to recommend me. My pride was hurt briefly, but overall, I couldn't argue with him. Perhaps the Lord had given him the spirit of discernment to see the true me that I was trying to hide from everyone: the queer guy who had a history of discreetly fooling around with other guys. So I remained an entry-level spiritual leader and didn't complain.

While I was having no luck with the ladies or leadership promotion, I was meeting my physical needs with non-BJU guys off campus. As an upperclassman, I could permanently park my car on campus, which allowed for unexpected opportunities off campus that I soon began to crave and capitalize on more and more. On various evenings, I would frequent places like the mall where I could find the means to satisfy my physical drive with men, but I was careful never to meet anyone (as far as I knew) affiliated with BJU or to disclose my experiences with anyone I knew on campus. This was purposely done so no one at BJU could potentially use this information against me.

Bob Is Watching Us

Even at this point, when I was still a fervent, optimistic defender of the university, I knew that its rules were strongly enforced. In my early years at school, I was unafraid to publicly sing a few bars of a random pop song here or there, depending on who was around me at the time. I blame that carefree attitude on my naivete combined with my lack of run-ins with the administration. I was even bold enough to parody a well-known pop song while simultaneously joking about the surveillance culture on campus. Bette Midler's cover of "From a Distance" had been a hit a few years before, so at times, among my friends, I would tweak the refrain and sing:

> Bob is watching us
> Bob is watching us
> Bob is watching us from a distance.

I thought I was being lighthearted and clever. I had always interpreted the original lyrics as encouraging: God was a loving figure always around to help us. But the more I stayed on campus, the more I realized how eerily true it was that the eyes of BJU were watching us, and not always in a comforting way.

News of this kind of surveillance crescendoed the longer I stayed on campus. At first, I heard about distant student figures who mysteriously disappeared when they were shipped. One of the first ones was the president of the Inter-Society Council. It was a scandalous story about her allegedly being off campus unchaperoned with guys, but I didn't give it much thought because I didn't know her. Sometime after that, I heard a rumor about a radio and television major who worked at the dining common. As the story goes, she had been shipped because she'd absent-mindedly left a pregnancy test in the trash can in her own dorm room. Again, I marveled at the story but didn't dwell on it that much.

But then, someone I worked with at the library disappeared abruptly. I heard she had been shipped for attending an innocuous, yet unchaperoned, co-ed party off campus, which was against the rules.[2] Because students who are shipped do not typically stick around long enough on campus (usually twenty-four hours at most) to report their fate to other students, we remaining students had to piece together information from various sources. The bottom line, however, was that someone had turned her in, and now she was gone. Bob was watching us. That's all I needed to know.

But BJU had other ways of procuring punishable information about students too. I witnessed how Bible Conference week was designed to physically test our fortitude and uncover anyone breaking rules. While enduring the intense daily schedule of sitting through many convicting sermons and altar calls with very little sleep, students subsequently felt pressured to turn themselves and their friends in for committing any infraction, such as listening to the wrong kind of music or watching any movie with a rating higher than G.[3]

Additionally, a section from the student handbook states that if anyone was aware of another student's breaking the rules, that person would also be eligible for the same punishment if it could be proved that they knew about it but did not tell.[4] These accumulating examples of surveillance convinced me that no matter how much I trusted anyone on campus, they could always be forced to use my personal information against me, especially if information from direct surveillance wasn't enough to convict me outright. Damning information was a form of currency on campus for opportunistic students, making it commonplace for them to turn people in to the administration. This kind of move could be advantageous for those wanting advancement in the spiritual leadership hierarchies on campus.

As I heard more rumors about students disappearing, I remained closely guarded about meeting men off campus. Even if I had ever seriously considered disclosing my "struggles" to my dorm counselor—an unlicensed, ministerial graduate student who lived in each dorm—I knew that anything I said would *not* be kept confidential and that I would be red-flagged forever in the eyes of the administration. So I kept my mouth shut.

"God's Special Place for You"

As an upperclassman, I noticed how BJU operated on at least two overlapping levels of control. Not only did it serve *in loco parentis* as a university figure, but it also served *in loco ecclesia* as the community church. Accordingly, it became difficult to distinguish whether the punishments, such as receiving demerits for missing a class, were meted out as academic penalty or as spiritual rebuke for disregarding authority. Every time we looked at our student ID cards, we were reminded that BJU was

"God's Special Place for You," so any action of the university's, academic or not, was done in the name of spiritual ministry, and any questioning on our part would be automatically labeled as rebellious. Because of that, we were supposed to passively welcome correction, and as someone who grew up in the fundamentalist system, I knew from a very early age the importance of obeying spiritual authority figures.[5] There was no way I would've ever felt comfortable openly contesting any of BJU's administrative policies, much less its disciplinary ones.

For me now, as a former fundamentalist, the doctrine of salvation is a tricky matter: we were always taught how to attain it, yet we were often emotionally manipulated into questioning our possession of it. At a place where we were constantly reminded that our spirituality was determined or evidenced by the amount of work that we put into evangelism and ministry-oriented activities, I could never effectively discern which came first, the faith or the works, or, more importantly, which spurred which, because we were regularly asked to question ourselves and our motives, to really ask if we were saved.[6] No wonder I felt so inwardly divided, spiraling through that cyclical question about the motives and authenticity of my salvation, all while trying my best to repress both that queer portion of myself and also the likely answer that being queer meant I wasn't saved.

Alternately, and perhaps ironically, I had developed a pretty strong, platonic connection with a guy in my society who shared many similar interests in music and culture. Andrew Bolden and I were the same age and from the Midwest, we participated in the same extension ministry (a spiritually based community service activity), and we even worked in the same department in the library on campus, so we began to spend a lot of time together. Throughout our friendship, we talked about our future goals and desires, including the kind of woman we wanted to marry and how we wanted our weddings to be, but never did we talk about anything even remotely suggestive of being attracted to guys. The danger was too great to trust anyone.

Another Warning

Suddenly, during the second semester of my senior year in 1998, I received startling news from someone I was very close to on campus. She told me unsavory rumors about Andrew and me, and while she didn't tell me to do anything other than "be careful," I knew that was coded language to "abstain from all appearance of evil" and distance myself from Andrew and the negative reputation I had been unknowingly creating for myself.[7] But I felt uneasy on several levels: I was terrible at interpersonal conflict, but more importantly, I shuddered that people might have thought I was gay.

I knew I couldn't pull off an Arnold Schwarzenegger–like masculinity. Instead, I liked to believe I exuded a "safe" masculinity akin to someone like Dick Van Dyke: someone musical, sensible, conservative, friendly, garrulous, and, most importantly, nonthreateningly straight—but I was fooling myself even then.

Even more unsettling than having to hear from a close friend about jarring personal attributes that I would rather suppress was that my questionable spiritual and existential integrity had been the subject of campus rumors. I figured I might have curated some kind of zany persona over the years at school, but nothing to cause this kind of attention. The images of those shipped students clouded my head. Bob was watching *me*. Rumors were dangerous on a campus that thrived on a surveillance system; they begat seemingly innocuous conversations with hall leaders and dorm counselors, which in turn could put me on their watch list if I said the wrong (or honest) thing. I couldn't deal with that kind of attention.

I'm ashamed to admit that I caved to pressure and shut Andrew out of my life. I was extremely impressionable and vulnerable and believed I was doing the right thing by distancing myself from Andrew, who was going through his own kinds of misery on campus. To this day, I still cringe at my actions. Andrew and I reconnected a few years ago on the other side of both fundamentalism and the closet, and he has forgiven me, knowing that my behavior at BJU was influenced by fear.

Back in May 1998, I graduated with my bachelor's degree and decided to stay on as a graduate assistant, partly because I was still holding on to the dream of finding a wife at BJU. I had hoped that my new circle of friends might lead me into a dating opportunity, but I was still searching for more information about the gay world at the same time. I soon found myself checking out gay-themed movies from Blockbuster Video and watching them in my dorm room. (Unlike undergraduates, graduate assistants were allowed to have TVs and VCRs in their rooms—and much more privacy with only one roommate and also locks on their doors.)

As thrilling as it was to secretly watch these kinds of movies, I could never really identify much with the Hollywood representation of gay

life. Yes, I enjoyed watching attractive characters, but they were also extremely fit, athletic, vapid, and likely self-destructive or narcissistic. I
knew I wasn't really that kind of gay person, but I hadn't seen many other
kinds represented.

I even took my curiosity and courage a step further into the gay world
by going by myself one night to The Castle, a local gay club. I didn't know
what I would find there, but I wanted to know more about this world. I
would have to be extremely cautious, though. I was paranoid about getting caught from some unidentified BJU surveillance source in the process, and rightly so: in April 1999 the rock band Aerosmith played a
concert at the BI-LO Center in Greenville. I had heard that the administration strategically placed hall leaders at various stadium entrances,
poised to catch any BJU students trying to attend the concert.

I don't know how many students they actually caught that night, if any,
but that kind of surveillance tactic from BJU didn't surprise me. It only
fueled my paranoia. I didn't want to be caught by anyone when I went to
The Castle, so I parked in an adjacent lot. While I was desperate to make
some kind of a connection at the club, I mostly kept to myself and wore
an oversized hat as a way of hiding. I didn't forge any friendships there,
but I considered the visit a success: I hadn't been caught.

"Name and ID"

That success was short-lived, though. My exploration into gay culture led
to my own expulsion. Encouraged by my secret trip to The Castle, I became a little bolder. One Thursday in early October 1999, I went to nearby
Furman University to research a paper for class, but while at the computer, I also visited certain gay websites. I was miles from campus, feeling discreet and safe. I'd never been caught by anyone for going against
the rules before. Why should today be any different?

But Bob was watching me from the next carrel.

I don't remember if he was a former or current BJU student, but after
a few minutes sitting next to me, he confronted me—as good BJU Christians do. He first asked me to step outside so he could speak more freely
to me, which was very considerate. His line of questioning immediately
indicated that he knew I was a BJU student. He asked about my actions
in this disappointed, fatherly tone, and my heart sank. Then, he bluntly
asked for my name.

"Name and ID. Name and ID." Immediately, this refrain popped into my head. It was usually said by hall leaders to student offenders during the turning-in process. My friends and I would jokingly parrot this refrain from time to time. But now, the jokes were over. It was happening to me for real.

I couldn't look at him. Instead, I just stared straight ahead toward the autumn trees in the distance on that sunny day. The leaves were falling, and I longed to be anywhere but on the front porch of the Furman library. I needed to get away. In a panic, I told him a fake name and saw no more reason to stick around, so I hurried toward the parking lot to my car, but I could feel an essence within me slowing dying with every step. This was my stupid water balloon moment my father had warned me about. I knew things would never be the same for me. Bob was watching me from a distance, and it was only a matter of time before the administration found me.

I couldn't focus on anything the rest of that day. My inner turmoil kept me withdrawn and under a trance, but I had to appear calm on the outside because who could I tell about this? I was a zombie going through the motions of living a life I couldn't belong to anymore. The next day, Friday, at the beginning of my 10:00 a.m. class, I received a note telling me to go directly to the dean of men's office. I wasn't shocked at being summoned; I was just surprised it took them less than twenty-four hours to find me. My senses were heightened, yet I felt numb on my surreal walk over there. My spirit had been hollowed out, and I knew how this would go: my time at BJU was finished.

I was told I had to be gone by Monday. I pathetically expressed my desire to stay, but the assistant dean wouldn't listen. I passively accepted the punishment like a good, spiritually convicted Christian who has been trained not to contest, negotiate, or bargain with authority figures. In an instant, I had been transformed from a model BJU student and employee to someone who was beyond their ability to reform. But unlike most people who are shipped, I was not shadowed by a hall leader for the rest of my time on campus. I assume it was because I was a graduate assistant instead of an undergraduate. For approximately the next thirty-six hours, I occupied such a bizarre in-between space on campus: I was neither employed nor a registered student, unrecognized by the administration as anything other than reprobate or unclean; yet, I was still there, attending the soccer games with my sister, a freshman, as regularly scheduled.

Word gradually spread on campus that I was leaving. I had become another rumor, just like those others who'd been shipped. Most friends showed support and love and compassion, even after I left; others kept asking for the reason I got expelled. I was too hurt and ashamed to tell any of them the real reason. I wonder now if any of them would've responded so supportively had they known. One minor silver lining during this time of shame was that my local extended family and my campus roommate were both out of town for that weekend, which meant I was spared from explaining my leaving to either of them in person. But that still left the dark task of notifying my immediate family.

My sister on campus had been the first one I told, but I couldn't bear the thought of having to tell my father. I was running out of time, though, and I needed to ask my parents if I could come home because I had nowhere else to go. I was relieved when my mom answered the phone that Saturday night. Her empathy comforted me during that extremely difficult phone conversation, even though she didn't know exactly why I got shipped.

That Sunday morning, hollowed out and mortified, I said my teary goodbyes to close friends and my sister. For the entire drive back to Illinois, my car stuffed to capacity, I was consumed with both the shame I had brought upon myself and the guilt for abandoning my sister during her first semester on campus. These emotions were compounded by the fear of the unknown: I had no clue what to do with myself next or what to tell my parents once I got back home.

Making My Own Opportunities

I won't sugarcoat this story.
I won't say that I'm glad I was expelled.
I won't welcome hardships as a form of appreciating life.

Getting shipped forever changed me. That next year and a half was the lowest point in my life so far. I didn't realize it at the time, but getting shipped articulated the beginning of my long, nonlinear journey away from both BJU and fundamentalism. Yes, I'm glad I arrived at this destination, but I'm less than thrilled with how that journey was prompted. During this time period, I worked my way out of my personal misery by writing down thoughts I couldn't tell anyone, and for approximately the next ten years, I cycled through times of intense church participation so that I could maintain the fundamentalist facade I had inherited and thought I wanted for myself.

But it didn't work. Age may or may not bring wisdom or maturity, but it certainly instilled a self-awareness in me. I could no longer hide behind the advantages of youth in this fundamentalist regime. As a new adult, I was expected to find a wife, create a family, and support my local church in ways that only a married man can. Otherwise, I would become even more conspicuous as that stereotypical creepy middle-aged man sitting alone in a church pew. With the help of social media in 2011, I became connected to other gay men who had also gone through the BJU system. Through their encouragement, I realized I was not alone: I walked away from a system that wasn't helping me.

It took many years, but I finally told my parents the truth about getting shipped while also coming out to them. I thought I knew fear back in 1999 when I had to call them about getting shipped, but that was just a precursor for the actual act of coming out: it's the absolute fear of the unknown, wondering how a loving, tight-knit family will react to a child embracing the biblical definition of an abomination. As is to be expected, my family needed time to process my revelation, but these days, we lovingly spend time with each other without talking about that issue.

I never had the courage to ask my father while he was alive about his specific thoughts on my surprise and shameful return home in 1999, especially after he discovered the real reason many years later. Had he replayed in his mind his original caution to me about getting shipped when I was a teenager, heading off to BJU as a student for the first time? I never doubted he would take the fundamentalist stance against homosexuality when I came out to him, so I knew he would be disappointed in me that I was gay. But I had other questions, too, for him and for me. Had he been disappointed in me because I got shipped? Was I part of that unsaved crowd he had once referred to?

I know he never stopped loving me from the day I was born, just as I know I earnestly asked Jesus into my heart many years ago. And if I was raised to believe in biblical literalism, then in that mindset passages about the eternal security of the believer, such as John 10:28–29, should overrule any cultural power that the Clobber Passages may hold. So I have no doubts about the accepting love of my earthly or heavenly father or my status in either family. But I have to admit that decades of internalized homophobia can still taint certain days, experiences, or memories.

Still, I never accomplished my goal of following in my father's footsteps at BJU and finding a wife or participating in what Jack Halberstam calls the "normative narratives of time."[8] But as much as I wanted to
replicate my parents' successful and loving marriage, which BJU helped
coordinate, I realized that BJU was not that kind of "Opportunity Place"
for me, no matter how much I wanted it to be. As long as BJU stands as
an expression of fundamentalism, I can resolutely keep it in my past. I
still hold many pleasant memories from college: the friends, the professors, the cultural events, the social activities, the fellowship. But Svetlana Boym warns that "the danger of nostalgia is that it tends to confuse
the actual home and the imaginary one. . . . Unreflected nostalgia breeds
monsters."[9] For Boym, reflective nostalgia allows us to view a place from
our past with a critical lens, and for me, that day in October 1999 prohib-
its me from seeing BJU as an imaginary home. It was the day that BJU
painfully revealed to me that I did not belong there. Instead, I was destined for other paths where I could use my fundamentalist past as a way
of connecting with others from all kinds of backgrounds. Most recently,
I am doing so at my current university as faculty sponsor of our Gender-
Sexuality Alliance student organization.

It's been tough openly navigating queer culture as an adult. There will
always be that residual fundamentalist part of me that shaped my life for
more than thirty years, but I've felt an intense amount of encouragement
from meeting others like me who have also left fundamentalism and accepted their authentic, queer selves. I'm still finding my way, but I'm definitely happier on the outside of BJU's fenced-in campus. As a gay man,
I've learned not to rely on a fundamentalist God for opportunities. If Bob
is still watching me from a distance, I hope he sees me creating and enjoying my own opportunities.

Notes

1. Lewis, *Romancing the Difference*, 75.
2. *Bob Jones University Student Handbook, 1997–1998*, 28.
3. Ibid., 22.
4. Ibid., 5. Dalhouse, *Island in the Lake*, 143, says that "This closely resembles the honor
code used by schools such as the University of Virginia, but at BJU this tradition is used
for much broader purposes. Traditional honor codes cover only the offenses of lying, cheat-
ing, and stealing. However, at BJU a questioning, critical attitude could easily be added to
the list."
5. *Bob Jones University Student Handbook, 1997–1998*, 16.
6. In my analysis of Aaron Hartzler's memoir, *Rapture Practice*, I note a similar phe-

nomenon: "Hartzler's fundamentalist family believes no one is saved by good works, as mentioned in the book of Ephesians, leading Hartzler to wonder if the works being done serve as a *reminder* of salvation, or as a *misled attempt* for salvation." Weldy, "Religious Cognitive Dissonance," 41–42.

7. I Thessalonians 5:22.

8. Halberstam, *In a Queer Time and Place*, 152.

9. Boym, *The Future of Nostalgia*, xvi. In Valerie Strauss's article, Philip Nel uses Boym's lens of reflective and restorative nostalgia when discussing how to approach certain racist books by Dr. Seuss. Strauss, "Breaking Up with Your Favorite."

If I told someone at BJU, I risked being tattled on,
called into the dean of men's office, and extensively
questioned about my masturbation habits, which
was the routine form of questioning that was meant
to trap a student into willfully admitting any number of sexual offenses. Even if I hadn't actually broken any school rules, I had learned enough about
how the system at BJU worked to know that I didn't
want to be placed under even more scrutiny, possibly losing privileges or being required to participate
in regular counseling sessions.

ACE: An Accelerated Program into Fundamentalism

In the fall of 1981, I matriculated as a freshman at Bob Jones University,
dubbed "the World's Most Unusual University." I was only sixteen years
old, and I didn't know I was gay.

How does that happen?

It starts by attending an independent fundamentalist Baptist church
with a healthy level of control on families, perspective, and permissible
future options. At the behest of my uncle, we (my mom, brother, and—on
occasion—my older married sisters) started attending that kind of church
in Maryland around 1975, when I was about ten. My dad, an atheist at
the time, didn't object to our going to church, but he did convert several
years later while I was in college. My conversion experience was personal
(praying in my bed late at night when I was eleven), and, sadly, frequent
(in much the same manner). I constantly questioned my salvation, and
the level of angst was directly proportional to world news and the level of
hellfire in the sermons I had heard that week.

The mid- to late seventies was an interesting time to be a fundamental Baptist, and not just because of the polyester leisure suits and wide ties. We were the recipients of several prevailing hysteria-inducing preoccupations, courtesy of our church. The communists were going to invade America at any moment, and first on their agenda would be burning all the Bibles and jailing or executing all the Christians. If not that, then surely Jesus' second coming was imminent, and we'd be raptured away so the world could be wiped clean during Armageddon. With both the communist and rapture scenarios firmly planted into my psyche, I seriously doubted I'd be alive or on earth long enough to graduate from college, much less become the middle-aged man I am now.

Our church had also started a Christian school, initially as a kindergarten program, adding grades as that inaugural class progressed, but in the fall of 1978, when a nearby Christian school closed, they decided to jumpstart grades 4–12. The jumpstart was made possible by using ACE (Accelerated Christian Education), a modern take on a one-room schoolhouse where students of all grade levels worked independently, completing booklets at their own pace. You could have lots of students with only a fraction of the staff normally required by traditional schools. The twenty- to thirty-page booklets were called PACEs (Packets of Accelerated Christian Education). Twelve booklets in any subject were roughly equivalent to one course year, so figuring in English, math, science, history, and other subjects resulted in sixty PACEs equating to the entire curriculum for any particular grade. We had traditional classes for Bible courses, a loosely structured recess that took the place of physical education, and a chapel service once a week.

The main drawback of ACE was that if one wasn't adept at learning by reading, or wasn't highly self-motivated, it could be a struggle to even get twenty or thirty PACEs done in a year. I didn't have that problem: I was motivated and easily soaked up knowledge. I think I completed ninety booklets that first year. In fact, I did so well that as I started my second year in that Christian school—which would have been ninth grade in public school—I realized I was going to graduate in one more school year, just a few months after my sixteenth birthday.

Naive at Fourteen: Robert Urich and College Choices

I was extremely naive, not just as a fourteen-year-old who'd suddenly figured out he was rapidly finishing high school; I was also naive about life in general, especially because I didn't know I was gay. Thanks to fire-and-brimstone preaching—and Anita Bryant, who went from Florida orange juice TV commercials to warning people about evil homosexuals—I had stereotyped gay people: they were effeminate perverts trying to molest and recruit children. Since I wasn't like that (never mind that I had no idea what gay sex or a same-sex relationship even was), I figured I was okay, and definitely 100 percent straight.

But there were signs. The men in the Sears catalog were so handsome. So were those older guys at summer Bible camp. And in a store at the mall, one poster of my favorite TV star, Robert Urich, would captivate me every time. I'd just stand there gazing at him, shirtless and in character as a private investigator on the ABC TV show *Vega$*, completely unaware of the implications behind how he made me feel warm and fuzzy inside.

But he wasn't the only thing controlling my thoughts at that time. After a summer of staring at Robert Urich in the mall, I returned to school (it would have been tenth grade in public school) and started thinking about college. As I already mentioned, my church held a significant amount of control in my life, especially with my educational curriculum, but this control included my higher educational possibilities too.

Our church approved of four Christian colleges, even though few members had attended a Christian college, or any college for that matter. Pensacola Christian College in Pensacola, Florida, and (the now-defunct) Tennessee Temple University in Chattanooga, Tennessee, were staunchly fundamentalist schools. Both offered a variety of majors, had huge on-campus churches, lots of rules, and used only the King James Version of the Bible. On the extreme right side of the spectrum was Hyles-Anderson College in Crown Point, Indiana, which made all the other fundamentalist schools appear positively liberal in comparison. Finally, our pastor's son (who was also our school principal at the time) had recently graduated with a master's degree from Bob Jones University in Greenville, South Carolina. He and his wife often spoke highly about the school.

To a naive fourteen-year-old, BJU seemed the most "collegiate" of my choices. It had chapel and all the church-related activities I expected, but BJU also had a museum, a planetarium, and a fine arts calendar filled with exciting things like plays, operas, and symphonic performances. As far as I knew, other schools didn't have those options, and the other schools seemed to emphasize Christian service to a degree that made an introvert like me uncomfortable.

But not everyone was thrilled with my choice. Some church families favored those other schools and tried to discourage me, saying BJU didn't have a church on campus, or that BJU allowed girls to wear pants (which technically was true, but only under strictly regulated, non-co-ed conditions). I didn't pay the naysayers much attention.

The idea of attending a local school—such as Towson State University, the University of Maryland, or even our local community college—was never an option. As a Christian school student, I was taught that the secular government schools were scary places, filled with people tempting you to listen to rock music, take drugs, and revel in a carnal lifestyle, or worse: lose your religion. At my ACE school, we had been on field trips to the Maryland State House in Annapolis not to learn how government works but to protest legislation requiring licenses for church daycares and private schools. These field trips made me wonder: Why would I want to subject myself to such "ungodly" people and practices by attending a state school?

But it was also odd: my church was concerned about how the government wanted to surveil and control the day-to-day affairs of churches and private schools, but I didn't realize at the time how Christian schools wanted the same kind of access and control over vulnerable students like me. This would be a theme I would recognize even more when I became more familiar with BJU.

I jumped at the chance to take a road trip with several other prospective students and attend BJU's "Get Acquainted Days" in the spring of 1979. Everyone on campus was friendly enough, and the rules didn't seem that bad. They had fine arts—concerts, plays, operas, and what seemed to me a massive art gallery—which I loved. My fifteen-year-old self envied the apparent freedom collegiate life offered, so I decided to enroll in BJU as a mathematics education major. Yes, the guy who learned math from a bunch of booklets was going to college to become a high school math teacher.

I graduated from high school in May 1981 in a convocation ceremony consisting of a single student: me. As the summer progressed, I was excited about leaving for South Carolina and starting my life as a college student. We made it a family trip so my parents and brother could see Greenville and BJU. Even my dad, the atheist, was impressed. He later told people that BJU was "just like you remember colleges used to be." In hindsight, I think my primary and secondary Christian school's quality (or lack thereof) translated into a healthy skepticism that my dad harbored about Christian education in general and even more so about a

Christian college, but his campus visit changed that mindset. I'm not exactly sure what on campus changed his mind. Maybe the conservatism he observed on campus was appealing from a parental perspective.

A Rough Start: Visiting an Off-Limits Restaurant

A highlight of that first family trip to Greenville was our unknowingly violating a school rule before I had even stepped on campus: we had eaten dinner at an off-limits pizzeria. At that time, students didn't receive a handbook until they arrived on campus to register. That BJU had rules was well known, but the extent of those rules was a mystery, and by the time a student arrived on campus to read the handbook, it was too late to have second thoughts.

A section of the handbook listed businesses that were off-limits to faculty, staff, and students. Some businesses were listed for obvious reasons (serving or selling alcohol within a certain proximity to the school); others, not so much. Had I visited that same pizzeria after I was officially a student, I likely would have been expelled. This wouldn't be the only time I unknowingly avoided expulsion. I escaped detection every time, but this initiation into learning places we could and couldn't visit off campus showed me just how much BJU cared to know where we were at all times.

Aside from that taboo pizza restaurant visit, my first semester was rather mundane, save for some academic challenges because of a lack of traditional high school experience. I had never been to a chemistry lab, never written research papers, nor had I learned advanced math concepts from an actual teacher. Aside from the chemistry labs, I quickly acclimated to academic life, to living in a dormitory, and to the rules.

But BJU is not only a place of abundant rules; it is also a place filled with abundant peer pressure to date because marriage is "naturally" God's plan for everyone and because you can't have sex outside of marriage. I managed to go on dates occasionally. It was easy because there were so many required events on campus to attend, so it was not only free but also low-risk. I never really dated anybody more than once or twice, partly because of my social awkwardness and introversion, partly because of my age (I was two years younger than other freshmen), and the rest because of disinterest (for reasons that are obvious now). Throughout this awkward dating process, I managed to distract myself by noticing all the good-looking guys around me.

Male-on-Male Backrubs and the IRS

Two memorable events occurred during my second semester that first year. One speaks to my naivete regarding homosexuality, and the other serves as the seed that would later mature into my full-blown skepticism of fundamentalism, allowing me to eventually leave fundamentalism altogether.

The first event occurred during an evening hall meeting. In the dorms, once a month, sometimes more, everybody from each room on a floor would assemble in the hallway for a series of announcements, some congregational-style singing, and usually a quick sermon from one of the hall monitors. At other colleges, they're called RAs, but at BJU, hall monitors were the middle layer of a pervasive campus hierarchy that enforced rules and assessed the spiritual lives of those underneath them.

Part of the announcements during hall meetings included clarifications of existing rules or, in some cases, the implementation of new rules. After attending a few of these hall meetings, I felt like there was a pattern: the administration kept adding rules of what not to do because of things that the administration had seen students do. It was like they wanted to control every facet of student behavior.

This particular hall meeting introduced a new rule that had me puzzled: we were no longer permitted to give back rubs to each other. I thought that was strange. (I was unaware of the gay porn trope where the action begins by giving a back rub to the pizza delivery guy.) I asked my friends why this had become a rule; they told me that somebody had walked into his dorm room and found someone giving a back rub to another student. Rumor had it that they were both naked or at least shirtless, depending on who was relaying the gossip, and that the guy giving the back rub was a hall monitor; this was especially scandalous because monitors were chosen for their outstanding spirituality. It still seemed like a strange rule, but since I wasn't interested in back rubs, I never thought about this again—until several years later. But at the time, it struck me again how rules materialize as a way of keeping tabs on student interactions.

The second event happened in January 1982, when I became aware of some disturbing information: BJU was featured prominently in the news when President Ronald Reagan reversed his support for legislation that would have granted tax exemptions to schools that practice racial discrimination. To my surprise, BJU was one of the schools seeking such a tax exemption, after having lost it in a court case challenging the decision. BJU eventually lost its appeal in the Supreme Court.

If, before 1982, someone had told me that BJU was a racially discriminatory school, I would have been incredulous. Surely, somebody at my home church, especially the people that encouraged me to pick any school except BJU, would have warned me about BJU's awful history of racism and segregation. Were they okay with discrimination as well? Or did they not know about it either? I have no idea. I myself never really learned the extent of BJU's racist past until more than twenty years later. At the time, I rationalized that the rule was okay because it was applied equally (Whites couldn't date Blacks, Blacks couldn't date Asians, etc.).[1] But the fact that I had accepted the rule and that, almost twenty years later, BJU eventually rescinded it, has had a lasting effect on me, namely, in leading me to seriously question everything I had ever been taught about the Bible, separation, and especially fundamentalism.

An Eighties Gay Education at BJU: AIDS, Stereotypes, and Purges

At some point during my college years, I became less naive about the meaning of being gay, which included an awareness about certain sexual acts. I can't point to one watershed moment, but in retrospect, I'd say it was a combination of events: summer breaks at home provided opportunity for activities not permitted at BJU, such as watching TV or reading science fiction. Also, the growing AIDS epidemic made discussion about sex rather unavoidable.

And while my knowledge increased, so did my determination that I was definitely not gay, a notion constantly reinforced by various aspects of BJU culture. For one concert, BJU hosted a performance by a boys' choir. The next day in chapel, Bob Jones III mocked the choir director's effeminate, flamboyant gestures. In other instances, preachers repeated the lie that homosexuals were child molesters. Also, one semester, rumors spread that homosexuality was the reason behind one particular men's dormitory having an unusually high number of expelled students. Some derisively called that dorm the Tower of Babel because it seemed that God was determined to drive everyone from it and bring it down. These rumors made me think back to both my pizzeria moment and that backrub hall meeting: there was always the potential of being caught by BJU agents of surveillance.

With all of these instances accumulating in my mind, I reasoned that I was not gay: I wasn't effeminate, I didn't want to molest children, and I didn't have AIDS, so clearly I was not gay. At the very worst, even if I did have the slightest doubts about my sexuality, I believed I could avoid the doubts and the attractions if I worked hard enough. No matter what I was, I knew I couldn't confide in anybody about this. If I told someone at BJU, I risked being tattled on, called into the dean of men's office, and extensively questioned about my masturbation habits, which was the routine form of questioning that was meant to trap a student into willfully admitting any number of sexual offenses. Even if I hadn't actually broken any school rules, I had learned enough about how the system at BJU worked to know that I didn't want to be placed under even more scrutiny, possibly losing privileges or being required to participate in regular counseling sessions. I had heard the same rhetoric at my home church, and I didn't want the extra scrutiny from those people either. I struggled so much to reassure myself that I was not gay, and I sometimes wonder now how I managed to keep my sanity.

As the years of my being a BJU student progressed, my excitement in returning to school diminished. Each time I crossed the state line into South Carolina, I became moody and silent. By the time I turned onto Pleasantburg Drive, I'd be dreading the scrutiny and pretense that I was as spiritual as everybody else on campus, but this was a necessary pretense to avoid being disciplined or counseled about general spiritual matters and being labeled as gay.

By this point in my student career, I knew that the administration cared about keeping track of students' activities. At BJU, I learned not to share anything negative with anybody unless I was in desperate circumstances. Otherwise, I was just providing ammunition that might be used against me, especially during a "purge," when a repentant student, attempting to avoid expulsion, would tattle on other students.

These purges were often started by somebody I knew who tattled on other students and informed the administration about a litany of student code violations. I often didn't know about these purges until after they happened, but I was always surprised that I had not been interrogated, if not expelled. I was naive, but not perfect. The worst of the rules I recall breaking was listening to contemporary Christian music while riding in a friend's car, which sounds pretty benign, but it was still a punishable offense. By the time I reached my senior year, I was less enamored with all the things that had made me fall in love with BJU as a prospective student, and I just wanted to finish my classes and graduate.

Attempts at a Christian Marriage and Career

I did my student teaching at a local Christian school in Greenville in the spring of 1985 and graduated in May. Earlier that year, during BJU's annual principals' recruitment conference, I had secured employment teaching high school math and science at a Christian school in northern Virginia. This school was associated with a church that was slightly more liberal than BJU, mostly with regard to music, but I was eager to see if I could successfully transition into a Christian work environment after all of that fundamentalist training.

I was only twenty years old when I started teaching, barely two years older than some of my students. The school tried to keep my age a secret, but one of the school board member's children leaked the information, which made things awkward. Socially speaking, I felt awkward too. I barely dated at all, and I didn't have a clue about how to pursue a hookup, straight or gay. The rental house I lived in had cable TV, which meant I finally could catch up on movies I couldn't see while at my parents' or at BJU. Since I was no longer under the viewing restrictions that a dorm student experiences, I received quite the education through pop culture. If BJU had given me a badly stereotyped idea of what it meant to be gay, eighties cable TV marginally counteracted that. Around this time, I finally understood that my desires could be labeled as gay, but I believed that if I continued to "do right"—as Bob Jones Sr. had famously said—these desires would go away.[2] I just needed to do right . . . more.

In June 1987, just over two years after graduating from BJU, I married someone I'd grown up with in church and who had also attended BJU. Would this work? I'd often heard preachers quote the Bible, saying, "it's better to marry than to burn."[3] I certainly had a genuine relationship with her, but as I look back on my mindset at age twenty-two, I can say that the strange dating environment at BJU combined with my lack of substantial relationship experience hindered my ability to recognize that this marriage wasn't a good idea. I still was attracted to men, even though I'd never acted on this desire.

The marriage didn't work, not only because of the arguments, disappointments, lack of communication, and sheer exasperation, but also because I was often internally confronted about whether I was gay. In a recent *Savage Love* podcast, Dan Savage described his own turmoil that also exactly described mine: "I lied under duress. I felt I had no choice but to try to learn how to be straight despite every cell in my body screaming about how much I liked men. Culture told me I couldn't be who I was, I couldn't have the things in life that I wanted, if I told the truth about these things to my partner or anyone else."[4] This duress meant I kept trying to make my marriage work. We had a child, which complicated things, but nothing alleviated the core problem I had been dealing with for a couple decades by then. After thirteen years of marriage, we decided to call it quits and separate. I still had not acted upon my attractions; I had yet to even kiss another man.

Disarming the Fundamentalist Threat of Eternal Damnation: A Better Me

I contemplated my doomed marriage and realized that absolutely nothing had worked to save me from my attraction to men. As I considered my thirty-something life as a divorced dad, I knew I was exhausted trying to be something I knew I could never be (a straight man), and that's when it dawned on me: if this was my lot in life, if God had predestined me for this, why keep trying to fight it? I would just live my life as a gay man. Sure, I'd go to Hell for it, but it felt like that was my destination regardless, so I was going to be true to myself. And this was the moment when I realized that who I was could not be controlled by any surveillance mechanisms put in place by BJU or fundamentalism. My failed marriage was proof of that. I couldn't participate in this kind of system anymore. It wasn't working for me, and I couldn't be held hostage to a religion like this.

To my surprise, my somber feelings of dismay about giving myself over to eternal damnation were extremely brief, immediately followed by an incredible feeling of joy and freedom I don't think I'd ever experienced before. I started dating men, and finally got to kiss one, which finally made me see imaginary fireworks and little hearts floating up out of my head like in the cartoons. I was almost giddy.

In the process of learning to navigate the gay dating scene, I accidentally came out to my ex-wife by not logging out of my dating profile on a computer she used. That precipitated my coming out to my family, because I feared what might happen if I wasn't the one breaking the news.

It was another surprise: my family was accepting, with my mother telling my siblings to treat me as they always have. A summer of dating turned into my first same-sex long-term relationship. When that first relationship ended, I wasn't in a hurry to start another one, but eventually I did, with my current one approaching fourteen years, five of which we've spent together as a married couple.

One guy I was dating asked me to go to the Pride parade in Washington, D.C. I had never been to a Pride event before. While I was there, I had expected to see drag queens, skinny twinks, and leather-clad hirsute men smoking cigars, but I was completely floored to see several church groups marching, including some Baptists! Suddenly, it hit me: if even a Baptist church could support and affirm LGBTQ Christians, then not only had I made the right decision to come out of the closet, but also my eternal plight—if there was such a thing—wasn't nearly as bleak as I thought it was many years ago. Walking away from BJU and its religious teachings was the best thing I could ever do to find freedom and myself.

During all that time I was trying to be straight, I had heard rumors that there were a few gay BJU students. One might have even been a porn star or something. But I figured I was one of a rare few who had managed to graduate without getting into trouble. I couldn't have been more wrong. By way of a BJU survivors' group on Facebook, I was invited to join a group of LGBTQ ex-students, alumni, and even former faculty and staff of BJU, some of whom I recognized as my contemporaries! It wasn't long after discovering this group that the BJUnity organization launched.

After decades of feeling like an outcast, I finally found people who understood everything I had been through—the fundamentalist culture I was raised in and, more importantly, the bizarre experience of attending BJU. Not only had I finally felt a sense of belonging, but BJUnity managed to do something BJU never could: turn me into an outspoken ambassador for something. The guy I was at BJU, who had hated knocking on doors to invite people to church, who had disliked going on extension (BJU-sanctioned community outreach groups), and who remains socially awkward at parties and mixers to this day, is now the guy who enthusiastically marches at Pride, hands out BJUnity business cards, and tells people it's okay to be gay, especially if you're gay and from BJU.

Finding this group of people helped me find self-acceptance in a way that I couldn't have imagined as that boy growing up during the communism-rapture scare in the late seventies. Back then, that boy didn't realize how influential the church could be in controlling every aspect of his psychological, emotional, and sociological development. Back then, that BJU student didn't see a way out of the rigid fundamentalist structure he had found himself in. But today, my life experiences show that I'm not tied down by my past's indoctrination. I can live without the religious fear and control of my childhood.

Notes

1. Bob Jones Jr. talks about this rationalization in *The Glory and the Power*.
2. Jones, "Do Right though the Stars Fall," 10.
3. I Corinthians 7:9.
4. Savage, "Episode 592: Teen Sexting."

chapter 3   ANDREW BOLDEN

> I could see the wheels turning in his head as he prefaced his next question with assurances of concern and promises to give me the "help I need," then paused for a moment, looked me in the eye, and asked, "Andrew, do you have homosexual tendencies?"

Opera at the Bob

She insisted on taking a photo as I prepared to leave the hotel where we were staying. My college graduation was over, but the cameras were still out in force; I was now off to sing at my friend Steven's wedding. As I stood there in my tuxedo, my mother caught a peculiar melancholy on my face that had become more frequent lately. In that photo, she captured more than just a look; it was a moment—an epiphany, really—that had bubbled up into a slow boil during my horrific final two years at Bob Jones University. I realized for the first time that I would never have what Steven had: I would never marry a woman like he was doing that evening; I would never experience that love, that joy, that bliss. No good Christian girl would ever want me—neither would my church, and possibly neither would my family—because I was the worst thing I could possibly be: a homosexual.

Though I would briefly step out of my very transparent closet about five years later, I quickly retreated back inside for years of depression, promiscuity, and praying away the gay. It would take a dozen years after that photo was taken before I would finally come to terms with my sexual orientation.

Overture: Learning Harmony in Church

I was born in Cumberland, Maryland, into a home of recent converts. My parents had gone to church all of their lives, but shortly before I was born, they attended an evangelical Baptist church where they discovered they weren't "real" Christians. They were formally received into the membership after their (second) baptisms, and church became a prominent feature in our family's routine.

We attended at least three services a week; any time the doors were open, we were there. In a brief ceremony that was basically an infant baptism without the baptism, I was "dedicated" by my parents alongside a number of other babies who would eventually become my Sunday school classmates and friends. We would be baptized by immersion if and when we made public professions of faith after reaching the age of accountability. In my case, I "asked Jesus into my heart" when I was four years old, kneeling beside the couch in our living room one Sunday afternoon after a particularly scary sermon about hell in that morning's worship service. To be sure about my salvation, I prayed twice. In fundamentalist culture, it's customary to be publicly baptized shortly after making a public profession of faith, but I put off baptism for a variety of reasons, though I think my delay largely had something to do with all the attention leading up to it.

Faith, then, became a central component of my life, and with that came music. My father was our pastor's favorite soloist, and my mother sang with him in the choir and played the piano for congregational singing. I understood harmony fairly quickly, and as my younger sisters came into the picture, other congregants began gravitating toward our family pew to be blessed by our hearty singing. When Dad accepted a better position back in his native Akron, Ohio, our church family mourned our departure.

As we settled into our new home and new school district, finding a church became a high priority. The first congregation we visited was nearby and twice the size of our old church. Their recently constructed building felt glamorous, with plush carpets and padded pews, but my folks became uneasy when the youth group planned to attend a concert by Carman, a Christian contemporary music singer affiliated with the Charismatic movement and a bit too much of a rock star for my parents' taste.

Shortly thereafter, one of my older sister's new friends from the high school band invited our family to her church: we found ourselves at Canton Baptist Temple, a huge Independent Fundamental Baptist church we had chuckled at a week before while passing their sign which said, "Home of the Christian Hall of Fame." Taking a page from Canton's Pro Football Hall of Fame, the walls throughout the expansive church campus displayed portraits of early church martyrs, theologians, and reformers alongside prominent nineteenth- and twentieth-century circuit preachers and evangelists. Before long, this five-thousand-member, highly polished, conservative congregation became our family's spiritual home for the next decade.

Touring Christian Colleges

One of an evangelical parent's greatest fears is witnessing their grown children harboring apostasy, which is typically nurtured through the faith-killing evils of a secular university education. My parents sent us to local public schools primarily because of the expense and the poor academic reputation of nearby Christian schools, but Mother informed me early in my high school days that I could only go away to college if I attended a Christian college. Specifically, there was a small handful of approved "fundagelical" schools: Jerry Falwell's Liberty University in Lynchburg, Virginia; Moody Bible Institute in Chicago; Baptist Bible College with campuses in Pennsylvania and Missouri; and Cedarville College (now University) in southern Ohio, where my oldest sister had attended for a couple years. Otherwise, I would be permitted to attend a secular school only if I lived at home and attended church with the family, limiting my choices to those colleges within reasonable driving distance, so basically Kent State University or University of Akron, both of which I dismissed with the contempt of local familiarity. Furthermore, Mother earnestly desired that I answer the "call to ministry" either as a pastor or missionary; while I wasn't opposed to the idea, I never "surrendered" to God's will as such, mostly because I knew I lacked the (heteronormative) charisma required to lead an evangelical church.

Not long after discovering opera with the help of mixtapes from my school choir friend Carrie, my church youth group sponsored a tour of several Christian colleges over spring break of my junior year. I was sure I'd end up at Liberty University, but I was shocked by the ungodly alternative rock music—Crash Test Dummies—played by the students in my dorm room; I was likewise unimpressed by the facilities and the classes. Disappointed, I looked forward to Cedarville, but in the meantime, we had to visit BJU, mostly because our youth pastor had attended there.

None of us was terribly keen to visit BJU because of its reputation for being stodgy and legalistic, a view my parents shared. Imagine my surprise to find a well-maintained campus and the friendliness of the people I met throughout my stay. Moreover, the classes seemed more rigorous and the music ensembles far more polished. In fact, after observing a choir rehearsal, I was invited to dinner with a couple of music majors who were very engaging. They told me all about the school and the music program, making a rather convincing sales pitch.

Visiting Cedarville after that was rather anticlimactic, and I surprised everyone at home by sharing my enthusiastic interest in BJU. Between its lack of accreditation and legalist reputation, my parents were not exactly thrilled. In a twisted form of teenage rebellion, I was insistent. I had to play the "God's Will" card for them to take me seriously. During my senior year, they visited BJU with the parents of a preacher boy from our church and returned home with a school sweatshirt for me. They had relented.

In my spiritual preparation for BJU, I had finally relented, too, and worked up the gumption to be baptized (by immersion, of course) during the evening service on Easter Sunday 1995. An extra-long, drawn-out invitation after that morning's sermon had pulled me down the aisle to make that decision. I was glad to have finally completed this rite of passage at my home church before I left for school in a few months.

When I told my friends at my public high school that I was attending BJU, most were rather confused: "They don't allow hugs? They only allow classical music? No movies? A strict dress code, too?! How will you survive? How could you possibly be yourself?" I fielded questions like these daily, always responding that I'd be fine, that it was only for a few years, and that I'd come out a stronger Christian and a better musician. I sincerely believed all of that and was eager to get there. I couldn't wait to meet roommates who, according to everything I was told, would become lifelong best friends; to soak up as much musical knowledge as possible; and most of all, to meet the love of my life and marry her. After all, what is a Christian university for if not finding a suitable mate?

Establishing Residency at BJU: Learning about Surveillance

I began in the fall of 1995, and, like any freshman experience, the first several weeks were rife with excitement, adjustments, and frustrations, but I was excited to study music seriously and ready for academic rigor. I saw my first BJU crush during my first trip to the dining common—she was the tallest girl on campus with big hair and a big smile, and soon I discovered she was also in one of my music classes. I was smitten. But my romantic notions of love at first sight were never requited by any of the young ladies who caught my eye. I'd start singing "So This Is Love" from Disney's *Cinderella* when a crush would agree to be my date for an Artist Series—the major concert and theater events throughout the year where we would actually be allowed to cross the threshold of the girls' dormitories and wait in the lobby to take them to the auditorium or concert hall. It never seemed odd to me that my natural inclination was to sing the princess songs.

Despite my own self-righteous tendencies that were encouraged there, I was bothered by my lack of independence and privacy: sometime during that first semester, I began to develop secret misgivings about my college choice. We couldn't leave campus without signing out or gaining written permission, and neither were we in control of our daily schedule, which was regulated by bells dictating when to sleep, wake, and go to class. Furthermore, we had no locks on our doors, and hall leaders—essentially a resident assistant with a Bible and a demerit pad—checked our rooms several times every day. We had to check in to the campus hospital in order to be excused from class if we were sick; otherwise, take your germs to class. I learned to be cautious about saying or doing anything that could be misinterpreted or grounds for getting turned in to any level of spiritual authority.

Likewise, we were encouraged—no, *required*—to report other students' violations under threat of our own similar punishment if we failed to do so, which naturally fostered a culture of distrust and suspicion on campus. Early in that first semester, during a break in our choir rehearsal, I sat next to a friend who spent her summers with her relatives at my home church. I was eager to share with her that I had seen the movie in theaters that she had recommended, *First Knight*, before I had left for school. Her eyes widened and she shook her head in an inconspicuous "no" when I mentioned the title. Attending movies was an expulsion offense, *even over holiday or summer breaks*. I realized an important lesson in that moment: to hold my tongue and be more discreet about my actions before I had been enrolled, lest any of our fellow singers who happened to be listening in feel convicted enough to report her. Even more audacious for my story is that, after that very same movie in Ohio, I had run into another local BJU student leaving that cinema with his family.

It's a wonder I wasn't called in to the authorities at BJU and forced to report both my friend and that student.

In spite of my second thoughts, however, I dared not renege on my earlier "God's Will" trump card by transferring elsewhere, though it never occurred to me that God might lead me to another school. I soldiered on, even adopting many of the spiritual standards practiced there, including daily devotions and participation in extension ministries; after all, we were evaluated spiritually every year, so it seemed I ought to at least appear like I cared about them. The school was literally training Pharisees and justifying it biblically.

My first experience with live opera was as a member of the soldiers' chorus in that spring's production of Gounod's *Faust*. Because students generally don't have voices or the dramatic prowess to handle the big (and often scandalous) roles of nineteenth-century grand opera preferred by the founding family, BJU hired professionals to sing the major roles. Advanced students might get a shot at the occasional *comprimario* role, but the selection process was typically clouded by politics of spiritual fitness rather than capability. The professionals gave spectacular performances, but I specifically didn't ask for the autograph of the bass hired to sing the role of Mephistopheles because he smoked cigarettes. Even if he was an amazing singer, he didn't seem to be aware that the body was a temple for the Holy Spirit.

Choir Tour and a Master Class in Betrayal

Early in my sophomore year, the University Chorale toured New England for a week in November 1996. Because we were recruitment ambassadors for the university, choir tours didn't often include much actual fun; instead, they consisted primarily of driving to a series of Christian schools or small churches where we would not perform but rather "minister in music" to the assembled students or congregation.

As part of this ministry, we stayed in the homes of church members along the way. Still, when we reached Maine, we enjoyed a lovely sunny afternoon at Cape Elizabeth, and for whatever reason, I demonstrated my sad excuse for a *tour jeté* in front of everyone. The upperclassman preacher boy rooming with me that night in a cold farmhouse began asking some probing questions as we settled into our beds. At first, I thought he was just getting to know me, but it soon began to feel more like an interrogation. Eventually he mentioned that after my balletic display, our conductor, one of my favorite professors in fact, had asked some of the guys to toughen me up. I couldn't say whether he meant for them to be physically rough with me or just point out every performance that didn't conform to their masculine expectations; regardless, it stung that I was somehow disappointing my professor simply by being my excitable, gender-non-conforming self. The next morning, we rose early to help our hosts by milking goats and gathering eggs, and I resolved to be more self-aware as I filled up with delicious homemade pancakes.

Just before my junior year, my friendship with a BJU student named Robin soured during our time working at my church camp.[1] In retaliation, she reported me and another student to the administration when we returned to school in September 1997. The other student, a friend I adored, was given a huge sum of demerits and placed on spiritual probation because of her rule-breaking actions during the *previous school year*, acts which she had told Robin about during the summer. The day after the drop/add period, when full tuition refunds were no longer given, I received a call slip—a BJU subpoena—in my mailbox to report to the dean of men's office. I was terrified. What had she told them? I had never been in any real trouble before, so the hours before this meeting were nerve-racking. My fears were confirmed when Tony Miller, the dean of men, interrogated me about my behavior that summer.

My offenses? I stood accused of such nefarious acts as dancing lewdly (any and all dancing is considered lewd by fundamentalists, so my ability to sway my hips to a rhythmic cheer, perfected in high school show choir, was practically a striptease); wearing my jeans so that the waistband of my boxer shorts was visible (I had forgotten my belt, but hey, it was the era of baggy jeans! It was on trend! Mr. Miller said I was imitating a prison fashion indicating my openness to homosexual sex); making inappropriate remarks in mixed company (racy discussions about body hair and referring to an uptight person as "anal"); and the *coup de gras*: intentionally acting gay.

In a voice that sounded like a cheap imitation of Peter Lorre, Mr. Miller worked his way down the checklist of my alleged misdeeds before asking about my dating habits. Even though the cultural norms on campus highly pressured us to at least be engaged by the time we graduated, I was only nineteen and pursuing a decidedly non-lucrative vocation. I thought my response reflected self-awareness and maturity: I told him that while I enjoyed going on dates with women, I thought it best not to pursue a serious relationship for another few years until I was more established. Frankly, I knew I wasn't ready for marriage, and that was the only reason to date seriously, right? I could see the wheels turning in his head as he prefaced his next question with assurances of concern and promises to give me the "help I need," then paused for a moment, looked me in the eye, and asked, "Andrew, do you have homosexual tendencies?"

I had seen it coming from a mile away, but I couldn't believe he had actually said those words, both ridiculous and nauseating. For good or ill, I had enough awareness to realize that nothing good would come if I admitted to it, so I struggled to explain that while I was no paragon of masculinity, I did not experience those "tendencies." I had even planned my wedding! Wait, that wasn't helping.

Alone in my defense, I listened as Mr. Miller twisted my words against me, even when I had repeated Christian buzzwords he had said moments earlier. When I mentioned my concern about my reputation because I wanted to maintain a good testimony, he invoked scripture and said, "Christ made Himself of *no* reputation!"[2] When I said I would be like Christ and endure the shame, he said I should want to live a life that is above reproach. It was an exercise in futility because he had the upper hand of spiritual authority.

To this day, I wonder why I didn't have enough sense or wherewithal to stand up and walk directly to the registrar's office and withdraw. The problems with his line of questioning, from the method to the content, were numerous. But I was stunned and afraid, and felt I needed to prove myself, both my true Christianity and my respectable heterosexuality. And while I remained in an earnest state of denial hoping for the wife and kids and picket fence that come with the American Dream, I remember feeling like a switch went off in my mind that day as I walked out of the administration building: after years of being on the receiving end of teasing and bullying and questioning, I told myself, "*Fine!* Everybody tells me I'm gay; I'll be gay!"

Days later, I was forced to attend a confrontation with Robin in which her exaggeration of the truth was apparent to everyone; however, the administration maintained my culpability without so much as consulting several other students on campus who were present at camp that summer or even speaking with the camp leaders. I was allowed to remain as my dorm room's spiritual leader (assistant prayer captain), but I was being closely monitored.

An Ensemble of Surveillance, Desertion, Spiritual Probation, and Counseling

Part of that monitoring required that I meet regularly with my dormitory supervisor, Stan Shelton, who would counsel me in developing Christian masculinity. At these meetings, he insisted that godly men are not emotional; thus, I shouldn't base actions or decisions on feelings. He tried coaching me on forming more masculine gestures, but that exercise proved awkward for both of us, especially as he wasn't very good at it himself, and I had better posture to boot. I remember looking at him, my eyes shifting around the room erratically, and thinking to myself, "Seriously, are we really doing this right now?" Somehow, I managed to avoid him after a few sessions based on the demands of my schedule, which seemed to suit him just fine.

But I was broken and alone. Robin had also turned all of our mutual friends against me, and now the eyes of Big Brother Bob were watching intently. Fortunately, a couple friends helped me deal with the fallout. Lance Weldy worked with me in the library's periodical room; Barney was a fellow voice major.[3] They kept me sane as I dealt with cold shoulders, rumors, and judgmental glares. Lance had an old Mustang he had won from his home church for bringing the most visitors that summer; with an Andrews Sisters soundtrack, he would often drive us to the local bookstore, where we would mostly just enjoy time away from campus. I purchased the original cast album of the new Broadway musical, *Titanic*, and in spite of its worldly music and inappropriate lyrics that made the CD uncheckable on campus, I listened to it anyway. Its soundtrack frequently inspired fantasies of running off to New York to audition for that show, but I had no idea how to make that dream a reality.

Just before exam week, a nursing major working a library shift with me remarked that my face looked thin, and she asked about my weight. Over Christmas break, I got on the scale and discovered that I had lost fifteen pounds that semester.

Returning for the spring term, I had gained some weight back and was finally feeling some equilibrium. But when Lance and I were bidding farewell to Barney, who was leaving with the itinerant musical ministry team that semester, Barney made a strange comment about no hugs or arms around each other when taking pictures. It was odd, but he was a university representative now. Maybe he was practicing official protocol with his testimony or something. Whatever it was, we said an awkward goodbye, and things were never really the same between us again. Lance and I continued as normal until about a month later, when I went home to Ohio to audition for a couple summer opera programs; I called him from my parents' house, but he was unusually reticent and awkward. When I returned, he actively avoided me with zero explanation. After a semester of countless hours together and supportive friendship, suddenly the bottom dropped out.

The freshmen in my prayer group, Luke and John, were there to catch me.[4] Throughout all the dormitories, adjacent rooms gather nightly for prayer in prayer groups; since Luke had gone to high school with me, he had requested to be in my prayer group. He had been my younger sister's show choir dance partner, and we had been in the school musicals together. John was a Buffalo bad boy, and he introduced me to his friends who managed to break rules and stay under the radar, leaving campus without permission and listening to rock music in their cars. They were close at hand when I finally confronted Lance in his dorm a few weeks later. Under great duress, he revealed that he had been warned to watch himself: people were talking about the two of us, being gay, together. The implications were devastating, and I was livid. Frustrated, I tried to reason with him, but he shut me down.

An unexpected lift came when I was asked by the dean emeritus of fine arts to understudy the tenor role for the spring opera; Beethoven's *Fidelio* was about a woman who rescues her husband from a slow death as a political prisoner in a secret dungeon. Though the heldentenor role was far too large for my small leggiero voice and would be performed by a professional, I studied and sang the part of the falsely accused husband for the bulk of the rehearsal process, and it felt like vindication.

At the end of the year, my hall leader changed his mind and did not recommend I continue as an APC the next year. My suspicion was that he felt I spent too much time with John, whose flouting of the rules was rubbing off on me. I was called back into Mr. Shelton's office to discuss the matter. The first thing he asked me was, "How does that make you feel?" Apparently, feelings mattered after all. Still, my honest admission of relief was wrong: because I was uncomfortable with my responsibilities as an APC, I was now primed for evaluation as a candidate for spiritual probation. Spiritual probation was a mysterious disciplinary restriction imposed on students because of a perceived or actual spiritual failing that typically included weekly biblical counseling sessions with one of the big guns in Student Life, a required chaperone to leave campus, and heavily restricted social interaction. We went through a questionnaire together, line by line, which included the question, "Are you happy here?" He was concerned; I was annoyed.

A week later, I received a sham form letter from the dean of men indicating my placement on counseling for the next semester; though not as restrictive as spiritual probation, counseling was nonetheless a mark against me that drew extra scrutiny from the administration and its student cronies. It was totally unfounded, allegedly due to my poor performance in several spiritual measurements: they cited my lack of daily devotions, which I did every day as prescribed; my lack of participation in extension ministry, which I did every month as required; my lack of attendance in local Sunday evening church services, which I did nearly every week. Along with other similar misrepresentations, I couldn't believe what I was reading. This action had everything to do with my honesty about my lack of enthusiasm for the school and my willing resignation from their spiritual leadership paradigm, but they would never actually state that.

Incredulous, and to my eternal regret, I ripped up the letter in the mailroom and threw it in the trash. I immediately called my mother to tell her I needed to transfer; I phoned a couple of friends at other schools who put me in touch with admissions personnel. After investigating some different options, however, I realized that I'd lose too much in the process, and would be practically starting over. So I reluctantly returned to BJU for my senior year, intent to do whatever necessary to get my hands on my degree and get the hell out of there.

My Final Year at BJU: A Duet of Tiny Victories and Larger Risks

That summer I purchased my first car, which allowed me some semblance of freedom from the constant surveillance of campus life. Also that summer, I secretly visited a gay porn site on the internet for the first time: after waiting for what seemed an eternity while the dial-up connection downloaded the page, I realized for the first time that men could have sex facing each other. All my life, I had been taught by heterosexual preachers with no imagination that gays couldn't possibly experience true love because they could only have sex from behind without looking into each other's eyes; intimacy could only be achieved through the missionary position. Or so I was told. This revelation was truly mind-blowing.

When I arrived for my senior year in the fall of 1998, I was relieved to discover that my assigned counselor was a first-year divinity student who had sung alongside me the previous semester in *Fidelio*. He had curried favor with the powers that be for his "sacrifice" to pursue the pastoral ministry rather than a career as an opera singer, even though they didn't want voice majors to do that either, and he couldn't read music anyway. Bill was generally kind and affable with a good belly laugh, but he was certainly not trained in any legitimate counseling techniques.[5] While the first sessions seemed harmless enough, my memory of our time together consisted almost entirely of Bill's bloviating about how my problems stemmed from my own sinful heart, a tactic that was in line with the university's standard teaching.

My twenty-first birthday was on a Sunday in Greenville, South Carolina, where alcohol sales were expressly forbidden, and drinking was yet another expulsion offense for a Joneser anyway. Luke and John joined a birthday celebration with my folks at the Olive Garden. The next evening, with my parents and grandparents in the audience, I presented my senior recital, which included the premiere of a new song cycle composed by my accompanist. It was something of a triumph, as I had made significant vocal strides that fall.

Based on another honest admission that I had missed daily devotions for an extended period of time, the dean of men decided that December to extend my counseling requirements into the second semester. To their minds, this failing warranted more attention than noticing that my actual problem was depression that needed medical attention. But then, they would say that's a spiritual problem too. One might think I would have learned not to be honest with them, but I was terribly naive and had yet to figure out that at BJU, the truth most decidedly will *not* set you free. I endured another term of the same snake-oil cure, which consisted of more Bible reading and Bill's bluster.

Several victories during my final semester gave me some endurance and hope for the future. First, I had been accepted to the Cleveland Institute of Music for graduate studies with a significant scholarship, and I performed the tenor solos for the chorale's presentation of Mozart's *Requiem*. Second, my voice teacher, Dr. Gingery, proved an empathetic advocate: when I told him my disappointment that I was never even considered for the traveling music ministry team to represent BJU, he noted that he himself, who had traveled on four different teams as a student fifty years before, would not have made the team with the current selection process.

Moreover, Dr. Gingery fought to remove my name from the blacklist and secured my place as a chapel soloist: my run-ins with the administration (the Robin incident and subsequent counseling sessions) prevented me from participating in anything considered "leadership," including singing for the student body. Dr. Lawson, the dean of the School of Fine Arts, eventually remarked to me backstage about getting me on the chapel special music schedule; I quipped with an exasperated smile, "Finally!" and he immediately threatened to remove me for not being grateful. I explained myself enough to hang on to my spot, but not without feeling the sword of Damocles dangling over my head. I sang Dr. Gingery's lone composition as something of a thank you, though we subsequently heard that Bob Jones III didn't appreciate its solemn minor key because he believed Christians and their music should always be happy. Additionally, Dr. G also arranged for me to sing for a former student who had become a prominent international opera conductor while he was visiting Greenville; nothing came of it, but it was a valuable experience.

My third personal victory came when I secured a spot as a men's voice finalist in the annual Commencement Competition alongside two other singers from Gingery's studio. It should be noted, however, that one of the original finalists from another studio was eliminated from the competition because he had accumulated too many demerits, so an alternate was bumped up with us. Still, as Dr. Gingery was nearing retirement and taking no new voice majors, this was the last year such a trifecta was possible, and it was indeed a singular tribute to his teaching. On all accounts, Dr. Gingery's office was a haven of music, coffee, smiles, and delicious stories, oft repeated but always relished. When he died in 2019, I debated returning to Greenville for his memorial service, but I realized the folly of opening psychological wounds and facing the judgmental glares from that community. Some friends later confirmed that I was justified in my decision not to return when they recounted unpleasant stories from their parents who had attended.

But that last semester was filled with fear too. I began noticing guys much more and became terrified someone would notice my lingering glance and beat me up or, even worse, turn me in. I began taking serious risks, calling gay chat lines from my dorm room and using my credit card to pay the membership fees. Mostly I just listened to the recorded ads, but a few times I would engage in a very quiet conversation. I still can't believe I was never caught, though possibly that was because I was using an outside line.

One Wednesday night, after driving around in circles for an hour, I dared to enter a gay bar, awkwardly confused by the term "cover" and completely ignorant about alcohol. They told me about the strippers at 11:00 p.m., but I knew I would have to return to campus by 10:15. There was a handful of people at the bar, including a saggy drag queen in a sparkly sack dress and an unfortunate wig. I sat in the corner by myself, vainly wishing for someone to proposition me, but no one did. Imagine my paranoia as I returned to campus with the sudden realization that I smelled like cigarette smoke: I racked my brain for names of local restaurants that had smoking sections and schemed a way to avoid as much contact with other students as possible. Luckily, Wednesday night meant room prayer group where each individual dorm room conducts its own prayer meeting, so I decided I would take the demerits for failure to check in by avoiding the front lobby and sneaking up the rarely used side staircase of my dormitory. I stuffed my bulky coat at the bottom of my laundry basket, and as soon as the bell rang to end prayer group, I stripped, grabbed my towel, and ran to the shower, hoping my hall leader didn't smell me as I hurried by.

I confided in Jason, my best friend from high school, who urged me over the phone to avoid taking such risks; he had read the rulebooks that I had smuggled to him—they were considered school property and not to be removed from the premises. He knew that I could lose it all, and he was right.

I tried to tell John, but when our attempt at a private conversation was interrupted, we never really broached the subject again until years later, when I finally came out of the closet. Near the end of the semester, I took Luke for a late walk to the isolated lake on back campus, insisting that I needed to talk to him with the utmost privacy; he joked that it must be bad if we were going all the way out there. When we sat by the big rocks by the edge of the lake, I told him that I was afraid I might actually be gay, just as everyone had told me all my life. He was near tears and insisted that it couldn't be true, that I didn't have to be that way, and that he would help me and pray for me. Luke never wavered in his friendship. Years later, when I did finally come out, his wife wrote a beautiful poem describing how the color gray arrived in her formerly black and white world.

Coda: Rejecting BJU's Symphony of Surveillance

I managed to stay out of the university's crosshairs for those final weeks and graduated in May 1999. I left the Cleveland Institute of Music after one semester, largely from the difficulty of transitioning to reality, exacerbated by my fear of being gay, which manifested in a strange desire to return to BJU with something to prove. I needed BJU's validation, for them to see me as a good musician and a great Christian; maybe they would even let me travel with the ministry team! When BJU delayed my admission because of my honesty, yet again, this time for admitting that I had tasted wine on three separate occasions *post-graduation*, I took that as a sign to stay away. Plus, a conversation with Jason gave me better clarity both about my miserable time there as well as the overall controlling nature of BJU.

He reminded me of the Bob Jones Sr. quotations riddled throughout those smuggled rulebooks, how the front of every classroom had a giant placard with one of those quotations mounted above the chalkboard. Why not scripture? Why not great Christians throughout history? Why not relevant artists and scholars? No, it was the founder above all, and BJU's policies reflected this control.

Control is exactly what BJU wants—at all times. We were not permitted to question or criticize the institution or its leadership. They tracked our movements and monitored our actions on and off campus, in and out of session, even after we graduated. They limited our access to multimedia, and they would withhold mail with "immodest" photos or objectionable material. They read our emails. The magazines in the library and the games in the student center were censored. We were only permitted to listen to approved classical and sacred music. They treated their people poorly, convincing them that their pitiful circumstances were better than what they deserved as wretched sinners, that their sacrifice was God's perfect will for their lives.

I began to recognize the twisted reality of the oppressive world I kept pursuing. Maybe the appeal was the structure, the formality; maybe it was the struggle. Regardless of what enticed me, it became clear that BJU is decidedly unhealthy, unsafe, and un-Christian.

Encore 1: Leaving Fundamentalism

My family and I began a theological exodus from fundamentalism. That process opened the door to my own spiritual curiosity, which took me in more liturgical directions, including a conservative Presbyterian church outside of D.C. and then a Continuing Anglican parish in the Atlanta suburbs. After years of praying away the gay, participating in an ex-gay therapy course with group counseling, and working with a litany of pastors and Christian counselors, I thought I had discovered my answer in Catholicism while studying historic worship patterns in one of my (liberal Methodist) seminary classes at Emory University, where I was pursuing a master's degree in sacred music. I thought converting and entering monastic life or the priesthood would allow me to practice my evolving faith and express my sexuality in celibacy, not to mention that Mother would finally get her prayed-for preacher boy. Problem solved!

But when I brought this plan to my parents during a summer visit, they were devastated, even more so than when they discovered my struggle with "same-sex attraction" many years before. In their view, Catholicism is not true Christianity, so I might as well have wanted to be Buddhist or atheist.

Still, the most telling moment was when my mother said to me, "So, no Bolden babies?"

"Mom, you have a dozen grandchildren already," I replied.

"But they're not Boldens!" My mother was counting on me to pass on the family name. Naturally, of course, within the confines of heterosexual Christian marriage.

Encore 2: Coming Out to Myself

I point to that moment as the beginning of the end of my sexuality struggle. Instead of converting to Catholicism, I finally came out of the closet very publicly in January 2012 due in large part to the quality psychiatric care I received at Emory University; I finally came to terms with the fact that I would never really be able to love someone fully until I acknowledged how and who I love. I said to my therapist on December 7, 2011, "I'm gay, and it's okay."

Likewise, I received profound encouragement and solidarity from a group of LGBT+ alumni from BJU that I had found on Facebook the previous summer, which also facilitated my reconciliation with Lance. He and I visited BJU together while in town for a gathering of the gays. In addition to making a statement by sneaking some photos of us kissing in the library, we found ourselves in the infamous dormitory stairwell where we had had our confrontation fifteen years before. As we lightheartedly recreated the scene, my breathing became heavy and labored; I ran down the stairs and out the door for fresh air to help me through a panic attack.

But after graduation from Emory, my life stalled. I couldn't find a job in my field, especially now that no evangelical church wanted an out gay man with Catholic inclinations. I returned to Washington, D.C., with my tail between my legs, disappointed and depressed. I clung to the idea that maybe Catholicism would still work out; however, after a year singing in the Schola Cantorum at St. Matthew's Cathedral in D.C., sitting directly under the pulpit of Cardinal Wuerl's coded rhetoric, I realized that I would always be right outside of the grace they offered, just like my experiences in fundamentalism and evangelical Protestantism. I left the choir and quit attending church for the better part of four years, inhabiting a darkness of hopelessness and hedonism, regret and recklessness. I doubted everything, from God's existence to my own will to live.

In the fall of 2017, a friend of mine had taken a new position as organist-choirmaster at St. Margaret's Episcopal Church, a parish that had welcomed the Washington, D.C., gay community at the height of the AIDS crisis. He asked if I would participate as a bass soloist for his choir. As a favor, I agreed to help him out for a few weeks. My first Sunday coincided with an acute family crisis, and I nearly canceled, but before I knew it, I committed to sticking around as a choral scholar. And then, on All Saints' Sunday, my faith reemerged. I expected the service to produce a few wistful tears of remembrance and anticipation; I was not prepared for the wave of love, swelled by winds of hope, that came crashing in to waken a long-dormant faith. I found myself blindsided by the individual elements all working in concert: the beauty of the liturgy, the vision of the scripture, the rhythm of the homily, the welcome of the table, the lyric of the anthem, the thrill of the soaring hymn descants. All these elements renewed my sense of Who and what and why. I was overcome.

For the first time I realized that the faith I was raised in was so loveless and literal, so introspective and hair-splitting that it could rarely manifest much real good in the world, and that true faith is so much more than just belief in a deity or a ticket to a comfortable afterlife. It is a force for positive change in the world, for love and grace and joy, for welcome and community and support.

I was forced to leave D.C. after a major health crisis cost me my personal assistant job; I retreated to my parents' home in Ohio, where I planned to stay no longer than a month or two while I regrouped and found a new position in a more exciting place than their quiet suburb. But a conspiracy of circumstances found me staying in my hometown, finally doing the work I've always dreamed of as the choirmaster in a local Episcopal parish and teaching private voice lessons to a host of young singers.

Encore 3: Fulfilling a Dream and Finally Living My Life

In another dream delayed, I was cast in a local community theater production of *Titanic*;[6] the director of the show had done just the thing I had wanted to do twenty years ago: run to New York and sing in one of the original Broadway production's national tours. I found myself in a strange emotional space, thrilled to be onstage again and singing this epic score yet negotiating the nostalgia, jealousy, and regret this opportunity stirred up, exacerbated by the news that BJU was mounting its own production of the show.[7] BJU's marketing video, which featured students dancing to ragtime music, seemed the peak of hypocrisy: I wondered whether they refunded tuition to students who had been kicked out for listening to that same music years ago, before they deemed the devil's ragtime fit for Christian consumption.[8]

But as I recount the difficulties I endured at BJU, it occurs to me that my trauma is as much vocational as it is emotional and spiritual. We frequently heard the message from the chapel platform and through marketing and recruiting materials that "BJU doesn't train students how to make a living, but how to live."[9] The irony here lies in the fact that they did not teach students how to live outside of a fundamentalist bubble; they were so invested in their fundamentalist separation that the education failed to present ideas or materials that might be contradictory to their understanding of the world.

We were taught how to conform to a particular standard of behavior—the only acceptable behavior in God's eyes—and any deviation was suspect and sinful. We were not taught to think critically or read widely; we were warned never to question authority, especially the Man of God. Curiosity beyond approved subject matter was not encouraged; rote memorization and regurgitation of facts were the order of the day. Scripture was the only lens for interpreting anything, and since they had already done that for us, we simply had to accept that. BJU didn't teach us *how* to live; they taught us the *only* way to live.

As a result, I could not live my life. BJU's perspective was so ingrained that it took me more than twenty years of struggling with an unattainable way of living before I finally found an equilibrium that made my current vocational contentment possible. And still, in spite of the happiness that I've stumbled upon, I continue to struggle with my professional competence due to the blatant holes in my unaccredited undergraduate education.

While packing up my D.C. apartment that fateful summer of 2018, a friend insisted on a final selfie together as we said goodbye; she cheered to discover that she captured a look that embodied my spirit, insisting that I faced life "leaning into joy." I cried. It sure took a while to get there.

Notes

1. Pseudonym.
2. Philippians 2:7.
3. Pseudonym.
4. Pseudonyms.
5. Pseudonym.
6. Players Guild Theatre, "*Titanic: The Musical.*"
7. BJU PR, "BJU Presents *Titanic: The Musical*"; Quigley, "BJU Presents Broadway Musical *Titanic.*"
8. Bob Jones University, "*Titanic: The Musical.*"
9. In the author's introduction to the original edition of Sr.'s *Chapel Sayings*, Sr. explains that people ask him the reason BJU alumni have been successful in finding jobs, saying they ask him "if this is because we teach our students how to make a living; and we always say, 'No, we try to teach them how to live; and if they learn how to live, they do not seem to have any trouble making a living.'" Jones, *Chapel Sayings of Dr. Bob*, 2.

chapter 4   FAWN MULLINIX

We ran down the hall and down the stairs together
and exited the building without any problems. Once
outside, I turned to her and asked if I could drive.
If the gate was closed, I was determined to find another way out because I was not staying another moment on BJU's campus, and I most certainly was not
calling my parents the next morning to confess to
them—in front of the dean of women and the dean
of students—that I was a homosexual. She agreed to
let me drive, and we headed to the main entrance of
campus to see what lay before us.

My Assurance

I grew up in a conservative pastor's home in rural Pennsylvania. My parents, aunt and uncle, and grandfather had all graduated from Bob Jones
University in years past. From the time I can remember as a little girl,
my immediate family and my grandparents attended BJU's annual Bible
Conference, where preachers from all around the globe were invited to
come for a week of nonstop services. It was expected that my siblings and
I would attend a private Christian college as well. I suppose we had "options" within that category, but the silent presumption was that we would
attend our parents' alma mater, BJU.

Not only was my dad the pastor of a small, nondenominational country church, but I was also homeschooled from second through twelfth
grade. I played sports with our local high school teams in summer recreational leagues, but other than that, most of my exposure to other kids
my age was limited to our church's youth group, which was quite small.
During my eleventh-grade year, I had my first experience with another
girl, the only other girl in our youth group besides my sister and me. We

began exploring things we knew nothing about, but, despite all of our experimentation, I never viewed myself as a lesbian. I recall reading Romans 1:26–27 and thinking, "That is not me. That's not what I'm doing. I'm just in love with my best friend. This is different from *that*." I earnestly loved God and believed in Jesus and His gift of salvation. But I couldn't deny my feelings for my best friend. What did it mean? How could I stop it?

I'd been taught that someone who *really* knew God and loved Jesus could not be homosexual, but I couldn't ignore this inconsistency with my own life experience. There were times I was so torn inside that I would cry to God on my bedroom floor, wondering if He still loved and accepted me, because I had heard those fiery sermons about homosexuals and impending doom if they didn't turn from their "perverted" ways. Conversations I overheard between my dad and my grandfather (who was also a pastor) further reinforced this anguish. When I was younger, they had talked about homosexuals, long before I knew what one was or that I was one, and I will never forget the words they used and the disgust that dripped from their voices as they described "those people."

As torturous as those moments were for a sixteen- and seventeen-year-old girl, I always came to the same conclusions: God *did* love me, He *did* accept me, and I *did* belong to Him. I repeatedly came to these conclusions because of verses like Romans 10:13, John 10:29, and Romans 8:31–39. These verses said that everyone who calls on the name of Jesus will be saved (no exceptions or conditions) and that no one can take us from the Father's hand. The verses in Romans 8 were the ones that gave me complete assurance. They told me that God the Father gave His only son, Jesus, for my sake and that nothing in Heaven above or Hell below—no demon, no angel, no fear, no worry, and no power—could separate me from the perfect love that God has for me. These verses helped me remember my devout mindset when I asked Jesus to save me as a young child. I understood what I was doing and why, and I sincerely believe God's unchanging love sustained me throughout the difficult journey I embarked on more than twenty years ago.

My First Confession at BJU

In fall 1997 I made a valiant effort as a freshman to dismiss my high school experience and turn my attention to the young men who were swarming on the BJU campus. As a criminal justice major, I saw no shortage of handsome, athletic guys to meet. I would sit in class and think, "This isn't so bad. I've got this! Nobody ever found out about my girlfriend in high school. I have a clean slate." With this enthusiasm, I interacted with a few guys I found attractive, but while they were always friendly, none of them asked me out. I was stumped then, but looking back now, I completely understand: I'm fairly certain their senses told them things about me that I hadn't yet come to understand about myself.

As my first semester unfolded, I learned things in criminal justice classes that concerned me deeply. We were studying the definitions of various crimes, one of which was statutory rape. In my inexperience, I jumped to conclusions about the relationship that I'd had back in high school with my best friend. She was a few years younger than me. Near the end of our relationship, she was sixteen, and I was eighteen. The fear that gripped me was paralyzing, although everything that transpired between us had been consensual. My mind raced to what could happen if she told anyone about our relationship. After a few weeks of debating with myself, I finally confided in my older sister, who was also a student at BJU. She was shocked but took the information well. Together, we decided to call our parents and tell them the whole story, especially because my high school girlfriend was still attending our church and was causing some trouble in the youth group. We did not know what she might be capable of.

On a Monday morning, I dialed my parents' home phone with trembling hands and heart to make my confession. They were devastated but loving in their response, noting that we all make mistakes and that God can forgive anything. Still, they wanted verbal affirmation that this sort of thing would *never* happen again. If so, we would all forget this whole ordeal. I couldn't have been more relieved. My parents still loved me, and we had a fresh start. This whole mess was behind me. Perfect!

An Unexpected Development

Perfect, that is, until an unexpected friendship began developing between me and an upperclassman who was part of my prayer group. Prayer groups were composed of three or four dormitory rooms of students who met on specified nights of the week to pray together and share a short devotional thought; they were mandatory for all on-campus undergrad students. She and I started spending more time together: breakfast and dinner, workouts, study time, hanging out in each other's dorm rooms, and shopping off campus. (As a junior, she was allowed to have a vehicle on campus, but underclassmen were not.)

That fall, the second president and chancellor of BJU, Dr. Bob Jones Jr., passed away. We attended his funeral service together, which turned out to be a significant bonding experience. Up to that point, she'd had very little exposure to funerals and death, while I, on the other hand, as a pastor's kid, had attended funerals all of my life, so I did my best to make her comfortable with the unfamiliar and unsettling event. By the time Christmas break came a few weeks later, it was rare to see one of us without the other.

Upon our return to campus for second semester, the charge between us intensified. We discussed sexuality at length, what we were feeling and experiencing, long before we crossed any physical lines. But once we crossed those lines, there was no turning back.

The first time we held hands was at a Vespers program, a required event that BJU held approximately twice a month on Sunday afternoons. Vespers consisted of devotional musical and dramatic productions provided by students, faculty, and staff. Most students dreaded going to them, but this particular one was enjoyable for me. We were seated in the balcony with the lights down to practically nothing. One of us draped our coat over our lap and the armrest between us, and at some point during the production we found each other's hands.

I knew we had to be very careful because certain faculty, staff, and even other students would love nothing more than to catch a couple of sinners like us committing some forbidden act. It was scintillating doing something so taboo on campus, surrounded by thousands of people who would have fainted at the thought of what we were doing, especially because BJU allowed little to no physical contact between male and female students. Couples were only allowed to hold hands on dating outings—chaperoned activities specifically designed for students to socially interact in a casual or romantic environment. That semester was full of adventure and close calls, and we enjoyed every moment.

After a long summer apart, we were eager to reconnect in the fall of 1998, which was my sophomore year and her senior year. Because the atmosphere at BJU did not foster any sense of privacy, we quickly became aware of our roommates' schedules so we could anticipate when they would come and go throughout the day; this knowledge gave us the ability to explore progressively further into forbidden territory.

In hindsight, I am amazed at some of the risks we took, such as my bright idea of sneaking into her room at night—which was across the hall and two doors down—to cuddle under the covers with her, all while we both had three roommates each! Because she was on the bottom bunk, she had the advantage of hanging a blanket from the bunk above her to cover her entire bunk area, a privacy screen of sorts that worked beautifully. Mandatory lights-out for all students except seniors was at 11 p.m., so I would set my alarm under my pillow and wake up at a certain time after that to head to her room. To keep my actions a secret, I had to pass several obstacles.

First, I had to make sure the hall leaders (upperclassmen who sat at a desk at the end of the hall to make sure everyone stayed in their rooms) and anybody else who might be heading to the community bathroom didn't spot me heading into the wrong room. Next, once inside her room, I had to be super quiet so her roommates didn't wake up and see me climbing into her bed. Finally, she had to set her alarm so that I woke up in time to go back to my room before morning rising bell, again without disturbing any of our roommates. And this is not something I did once or twice; this was our normal routine most nights of the week. Again, in hindsight, I can't believe I did that, but it just goes to show the lengths I would go to maintain a special connection. It may be hard to believe, but this risky behavior is not what exposed our secret relationship.

The Betrayal

Just after returning from Christmas break in January 1999, we had been out shopping for roller blades at the local sporting goods store and returned to campus just minutes before prayer group was to start at 10:30 p.m. When we walked into my girlfriend's room, a hall leader was waiting for us and told us we needed to come with her. Instantly, I knew we'd been discovered. My stomach sank and my adrenaline rushed as we followed the hall leader to the dean of women's on-campus apartment. The dean of women was a single woman who had never been married, never had children, and had never experienced, well, you know, the good stuff. She was widely regarded on campus as an "old maid" with little compassion for the human condition or the raging hormones of college-aged people. We knew she would not be empathetic during this meeting. The meeting consisted of two interrogators—the dean of women and the dormitory supervisor, yet another unmarried, unsympathetic, older woman.

They questioned us separately, my girlfriend first, then me, so we had no idea what the other had revealed. They asked all kinds of probing, demoralizing questions and finally disclosed their source: one of my girlfriend's roommates had rifled through her things without her knowledge, including her Bible, which carried an incriminating note from me. That roommate read it, then took it to the dean of women's office, which made a copy of it, and then she put the original back in my girlfriend's Bible. Talk about duplicitous and cunning! This is the type of behavior that was condoned and rewarded at BJU. If you could catch someone breaking the rules, you got brownie points with the administration.

As it turns out, we both had admitted to enough; we would be expelled from BJU the next morning. We also would be required to call our families in the morning to tell them we were being expelled because we had "homosexual tendencies and behaviors." To make matters worse, the dormitory supervisor informed us that a hall leader would be sleeping on the floor in each of our rooms that night to guard and watch us during the night to ensure we didn't commit any more immoral acts.

The Escape

My head was spinning, but I could only focus on figuring out how to escape this gated campus immediately. There was *no way* I was calling my family. Absolutely not happening. So I devised a plan. Their biggest mistake was letting us get ready for bed without supervision, so I told my girlfriend to pack a quick to-go bag with essentials before the hall leader came to sleep on her floor. Next, I told her to set her alarm for 1:00 a.m., and to stick it under her pillow so nobody else would wake up. (At least all those nights of sneaking back and forth counted for something.) Finally, once we left the dorm, we would use her car for our escape. But there was only one problem: at night, all the gates and entrances to campus are locked, except the front gate, which was watched by campus security. The official reason for having a gated campus was for security from nighttime riffraff, but we all knew the gate also served as a control measure to keep students on campus throughout the night.

Our one exit route, the front gate, resembled a toll booth that was placed in the middle of an entrance road and an exit road. The booth had a window facing both the entrance and exit sides that allowed the campus security officer to converse with the driver of the car, get the driver's name, and then open the gate to either side, which resembled a railroad crossing bar. I'd never left campus this late before, so I didn't know if it would be locked as well. What would we do if we had to talk to the officer in the booth? It was a chance we had to take. We had no other choice.

At 1:00 a.m., we woke to our alarms and met in the hall with our small bags of necessities. We ran down the hall and down the stairs together and exited the building without any problems. Once outside, I turned to her and asked if I could drive. If the gate was closed, I was determined to find another way out because I was not staying another moment on BJU's campus, and I most certainly was not calling my parents the next morning to confess to them—in front of the dean of women and the dean of students—that I was a homosexual. She agreed to let me drive, and we headed to the main entrance of campus to see what lay before us.

End of the Road

As we approached front campus, I let out a sigh of relief because I realized that the front gate was only partially closed. There was just enough room to drive around the bar safely, so I drove through without stopping to check in with the guard. We were free! We were out of that horrible place. We had the world at our fingertips—but where did we go then?

I had been so intent on leaving campus that I hadn't considered what to do next. We didn't have jobs or money, so, without many options, we dutiful daughters headed back to Pennsylvania. Her family lived near Pittsburgh, mine in south central Pennsylvania.

That drive to her folks' home in Mars, Pennsylvania, was such a long and sad journey. We talked about what we had just lost in the blink of an eye. At one point, we pulled off the side of the highway and sobbed with each other. She was in her last semester, and we knew our families would keep us apart once they figured out our news. In a bizarre turn of events, we arrived at her house only to discover her parents were out of town, which gave us time to regroup and collect our thoughts, but we knew the end was inevitable.

Like a good girl, I called my parents to let them know I was safe, but I was not prepared for their response. My father said my mom was physically ill, both about not knowing where I was and also about my homosexuality. Jim Berg, the dean of students, had called my parents to notify them that the university had no idea where I was because I had broken out of the school in the middle of the night with my lesbian lover.

When her parents and my parents made contact with each other, it was all over. Her parents drove me halfway between Pittsburgh and Harrisburg to reunite me with my parents. I was beyond broken. The pain was so deep in that moment that I couldn't even muster the energy to speak to my siblings when I slipped into the car. It felt like my world was ending. In some ways it was, but I learned something about myself—I always rise. I don't stay down.

A few weeks later, Dad and I drove to BJU in a friend's minivan to collect the belongings I had left behind that fateful night. I was a nervous wreck. What would my roommates say? How would people on the sidewalks and in the dorm treat me as I passed by? To my surprise, my roommates were very cool about it all. They were blown away that I had broken out in the middle of the night and told me how the hall leader had "freaked out" when she realized I had snuck out on her watch. One of my roommates had a pretty good idea I was a lesbian, so she wasn't totally shocked to hear what had happened. None of them treated me poorly. They were very kind to me despite the school's demoralizing approach to the situation.

Rejecting the Rejection

The next year was challenging. I lived with my parents, and I know it sounds incredibly ridiculous, but I reapplied to BJU one year later. When they expelled me, the school had told me and my parents that I could reapply after one year. It may not make sense, but I was determined to prove to myself that I could succeed there.

To our surprise, BJU turned down my application, adding that I could not return until everyone who was in my class had graduated. BJU didn't want those students exposed to the scandal I had created. It was just another example of BJU's desire for complete control over its students: the school feared that my presence would weaken its influence while I was on campus. I was a risk it couldn't handle. My dad called Jim Berg to say he was disappointed that BJU was only interested in pointing out people's sin but not in restoring them. As a result, my dad no longer financially supports the school, and my parents never attended another BJU Bible Conference.

But that rejection turned out to be a blessing. As it turned out, I didn't need to prove anything to BJU, myself, or God. I resumed my studies at

Clearwater Christian College beginning in January of 2000. I had a much better experience there and earned my BS in psychology in December of 2002, so I only lost one semester's worth of work.

True, I did attempt to change my sexuality there by immersing myself in church, surrounding myself with good influences, and not looking at attractive women. But after three and a half years of beating myself up for feelings that came naturally to me, I finally realized that I was who I was. Unlike many others I know who went through similar experiences at BJU, I did not lose my faith through these experiences or turn away from God completely. I certainly rejected what BJU stood for, and I never returned to campus, but I also discovered God in new and amazing ways over the next decade. Those same biblical passages of assurance that I mentioned earlier in this chapter resurfaced in my psyche and quashed any power that Romans 1:26–27 could ever hold over me.

I came to a realization that I needed to stop fighting myself and being miserable. I knew that sharing this news with both of my parents simultaneously would be too much for me to manage, so I chose to come out to my mom in October of 2005. She was devastated and said I was "giving up" on fighting against what she called "my struggle." I told her that I had been fighting my sexuality at different times for most of my adult life and that I was finished trying to be something or somebody that I was not. It was time for me to be authentic with myself and the rest of the world, and that world included my parents.

It's one thing to be authentic to myself, but why in the world would I go through all this hardship in coming out to my parents, especially when I had already put them through so much grief when I got expelled from BJU? To be frank, I needed to make sure that my parents knew where I was in terms of self-identity for two reasons. First, I had lied to them on and off for years to cover up my relationships with women because I knew my parents would disapprove. I needed to be transparent with them now so that I could start building their trust again, even if they didn't like what they were hearing. Second, I needed to know if I would still be accepted and loved and included in the family dynamic. We have always been a close family, and their acceptance really mattered to me. It still does to this day.

We went through some tough times after I came out to them. During some of those times I had to create some space between us so that we could keep the overall relationship healthy. I learned that boundaries are important and healthy. More importantly, I learned how to set boundaries with them instead of allowing them to dictate their rules and boundaries to me. Almost fifteen years later, my parents and I have a stronger, more open relationship now than we ever had. We work together to live peaceably with each other, as much as lies within us.[1]

I will never forget that night I escaped from the clutches of BJU's surveillance. My then-girlfriend and I managed to at least temporarily take control of our own lives in an attempt to foil BJU's outing us to our respective families. That night taught me that nobody else gets to determine my value or define my relationship with myself or my God. If God wanted us to all be the same, He would have made us the same. Instead, I know that I am truly "fearfully and wonderfully made,"[2] and it brings Him joy for me to share my unique self with the world around me. I want my breakout from BJU's fundamentalism to inspire others who have been marginalized to take that first step toward self-acceptance. That first step doesn't have to be as dramatic as mine when I made my escape from BJU in the middle of the night, but any step that rejects the oppressive, controlling nature of fundamentalism is a step in the right direction.

Notes

1. Romans 12:18.
2. Psalm 139:14.

chapter 5   MEGAN MILLIKEN

Immediately, I jumped out of my seat and literally ran across the campus to my dormitory. It
was locked. I panicked. I knew why that door was
locked; it was locked so people just like me couldn't
hear of the inspection and try to stonewall it. I
banged on the door with the side of my fist as hard
as I could. I was thinking as fast I could when the
door flew open from the inside and a member of the
administration's eyes met mine with a look of evil
interrogation I'd never seen before and have never
seen again.

The Smell of Sex

The bell rang at 10:50 a.m., signaling the end of third hour at Bob Jones
University, and I still had the smell of sex on my skin. That bell meant the
entire campus—from students to professors to deans to custodians and
gardeners—had approximately ten minutes to gather in a gigantic auditorium for the daily campus-wide mandatory meeting. It was time for
chapel.

My heart had been racing the entire hour, so when that bell rang, it
heralded both relief and dread. It was the fall of 2003, and that semester's
custom had been for McCall and me to walk to chapel together after third
period. But this would be the first time I would see her since she had left
my bunk bed in the wee hours of that morning. I was *freaking* out.

In my nineteen-year-old mind, nightmares swirled: losing my best
friend because we had gone too far, getting expelled from college, ending my dreams of becoming a lawyer, and spending eternal damnation
in hell. The anxiety became overwhelming as I spotted her waist-length
dark hair and her ankle-length dark skirt. I sheepishly waved and walked

through the sea of rushing students to get to her. She smiled casually, leaned over the water fountain, and took a sip. Then she looked up at me and said with a baffling nonchalance, "I am so tired."

She wasn't freaking out! This realization made me instantly relax. I don't know what we talked about on the across-campus trek to chapel that day, but I know it wasn't about the sex we'd had that morning or what would become of our situation that now seemed irreversible.

How could we go back to being "just friends"? As if I hadn't been her first kiss or she hadn't been the one to whom I first made love? Even more pressing, at the time, was the impossibility that we could ever redeem ourselves from the certain consequence of our bliss, which was eternal damnation in hell.

And how could I go back home? I had gone to BJU to escape the chaos and violence of my home. When I had visited campus as a high schooler, I was struck—truly struck—by the calmness at BJU. It was so regimented and controlled; no one would break my door down in the middle of night to attack me as I slept. I needed the safety that BJU provided. I couldn't go back home to the belly of the beast.

After that day, McCall and I grew progressively closer. Suddenly, we weren't hanging out with our other friends or visiting our respective homes as much as we once had, since we both lived within a few hours' drive of the university. We were in love. I called my very serious boyfriend of a few years who was a student at North Carolina State University and told him I had found someone new: a boy named Mike. Yes, that's what I actually told him. It would be years before he or anyone else would know or confirm the actual truth.

From 2003 to 2005, whispers grew about McCall and me, whispers that developed into an intervention from "concerned friends." She and I were aware of these whispers, but I did everything I could to keep them at bay. I tried not to let people see us stealing glances. I tried to tone down my very obvious glee when she walked into the room. I tried to convince my friends I was interested in this boy or that boy. As it turns out, though, I was really bad at hiding our pulsating and uncontainable love.

It seemed like nearly every day I would encounter someone making a comment about McCall and me being "close friends," which felt like a dangerous euphemism. One night specifically stands out when McCall and I were hugging goodnight. We were in the hallway of the dorm surrounded by dozens of milling and busy students preparing for the end of the day, and we innocently and quickly hugged goodnight. The hall leader—a fellow dorm student designated by the administration to oversee and penalize students for "bad behavior"—saw us. She moved with a quickness and precision that instantly worried me. In front of all those other students, she pulled at my arm like a chastising mother and said, "Uh-uh, we don't do *that* here!" I jerked my arm away from her grip and said, "Do what? Say goodnight?" She was left speechless, while I remained furious. I interpreted that encounter to mean that the administration had its eye on us and that its concern had trickled down to the student leaders. They had been told to watch us. And they were doing just that.

So many students I knew had been expelled from school for far more minor offenses than the whispers against us: kissing a boyfriend, listening to an unapproved radio station or song, watching television, or even going to a movie theater. I took the threat of the whispers seriously; I couldn't let this be our fate too.

At the time, BJU was not regionally accredited, so despite our hard work in our rigorous academic programs, the credits we had earned thus far would likely count as very little or potentially nothing because of their unaccredited transfer value to other schools. That meant we became absolutely captive to BJU the longer we invested our time, money, loans, and credit hours into our education there.

Given the severely restrictive social and academic nature of the school, McCall and I told no one of our relationship, and we continued to fall in love with each other over the next few years.

Why Go to BJU?

I've noticed a pattern of responses when I tell people I am a BJU graduate. Invariably, they give me a look that's 90 percent shock and 10 percent horror. What comes next is some minor variation of, "*What?* Oh, you must've been forced!" They don't understand why I—a hard-charging trial lawyer and openly proud lesbian—could have *willingly* attended an institution defined by societal exclusion and female submission, but it's the truth: I not only willingly applied to BJU, but I also did so with eagerness, earnestness, and excitement.

Next, in this pattern of responses, I'm always asked, "Why? Why would you *willingly* go to BJU?" And every single time, I answer the same way: "Well, you'd have to enter the psyche of a seventeen-year-old." My response usually ends the well-meaning inquisition as I always intend to do because the honest answer is too long and too personal. If I were to answer that question, they would understand that a glimpse into that seventeen-year-old's psyche goes a little like this:

My parents divorced when I was a young child, but it wasn't your garden-variety divorce with the occasional bad blood. This was a divorce so nasty and so intense that the litigation lasted for years. In fact, my parents' divorce made state law in North Carolina, where I was born and raised, and if anyone is truly interested, they can read all about a three-year-old Megan in North Carolina case law. As a result of the divorce, I was raised predominantly and nearly exclusively by my mother, whom I loved very much. She was charismatic, intelligent, and crowd-silencingly beautiful. But she had substance abuse problems—likely from the divorce—that made my childhood home unpredictable at best and terrifying at worst. I needed a safe haven, so I started attending the closest church to my house, which happened to be a fundamentalist Baptist church and where my youth pastor was a BJU grad.

Because the church provided what I perceived as a safety net from the chaos and violence of my home, I attended three services per week from fourth grade until I went to BJU. During this time, I accepted Jesus as my Savior at age ten, and I participated in youth group trips to BJU and a summer camp called The Wilds,[1] which was run by BJU graduates. At that camp, I met a woman who would change my life forever. I was sixteen or seventeen years old, and she was my camp counselor. She was the first and only person I had ever told about what was going on in my home; conveniently enough, she was also an admissions counselor at BJU.

She captivated me and was somehow able to extract from me the hellish psychological traumas of my home. Once I realized her comforting power, I knew I would've done almost anything to be around her. She was the first person in my entire life with whom I felt like I could truly exhale. After meeting that fateful summer, she would call my house from time to time. Invariably, she would hear my mom screaming at me in the background about anything or nothing, and she would comfort me. Her words were like salve I had never known. They healed me yet left me craving for more. I had never known true comfort and understanding until I met her.

Over the months, she convinced me to consider attending BJU. I had excelled in school and could have likely gone to any college I applied. But those colleges didn't have her. So I agreed and went to campus for a visit.

That visit changed my life because it offered me a three-day, two-night glimpse into what a calm life could be. In hindsight, I mistook the controlled environment for calm and tranquility, but at that point, the veneer hadn't yet been ripped off, so all I could see was the quiet environment. And quiet was what I desperately needed.

The Intervention at BJU

One of the saddest realities of having an LGBT relationship at a place like BJU is not that your romantic partnership is extremely stifled; rather, it's that your platonic friendships suffer greatly. Because we were forced to live a deeply cloistered and fear-driven romantic life on campus, we couldn't perform all those rites of passages I had normally heard about from other ladies on campus when they fell in love with a guy: McCall and I couldn't tell our group of friends how we had blindly stumbled into this great love; we couldn't dish about how great the sex was or rehash our latest row; nor could we flee to them for comfort because, as it turns out, they were sometimes even more dangerous than the university administration.

No matter how conscious we were of our need for secrecy, we still found it difficult to hide our real and life-changing love. We did our best by never telling anyone about our relationship. Plus, we tried to hide our longing looks from across the room, but we weren't as successful as we thought. One Saturday afternoon, our group of friends came to "confront" McCall and me about "our sin": they suspected our relationship had progressed beyond a mere friendship. The evidence they offered was from the night before, when they had noticed our "sex-me eyes" at dinner. I remember that Friday night well. We had gone to Fuddruckers, a burger joint, with nearly a dozen of our friends. McCall and I had chosen to sit as far apart as we possibly could in an effort to hide the most beautiful connection we'd ever known. But we had shared a glance that our "friends" had detected, logged, and concluded was sinful.

In that moment of purported "love" through their confrontation, I felt a flurry of emotions I should never have to feel when speaking to people I considered friends about something deeply personal and serious like love. I felt enraged, terrified, and, above all, deeply betrayed. Here were my friends, our friends, trying to extrapolate information from McCall and me so they could turn us in to the administration and have us expelled. It was crushing.

Back then, I always felt like it was my responsibility to protect the true nature of our relationship. I suppose it's the same responsibility I still feel today to protect McCall when I know she's going to be in a large crowd or go for a jog in an unfamiliar city. So, in that moment, I acted. I immediately—and justifiably—turned the accusation onto the accusers by questioning their motive and their friendship. I also questioned their own friendships with each other by asking if it was a sin to have a best friend. As I responded, I intentionally reacted in a big way because I needed them to know that they never should've felt entitled to approach me with such a personal question. None of those friendships recovered from that afternoon. I told them to get out of my dorm room immediately, and to this day I've never spoken to them again.

That failed intervention ignited the whispers into an inferno of rumor. On a controlled campus like BJU, the administration was bound to notice. In fact, the campus culture encourages students to curry favor with the administration by reporting any and all salacious gossip. Besides gathering information from students, the university administration would also routinely inspect our dorm rooms, which did not have locks on the doors. The administration would even read our most personal journals.

One time, I was in a class where I heard whispers that the administration was doing a "room check" in my dorm. A room check is when the administration's agents would scour your dorm room looking for any sort of contraband whatsoever. I knew I had to act quickly or my secret would be out. I had written dozens, if not hundreds, of poems and journal entries about the revolutionary love I was experiencing. I had to get that notebook. Fast.

Immediately, I jumped out of my seat and literally ran across the campus to my dormitory. It was locked. I panicked. I knew why that door was locked; it was locked so people just like me couldn't hear of the inspection and try to stonewall it. I banged on the door with the side of my fist as hard as I could. I was thinking as fast I could when the door flew open from the inside and a member of the administration's eyes met mine with a look of evil interrogation I'd never seen before and have never seen again.

She asked me what I was doing. *Think fast, Megan!* And with that internal rallying cry, I yelled out, "I'm bleeding. I need a tampon!" She replied that she'd get me a tampon, but she also turned her back, and when she did that, I bolted past her. I swear I was running at Olympic speed as I tore down that hallway in an ankle-length skirt. She yelled at me to "Hold on!" but I kept running. I got to my room, grabbed my journal, stuffed it into my waistband, and grabbed a tampon just as she opened the door. "Whew!" I said. "I gotta get to the bathroom," and I quite literally pushed my way past her. Later, after my heart rate returned to normal, I said an inner prayer of thanks. We were safe—at least for the moment.

But I knew time wasn't on our side. With our friends, the culture of the student body, and the regular invasions by the administration, I knew the administrators would notice us eventually. And notice they did. I was called in to meet with an administrator who clothed herself in the deceitful title of "counselor," but she was no counselor whatsoever. She was, however, someone who had the authority—if I confirmed the true nature of my relationship with McCall—to remove me from BJU and destroy my lifelong dreams of going to law school.

When I sat down in her office, I already knew what was coming from her. Time slowed down. It was bizarre, but it felt like I was in slow motion as I made the conscious decision to play the greatest part I would likely ever have to play. So, just like with my "friends" during their intervention, I made the knee-jerk decision to play it up *big*. The counselor asked point-blank if I was having a sexual relationship with McCall. This was my moment to exterminate the whispers and rumors. I stood up, started crying very real tears, and screamed, "How could you think such a thing about me? I am so offended!" I then ran out of that room and slammed the door harder than I've ever shut a door before or since. I ran to my room, fast. For some reason, I believed that if I got back to my room, on my own turf, whoever might be following me would have to meet me on my own terms. But no one ever came. I smiled a little because it felt like I had beaten them at their own game of emotional manipulation.

Because the administration could not extract damning information from me or McCall, even by using our friends, it tried other means. In every dorm building, there was an internal camera facing the entrances and exits to the dorm. They were intended, presumably, as a safety measure. But these cameras were conveniently located between my room and McCall's room. We learned how to hug the walls and sneak past their gaze to connect with each other.

The administration then adjusted the cameras between my dorm room and McCall's dorm room to eliminate any blind spots. It was clear that the administration figured we were sneaking into each other's dorm rooms at night, so they moved the cameras. I can remember the day I came in from class and saw the maintenance men on ladders moving the cameras so that they'd now capture us; I panicked. But like always, we devised a plan. We would climb the stairwells, stealthily move across the other hallways and then descend the closest stairwell to our destination. Because what is love if it isn't evading cameras?

(Questioning) Life after BJU

Thankfully, we both graduated—McCall in 2005 and I in 2006—without further traumatic confrontations. We had learned to live in isolation with ourselves. McCall entered a career in the medical profession while I began law school. But even though we had geographically distanced ourselves from BJU, we both couldn't quite psychologically shake the fundamentalist teachings and the fears that accompany those teachings. McCall became preoccupied with the feeling that our love, despite it being sacrificial, faithful, and selfless, was an eternal sin damning us to hell. I have to admit: I wasn't fully convinced she was wrong.

It's impossible to immediately and irrevocably shed the teachings, culture, and beliefs that have absolutely defined one's previous life simply because something changed, even if that something that changed was meeting the love of your life. McCall struggled immensely with the meaning of certain verses in the Bible—specifically the two or three verses that claim a man lying with another man is "an abomination." So after four years together, she called me and ended the relationship. Philosophically speaking, with that one phone call, my life as I had known it thus far had ended. I found myself in that uncomfortable position of being forced to evaluate my entire life's religious history to figure out how and why I could be held hostage to these beliefs.

While attending law school, I shunned my classmates and spent my time in solitary confinement as I completed my coursework. But also during this time, I read the Bible, tried to love a guy here and there, visited a Baptist church, and even saw a Christian psychologist. I wanted to know who I really was.

Self-Discovery

My journey of self-discovery led me to a firmer belief that the love between McCall and me *is* the defining aspect of my life: it is where I began, and it was where I knew I was supposed to end. The love we shared was the safety I had always needed growing up. It wasn't fraudulent, like the "safety" at BJU, which was clothed in control and manipulation and retribution and negative consequence. Our love was pure, authentic safety, the result of two people falling madly in love with each other in a relationship full of sacrifice, loyalty, trust, understanding, and compromise. My journey of discovering myself was recognizing who I was, both inside and outside the prism of our love, and that discovery led to only one conclusion: I am her and she is me. To put a twist on that oft-quoted verse heard in weddings: our love joined us together, and there is no man that could tear us asunder.[2] I just needed patience for McCall to realize this too.

Those same people who ask me *why* I went to BJU also ask me *how* I became the openly proud lesbian I am today—the one who utterly rejects the verses that fundamentalists manipulate to clobber you if they suspect you might be "struggling with homosexuality," the one who rejects all forms of organized religion and even doubts the existence of an actual creator or benevolent God. I tell them: There was no epiphany. I wish there had been. It would've saved me years of belabored torture of doubt, confusion, and the very real conviction I was going to hell for all of eternity. Instead, my beliefs are a direct result of that belabored torture. Years of researching, studying, praying, and tormenting myself over what the Bible says has led to my complete rejection of it.

My path back to McCall took a little longer. After I graduated law school, I moved to Charlotte with a brand new sense of self-acceptance. There were times I couldn't completely shake the vestiges of my old beliefs, though. For example, I recoiled when someone would take the Lord's name in vain in front of me, and I'd shamelessly ask them to never do it again in my presence. But overall, I began to slowly embrace my true identity as a lesbian. I became friends with other lesbians who introduced me to the greater LGBT community. While in Charlotte, I was in two relationships, but they were both short-lived because all the while, no matter how hard I tried to forget about McCall, I simply couldn't.

During this time, McCall enrolled in a seminary course to better understand the very text that was keeping her from the love of her life. She also saw a fundamentalist Christian counselor and even once asked me to come meet with him and her for a session. I wasn't optimistic about the session, but I was willing to give it a try if it meant getting back with her, so I drove down to Charleston, South Carolina, where she was living, and met with them. While the "counselor" berated us and told us we were going to hell, I was overcome with the obvious reality that he, too, was gay, but he was so severely closeted that he directed his anger and misery toward us. I left the session and told McCall I wouldn't endure that kind of abuse ever again, but I also told her to call me if she ever figured out her life.

Two key factors proved to be influential in our reunion. First, she moved to Asheville, North Carolina, where her horizons began to broaden as a result of the very inclusive, loving, and accepting culture that defines that city. Second, I got sick, really sick. I needed surgery, and despite my being in a relationship with someone else who I truly cared for, I only wanted McCall with me. She came to be by my side, and we have never been separate since.

We are engaged and living together with two dogs and two cats. Notwithstanding their very conservative and even Trumpian beliefs, my family is very accepting and loving toward McCall. In fact, sometimes I think they like her more than they like me. McCall's family is a different story entirely. For the better part of the last fifteen years, they've deployed a litany of battle strategies against us—everything from banishment to shunning to degradation. They are the reason I came up with the proverb "There's no hate like hating for Jesus." But I am happy to report that in the last year a few of them have begun to show us more kindness.

Reevaluating My Life

While writing this story, a persistent question crept into my thoughts, causing me to reevaluate my life: besides falling in love and creating a life with someone I'll love forever, what was the point of all this? And then, it hit me. Recounting my story showed me what I needed to hear—all of this has made me tough as nails.

I fought for years against nearly insurmountable obstacles for McCall and for my own peace of mind. I have lived in the depths of depression, convinced I was offending a holy God just by being alive, and even struggled with suicidal ideation as a result. But I made it. I made it because it really *does* get better. Recently, I told someone that I am the strongest person I've ever met. And I believe that. Since emerging from the pile of ashes that was my life, I haven't faced one single problem where I didn't *know* I'd be just fine. I've made it through hell, and I'm not going back.

In the greater sense, my story serves as a testament that even the most immutable, immovable, and unrelenting beliefs can change. In the news recently, some man did some great thing, but then the media found inappropriate tweets from when he was sixteen years old. The great thing he had done was now cast in a different and unforgiving light. I look at that story and am so thankful I didn't have social media when I was sixteen. Otherwise, you might've seen a post from me about how gays should burn in hell forever, or how those who reject the Bible should suffer, or how those that don't believe in Jesus Christ as their Savior are lost and ignorant.

That sixteen-year-old version of me was happily attending that summer camp run by BJU graduates. That camp had a mantra. The speaker would say a line and the children, in grades six through twelve, would finish the mantra in unison, the same mantra, I am told, that was also spoken at one time by Bob Jones III to the student body during BJU chapel sessions.[3] The speaker's line was "The most sobering reality in the world today is that . . ." and the children, the hundreds and hundreds of children, in robotic fashion would reply, "people are dying and going to hell today."

But the most sobering reality isn't that one. At least not to me. If I could reply to that speaker's line today, I would say that the most sobering reality is that "we aren't slaves to someone else's beliefs or dictates." What sobered me up was understanding life for myself. Just because BJU believes something doesn't automatically mean that I do too. Self-discovery is the most sobering, and wonderful, reality in the world today.

Notes

1. *The Wilds.*
2. Matthew 19:6.
3. According to web archives, the chapel summary for Monday, September 9, 1996, included the following: "Dr. Bob reminded us to keep before us the quote that we often recite responsively in Chapel, 'The most sobering reality in the world today is that people are dying and going to hell today.'" Bob Jones University, "September Chapel Messages."

PART TWO   *Other Institutions*

And other sheep I have, which are not of this fold:
them also I must bring, and they shall hear my
voice; and there shall be one fold, and one shepherd.

JOHN 10:16

The reader might wonder why this section contains only two chapters. True, these contributors could have been grouped in another unit. Both Curt Allison and Micah J. Smith still identify as religious or spiritual, for example. But both of these voices carry a unique perspective because they provide insight into other conservative Christian colleges. Curt's choice to attend Oral Roberts University for graduate work is certainly unexpected because of some striking differences between BJU and ORU. The casual secular outsider may not be aware of these differences between nationally known religious colleges like BJU, ORU, or even Brigham Young University, but a fundamentalist would. As the ORU website states, "ORU was founded by Oral Roberts in 1963 upon the power of the Holy Spirit and the authority of scripture." Self-labeled as a "charismatic, Christian, liberal arts university," ORU sets itself apart from schools like BJU through its emphasis on the Holy Spirit in addition to scripture.[1]

George W. Dollar lists "three kinds of modern *professing* Fundamentalists: the militant (the genuine, historic Fundamentalists), the moderate, and the modified," and he places ORU in the modified group, claiming that the school believes in the same major doctrines as fundamentalists but are technically more evangelical because they "play down the importance of separation from all forms of apostasy and compromise."[2] David O. Beale would concur with Dollar's point that ORU is more evangelical than fundamentalist. In his chart of different subcategories of evangelicalism, Beale lists ORU as "Ecumenical charismatic" because of its "emphasis on baptism with the Holy Spirit; extraordinary gifts; experience above Scripture."[3]

Curt Allison writes about his journey from fundamentalism to evangelicalism and beyond. Attending BJU for a few semesters in the early

eighties, Curt emphasizes his positive experiences as a student in finding a community of like-minded believers. However, his zeal for fundamentalism waned after his parents joined a non-fundamentalist church,
which made him question why fundamentalism teaches that secular music, movies, and other denominations are considered bad. After transferring and completing his studies at a state school, Curt completed a graduate degree in church music at Oral Roberts University. He is the only
contributor to this book who participated in the ex-gay ministry from
Exodus International. Realizing the ex-gay therapy wasn't working, Curt
discusses his success in affirming his gay identity and also being ordained
in the United Church of Canada.

Micah, on the other hand, attended Pensacola Christian College, which
was founded in 1974 by Arlin and Rebekah Horton, who were both 1951
BJU graduates.[4] The 1993–1994 catalog notes that "100 students arrived
at Pensacola Christian College's one building" for that first year. While
students who attend ORU typically do not come from the same network
of churches and schools as those who attend BJU, the same cannot be
said for PCC. Given that PCC was founded by BJU graduates, it is not
uncommon for traveling ensembles from PCC and BJU to visit the same
churches for promotional campaigns, though the schools have had their
share of differences. Still, it is easy to spot the close similarities between
the two schools when looking at the inside front cover of the 1991–1992
catalog, which provides a very similar statement about a student's privileged status that BJU does: "Attendance at Pensacola Christian College
is a privilege and not a right. Students forfeit this privilege if they do not
conform to the standards and ideals of work and life of the College, and
the College may insist on the withdrawal of a student at any time that the
student, in the opinion of the College, does not conform to the spirit of
the ministry."[5]

As a third-generation BJU student, Micah J. Smith attended BJU in
the early 2000s. He expresses his enthusiasm at finding his independence
at BJU after such a supervised childhood. However, Micah's time at BJU
was short-lived because of his father's disagreements with the school, revealing just how vulnerable children of fundamentalist households are to
their parents' influence, even as those children grow into early adulthood.
He was allowed to transfer to PCC, but his time was cut short there because of rumors that he was gay. Unfortunately, Micah experienced firsthand how tenuous it is for a student to maintain the subjective privileged
status as a member of the PCC community. Both stories in this unit show

that BJU is not the only strict religious college campus in this country and that queer Christian students can be attracted to colleges across the spectrum of fundamentalism and evangelicalism.

Notes

1. Oral Roberts University, "General Information about ORU."
2. Dollar, *A History of Fundamentalism in America*, 283, 285.
3. Beale, *In Pursuit of Purity*, 269.
4. Pensacola Christian College, "History of PCC."
5. *Pensacola Christian College Undergraduate Graduate Catalog, 1993–1994*, 6; *Pensacola Christian College Undergraduate Graduate Catalog, 1991–1992*.

chapter 6   CURT ALLISON

> While I was at BJU, I noticed a crack forming in my
> fundamentalist armor. Everything outwardly fit the
> mold, fit the expectations of others, and fit my own
> idea of how I believed I should be in this world. But
> looks can be very deceiving. If anyone had peeled
> away the layers of my rock-solid, ironclad presenta-
> tion to the fundamentalist community on campus
> and beyond, they would have found a very confused
> young man whose sexual identity was demanding to
> be acknowledged.

The Poster Boy for Fundamentalism

I was born in Greensboro, North Carolina, on a hot summer day in 1964.
Raised by loving parents who cared for me and provided everything I
needed, I remember a happy childhood filled with lots of laughter. Being good southern folk, we attended church every single Sunday, but the
church we attended was an independent Baptist church. Our church was
not part of the Southern Baptist Convention, which we viewed as heretical and not strict enough with its theology, nor in what it allowed its
members to do. For example, Southern Baptists could attend movie theaters, but we did not think Christians should do so because of the potential worldly content of the movie and its damage to our testimonies. To
an outsider, this notion may sound unbelievable, but this type of conviction was a big deal for us. Strict beliefs and exacting theologies were required to be a good, faithful Christian. When I was around eleven years
old, our family began attending an Independent Fundamental Baptist
church, which would impact the trajectory of my life in unthinkable ways.

I also attended the Christian school connected with the church, but
even though I had attended the church since grade school, it wasn't un-

til September of 1979, when I was fifteen, that I personally made a public profession of faith. I was at a Christian camp, and on the final night
during the evening worship service, I personally accepted Jesus as my
Lord and Savior (the phrase commonly used in my church that meant
I now publicly identified myself as a born-again Christian). After that
point, I attended every single service of the church and especially looked
forward to special week-long services called "revival services," which occurred about once or twice a year. I was heavily involved with the school,
too: I played the piano for various choir groups; I was Senior Class President, co-captain of the basketball team, and also recipient of the Christian Leadership Award at graduation. In short, *I was the poster boy for
fundamentalism*, and I wholly believed in the fundamentalist Christian
institution.

I began to sense my same-sex desires in seventh grade. My first recol-
lection occurred in the locker room after basketball practices. I couldn't
deny the strong rush of hormones while there. But because of the weekly
preaching I had heard from the pulpit at my Independent Fundamental Baptist church—preaching from the "clear word of God" that homosexuality is an abomination—I interpreted these hormones as part of the
Devil's work to draw me away from God's plan for my life. So instead
of talking about these same-sex desires, I stuffed those feelings deep inside and made sure to live as a good fundamentalist young man at home,
school, and church. I would not openly recognize my same-sex desires
again—to myself or anyone else—until I was twenty-five years old.

The next logical step for me was to attend Bob Jones University, which
I had heard about at my Christian school. Not only had several teachers
and administrators graduated from BJU, but our church and school also
hosted traveling music ensembles from BJU. Plus, every year, a group
made up of mostly BJU graduates helped us produce a student-run play,
complete with costumes, lighting, and music. Since BJU was heavily promoted in our school as an ideal place, I always assumed I would go there.
So did everyone else in my group of friends. The only person who questioned my choice was my dad, but I could easily ignore his questions because he was not a Christian at that time. He didn't get it.

To this day, some people question why I would willingly attend this
strict, fundamentalist university. I usually respond with the following
point: growing up as a fundamentalist, my worldview was carefully controlled through a rigid fundamentalist lens. Anything outside that lens
had no place in my life, and that included my choice of university, so I

never considered attending anywhere else but a fundamentalist Christian college. Plus, I was genuinely *excited* to attend BJU. For me, attending BJU was part of being a faithful Christian. It wasn't some crazy school with strict rules and regulations; it was a school that was serious about following Jesus. In fact, the rules *proved* that the university took the Bible seriously because, in my mind, the strict rules were based on the Bible. BJU was serious about being a Christian university, and I was serious about living a Christian life. It was a match made in heaven.

In total, I attended BJU for three semesters, starting in the fall of 1982 through the end of the fall semester of 1983, and during that time, I enjoyed most every aspect of the school: I made friends almost from day one, I loved my classes and my professors, and I was involved in my literary society—BJU's equivalent of a college Greek system—and sang in our society choir. I distinctly remember feeling at the end of my first semester an intense gratitude that I was at BJU, that God had led me there, and that I was someone who believed in the true Christian faith, not a faith that had been watered down by more liberal churches. The rules at school actually gave ine a sense of security in the world, and, as I stated before, I felt like I was following God's plan for my life by going to BJU.

During my first year there, we received an announcement in one of the chapel services that the IRS had revoked BJU's tax-exempt status over the school's ban on interracial dating.[1] Even though I was raised in the South in the 1970s and 1980s, I lived in an overwhelmingly White bubble. My church, my neighborhood, and my friends were all White. Because of this White bubble, I held the unexamined theology of my church which stated that interracial dating is not part of God's plan. So this announcement at BJU fell neatly within my worldview at that time.

Furthermore, that moment instilled in me a sense that we as "true" Christians were being persecuted by the world for our beliefs, and in a strange way, that sense of persecution gave me an even greater feeling of security: a security that tells you exactly what to believe theologically, a security that gives you strict rules on how to live outside of church, and a security that promises you an approval by God and admission to heaven because of your beliefs, even if people make fun of you. That approval by God provided a sense of security for my present life and the hereafter. My identity while at BJU was strongly linked both to fundamentalist practices and (what I believed to be) the consequential persecution from the world because of those practices, persecution which reinforced my assurance that I was exactly where I needed to be.

The Filtered BJU Life

Students live a filtered life at BJU. Fundamentalism filters out reality and critical thinking, especially about race, so I filtered my entire experience at school to mirror that fundamentalist reality, even if life wasn't really that way. Because of the way BJU structures its student restrictions for going off campus, I didn't spend much time off campus my first year to acknowledge the racial diversity of Greenville residents. The times I did go off campus, I instinctively had my guard up to "be careful about the world," even if I was just going to the bookstore or the mall. I could only relax when I returned to the secured whiteness of campus, the place where God's people are. This lack of racial awareness is one of the nasty residues of fundamentalism that I still deal with today.

But my identity was much more than being a fundamentalist, more than I could admit, even to myself at the time. While I was at BJU, I noticed a crack forming in my fundamentalist armor. Everything outwardly fit the mold, fit the expectations of others, and fit my own idea of how I believed I should be in this world. But looks can be very deceiving. If anyone had peeled away the layers of my rock-solid, ironclad presentation to the fundamentalist community on campus and beyond, they would have found a very confused young man whose sexual identity was demanding to be acknowledged.

Moments of Grace: My Jazzy Piano Audition

The crack formed when my parents back in North Carolina started to attend a Southern Baptist church (non-fundamentalist, non-BJU-approved). My concern about their choice progressed toward curiosity. Why were they going to this church outside my fundamentalist filter? I was so happy at BJU throughout my first year that I fantasized about graduating from BJU with my undergrad and grad degrees and then joining the faculty and literally living on campus. But if I were so happy at BJU, why would I be so curious about my parents' new church?

I refer to this unexplained curiosity as a "moment of grace" that was the beginning of my journey to freedom, my first step toward allowing my true self to emerge and begin learning the spiritual practice of questioning. This moment was leading me to life outside of a structured religion and was the beginning of a life of abundance in every sense of the word, but it would take me years to reap the rewards of this journey.

True, I was happy that first year at BJU, but in the sense that happiness is a confirmation bias. I experienced many blessings there. I was happily involved in my society and was elected by the entire freshman class to be their freshman class pianist. Plus, all my roommates got along. All of this was proof that I was in the right place—complete with all the filters that gave me a sense of security that I was actualizing "God's perfect plan for my life" at BJU. In this case, "God's perfect plan" meant critically unexamined theological language that I no longer use, but it was standard jargon for me and my community at the time. I felt happy there because I felt so secure. It was a false security, but a security nonetheless.

Yet in the midst of these filters, I experienced further eruptions of unexplainable moments of grace. My audition for freshman class pianist is a good example. This role was considered a position of leadership. At the time, people interested in the position would put their name forward, and then each candidate would play a little bit on the piano to show the entire freshman class how well they could play. Most candidates played their audition piece in a BJU-approved style: very traditional, standard chords, very little syncopation, no jazz idioms, no diminished chords or flat nines. But my song—a jazzy, bluesy, toe-tapping version of the traditional hymn "What a Friend We Have in Jesus"—was a hit with the freshman class. I got elected.

How did I muster the courage to do that? To perform that song in a decidedly non-BJU style could have easily gotten me in trouble. This audition piece was certainly outside the filter I had constructed for my life. At that time, auditions for the freshman class pianist were not preapproved or checked by the administration, either, which also factored in to my ability to just play how I wanted. This kind of moment of grace demonstrates how even then, when I was at my peak happiness at BJU, my human spirit was still looking for ways to voice my desire for freedom. My state of happiness would be completely different during my second year there.

The Beginning of a Change:
Switching Churches and Getting Campused

Back home over the summer after my first year at BJU, I accompanied my parents to their new church and was shocked to see how much in common this church had with my fundamentalist church. At this new church, they sang the same hymns, read from the same Bible, and, most importantly, seemed very committed to Christ and were serious about their faith, which was extremely important to me. I wanted an authentic, vibrant faith, and this new church had that. I don't know what I was expecting to see at this new church—human sacrifices or something equally heinous—but I realized that the boogeyman wasn't the boogeyman anymore. Our churches were more alike than not. I was thoroughly convinced—and joined the church toward the end of the summer.

That wasn't the only kind of change happening for me that summer. I also started tentatively dipping my toe into this newfound freedom away from fundamentalism. I attended movies. I let my hair grow out. I even remember pondering—just pondering—that dancing might be okay too. This summer represented another step forward in this sometimes awkward but incredibly exhilarating journey toward freedom, authenticity, and abundance.

When I returned to BJU in the fall, I was not the same Curt as before. I snuck off campus to attend dances at nearby Furman University. Around the middle of that fall semester, I played the song "Weekend in New England" by Barry Manilow in the music practice rooms. Someone heard it, turned me in, and that infraction put me over the demerit limit to get permanently campused. For the rest of the semester, I was not allowed to leave campus for any reason except to go to church on Sunday nights. What a difference a summer makes. In my freshman year, I was the righteous man. The good Christian. Sold out to Jesus. An insider. Now in my sophomore year, I was a troublemaker. One to be watched carefully. Needing to "get right with God." An outsider to true spirituality. The semester worsened for me, and my parents said I needed to transfer. At the end of the first semester of my sophomore year, I left BJU. I was there for a total of three semesters.

Learning New Things at a Secular School: Democrats Can Be Christians

At the time, BJU's second semester didn't end until the third week of January, which made it difficult to transfer anywhere until the fall, so I basically had the whole spring of 1984 off from school. At home, I became very involved in my new Southern Baptist church. I also continued to go to movies, let my hair grow, and listen to popular music. I transferred to Appalachian State University in Boone, North Carolina, in the fall of 1984. Most of my credits transferred, and I graduated in 1987 with a piano performance degree. By the time I got to ASU, I was more comfortable with myself as an evangelical. But throughout my time there, as I slowly became less fundamentalist in my life and theology, my struggle against same-sex desires intensified.

While at ASU, I joined the Baptist Student Union and felt like I had found my people. I played piano for the BSU choir, and I remember two other notable events. First, I started drinking beer, which was a big deal for me, but even more noteworthy was when I first met a Democrat who was also a Christian! I didn't know that you could be both. Because of the election going on in North Carolina, one student wore a button for the Democratic candidate for governor. It prompted me to have a conversation with her, and I could feel my worldview continue to broaden.

Toward the end of my time at ASU, I experienced another moment of grace. Spiritually speaking, I needed a shot of something. I needed more of a felt faith or an embodied faith that's not just about a theology of creeds but a theology of experience. I didn't want to throw out theology; I just needed it to make the journey from my head to my heart and throughout my body in a holistic manner. This search led me to a Charismatic church, and I was hooked. This church brought together a theology on paper with an experiential, embodied faith. The preaching was excellent, the people were serious about faith, the music style was contemporary, and the worship involved the body with lifting hands and bowing in prayer. At this church, I felt the embodied faith, and it was electrifying.

Making a Charismatic Change: Life at Oral Roberts University

After I graduated from ASU, I felt a call to music ministry. I wanted to go somewhere where my Charismatic faith would be nurtured within a strong, evangelical theological setting. I learned that Oral Roberts University in Tulsa, Oklahoma, was accredited by the Association of Theological Schools and that it was an evangelical Charismatic institution. ORU provided me what I wanted in a seminary education: a place that was both credible and Charismatic.

Life at ORU was a breath of fresh air compared to BJU. The general atmosphere on ORU's campus was much lighter. There weren't as many rules—I could go to movies, for example. But there were still rules. We couldn't organize a dance on campus, but I got the feeling I could probably dance off campus and be OK. The big rules were still in place there too—no drinking or smoking on or off campus—which gave me a bit of security that ORU still had standards that I respected.

I loved the Charismatic nature of the school, which was most evident during the school chapel services. A live band played as we lifted our hands and sang, and we had an extended time of prayer. This was what I wanted with spirituality: an embodied, felt experience informed and supported by a strong theology. I was well aware of this strong theology during seminary classes, where I was introduced to the historical-critical method of biblical interpretation. I was taught the seven theories of creation, the Q source and Marcan priority in my studies of the Gospels, and also redaction criticism in understanding how the Bible was compiled. I learned that biblical criticism is a helpful way of understanding scripture that honors both the message and the culture of the time it was written. But I was also very aware that this kind of biblical teaching would not have been sanctioned in the fundamentalist classrooms at BJU.

I continued to move away from the strictures of fundamentalism into a more open, inquisitive, and affirming approach to all things spiritual. This movement away from fundamentalism was juxtaposed with a gnawing, growing awareness of my sexual orientation. As my openness increased, so did my awareness that I had to deal with being gay. When I was a fundamentalist, my sexuality had been stuffed away and detached from my life. But now as I continued my journey toward freedom, authenticity, and abundance, I had to start dealing with my sexuality.

I graduated from ORU in 1989 with a master's degree in church music and then found my first church job in Norman, Oklahoma, in 1990. I was ordained in 1991 and worked on staff at a Charismatic Pentecostal–type church. I had always felt a call to serve in the church, but at that time, the only way I could hold on to my calling into ministry was to deny and suppress the reality of my same-sex desires. I had even married a woman. Everything on the outside was going according to plan. But inside I was dying.

Looking to Exodus Ex-Gay Ministries for Relief

I didn't know how much longer I could deny my sexual orientation. I didn't hook up with guys at this time, but I liked porn magazines and phone sex. With each passing year of marriage, my struggles intensified. Finally, after being married for two and a half years in 1993, unable to bear the weight of my secret any longer, I sought out therapy and began attending an Exodus ex-gay ministry. I had been listening to a Christian radio station one day and heard an advertisement for an Exodus ex-gay ministry in Oklahoma City. Of course, I took this as a sign that God wanted me to finally deal with my homosexuality by attending this ex-gay ministry.

So what does an ex-gay ministry do?

Well, an ex-gay ministry seeks to "heal" LGBTQ people through individual counseling, group therapy, worship, and prayer. The idea is that in childhood and adolescence, several factors can stop "normal," healthy, heterosexual development. These can include incidences of abuse, an emotionally distant father, or an overbearing mother. Ex-gay therapy seeks to identify which factors are at work, bring healing in those areas, and then nurture and guide the client toward the path of heterosexuality.

At that time, I believed in ex-gay therapy, and I started attending sessions regularly. Ironically, my decision to join Exodus was the beginning of my journey to a different kind of freedom than Exodus had intended. I was not happy in my marriage, nor was my wife supportive of my attending Exodus. She just wanted out of the marriage, period. So our marriage dissolved, and for the next fifteen months, I threw myself into the ex-gay ministry, seeking a change in my sexuality: I attended my individual counseling and group meetings; I talked about my feelings of same-sex desires; I cried as I poured out my heart, trying to figure out what had thwarted my path to developing "normally" as heterosexual; I attended church regularly; and I shared my secret with close friends. I did all of this with a sincere heart. I believed I would be healed one day.

Exodus was an umbrella for local counseling centers primarily in the United States and Canada. Each counseling center teaches reparative therapy and signs on to the Statement of Faith of Exodus International. I attended an Exodus referral ministry in Oklahoma City called First Stone Ministries. Each Exodus ministry had their own theological flavor. First Stone was more Charismatic, which was great for me.

During the group meeting held once a week, we spent some time in praise and worship, prayer, and then working through an ex-gay curriculum called Living Waters. This was a program of reparative therapy complete with teaching, a study guide, scripture, and reflection questions. Then we would move into small group meetings. It was almost like a support group, where you would talk more in detail about your life and about the teaching discussed earlier in the evening. I also attended an individual counseling session weekly, where I endured more reparative therapy.

The Exodus program taught that any of the three areas that I mentioned—molestation or sexual abuse, a distant father, an overbearing mother, or lack of bonding with the same-sex parent—is where the enemy (their word) hinders our developing in a healthy, heterosexual way (again, their words).

I started going to Exodus in December 1993 and went twice before I told my wife, but then my life began to crumble: the church asked me to resign, and my wife and I split up. So I left Norman and moved to Oklahoma City, where I threw myself wholeheartedly into Exodus. I went into therapy believing it would work. I was so vulnerable and hungry for lasting internal change; I would have done whatever they told me to do.

But nothing changed.

The darkest night of my soul came in January of 1995, when I decided to leave the Exodus ministry. In my last five or six months at Exodus, I slowly realized I was not going to change. I was so tired of trying to be what others expected me to be by putting on false personas. I was ready to be honest and authentic.

As much as I wanted to live honestly, I left Exodus in a quandary. I still believed homosexuality was sinful, but I couldn't keep going through the outward motions of change, knowing I wasn't changing inside at all. By leaving this Exodus ministry, I felt like I was leaving God, like I was leaving authentic faith.

Finding My Authentic Self: Losing My Interpretive Virginity

After I left the Exodus ex-gay ministry, I started attending a wonderful United Methodist church in Oklahoma City, and over the next four years I firmly planted myself in the midst of this new kind of Christian community. This particular United Methodist church was part of the Reconciling Congregation program within the denomination that officially opposed UMC's doctrine against the full affirmation of LGBTQ people and instead worked for change within the denomination. So over time I fully reconciled myself as a gay Christian man.

The entire time I participated in fundamentalism and evangelicalism, I sought to be authentic by following the rules, ascribing to the approved theology, and doing or not doing whatever my church and school told me. I understood all those restrictions to be the tools to achieve authenticity. But that moment of pure awareness—when I understood that I couldn't change my sexuality—was the beginning of pure authentic living for me.

It was a moment of grace that awakens the compassionate stirrings of love and tenderness toward yourself, a moment that comes as an internal response to the recognition of the beauty, value, and love within our very selves. That particular grace ignites a power within. My entire life has been one long, beautiful movement toward a realization and awakening to this grace of love and tenderness toward myself.

There is a saying within the community of those who have left the ex-gay movement (we fondly call ourselves ex-ex-gays or gay squared) called "losing your interpretative virginity." When you work through and wrestle with the six or so passages in the Bible that have traditionally been used to clobber LGBTQ people (called the Clobber Passages), then you can truly understand them in their proper biblical, historical, theological, and exis-tential context and look at them in a non-literalistic way. Once you apply those principles of interpretation to the Clobber Passages, then you have lost your previous way of reading scripture in a more literal manner. Con-sequently, you have lost your interpretative virginity and can apply that same biblical hermeneutic to the rest of the Bible as well. Thanks to the strong theological education I had received at ORU, this was how I was able to reconcile those Clobber Passages.

That amazing United Methodist church literally loved me back to wholeness. Within the context of a Christian community, I experienced the freedom of living my life authentically: no secrets, no lies, and no hiding.

Ordained and Committed to Inclusive Christianity

Today I live in Vancouver, British Columbia, and I own a small business. I am also an ordained United Church of Canada minister, serving as part-time pastoral staff in a downtown Vancouver church. For me, my ordina-tion by the United Church of Canada represents the full cycle of my life on this journey to affirmation: I was ordained in an anti-gay church, I went through Exodus to make myself something I wasn't, and then I had an experience of grace that empowered me to begin the long journey to-ward reconciliation.

My ordination on June 3, 2018, has cemented that journey into my current community of faith—fully affirming, fully accepting, fully Chris-tian. What's more, I am happily married to my husband of twenty-three years. I am one of a small percentage of those who made it out of the ex-gay and fundamentalist world who is still committed to the Christian faith. This certainly isn't the faith of my childhood; rather, it is a broad, expansive, inclusive vision of Christianity. Today, my parents aren't fully accepting of who I am, but things with them have greatly improved since I first came out.

As I look back at the unfolding chapters of my life, I see different threads. I see the thread of fundamentalism. I see the thread of my sexuality. I see the thread of my Exodus ex-gay experience. And I see the thread of my current work within the church. I once viewed these as separate, compartmentalized threads. But now I see them as one consistent, beautiful braid, woven together over time with tears and laughter and with joy and despair that has brought me to this place. And the result has awakened in me a greater compassion for LGBTQ people like me who are caught in damaging faith communities.

I hold no ill will toward Exodus or reparative therapy. While I strongly oppose everything this therapy represents, my heart goes out to those caught up in its deception. I could never endorse this sort of counseling, but I will always be thankful for the people in that Exodus group in Oklahoma City that saw a scared Christian young man who thought he might be gay, welcomed him into their fold, and held him as he cried. In that specific capacity, they showed compassion as Jesus would have done.

Companioned on This Journey: We Are Not Alone

The church I serve in Vancouver is progressive, open, and affirming. Each Sunday morning at the beginning of our service, we begin with these words: "Welcome this morning to St. Andrew's-Wesley United Church. We are an open-hearted, open-minded, LGBTQ affirming community that follows in the Way of Jesus." A big part of my church work now includes outreach to the LGBTQ community, in particular those queer people who are coming out of non-inclusive, even abusive religious communities and who still long to honor and nurture their spiritual lives. My work involves welcoming them, listening to their stories, and being a companion with them along their own journey. Most of all, I want to counter the fear and alienation they feel—that I felt—by reminding them both in word and in the community I serve in Vancouver that they are never alone.

I want to offer an encouraging, final thought: we always have a companion on our journey. That companion can be however you define God (as a presence, higher power, spirit, something-beyond-ourselves, etc.), or a community that loves and surrounds you, or even your authentic self who yearns to be recognized and expressed. Whichever companion you want to focus on, you are never alone on your journey. As an affirming Christian, my days of converting are over, but I must admit that I love the Emmaus Road story told in the New Testament because it highlights the point that we have companions at every part of our life journey, even in the sorrows and dark nights of our soul.

Because I was aware of my companion, I never gave up hope and knew there was going to be a way to eventually figure it all out. Leaving BJU, attending a Southern Baptist church, going to a state university, attending ORU Seminary, going through the ex-gay ministry: I thought all these parts were *the* answer. But these were just parts of my journey, parts that continually evolved and changed. However, the constant in the midst of all these changes was the fact that I was not alone: I was always companioned. And you are always companioned too. Always.

Note

1. *The Bomb and Its Fallout.*

chapter 7   MICAH J. SMITH

To be honest, I felt comfortable around pretty much anyone besides the typical "boj," which was an unofficial term used on campus to describe a student who religiously believed in the student handbook rules and would not hesitate to enforce them, even if it meant turning in fellow students to the administration. Typically, bojes desired or held positions of spiritual leadership on campus as a symbolic indication of and reward for their piety. I wasn't interested in hanging around or becoming that type of person. Interestingly enough, I again found myself with lots of female friends, which was great because at BJU, I could connect with females platonically and not worry about anyone wondering if I was gay.

A PK's Life

My sheltered upbringing may appear bizarre to those not raised in the fundamentalist subculture, but I hope my story provides a rationale for my theological upbringing, outlook, and behavior. I was raised in an extremely conservative, fundamentalist Baptist family. My father was the senior pastor of a fundamentalist, premillennial Baptist church in Maryland for most of my childhood, giving me the distinction of being labeled a preacher's kid (PK). To this day, most of my immediate family members still identify as fundamentalists.

Although I was born in Denver, Colorado, I've always considered myself a Marylander, since we moved to Maryland when I was five. Shortly after our move to Maryland, I made a profession of faith and was baptized at my father's church. However, I don't really think I fully understood what it meant to be "saved." I was clinging to an experience as the basis for my salvation, and throughout my childhood I struggled constantly with my assurance of salvation.

It wasn't until I was much older and had finally left the fundamentalist movement that I realized that it's not an experience that saves, such as walking down a church aisle and praying a prayer. Rather, God saves us through his son, the Lord Jesus Christ. There is nothing we can do to save ourselves. Furthermore, I found comfort from different examples in scripture that reveal how God connects with each of us in a slightly different way.

A quick survey of biblical characters such as Enoch, Abraham, Jacob, and the thief on the cross demonstrates that nothing we do or don't do can save us: only the realization and acceptance of what Jesus Christ already did can save us. I'm comforted especially by the example of the thief on the cross, whose conversion story lacks the typical fundamentalist ritual and fanfare.[1] He simply acknowledged that he was a sinner and turned to Jesus and asked, "Lord, remember me when thou comest into thy kingdom." No aisle was walked, no fancy prayer prayed, no priest consulted, and no sacraments received. Salvation doesn't need fundamentalism.

After completing first grade at our church's Christian academy, both of my parents decided to pull me out of the academy and homeschool me. I never did fully understand their reasoning, although I assume it was because my dad was bothered that most of the academy's teachers lacked basic teaching credentials. When my father was voted in as the new pastor of the church and principal of the school in 1989, he essentially inherited an academy with very few qualified teachers and considerable financial problems. My parents homeschooled me and my five siblings all the way through high school.

For most of my childhood, we literally lived on the church campus, which was thankfully relatively large, complete with an auditorium (450 capacity) and an adjacent large building; two Sunday school, office, and educational wings; and the parsonage, where we lived. Needless to say, people were always in and out of the campus, so our parents' rule was that as long as all of the Faith Baptist Academy classes were out and the kids had been picked up, we could leave the parsonage and pretty much go wherever we wanted. I loved taking long walks, sneaking into the auditorium to play the piano or organ, or rummaging through the school library. There was always something to do.

While I have fond memories of exploring the church campus on my own as a child, I did experience major health complications from an early age, when I began having grand mal seizures. These seizures continued until my first year of high school. Throughout these years, my neurologists experimented with many dosages and types of medications to minimize the seizures, and some of the side effects from those medications continued into my high school years.

My Only Choice

As I neared the end of high school, I had few conversations with my parents about college because they had already made clear to all five of us kids that spending any time studying in a secular institution was a complete waste of money and would threaten our personal faith. In my upbringing, Bob Jones University and Pensacola Christian College were the only Christian institutions of higher education that I had been exposed to, so my college choices were slim. However, both my immediate and extended family were critical of PCC because of the "wild" southern gospel–style music they used in some of their advertisements and on their radio station. Given their criticism of PCC's liberal music standards, I understood that my only choice for higher education would be BJU.

Further solidifying BJU as my only choice were all of my family connections to the school. My father earned his master's degree from BJU in 1979. My mother attended BJU for several years until she married my father. One of my grandfathers graduated from BJU, while my other grandfather had Dr. Bob Jones III on speed-dial; Jones was often a guest speaker at my Grandfather Smith's church and school, the same church where my father later became senior pastor. One of my aunts had a brother who was on faculty at BJU, and three of my aunts, two of my uncles, and three of my cousins also graduated from BJU. Needless to say, we were pretty much a BJU-only family.

Around this time, I began to recognize an identity crisis that had been developing since childhood. I was different from everyone in the family in more ways than one. In part, I was different because of all the seizures I'd had as a child, along with the side effects brought on by years of high-dose medications. Because of my health problems at a young age, my parents steered me away from sports and more in the direction of music, gardening, decorating, designing, and arts and crafts: activities safer for someone suffering from seizures.

By the time I was seizure free, I wasn't outside playing baseball, basketball, biking, or football with my brothers; instead, I was the full-time organist at my father's church, in charge of designing most of the florals used in the main auditorium, helping my mom plan, clean, decorate, and prepare for luncheons with missionaries and pastors, and designing the landscape around my father's church campus. I was busy and loving what I was doing, and most people never questioned why I wasn't engaged in the same hobbies as my brothers were.

However, I started feeling very distanced from *all* of the males in my family and much closer to the females in my family. The older I got, the more difficult it was to spend time around other males and the easier it was for me to hang out with the ladies. I was a "ladies' man," but *not* in the strictest sense of the standard dictionary definition. Obviously, I'm not trying to insinuate that a lack of interaction with males somehow made me gay. To the contrary, I believe I've always been gay and have never been sensually attracted to the opposite sex. My point is that a combination of factors, such as my hobbies and medical restrictions, allowed me to connect better with ladies; we just seemed to have much more in common.

During these years of trying to figure out why I did not connect or relate to men, I thought it odd that I actually found a few men to be rather attractive—in a sensual way. I don't believe it had anything to do with my hobbies or with a lack of interaction with men. However, this awareness was troublesome because if there is anything a good Christian can never be, it is to be sensual. I was always taught we were made to be spiritual beings, *not* sensual. This meant that anything that aroused sensual feelings was a sin to be confessed immediately.[2] Colloquially speaking, we were to "turn or burn," that is, repent or be consumed by our earthly lusts.

We Can't Say "Gay"

To complicate matters, I had not been equipped with any vocabulary to make sense of this new phenomenon of being attracted to men or, for that matter, of human sexuality in general. After all, it wasn't until I was twenty-three and a student at PCC that I first found out from a nursing student how babies are made. At that time, several of us were on our way home from volunteering at a local nursing home, and one of the guys who was a nursing student told a joke. My brother and I were the only guys in the car who didn't laugh. Next thing I know, the guy who told the joke turned around, looked at my brother and me sitting in the back seat, and said, "You guys don't even know where babies come from, do you?" He then gave us a rather graphic description of the birds and the bees.

Given my lack of sex education, there was no way I could have possibly known as a teenager what it meant to be gay. At that time, I only knew we weren't supposed to call my Aunt Gay by her given name anymore because now the word "gay" meant something bad. (We had to call her "Aunt Wendy" instead.) I also vaguely remember people in church talking about the horrible "lifestyle choice of homosexuality" and about ministries to free people from the "sin of homosexuality," but no one ever explained what these things meant, much less mentioned anything called the Clobber Passages either. It felt like the very mention of anything related to homosexuality was an abomination, so I never had any desire to ask for clarification. All I knew was that both "gay" and "homosexuality" were bad words, but it wasn't until my college years that I was educated as to what these terms meant.

With all of this internal turmoil, I actually looked forward to going to BJU. I had almost never been away from my father's church campus without the direct supervision of one or both of my parents, so going away to college on my own had an appeal of independence that I had only dreamed of. I also thought that with all the students down there, I might actually find other guys that were more like me (artistic) and not like my brothers (jocks).

From My Bubble to the Bubble

In August 2002 I arrived on BJU's campus quite early and moved into the first floor of the men's dorm then named after Bibb Graves. In fact, I was one of the first students there because my parents wanted me to get settled in before the masses arrived. I really appreciated that because it gave me plenty of time to get unpacked. Before leaving town that weekend, my parents wanted to make sure I joined a local church, so I promptly joined Faith Baptist in Taylors, South Carolina, the one we attended whenever we visited my mother's parents, who lived in the area. My parents seemed very pleased, which made me happy.

My first weekend at BJU was great, especially because I had my dorm room to myself for about a week. It was like I had moved from a small, protective bubble of my father's church campus to this huge "bubble" of BJU's campus, which was like a self-sustained city. I loved it. Then, by the end of the second week, all three of my roommates had arrived, so there were four of us in one tiny room. At first, I was encouraged to discover that three of us in the room were PKs, while the other one was a missionary kid. Certainly, we would all get along because of our similar background and experiences, right? Sadly, this would not be the case.

One of the PKs was our room's assistant prayer captain—typically an upperclassman who is supposed to be the spiritual leader of the room—and he admitted to us that he only took the position because of the perks. His actions after this revelation certainly proved his lack of spiritual leadership: he started harassing us for more storage space and also openly used curse words. After a few days, he learned that two of us had been homeschooled and began to mock us, implying that we had a deficient education. For shock value, he walked around us naked, laughing at how sheltered we were. To this day, I have no idea why he did this, but it made both of us homeschooled PKs upset. I'd had enough, so I went to the dormitory supervisor and requested to be moved. Thankfully, he agreed, and I moved down the hall.

After that mess with my former roommate, I began to find my social stride in making friends. I am non-confrontational by nature, so it wasn't too difficult for me to find people to hang out with, most of whom could be classified as geeks or rejects. To be honest, I felt comfortable around pretty much anyone besides the typical "boj," which was an unofficial term used on campus to describe a student who religiously believed in the student handbook rules and would not hesitate to enforce them, even if it meant turning in fellow students to the administration. Typically, bojes desired or held positions of spiritual leadership on campus as a symbolic indication of and reward for their piety. I wasn't interested in hanging around or becoming that type of person. Interestingly enough, I again found myself with lots of female friends, which was great because at BJU, I could connect with females platonically and not worry about anyone wondering if I was gay.

As far as academics go, my first semester was a little rough. It was quite a transition to go from a more calming, homeschool environment to an extremely rigid one where everything was time sensitive and impersonal. However, I acclimated by the second semester, finishing my freshman year with a cumulative GPA of 3.63.

Dancing Disagreements

My father came to campus a little early to pick me up at the end of my freshman year. He wanted to spend some time getting to know some of my friends and also to attend the last Artist Series event with me. Every year, the Fine Arts Department of BJU organizes various productions as part of the Concert, Opera and Drama Series. These events are called Artist Series, and students are required to attend them. My father had not been to an Artist Series event since the seventies, which may account for how scandalized he felt at watching a stage adaptation of William Shakespeare's *Macbeth*.

As we were leaving the auditorium, my father said, "I almost walked out." He was referring to a brief scene toward the middle of the program in which several actors and actresses engaged in dancing. I understand his point. It is hypocritical when fundamentalists preach that Christians should *never* dance, yet the university showcases a dance in its play that is open to the public. I think BJU might have pointed out the differences between dancing from earlier centuries and contemporary dancing, but that would not have made a difference to my father.

At any rate, I was proud of myself for having successfully completed one year at BJU. I worked hard at my summer job at home and was looking forward to returning to BJU in the fall. What made my first year such a positive experience was all the friends I had made and the fact that none of us had been enticed to become bojes.

Instead, we had realized we were all at BJU because our families would *never* allow us to study at any other college, so we were simply content to make the best of it. We all wanted to be good Christians, but most of us were turned off by those who practically worshiped BJU and its leadership, not to mention all the scripture being taken out of context in daily chapel sermons and the conflicting messages between what the leadership told us the Bible says versus what it actually says.

For example, anyone familiar with BJU recognizes its history of stringent rules regarding music standards: no secular music, no music with a beat, and so on. But I was puzzled how BJU could interpret random passages to support its radical belief that good, Christian music should sound distinctive from the world's music. They would argue that the "new song" mentioned in Psalm 96:1 corroborated their beliefs that godly music was distinctly different. Next, they used the passage that "God is not the author of confusion" from 1 Corinthians 14:33 as further evidence that godly music should be ideologically coherent. Finally, they provided 2 Corinthians 5:17 as a reason to suggest that part of being a "new creature" requires a Christian to put away secular music. I remember reading and studying the context from which each of these verses was pulled and thinking to myself, "How in the world are they getting that belief from that verse?" The more I studied my Bible, the more gaping holes I found in many of BJU's most advocated beliefs. It really made me wonder if the origin of these treasured beliefs postdated the Bible itself.

About halfway through that summer, my father called me and my sister—who was enrolled to start that fall—into the living room to chat about our futures at BJU. For months, my father had been back and forth with the administration on a number of issues, one of which I had brought up because it sincerely bothered me. I couldn't understand why BJU would not allow me to attend Sunday school and Sunday morning worship services at my church in town, one that I'd joined during my first week as a student.

After all, my church was on the BJU-approved list, yet at that time, all freshmen were required to attend Sunday school services hosted by their respective society—BJU's version of fraternities and sororities that all students are required to join during rush week of their freshman year—and then attend the morning worship service held on campus at the Founder's Memorial Amphitorium. At the time, BJU had intentionally scheduled these services so that they overlapped or coincided with the morning services of all the churches on their approved list. I never learned all the details, but basically my father disclosed to us that he'd had a pretty bad fallout with Jim Berg, the dean of students, which confirmed his decision that he no longer supported our attendance at BJU. My sister and I withdrew from BJU that same day.

It was devastating at the time, but looking back, I am thankful my time at BJU was cut short because I now fully realize how much more negatively than positively affected I was by the training I received there. Had I stayed at BJU longer, it would have been that much harder for me to leave fundamentalism as early as I did. Ironically enough, as I was writing this chapter, I discovered that BJU has recently changed its policy concerning mandatory services on campus. It turns out that BJU now requires students to attend church off campus—including Sunday mornings—and to report those attendances to the administration.[3]

Naturally, I think it's good they changed this policy, but I still think that heavily regulated church attendance stifles the relationship I believe God wants to have with us; put another way, if God wanted us to never miss a church service, He would have slipped that message in somewhere between His First and Tenth Commandments. Regardless, I have to shake my head at this change in policy because it contributes to BJU's overall profile of strictly enforcing rules one way because of religious reasons until it decides to change those rules and strictly enforce them the opposite way for religious reasons.

Off to a Different Bubble: Pensacola Christian College

When terrible things happen to people, other people try to offer encouragement by saying things like, "When one door closes, another opens." Well, another opportunity certainly presented itself to me in the form of attending Pensacola Christian College after my time at BJU. But as my experience there shows, I'm not quite sure how encouraged I felt by the time I left PCC.

By the summer of 2006, two of my siblings and I had talked our parents into letting us enroll at PCC. We arrived in June 2006 because we had been accepted into a summer internship program that helped us afford our first semester that fall. Being there over the summer definitely made the transition from BJU a smoother one. I learned where everything was located and familiarized myself with the PCC student handbook.

Generally speaking, PCC's rules about social interaction between the sexes were the same as BJU's, but probably one of the more memorable differences in rules concerns PCC's gender-segregated elevators and stairwells. The easiest way to keep track of which elevators and stairwells were assigned to which gender was to remember that the "male-only" elevators and stairwells were always closest to the main entrance of the building.

Besides the music standards, which I discussed earlier in this chapter, the other major difference I noticed between PCC and BJU was PCC's rule about the King James Version of the Bible being the only version allowed on campus. True, BJU used the KJV as its official Bible during chapel messages and all its classes, but it never went as far as saying that the KJV is the *only* allowed version for a Christian. I never could understand why it was so important for PCC to only read a Bible version that used vocabulary that most contemporary English-speaking people wouldn't know how to properly pronounce, let alone know how to use in everyday conversation. But I held my tongue about this issue and immersed myself in PCC culture as best I could.

The Interrogation

I completed the fall 2006 semester but sat out the spring 2007 semester to save up more money to return. When I returned for the fall 2007 semester, I was unprepared for how my personal "differences" would be called into question there. The weekend before Thanksgiving 2007, I received a pink slip in my mailbox, summoning me to the dean of men's office. This was quite odd. I almost never got demerits. Plus, I had been so busy the whole semester that I'd hardly had time to think, much less do something wrong.

When I arrived at his office, the dean asked if I was dating anyone and if I had ever had a girlfriend. I quickly realized where this interrogation was headed. A group of women had informed the Student Life office that I was not dating anyone and that it seemed I had no interest in starting a relationship with any of the female students on campus. The dean then asked me if I was or had ever been attracted to the same sex. At that point, I totally lost it and broke down in tears. Why in the heck would he even care? Why does it even matter who I'm attracted to if I am *not* acting on it? I was totally baffled.

After I had settled down a bit, the dean gave me two options: either I call my parents and confess my struggle with the sin of homosexuality to them, or he would call my parents right then to tell them of this "very serious sin" I was being tempted with. I told him I wasn't calling my parents because I didn't see the need to drag them into my personal burden, so the dean called them instead and put them on speaker phone. Naturally, my parents sounded devastated, and my dad said he would be on the next flight down. The dean told him my next meeting was scheduled for 10 a.m. the next day and said he looked forward to seeing him.

The dean then informed me that I was immediately "socialed," which meant I was forbidden to speak to any student, with the exception of a spiritual leader they assigned to me. I was then escorted back to my room, where I collected my bedding, a few toiletries, and a set of clothing for the next day before I was escorted to an assigned room for that evening. Next, I followed the spiritual leader to the dining hall for dinner. I felt disgraced and violated, paraded around like a criminal, and for what? All I had done was tell the truth when I was asked those pointed, humiliating questions. I hadn't flirted or "looked sideways" at any guys. I hadn't said or written anything off-color or inappropriate.

The next day, the dean said I had two choices: either I could voluntarily withdraw from PCC, or I could agree to be subjected to a committee hearing which would evaluate the "sin I was struggling with" and then decide whether I could remain at PCC as a student. My father wisely asked what my chances were with the committee, and the dean responded that no case like mine had ever made it through the committee proceedings. Then he slid over the papers for me to voluntarily withdraw, smirked, and said, "This is your best option." I signed the paperwork.

The Fallout

After that interrogation and harassment, I worried that my being forced out of the closet would negatively affect my father's ministry, especially because I'd heard many preachers cite I Timothy 3:5 to argue that any pastor or church leader should immediately be removed from their leadership role at any point in which one of their children is discovered to have "succumbed" to a life of sin. Though it was certainly traumatic being outed by PCC, I also felt a huge relief because my parents now knew the greatest burden I had struggled with for many years. I was even more relieved that, fortunately, my dad did not lose his ministry. But I was still bothered by how fundamentalists interpreted my identity as being sinful.

By this point in my life, I had heard several chapel speakers at both BJU and PCC condemn homosexuality as an "unpardonable sin." They might not have necessarily come right out and called it that, but they would interpret Romans 1 in such a way that, by the end of the chapel message, it was clear they meant that homosexuality was the absolute worst sin anyone could possibly commit, despite the fact that it hadn't made the Ten Commandments. I had even heard one evangelist claim that the primary point the Apostle Paul was making in Romans 1 was to define homosexuals as the one and only category of human beings who absolutely cannot be saved. I was astounded by his assertion.

To this day, that interpretation does not make sense. If we look at Ephesians 2:8–9 as a representative biblical passage about salvation, we can see the following phrases: "by grace," "through faith," "not of yourselves," "the gift of God," and "not of works." How can anyone look at this passage and claim that a homosexual cannot be saved? I've studied the Bible for more than twenty-five years, and I cannot find even a small verse that suggests that salvation is "through faith . . . and also in not being homosexual." Not one single verse can logically support this theory without contradicting the overwhelming evidence that salvation comes very clearly "through faith" apart from any action we do or don't do.

The Epiphany

Looking back on it all, I believe the greatest good that came from my departure experience at PCC was my realization that so much of what I had been taught to believe could *not* be what Jesus had intended. So much of what fundamentalist Christians consider to be "priorities" has little or no biblical support. The few months that followed my departure from PCC were my great awakening. I finally began to see very clearly the contrast between what the love of Jesus is all about versus how fundamentalists were adding to and distorting the Bible to nullify the two commands that Jesus clearly defined in Matthew 22:37–40 as the greatest commandments.

Basically, leaving PCC was the final straw that led me to return home, work extremely hard, and finally make that bold step of faith to leave fundamentalism (literally in the middle of the night) at the age of twenty-three. I admit I did it in a bit of a drastic way, but at least I got out. Within a few months of leaving fundamentalism, I joined an inclusive nondenominational church, and a little less than a year later, I met a wonderful, godly man who was an active member at that church. I started dating him early in 2009, and by that summer, I moved in with him and his two daughters. We celebrated ten years together in April 2019. I am so blessed to have a partner who is the best lover, friend, and confidant. I have definitely come a long way since my year at BJU and my short time at PCC.

Before I close, I need to dispel this narrative that all former BJU students and fundamentalists are bitter. Being stigmatized as bitter has long been an emotional, manipulative tool by fundamentalists to prevent insiders from making any waves against an oppressive system. It has also been an easy method for writing off those who have left fundamentalism. Based on what I have read in the New Testament, I believe our Lord Jesus Christ was all-inclusive and only condemned pious religious leaders. With that being said, I make an effort in being all-inclusive like Jesus was by remaining friends with people I met at BJU, some of whom are still there.

Nevertheless, I must speak out about the damage done by organizations, churches, institutions, and movements that adopt and force Pharisaical or separatist ideologies on others. While still in the fundamentalist movement, I experienced times of great depression, and the only thing that kept me from killing myself during those dark times was that I'd heard some preacher claim that a Christian would lose their salvation if they killed themselves. That's messed up!

When I first came out and started meeting people outside of the bubble of fundamentalism, I was constantly asked to share my story because it seemed so bizarre to others. To be honest, I didn't really want to. I was so relieved to be away from all the rules and fear of failure that I didn't want to relive the first twenty-three years of my life in fundamentalism. But, after a few years, I finally realized that I needed to share my story for other people who could benefit from what I learned through my time in and departure from fundamentalism. I hope that my story helps prevent similar damage in others' lives and also shows that you cannot love God without loving all people.

I feel so blessed to be free at last: free to connect with a Christian church family that really cares about Jesus versus the burden of religious ideologies, free to love people the Lord brings into my path, regardless of their religion, gender, or race. Most importantly, I'm free from being defined by who I do or don't sleep with. I'm not defined by my sexuality. Just like everyone else, I was created "in the image of God."[4]

Sure, I may be guilty of having a little too much "sugar in my tank" compared to most gay guys, but I still matter. Why? Because God created us in His image for a reason, for a purpose. As a dear friend of mine used to say, "God never makes junk." And as my partner likes to say, "Every *body* is different." That doesn't make any of us unsavable or unusable. We were all created different on purpose, and that doesn't make any of us any less of a mirror of God. Every one of us is more important than we can comprehend.

Notes

1. Luke 23.

2. In the most recent student covenant, students are warned to avoid "sensuality on the internet or in publications." *Bob Jones University Student Handbook, 2020–2021*, 74.

3. Ibid., 14.

4. Genesis 1:27.

PART THREE   *Intersections*

> Then saith the woman of Samaria unto him, How is
> it that thou, being a Jew, askest drink of me, which
> am a woman of Samaria? for the Jews have no deal-
> ings with the Samaritans. . . . The woman answered
> and said, I have no husband. Jesus said unto her,
> Thou hast well said, I have no husband: For thou
> hast had five husbands; and he whom thou now hast
> is not thy husband: in that saidst thou truly.
>
> JOHN 4:9, 17–18

The story of Jesus and the Samaritan woman at the well is likely a familiar one for fundamentalists who have spent a significant amount of time
in a church pew listening to sermons. This story includes Jesus teaching the woman the difference between the physical water from the well
and the spiritual water of everlasting life that He offers. But this story
also raises conversation about different power dynamics and overlapping
identities that affect one's position within a social system.

A fundamentalist preacher covering this chapter would probably provide historical context about the friction between Jews and Samaritans
that dates back to the Babylonian exile in the Old Testament. He would
also probably mention why it was such a big deal for Jesus as a Jew to
engage in conversation with a Samaritan woman who had not only had
five husbands but was also living with a man who was not her husband.
Grace Ji-Sun Kim and Susan M. Shaw explain that "Jews considered Samaritans as foreigners" and that Jesus' conversation with the woman was
a significant act that "reaches out across differences of gender, ethnic-
ity, religion, sexuality, and class to welcome this woman in a theological conversation." Kim and Shaw argue that this story is a good example
of intersectionality, which they define as "a lens for understanding how
gender, race, social class, sexual identity, and other forms of difference
work concurrently to shape people and social institutions within multiple relationships of power."[1] BJU's campus certainly qualifies as a location

where power relationships affect queer students in different and significant ways.

The title of this part takes a nod from Kimberlé Crenshaw's term "intersectionality" by considering the different power relationships that queer BJU students from different backgrounds must negotiate while on campus. The five stories in this part highlight various "forms of difference" while also sharing at least one common denominator by virtue of taking place at BJU—religion. We can appreciate how each voice highlights their unique challenges as BJU's fundamentalism connects with or reacts to such prominent forms of difference as economic class, gender performance, international status, geography, race, sexuality, gender roles, and gender identity.

First, Marshall, who attended in the mid- to late eighties, exposes the students' financial burden because of BJU's lack of accreditation, which greatly restricted chances for financial aid. They also adeptly reveal the school's mixed signals of being expected to take care of their own financial matters like an adult, while also being expected to honor BJU's spiritual and physical control like a child. Marshall's financial struggles also connect to their costly investment in trying to conform to gender expectations on campus. After their time at BJU, Marshall finds authenticity as a transman. Next, Sandra Merzib eloquently describes life at BJU as a social outsider in the late nineties and early 2000s. As a Canadian with no real connections to the university other than attending a BJU-oriented church, Sandra describes the xenophobia she experienced as a bilingual Canadian, the oppressive spiritual and social hierarchy on campus, and, most importantly, the damaging effects of reaching out for counseling about being a lesbian. Referencing Bob Jones III's famous interview on *Larry King Live* in 2000, Sandra explains that she was expelled under false pretenses because she was a public relations liability to the campus.

As an Asian American growing up in Hawaii, Reid notes his affinity for a culture that BJU considered pagan. Reid is our only non-White voice in this book, and his story provides a thought-provoking perspective about feeling culturally, geographically, and socially isolated because of his fundamentalist upbringing. A student from the mid- to late 2000s, Reid recounts the chapel services about homosexuality in April 2007, which prompted him to question his beliefs about homosexuality. Through his extended metaphor about living on an island, Reid exposes fundamentalism's tactic of stigmatizing homosexuality to keep gay men isolated. The fourth story in this unit comes from Rachel Oblak, who articulates the linguistic, psychological, and physical complexities unique to her situation as a young fundamentalist woman attracted to men and women. Attending BJU in the mid- to late 2000s, Rachel describes being present on campus the day the activist group Soulforce attempted to visit BJU in April 2007. After leaving BJU, Rachel learned about bisexuality and came to better understand herself outside of fundamentalism's strict gender roles.

Blair Durkee's story finishes this part on intersections. She notes that her attending BJU in the mid- to late 2000s was the result of little choice on her part: because her mother worked there, she could attend tuition-free. Through the extended metaphor of a treadmill, Durkee adeptly describes how the participation expectations at BJU work effectively to keep students too busy with spiritual exercises to question the fundamentalist system. She mentions the Soulforce visit to campus in April 2007 as a way of describing her growing inability to articulate her personal disagreements with BJU's fundamentalist stance against gender identity. After she left the BJU community, she learned to live authentically as a transwoman. The five stories in this unit can only begin to address the different ways that queer students from different backgrounds have been shaped by the religious power structures on campus.

Note

1. Kim and Shaw, *Intersectional Theology*, 75, 2.

chapter 8   MARSHALL

Despite being told repeatedly by BJU that businesses didn't care about its lack of accreditation, I
learned that other schools did care about accreditation, especially when transferring credits. Thousands of dollars. Countless hours of anguish. Years
of my life. All that I could show for my investment
in BJU was like vaporware, something that was advertised as real but was only a theory, a prototype if
you will, that wasn't what it represented itself to be,
and never materialized. In this case, BJU promised
a quality degree that would lead to a worthwhile career, but it didn't deliver on that promise because my
unaccredited hours could not be transferred to another school so I could complete work on that degree. All of my hard work at BJU could be seen but
not touched and had no substantial, tangible value
for advancing my career. It was the punishment that
kept on giving.

The Sociological System of Fundamentalism

When I was around eight, I spent a warm summer day lying in my aunt's
backyard, watching summer clouds against a beautiful blue sky.[1] That description may sound like an idyllic kind of childhood summer activity, but
there was nothing traditional about my developing concern that I wished
I had been born a boy. If there were a specific moment I could identify as
being the start of my "identity journey," it would likely have been then. On
that day, my thoughts about identity passed through my consciousness
like the summer clouds floating by above me.

Since that day, I have experienced a series of ups and downs, yeas and
nays, closets and transparencies, but on that summer day, I remember

being aware that I never understood why my cousins and sisters liked dresses or dolls. What's more, I was forever baffled by the boy-crazy phases of female puberty, the obsession to have a boyfriend, and the desire to hone those housewife skillsets highly expected of girls in the mid-seventies. I thought my teenage angst about being different was typical, and occasionally in junior high and high school I would put in the effort to fit that standard, gendered mold, but nothing ever had any solid footing. My feelings of not belonging anywhere went far beyond those traditional and expected awkward phases associated with emerging into adulthood.

To be fair, while I never fully conformed or identified with traditionally feminine behavior, I also never felt any intense attraction to women at this point of my life, either. Growing up in a Baptist environment, I never had the vocabulary or any concept of what it meant to be transgender, but I can't be completely sure if this is because I spent my teenage years in a very small town in Colorado or because of my Christian-indoctrinated education from birth. Perhaps it was a combination of both, but, then again, how can one even realize what they don't yet know is missing? It wasn't until I reached college age that I discovered my attraction to someone of the same physical gender, which is when my journey to awareness began in earnest.

I transformed from a rebellious, disjointed, immature, small-town teenager to a rebellious, disjointed, immature, Christian-college student. If it weren't so tragic, I could humorously label this as being a series of unfortunate events. I felt the effects of this transformation for years to come, and my time at Bob Jones University intensified them.

But how in the world did I end up at BJU, one of the most fundamentalist, repressive schools in the United States that fostered notoriously strict gender roles and expectations, and that has zero tolerance for breaking rules designed to eradicate any drift from its definition of acceptability? It's easy to say I didn't know better, which is technically correct. But it really goes beyond a pat answer about ignorance and concerns the sociological system of fundamentalism.

Let me preface my next statements by saying there is nothing wrong with identifying as Christian. I personally still identify as such, albeit in a different way from my early years. Growing up, we were Baptists who faithfully attended church at least three times a week: twice on Sundays including Sunday school, and usually once on Wednesdays including youth group, with occasional additional church events like Vacation Bible School and Christian summer camps. Our family's immersion in the church, short of being in the ministry, was just about as complete as one could imagine. When I was seven, I made a profession of faith and was baptized shortly thereafter at church, but years later, during the week-long preaching services at Bible Conference at BJU my freshman year, I experienced a similar kind of conversion, likely because of the intense pressure exerted on students to be perfect. If we weren't perfect, then surely we must never have been saved in the first place.

When I applied (at the insistence of my parents) and was subsequently accepted to BJU, I felt an odd, perverse sense of pride. Making this decision meant I was special and had a higher calling. An added benefit was the admiration from my senior and youth pastor, whose approval I rarely received. Finally, I had managed to do something right to please both my pastors and my parents for a change. It didn't matter that nearly everyone else thought I was making a mistake. (My school counselor advised me against attending because BJU wasn't accredited, and other teachers and peers were amazed I would attend such a strict school.) I was enchanted by the approval from those in spiritual authority, a simple nod that put me in higher standing. Again, I still consider myself a Christian who constantly fails when following the teachings of Jesus, but I cannot in good conscience identify as a fundamentalist.

Fundamentalist indoctrination begins, largely, with young children, through churches and religious schools founded and funded by those who successfully moved through their educational system. In third or fourth grade, our Christian school was visited by a traveling BJU team, all perfectly coiffed, smiling, and with sugar-sweetness dripping from them like molasses. They wowed us with an exciting promotional film showing happy college students who were fulfilled and smart, having fun, studiously learning, and reverently worshiping. It made an impression, which is exactly what it was designed to do. For so many, BJU was revered as this shining star, this God-chosen place where parents could send their children and not worry for their physical or spiritual safety: it would protect all the parents' hard work of instilling both morals and a biblical, rigorous work ethic while also preparing them for life out in the "evil world."

My fundamentalist indoctrination began at our church-run elementary school. Our curriculum, chapel, dress code—even the punishment and reward system—closely mirrored the popular fundamentalist Christian colleges of the seventies and eighties. Unsurprisingly, our school also enforced gender-defined expectations from the top administrative offices down to the very youngest students. In hindsight, perhaps these earliest memories of enforced gender roles contributed to my discontent with attending a Christian school. I chafed under the double standard that some things were okay for boys but not for girls. Primarily, I despised wearing dresses: they didn't make me feel pretty, nor did I want to feel pretty. Instead, I wanted to run and play dodgeball and slide into the bases during the recess kickball games rather than allowing myself to be tagged out. Beyond that, I wanted to be viewed as smart and capable, not just as someone preparing for a husband someday.

In due course, I realized that I wanted to do all the things proper "ladies" weren't supposed to do not because I was rebellious but because I naturally wanted to do them. Simply put, being a "lady" (for me) was restrictive and limiting; after all, certain activities shouldn't be done in a dress. Being confined to a dress was a constant source of irritation, so when my parents announced we were moving to a small town four hours away, I was elated. Finally, I wouldn't have to attend that dreaded school or wear dresses every single day. I had never been so happy.

One thing didn't change, however. Even though I convinced my parents to let me attend a public junior and senior high school in my new city, my family still eventually managed to find and attend a church with strong ties to BJU. The immaculate image of BJU from our previous church didn't change. In fact, it was perpetuated at our new church through its leadership: the pastor, his wife, and our youth pastor and his wife were all products of BJU, not to mention the frequent visits from those BJU "preacher boy" students who returned to church on break to try out their new preaching skills on a receptive and enthusiastic audience. The influence of BJU was pervasive and punctuated, for good measure, with occasional visits from BJU ministry teams that were traveling the mission field of the United States, recruiting the next class of faithful soldiers for the Lord's army. Clearly, I was heavily steeped in this indoctrination and had little chance of resistance. Those who did resist, ultimately, would live tragic lives of sin and depravity (or so we were told).

The High Cost of Attending BJU

This period of attending BJU during the mid- to late 1980s magnified my internal dissonance that I couldn't yet articulate, and a lot of my conflicts on campus revolved around either my lack of finances or my gender performance, or sometimes a combination of the two. It felt like my career at BJU was doomed before I even arrived. Because my family did not have the means to provide transportation for me to get to South Carolina, I needed the assistance of the dean of women's office database, which worked to pair me up with another student geographically close to me. Though I didn't have any proof, I felt like this asking for assistance was automatically viewed as a burden by that office, which by default put me on its radar.

If my lack of resources in getting to campus didn't put me on the administration's radar, then my financial inability to conform to BJU's gender expectations most certainly did. It began with my not being feminine enough. For the first year and a half I was a student, I owned one coat—a jean jacket. Truthfully, I only needed one coat in the South, but my jean jacket was deemed not to be "feminine" attire. It didn't matter that it was the only jacket at my disposal; all that the administration saw was my jacket as a reflection of my rebellious nature and nonconformity.

Another such "problem" was my struggle to conform to feminine hairstyles. In the era of eighties big hair, my super-fine, super-straight hair wouldn't cooperate, so I resorted to perms. But perms were expensive, so I was determined to make that perm last as long as it could from the most inexpensive source: BJU's cosmetology school. About twice a year, I would scrape together approximately twenty dollars to get a perm with the smallest rods so I could keep the tightest curls as long as possible, but my eighteen-hour days that began with my morning shift at the dining common didn't give me much time to style my hair. I did manage to keep my hair from turning into a frizzy hot mess by applying a healthy amount of mousse, but my hairstyle worked against me and only managed to make me look too masculine.

I tried to remedy the masculine look by adding a dash of bright red lipstick for flair, but that only made matters worse. My tight perm, jean jacket, and red lipstick landed me in the dean of women's office. They said my reprobate image indicated my need for counseling and a wig. I refused to wear a wig but promised to comb my hair out and to lay off the mousse. I found myself dangerously close to being put on spiritual probation, which would disqualify me from one of my on-campus jobs as a student referee in the women's intramural athletic program. Instead, I was required to attend weekly one-on-one counseling sessions with my dormitory supervisor to help me learn how to be a proper lady and to parse out my seemingly rebellious nature against such things.

And, yes, those detested, required dresses from my childhood were back with a vengeance. In my parents' eyes, BJU served as the ultimate answer to shepherding me—the rebellious, angry kid—into adulthood so that I could either become my own problem or a fundamentalist success story. What neither they nor I realized at the time was that this "solution" to a thorny issue actually exacerbated everything. It would be years before my parents would understand just how detrimental my time at BJU really was, yet, though they remained unaware, I was just beginning my immersion into BJU culture as a college student where I was treated like a child yet expected to be an adult.

Mixed Messages

This confusing treatment was further compounded by self-discovery, self-loathing, and doubt, all heaped on me during my time there. At BJU, a constant theme running throughout the culture was that my core is corrupt; I have nothing good within. Only through conformity to BJU's perception of biblical standards could I claim to be Christian. If I deviated from those standards, my words would become hollow deceptions of my wicked heart. Despite my sincerity and devotion, I began to believe that I could be blinded by my own depravity and ultimately have no communion with the Body of Christ or with God.

The very first grown-up responsibility I faced there concerned how to finance my education. College was expensive, and if I wanted to go to school (and I did), I would have to figure out a way to pay for it myself, especially because my parents had no financial means to support my education alongside my four younger sisters, who were all in private Christian school. At that time, because of its unaccredited status, BJU did not allow any sort of federal education grants or loans, and the money I had saved working through high school did not go very far. As a result, I applied that work-hard ethic from my fundamentalist background and found a work scholarship job on campus to cover the rest of my school bill.

But the major problem was that working hard wasn't enough. At $2.85 an hour, even at forty hours a week, which was taxed as income, it was impossible to pay for classes and room and board on a work scholarship job alone. That bill amounted to more than $650 a month, which doesn't seem like much today, but back then, the cumulative (*with interest*) $200-plus deficit every month felt like an insurmountable climb. Furthermore, we were told that BJU could pay substandard wages because it was a work scholarship. I, and countless others, worked at the dining common without the possibility of overtime, while doing demanding, dirty, and sometimes dangerous jobs—all for the privilege of attending BJU.

Other cost-saving endeavors like shared off-campus housing were forbidden for underclassmen who did not live with an immediate relative. Additionally, we weren't allowed to work off campus, either. In retrospect, I have a theory that some of those rules were designed to organically weed out the students or families who weren't as committed to their teaching, their particular ethic, or their desired social class. From a young age in a fundamentalist environment, I had been conditioned to accept authority without question and had been programmed to view BJU as a spiritual and educational authority. When BJU speaks, it is almost as if the very mouth of God is speaking. In light of my theory, I interpreted BJU's financial test as a spiritual challenge, and I accepted it. Stubbornly, I decided I was going to succeed, that I was good enough and elite enough to get my diploma at this proving ground of the spiritually faithful.

Since paying for school on work scholarship alone wasn't a possibility, I found myself forced to stay out of school some semesters so I could earn regular wages to pay down my school bill. Most of the time I would attend two or three semesters and then travel back west to work full time through a summer and fall semester. I used these times away from school to save additional money for everyday expenses like laundry, books, shoes, nylons: all those little things we were expected or required to have while a student.

In 1986, during one of these furloughs back west, I took a course at a junior college. In-state public college was shockingly inexpensive, and the class cost about one hundred dollars. During this course, I developed a friendship with one of my classmates who then introduced me to female friends of hers. Over time, one of those friends ended up being much more than a friend.

The best way I can describe how this felt was that it was like finally finding a key to a lock I didn't know I had. It was both confusing and clear at the same time. This sense of coming home to a place I'd never been before left me terrified yet whole. My fundamentalist indoctrination provided me with a specific set of rules regarding physical intimacy, and anything outside that framework was immoral. Those who strayed, especially from the heterosexual path, were on the road to death and destruction. How could anyone find communion with God while living an intentionally promiscuous, craven "lifestyle"? My internalized condemnations reverberated through my soul as I contemplated how the one thing that finally made me feel whole and complete was described by my religion as one of the most depraved.

During this time, six or seven passages in the Bible were conveniently fashioned into a spiritual sledgehammer and delivered with vehement force designed to scare and dehumanize its target, which certainly stunted my own personal understanding of what the Bible really says about being gay or transgender (which in the whole context of scripture really isn't much). That message from the Clobber Passages is the same one still hammered today, only with more flair and venom. From the vague and sinister telling of Sodom and Gomorrah to the New Testament railings about being given over to a depraved mind, these stark images scared me into imagining some reprobate on Skid Row in abject misery. It was a brutally effective deterrent as it ultimately doomed the only relationship that had made me feel like an equal, valued partner up to that point in my life. During the onset of the AIDS crisis, I noticed the church using the spectacle of men dying of this cruel disease to reinforce its myopic vision that God had rejected this community. Even today, a large portion of the evangelical church still passes this judgment on the queer community.

Within months, in January 1987, I inexplicably found myself back at BJU for another semester. Heartbroken over the loss of my first relationship because I couldn't reconcile being whole with my spiritual upbringing, I suffered in silence because I knew that BJU would expel me if I told anyone what had happened. The specter of losing my grip on my educational goals was more than I could fathom giving up. Like a good fundamentalist, I attached my personal value to my ability to persevere through all the trials that it took to attend BJU and work toward my degree.

Expected Sacrifices

The administration liked to sound sympathetic toward our plight. During one of the daily required chapel sessions, we were told by the school president and namesake, Bob Jones III, that being a student at BJU would require sacrifices and that those who didn't make it to graduation weren't worthy of the diploma. Those who did graduate, however, were regarded as special, exceptional individuals in the eyes of the university and our future employers. I wanted to be exceptional, so I was determined to graduate, no matter what it took or how long it took. No amount of personal anguish would stand between me and my goal. I was literally willing to sacrifice myself to achieve it: my new mantra was "graduate or die trying."

But my goal of graduating soon became challenged in strange ways. Before my first relationship, I was largely oblivious when it came to recognizing women on campus who were like me. Now, I saw them everywhere, including on campus. It also seemed that conversations around me always drifted into this topic: debates about maintaining friendships with gay people at home, or even quieter conversations about specific people we knew on campus. I had friends on campus who I am convinced were in a relationship, but I was too scared to ask, and they were likely too scared to be open around anyone because of the potential danger of expulsion.

However, there was one woman in particular, I'll call her Kristine, whose friendship with me morphed into a relationship in which I could discuss all of this without fear. She bravely told me her radical thoughts about the biblical David and Jonathan that would have been considered blasphemous at BJU had anyone heard her. She also opened up about her relationship with another student on campus. I noticed they began to dress alike—as straight couples on campus were prone to do—as though they weren't trying to keep their connection a secret. Over the course of a semester, Kristine and her girlfriend even tried to fix me up with another female student, who I'll call Jill, on campus who was obviously interested in me. Jill happened to be in my same row during chapel and was always trying to get my attention by using that special "dating" stare used by straight couples on campus: coy smiles designed to elicit an acknowledgment of her interest and sly side-eye glances to see if I would reciprocate.

My personal goal of finding success at BJU, however, caused me to reject the realization that I was attracted to women, and to this day I feel bad about the way I treated and rejected Jill. I wish I could tell her how sorry I am for being a coward and not allowing her to express her feelings for me then. I also wish I could say that rejecting her was the worst thing I did to maintain my goal of succeeding at BJU.

But it wasn't: I also betrayed Kristine.

So desperate was I to conform and be accepted by BJU that I disclosed Kristine's relationship to the dean and assistant dean of women. How could I do such a thing? I can rationalize my behavior by explaining we were expected to report transgressions, no matter how small; otherwise, we were just as guilty as the transgressor. I can also downplay my betrayal by reporting that nothing ultimately happened to Kristine and her girlfriend, likely because one of their parents was a considerable donor to the school. But I can't shake my memories. I owe those two women an apology, and my horrible betrayal will remain one of the deepest regrets of my life.

The Price of Passing as Straight

In what would be my last semester, I was old enough to live off campus and work part time off campus while attending school. Four of us shared an apartment: me, a friend, and identical twin sisters. The sisters took the BJU code of conduct to the next level, at one point reporting me to Jim Berg, dean of students, because one of them had caught me with a cigarette. There was no question now: I was on Mr. Berg's radar.

During this phase, I managed to pass as straight by dating men and appearing to be serious about marriage. Sadly, I was serious enough to marry someone I did not love. We were both too young to appreciate the social and practical expectations of building a life together, but we had known each other since junior high and had sporadically dated over the years. I decided I could tolerate him, which would allow me to maintain an acceptable relationship without having to accept myself as I was and also avoiding the "sorrow of love"—that longing for what I believed I couldn't have. He was in the military, gone for considerable stretches of time, so while on leave one year, he came to BJU at the end of the semester so I could take him back to his military post in San Diego. When he arrived in town, we spent the next few nights together in his hotel. We married a couple of days before commencement with the justice of the peace in a quiet, short ceremony, and then the next day, during commencement, we left campus to head west. I would never walk on that campus again.

While my then-husband was deployed for most of the summer, I mentally planned how I would return to school in the fall and navigate this new married life for the next year and a half until I completed my degree. Three semesters left to graduate. Simple. I could do this.

But by late summer when I had not received my enrollment package, I called the school. Mr. Berg told me I could not re-enroll for two years. As it turned out, my absence at the off-campus apartment had been noticed. The dean of students was made aware of this and subsequently saw the announcement of our marriage ceremony listed in the public notices of the local newspaper. My transgression? I had married before commencement without the school's permission. I don't remember knowing it was against the rules to do so; my husband and I were more focused on being married so we wouldn't be traveling and cohabiting "in sin." But if I wanted to return to BJU, I would have to pay all my outstanding debt to the school and provide a pastoral recommendation from an approved pastor.

I was adrift and rejected; my one driving focus had been crushed. I lived in a large city where I only knew one person who was usually gone, and my family didn't even know I was married (most still don't). I had no home to return to, no career, no diploma. Essentially, I was unskilled labor with "some college"—all because I tried to fill BJU's required heteronormative mold. I slowly had to learn I couldn't build a long-term life of integrity by lying about who I am or who I love. About a year after I got married, I had our marriage annulled. I was on my own with a chapter of my life, so full of promise and expectation, shut by people and circumstances that tormented me for years to come.

At the time, I was convinced higher education had effectively become unobtainable. What could I do? My hands were tied. I was barred from returning to BJU, and I couldn't continue elsewhere without starting over because BJU also refused to release my transcripts until my bill had been paid.

Twenty years later, when I finally did pay my bill, I discovered my transcripts were worthless. Despite being told repeatedly by BJU that businesses didn't care about its lack of accreditation, I learned that other schools did care about accreditation, especially when transferring credits. Thousands of dollars. Countless hours of anguish. Years of my life. All that I could show for my investment in BJU was like vaporware, something that was advertised as real but was only a theory, a prototype if you will, that wasn't what it represented itself to be, and never materialized. In this case, BJU promised a quality degree that would lead to a worthwhile career, but it didn't deliver on that promise because my unaccredited hours could not be transferred to another school so I could complete work on that degree. All of my hard work at BJU could be seen but not touched and had no substantial, tangible value for advancing my career. It was the punishment that kept on giving.

Changing My Shoes

For nearly the next fifteen years after leaving BJU, I lived in a state of self-imposed spiritual exile. I'd never been willing to abandon core Christian values of loving God and your neighbor, but I also refused to attend churches that were anti-LGBT. The seeming enmity between Christianity and the LGBT community just felt out of alignment with the primary arc of the biblical message. All of this spiritual unpacking felt like I had been wearing bad shoes all my life. It's funny, because you don't realize how damaged things have been made by wearing bad shoes. It's only once you change out the problem that your gait improves, the pain in your hip starts to fade, and you stand up a little taller. The challenge is realizing that the shoes you've had your whole life—the only ones you've ever known—are the bad fit. It took me a while to think about changing shoes.

I began that journey of changing my shoes by finding gay Christian websites online, reading, and listening to podcasts and sermons. My epiphany came one day as I listened to a sermon by Mel White about the New Testament centurion and his *pais* (lover).[2] I couldn't stop crying, realizing that the Bible doesn't say all the horrible things that the evangelical church would have us believe.

I began in earnest to end my exile. *The Children Are Free*, cowritten by BJU alumnus Jeff Miner, was particularly enlightening.[3] I found and became involved in our local Metropolitan Community Church in Kansas City called the Spirit of Hope Metropolitan Community Church. In this congregation I finally found spiritual healing in my community. But it's strange how tough it is to get rid of old fundamentalist habits. After several years, I began to view MCC with a critical eye, and a group of us formed our own congregation to be a more biblically "true" church.

The one lasting poison of fundamentalism is its view of superiority above all others: that somehow, we are more special, more broken, more forgiven, and more righteous than the next Christian. Fundamentalism loses the message that we are all the body of Christ and instead believes that only its view, interpretation, and sect matters. I had to completely shed this perspective to return to a relationship with the church. After a relocation for work, I discovered, quite by accident, the Episcopal church in my area. Almost immediately I found the spiritual balance and peace that had been so elusive my entire life. I discovered that Christianity isn't a contest; rather, it's a life, a walk. It is supposed to bring peace, not contention; love, not division; compassion, not rejection.

For many years after BJU, I tried to understand myself as a lesbian because that was the only identifier that seemed to fit. But it felt like a difficult fit. I never cared much about things I believed most feminine women traditionally did: clothes, cooking, jewelry, makeup, babies, homemaking, fashion, or shoes. To me, all those interests made women wonderful and mysterious at the same time, yet there was still nothing feminine about my person or thinking processes.

I occasionally met and associated with those who seemed to fit the profile of people who were fascinated by women yet were not focused on *being* women. Being raised in a binary, either-or environment made it difficult for me to think beyond this paradigm. You are either female or male, Christian or heathen, gay or straight; there was no real discussion of existing somewhere on a spectrum. In fundamentalist circles, it still is a yes-or-no, this-way-or-that-way proposition. But I have discovered that all of us, to varying degrees, have some elements of spectrum existence. Some more than others, as is the case for me.

Transgender Validation

One of my first encounters with the gender-spectrum concept was when I watched the HBO special *Southern Comfort*, about a transgender man. As I watched this documentary, I recognized that familiar sense of something fitting right, just like my very first same-sex relationship. But unlike that relationship, that remaining dissonance of not having the proper identification was gone. It felt like I was wearing custom-made shoes now. No more mass-produced, one-size-fits-most for me.

The more I read and listened to stories of transgender existence and experience, the more I realized that I had finally found my authentic self, much in the same way that I had found my spiritual self when hearing Mel White's message. Brent Walsh's journey as a transman, as recounted in his sermons "Full Frontal Faith" (given in 2010 at BJU alumnus Jeff Miner's church) and "Fearless Authenticity," so closely mirrors my own story that it allowed me to finally accept my own internal reality. But the implications of that reality were frightening.[4]

While I think many would agree that openly identifying as transgender is dangerous, I would like to add just briefly that openly identifying as a transgender man can result in pushback from several fronts. The first front is likely the most obvious—the patriarchal misogyny woven into our societal fabric. Some men feel threatened, as if we are challenging the notion that a biological male birthright affords him the dominant position in society. True, we as transgender men certainly subvert this patriarchal system by merely self-identifying, but we do not seek to lessen a cisgender male's value. Still, we are perceived as doing so and are often met with violent reactions.

The second front comes from some women. We as transgender men are perceived as having some prejudicial view of women. Some have accused us of betraying the "sisterhood" and of viewing the identity of womanhood as beneath us. Again, we do not seek to lessen a cisgender woman's value either. We are who we are, and we just want to live our lives in peace with the same opportunities as anyone else.

My awareness of being a transman took me down a path that is difficult to explain to those outside of our small subset of outsiders. It still feels like an "Awkward Bros" club where we live in the shadow of humanity. We have our own language, but we don't have our own voice. We are largely transient in both physical and emotional senses because it is harder to hit a moving target, meaning we must be prepared to move as a means of self-preservation should any physical danger come from our being completely transparent about our true selves. And this transience also affects our finances, as we cannot always rely on economic stability through maintaining consistent employment, a luxury typically afforded to our heterosexual and cisgender counterparts.

The Price of Transgender Living

As much as I would like to say that my gender identity affects only me, that is not the case. Some of what it means to be trans is tied to my own immediate social concerns. I have learned to be flexible with pronouns in real-world situations because any potential injurious consequences affect not only me but also my family, who depend on me. Naturally, I appreciate when supportive, affirming people ask my pronouns, but I always hesitate to respond: it feels good to be seen and accepted, but it is also dangerous in my relatively small town with deep conservative roots, especially when in past election cycles I've received robocalls about the "dangerous" transgender bathroom policies. I've been on the receiving end of dirty looks and second looks when coming out of the "proper" public bathrooms, so I can imagine how I would be viewed if I were out with my pronouns.

In the real world, I can't financially afford to physically transition. Does this cause me internal dissonance? Absolutely. But it's a price I'm willing to pay for now. One of Bob Jones Sr.'s famous chapel sayings was "Don't sacrifice the permanent on the altar of the immediate," and as much as I hate to invoke any quotation from that school, it's one that I can't get out of my head.[5] Plus, it actually applies to this situation. I can't ask my family to sacrifice their permanent safety on the immediate altar of my being out in this unsafe climate. Because of that, I must remain anonymous in this chapter.

My story doesn't offer a happy or wise conclusion because after fifty-some odd years, I can't say I have it all figured out. Every day can feel like yesterday's contradiction. But I try to be honest, faithful, hard-working, loving, kind, and—most days—patient. My parents and sisters, in theory, have accepted my trans identity more easily than when I thought I was a lesbian, probably because they intuitively know that this is who I have always been. They grew up with me; they know I wasn't ever a very good girl, but I was a pretty decent boy.

I have learned to see that the threads of my Christianity and my otherness are not separate threads made of different material but rather strands that intertwine to make me who I am. Christianity is based on my individual understanding of God, Jesus, and the Holy Spirit and how the church fits into that relationship, not the other way around. With the help of people like Mel White, Jeff Miner, and Brent Walsh, the Clobber Passages hold no power over me anymore, because now I see that the church can be fallible in how it interprets scripture. Instead, I'm more concerned with the message of Matthew 15:11: "Not that which goeth into the mouth defileth a man; but that which cometh out of the mouth, this defileth a man." As a transman, I gravitate toward the overarching message of the scriptures, which calls us to love God and our neighbor. People get hung up on labels. God just wants to know that you love Him.

In some ways, the first person who benefits from telling my story is me. I haven't been to BJU in thirty years, yet recalling events from my experience there invokes religious trauma that I hadn't realized still existed. But I'm not afraid to tell my story now. I might have been scared twenty years ago. Now, I'm old, and I just don't give a shit.

I've spent most of my adult life with one woman, and I hope we spend the rest of our days together. I have also determined that nobody and no institution should take away someone's dreams, so I've gone back to school. I have had to start over—not one of my BJU credits transferred—but seeing this goal through may mean more to me now than it ever would have before. I'm majoring in business administration, and on my current timeline, I should be finished in approximately two years. Just like that teenager so many years ago, I'm determined to get my degree or "die trying," but this time, it's on my own terms.

Notes

1. The author of this chapter is writing under a pseudonym.
2. Matthew 8:5–13 and Luke 7:1–10.
3. Miner and Connoley, *The Children Are Free*.
4. Walsh, "Full Frontal Faith"; Walsh, "Fearless Authenticity."
5. Jones, *Chapel Sayings of Dr. Bob*, 5.

chapter 9   SANDRA MERZIB

When you become a student at BJU, you unknowingly become part of an unspoken, hierarchical
point system where you're awarded points for elements in your life that are out of your control. If
your point total is high enough, you enjoy the perks
of being at the top of the hierarchy, which include
bypassing administrative scrutiny and treating
poorly those with fewer points. Here are some of the
ways you earned points: being male, being a child of
a BJU graduate, being the child of a pastor, being a
child of missionaries (bonus points if they are currently serving in the mission field), having attended
a Christian high school, having been homeschooled,
being from the United States, being White.

First Impressions

People often ask me when I first knew I was gay, and they are usually surprised when I tell them I can trace it as far back as six years old. I remember having an adorable crush on my grade-one teacher. One time, when I
was a student in her class, I was sick with the flu. I cried for days because
I couldn't go to school and see her. I never thought these feelings might be
perceived as wrong or different until I was older. At thirteen, I first heard
the word "lesbian" flung around in a derogatory way on the bus ride home
from school. When I found out what that word meant, the brief moment
of realization I had gave way to a sinking feeling of dread—that word described what I was. The derision in the students' voices coupled with the
anti-gay rhetoric I had heard in church for years confirmed that this was
not a good thing.

It was 1997 in Calgary, Alberta. My mom, dad, sister, and I were attending a fundamentalist Baptist church pastored by a Bob Jones University grad from the United States whose wife was also a BJU grad. Also, two other boys who attended that church went to BJU. My parents were influenced by this pastor to believe that BJU was the place God wanted their daughters to be, and attending a secular university would mean their children were out of the will of God.

The decision to attend BJU was made for me. My parents presented me with two scenarios: go to BJU and have all expenses paid for by them, or move out of the house and be on my own. Their reasoning was that they would not financially support me being out of the will of God. Since their second scenario was not exactly ideal for an eighteen-year-old fresh out of high school, I conceded to BJU as the better of the two options. I knew the school was strict, with lots of rules, as I had an older sister who went there. They had presented her with those same two scenarios, but she had never divulged any specifics about her experiences there, giving me only a vague understanding that it was far worse than I could possibly comprehend. I truly had no idea what I was getting myself into.

At that time, I believed in God and did my best to be spiritually earnest, but there was always something blocking me from being completely immersed in the way of thinking that permeated the church culture all around me. I had gotten "saved" and baptized at around twelve, but doubts around my salvation always loomed. These doubts continued, and the constant servings of spiritual guilt heaped upon us at BJU prompted me to get "saved" and baptized a second time. I wanted to believe, and in my own way I think I did—I just didn't seem to believe the way the church or BJU wanted me to. Even as a child, I found it difficult seeing everyone blindly following everything they were told without question, and I couldn't quite bring myself to do the same. I didn't understand it at the time, but it's clear to me now that this discomfort was the initial seed of critical thinking being planted. To my parents and my church, however, it was perceived as rebellion. Despite my many doubts, I was willing to give this school a try, especially if it could help me with this secret I had been harboring for many years.

At this point in life, my being gay was probably not a complete secret from my parents. When I was young, I was absolutely in love with Mariah Carey (still am!). I had posters of Mariah on my wall and would listen to her music incessantly. I was teased at school for having pictures of her in my locker while other girls my age had pictures of boy celebrities in theirs. I'm sure that, much to their disdain, my mom and dad had an inkling that I wasn't completely straight.

My teenage self made the mistake of keeping a diary as an outlet for all of my feelings. I divulged to that diary that there was a girl at school that I liked. My mom found my diary and read it, which caused her to become upset in a way I'd never seen before. She picked me up from school and was unnervingly silent all the way home. Once she had parked in our driveway, she lost her temper and yelled at me, including such questions as "How could you do this to us?" and "What would people think of us?" She was more concerned with how this affected her reputation at church than it did me during this fragile, confusing time.

I learned that a person's mental and emotional well-being wasn't really valued in a fundamentalist church. This was in keeping with how society viewed mental health in the nineties. People who saw therapists were punch lines in sitcoms, were considered crazy, and were talked about behind their backs for being weak or mentally unstable. I never saw anyone positively emphasize or even mention self-care, emotional well-being, or good mental health in school. It was even less so in the church, which would go as far to say that self-esteem was satanic and that mental health problems were actually "sin problems."

It was an unspoken understanding that my attending BJU was an act of conversion therapy. After the diary incident, my family didn't talk much about my "tendencies," as my mom referred to them. Attending BJU became a way for me to appease my parents and a way to fix myself. I didn't want to be gay, so if there was work I could do to make myself straight, I was willing to do it. In late August 1997 I got on the first of three planes with my older sister and headed to Greenville, South Carolina.

After some issues with customs, a missed flight, and a delay of several hours, I finally arrived on campus on August 31, 1997. Exhausted and nervous, I discovered that I was the last of my room's four occupants to arrive. My roommates had already unpacked, so I was relegated to the least desirable bunk and the least amount of storage space. I had had the option of rooming with my sister, but considering the closeness of the quarters, we decided it was in the best interest of our relationship not to room together. Still in shock at how far away I was from home, I couldn't shake the feeling that I had stepped into another dimension.

To make matters worse, I found out that Princess Diana had died in a car accident earlier that day. Since I had spent the day traveling, I was clueless about her car accident. Hearing this news through the filter of my exhaustion magnified its tragic nature—I was completely gutted. I am Canadian; many of us love the monarchy, and most of us really loved Princess Diana. I remember shedding tears thinking about how young she was.

To my horror, I soon heard negative reactions from fellow students and campus leaders. I was shocked into silence when I heard people bluntly stating that she had met the fate she deserved because she was living in sin. There was no sympathy for a young life taken, no sympathy for the two young sons she left behind. They adamantly and almost gleefully stated that she was in hell now, since she had died in sin without being saved. I couldn't believe the lack of compassion and sympathy. Even if she didn't share the same beliefs, couldn't we meet this tragedy with kindness instead of derision? I would come to understand that this attitude was the norm at BJU, and this incident set a precedent for future behaviors and attitudes I was to encounter on campus.

Culture Shock

BJU dormitory life was the biggest culture shock I have ever experienced. I was not used to being at a place where everyone was so inauthentic and everything was regimented. I had to share with three other girls a very small room furnished with bunk beds and a door that didn't lock. Privacy was not a thing; your possessions and space were subject to search at any given time, and if you were caught with anything that "didn't check" (meaning was not permitted), you were given what was deemed the appropriate demerits or punishment. In our case, things that didn't check included drugs and alcohol (possessing these called for immediate expulsion), but these things were so far out of our orbit that they were easy to avoid. The things we were most worried about being caught with were comically innocent: headphones, music that wasn't classical or BJU-approved Christian music, or "worldly" books, magazines, or pictures.

In 1997 my music collection was housed in two large CD books. We had the option of turning in our uncheckable music at the beginning of the year with allegedly no fear of repercussion in the form of demerits, and the dormitory supervisor, who actually lived in our dorm, would hold on to our music until the semester break, when we could reclaim it. The same held true for headphones. But I could not imagine parting with my CDs for a couple of reasons: first, I felt sure my collection would label me as a sinful rebel. Second, I wanted access to my music should the opportunity ever present itself—it did, but it was rare, and I had to be extremely sneaky.

Most nights I stayed up a couple of hours past our required lights-out time of 11 p.m., flipping through four or five different radio stations on my little Sony Walkman. I had contraband headphones jammed into each ear and a blanket bundled around my head in case my headphones leaked music and gave me away to my roommates. Because the campus cultivated a culture of tattling, or turning people in, you never knew who you could trust, so it was best to keep these actions a secret from every-one, even supposed friends.

I remember digging my uncheckable CD books from the bottom of my dirty laundry hamper (the safest place I could think of to store them) and pulling out a chosen CD that I would play over and over as a way to soothe myself, to work through my feelings, and to remember what it was like to be normal. The burden of being in this extremely artificial environ-ment while living with the secret of being gay was becoming too big. I had friends, but would they still like me if they knew? I would soon find out the answer.

The Hierarchical Point System

When you become a student at BJU, you unknowingly become part of an unspoken, hierarchical point system where you're awarded points for el-ements in your life that are out of your control. If your point total is high enough, you enjoy the perks of being at the top of the hierarchy, which in-clude bypassing administrative scrutiny and treating poorly those with fewer points. Here are some of the ways you earned points: being male, being a child of a BJU graduate, being the child of a pastor, being a child of missionaries (bonus points if they are currently serving in the mis-sion field), having attended a Christian high school, having been homes-chooled, being from the United States, being White.

I am White, so I could check that off the list, but that was pretty much it. As a female who went to public school and even (gasp) Catholic school at one time, and whose parents were not missionaries and hadn't at-tended BJU, I was screwed from day one. On top of it all, I was labeled "foreign"—I kept thinking, "I'm from Canada, not another planet"—so I never really had a chance. When I spoke in Greek to my parents on the phone, a roommate would yell, "Speak English; you're in America now." There was absolutely no room for otherness of any kind there.

I also made the mistake of having a personality. It felt as though many around me removed their personality as a way of being careful, conforming to this image of a godly person they thought they needed to be for those in charge. I tried to be cautious, but my personality leaked out and was interpreted as rebellious.

On paper, each dorm provides a system of individuals to foster spiritual growth. In actuality, these spiritual leaders were designed for surveillance purposes. Each dorm had a live-in dorm supervisor who was older than the residents. Some were decent people, but most were not, especially if your hierarchy point tally wasn't high enough. Next, each dorm had a live-in dorm counselor, typically a graduate student. Each floor of the dorm was divided into two halls, and each hall had a hall leader, who was usually a junior or senior undergraduate. Within each hall, a cluster of three or four rooms constituted a prayer group, and each room had either a prayer captain or an assistant prayer captain. It was a strange system that granted certain individuals the power to spiritually lord authority over others. We received constant pressure to attain one of these spiritual positions, while people in these positions were pressured to turn in their fellow students for any infraction, big or small. Earning this position was entirely through the discretion of the spiritual leader in your room, who evaluated you at the end of the year.

If your closest spiritual leader decided that wearing combat boots and dyeing your hair (as I did) were not good examples of spirituality, you would receive a bad review. As a result, I then had to explain to the dorm supervisor why my prayer captain didn't view me as spiritual enough to lead the occasional devotion in prayer group. Throughout my time at BJU, I was never made any kind of spiritual leader.

Taking a Risk: Asking for Help

For whatever reason, my eighteen-year-old self told my hall leader I needed counseling. I matter-of-factly told her I was gay and that I wanted to overcome it. For the majority of my life, pastors had preached that homosexuality was a sin that God could help overcome. I wanted that, so what could she do for me? She panicked. I could tell she had never knowingly met a gay person and was clueless how to respond, so she did the only thing she knew—took this issue straight to the dean of students, Jim Berg.

Being new to the BJU system, I sincerely believed this man could help me finally take this gay thing away, so that I, too, could participate fully in this campus culture. I wasn't prepared for his invasive questions. He was looking to blame my being gay on any sexual abuse in my past. Furthermore, he asked me how often I masturbated and what I thought about when I did. Out of the corner of my eye, I noticed my hall leader squirming in discomfort. To this day, I marvel at my courage in responding to him that I found these questions incredibly inappropriate and that I did not feel comfortable answering them. I have no idea why he accepted this and didn't push the issue further, but I am proud of my eighteen-year-old self for recognizing a bad situation and not perpetuating a cycle of power abuse.

If only that was where it stopped.

Mr. Berg decided counseling was the best recommendation, and he would oversee it himself, with the help of my hall leader. What followed was three years of reading and re-reading my Bible, a lot of prayer, and invasive questions about so many aspects of my life including my thoughts and my habits, but no mention ever about my being gay and what to do about it. When I inquired about this, Mr. Berg replied that once we sorted every other sin in my life, this one would just go away. But it didn't. If anything, it intensified, ironically, because I tried so hard not to think about it. I was miserable: I was still gay, still surrounded by girls, had developed a few crushes, and now it seemed more people knew my secret—without my telling them.

Finding a Boyfriend . . . and Misery

To satisfy the scrutiny of Mr. Berg, I found a boyfriend. Dating at BJU is low pressure in some ways and very high pressure in others. It's low pressure because you aren't allowed to touch, to be alone together, or be off campus together. You "date" simply by being in each other's presence, which is ideal for a lesbian who doesn't want to touch a guy. On the other hand, dating is high pressure because you were expected to graduate with a serious potential marriage partner in tow. If not, you were considered a failure, which is sad and dangerous when you realize most BJU students are essentially overgrown children with no experience of real relationships. We were expected to marry a person we had never touched, never kissed, and never seen outside of this rigid, rule-laden fishbowl. It was a recipe for failure or worse, especially because, in that artificial environment, people could be extremely different from their BJU personas.

Unfortunately, I picked the worst guy to date during my sophomore year. He was jealous, possessive, and emotionally abusive. He alienated me from other people by monopolizing my time and not allowing me to socialize with anyone but him. I finally worked up the courage to break up with him over the summer, but the breakup was hard on my good female friend since her boyfriend and my ex-boyfriend were still best friends. My ex did his best to poison my friend against me, and soon she stopped talking to me.

Because this guy had kept me from talking to anyone, male or female, for so long, I suddenly found myself in my junior year without any friends. Meanwhile, I continued to receive invasive and ineffective counseling from people who had no idea how to "cure" me of my gayness. It was also becoming apparent that more people knew my secret without my consent, as other friends were alienating me for no other discernible reason. For example, my roommate my sophomore year told me that somehow her mother had found out about me being gay and no longer wanted her daughter to room with me. I was understandably blindsided by this. The awareness of people suddenly finding out combined with a national controversy involving BJU served as a catalyst for one of the lowest points in my life.

Presidential Exposure

In February of 2000, George W. Bush spoke at BJU while campaigning for his initial run for the U.S. presidency. This visit sparked a media spotlight on questionable practices at BJU, including its interracial dating policy, which carried the penalty of expulsion. In 2000 this rule was still very much enforced. Bob Jones III, the university president at the time, met with Larry King on his show in early March 2000, and what most people remember from this interview is his repealing the interracial dating policy right there on the air.[1] We, the student body watching from the Founders Memorial Amphitorium, all let out a collective gasp, incredulous that the administration would change its stance on a topic it had spent decades defending as a biblical principle.

Time seemed to stand still as he made that announcement. BJU is not known for celebrating differences. To the contrary, the school judges students daily by their ability to conform to both internal and external standards that make them look, talk, act, and think like everyone else. Earlier, I mentioned my take on the hierarchy of privilege on campus and how I did not fit into their criteria of value. I learned very quickly that if people were currency, I was virtually worthless. But even back then, when I lived as an outsider in so many ways, I still couldn't fully recognize the true severity of the campus's lack of diversity and my White privilege. It would take me a long time to dismantle BJU's way of thinking to appreciate the beauty and strength of diverse cultures, backgrounds, and faiths, expanding to the queer community. When I finally did gain perspective, I felt a pang of regret that I ever partook in a system that promoted racism and xenophobia as core values.

As miserable as I was, I know my experience cannot possibly compare to any of the students of color who were recipients of daily active racism. I knew firsthand that the dean's office summoned "ethnically ambiguous" looking people in to officially declare their race and let them know what race they were allowed to date. I knew firsthand of people who were expelled for dating a person who was not the same race as them. This was all done in the name of control, and some tactics were more horrific than others.

The fact that Dr. Bob (as we all called him) dropped the interracial dating ban in 2000 doesn't mean the school stopped being racist. It doesn't even mean that they truly dropped that ban. It simply meant that the school was reinventing its image without relinquishing actual control. Honestly, as a White person, I don't feel fully qualified to talk about the experience of race and the direct ramifications of Dr. Bob's decision because that experience is not mine to tell. All I can continue to do now is educate myself and do my best to no longer be part of that problem. But what I can address is another part of Dr. Bob's announcement that directly affected me, and which is often overlooked when people discuss his TV interview.

Without a doubt, his announcement about the interracial dating ban was revolutionary, but a different part of his interview left me breathless. Larry King asked Dr. Bob about the university's stance on homosexuality. He responded that they believed it was a sin, which was no surprise. But Larry King then asked if you could be a student if you were gay; Dr. Bob replied, "No." I sunk down in my seat. Here I was, a gay student at BJU, and it appeared that the people who knew were growing larger in number.

Three weeks later, I was expelled.

The official reason? I had accumulated too many demerits. Demerits for unknown, conveniently un-itemized offenses, but demerits nonetheless. The unofficial reason? Too many people knew I was gay. I was becoming a potential PR liability, and BJU needed me to leave. I knew they were lying about the real reason I had been expelled the minute they told me I would have to wait two years to re-enroll, as opposed to the customary one year.

Another Culture Shock

After my expulsion, all I could think of on my way home was that I had reached out to them for help, put my trust in them, and in return, they put me through hell, gossiped about me, and then shipped me off to preserve their reputation and their statement that there were no gay people at BJU. But I reacted to this betrayal strategically, biding my time during those two years away from BJU by participating in activities that were instrumental in getting me to the place I am today. Both BJU and fundamentalist Christian sects warn against spending too much time in the "secular" non-Christian world for fear of having your Christian faith dulled by its influence. I admit that it was a bit of a shock to my system to go from being immersed in this Christian world to now being fully part of the regular world.

But this culture shock turned out to be a welcome one. I was exposed to the secular world through working a couple of jobs and attending the University of Calgary. Through these experiences, I learned that the people I was cautioned most about, the people who were supposed to be the most terrible influence on my faith, were actually some of the kindest, most compassionate people I had ever met. (Conversely, some of the worst people I have ever met to this day were people I met at BJU.) I was astonished to see people who were kind and decent for the sake of being kind and decent, not because they were told to be this way in order to get to heaven. For years I had heard that any good a person does comes from a directive from God, and therefore godless people could not do good because they did not have God to direct their goodness. I was surprised to see for myself that this message was completely false.

In contrast to my experience at BJU, my time at the University of Calgary was profoundly liberating. I had teachers from all kinds of backgrounds expecting me to think critically—a skill I had never developed because I had been taught it was evil. I learned to see other perspectives and was challenged to know why I think the way I think. More importantly, the U of C served as a safe space where I could dabble in coming out and see how it felt.

The most astounding phenomenon was meeting other gay people—both students and professors—who were completely unfazed by their gayness and who treated it as just another part of their identity. Before my time at the U of C, I had never met content gay people who lacked internal struggle and self-loathing. Now that I had met so many, I imagined that I could have that same peaceful feeling too. I began wondering, "What would happen if I viewed my gayness as the way I was actually designed to be? How would that change my relationship with myself, with my gayness, and with God?" Even though I still had a difficult time accepting myself, this thought gave me permission to explore the way I was designed to love.

When I gave myself that permission, I felt liberated in a way, yet still ensnared by the guilt this decision made me feel. I had finally landed on my truth, but felt that I would pay for it eternally. Eventually, I was so desperate to stop feeling like I was swimming upstream that the liberation outweighed the guilt, if only by a hair. Soon after, I met a woman, and we started dating. Because her family went to church with my family, she understood that I was precariously straddling two different worlds: one foot in the church and the other one trying to find solid ground in the gay community. I did my best to split myself between these two worlds to keep my gay world a secret from my friends, my family, and my church, but this put a strain on my relationship with my parents because I couldn't be honest with them about who I was.

To complicate matters, my two-year exile from BJU was almost up, and I knew how important it was to keep BJU unaware of my personal and intellectual growth when I returned there as a student. But why in the world would I go back to BJU? I had two major reasons for wanting to finish there. One, as an interpretative speech major, I wanted to perform my senior recital that I had worked so hard preparing. Two, I knew they would never expect me to actually re-enroll, and if I proudly returned with my spirits unbroken, they wouldn't know what to do.

Turns out, I was right.

The Comeback

Unlike the first time I set foot on campus, I was fully prepared for the culture when I reenrolled for my final year at BJU. They didn't play by their own rules, so I didn't play by them either. They relied on guilt as a form of control, so I determined I would not be controlled. They had betrayed me in the past when I showed vulnerability and honesty, so this time around, I was prepared to lie about anything—something I would never have considered in the past—so I could finish the year and graduate. Survival was the name of the game, and that's what I did—survived.

Part of my return after expulsion required that I endure mandatory counseling, but I knew just what to say this time around. I asked my assigned counselor if she had ever counseled a gay person. She hadn't. In a bold move, I told her, "I'm going to make this simple for you. I've had two years to deal with it, and it's dealt with. I will not talk about it with you. It is off the table." She agreed, and we carried on. She didn't need to know that "dealt with" actually meant I was dating a woman and had come out to myself. Sure, it was an imperfect coming out, but it was my first step in taking control over my own life. I finished my final year, completed my recital, and graduated. I walked off that campus in May of 2003 with my head held high, on my own terms, and I never looked back.

After I graduated, I began the process of working, applying for grad school, and figuring out the general trajectory of my life. The relationship with my first girlfriend didn't work out, which was devastating at the time, but it was for the best. I will always be grateful to her for introducing me to gay culture and helping me realize that I was worthy of love just the way I was.

I continued to attend church for about nine more years, all the while getting more settled in the LGBT community. I left the hypocrisy of the fundamentalist Baptist church and attended a Presbyterian church where the people were generally more accepting. I began to think that maybe I could have this balance between my faith and my life, until the pastor preached an anti-gay sermon. Granted, it was much kinder in tone than the sermons from my fundamentalist days, but even a message that kindly asks "lost" gay people to come to Jesus was too much for me. I was insulted that the pastor called on the congregation to "love me back to Jesus" when I was already sitting there in his presence. I walked out of church that day and never went back, not because of anger or any other strong emotion; I just knew in my heart that I was done.

Time, distance, and the compassion of those outside of BJU have helped me rid my self-loathing. I admire my six-year-old self for her ability to love so openly. I wish I could tell my teenage self that everything would be okay, and I stand in awe of my strength as a BJU student. In addition to my own self-therapy, I needed the consistent support of the people I encountered in the real world to set me on a path of self-acceptance.

It took the unwavering love of my amazing wife to see myself as a person worthy of love the way I was designed to love. It took Lady Gaga's *Born This Way* era to truly set me free and see myself as the beautiful, fabulous gay unicorn that I am. Finally, it took both my gay friends and my straight allies rallying around me and stepping in as my chosen family when my own family would not accept me. In the end, what brought me closer to God was everything that BJU warned me against.

After much time, many conversations, and some tragedies, my family has learned to accept that my life is the way it is, and that I am who I am. It took my grandma passing away for my family to finally meet my wife. It took my dad's deteriorating health and eventual passing not fifteen months after my grandma before my family began to accept Kaitlyn as a part of family gatherings. It's by no means a perfect situation, but it is several steps in the right direction. The fact that I no longer have to split myself between two worlds is the most liberating aspect of all. It's a happy ending I never thought I would find and, frankly, one I never thought I deserved.

I hesitate to say that my current faith is complicated: the journey to where I am today was certainly complicated, but my faith remains relatively simple. I still believe in God, and I believe He created me this way. But faith is personal. Everyone gets called to believe what they believe in their own way, and for me, I can't read the Bible because I can't shake the interpretations BJU hammered into my head. I'm glad there are people who have studied the Bible in its original language who have proved that faith and sexuality don't have to be at odds with each other. But for me, I'm not sure I'll ever set foot in a church again because of the hypocrisy I experienced.

I look back at my time at BJU and shake my head at the people who got it so incredibly wrong in the name of God, but I don't hold what any of those people did to me against God himself. Following what Jesus said were the two greatest commandments—loving God and loving your neighbors as you love yourself—is enough spiritual guidance for me, even if the people who claim His name consider that message too simple to be the whole truth.

Why can't it just be that simple?

Note

1. Jones, "Dr. Bob Jones III Discusses."

chapter 10   REID

Oddly enough, the teachers at BJU were the ones who shaped my thinking on homosexuality. Change didn't come from activists outside our fortress; it came unintentionally from faculty within our own walls. During my first year in grad school, a teacher said, "Before college you should just take education at face value, but now that you're an adult, you should question everything." I think my teacher meant we were to become stronger in our faith through all the questions, but this moment gave me permission to ask myself the most taboo question: is my homosexuality really wrong?

Traditions: Hawaiian and Christian

Yes, I get it. I'm that typical millennial: always trying to remind everyone how unique I am.[1] But seriously, as long as I've known myself, I've never seen another person quite like me. I've never had a role model, so my aspiration was to be me, but older. And I've never had a group that I identified with: not the athletes, not the musicians, not the nerds—not even the outcasts. Without any group of belonging, I had no comfort zone either. Instead, I just wandered around an unending un-comfort zone of "it could be worse."

My driver's license allowed me to pick only one race, so according to the state of South Carolina, I'm Asian. But my ancestors are from all over the world. About two centuries ago, a European sailed across the globe and married a Pacific Islander, and their descendants married Asians from China and Japan. In Hawaii we call that hybrid *hapa*, which translates to "half," but I can't really claim that identity either because *hapa* is almost always understood in Hawaii to mean "half-White," which I clearly am not. The early Christian missionaries to the islands of Hawaii brought many things that the Hawaiians grew to cherish, like written language and Western music. On the other hand, they also brought their religion.

As a child of so many interesting cultures, I always loved exploring more about the fascinating places and cultural traditions that represented my ancestors: Obon from Japan, Chinese New Year, and hula from Hawaii. I loved these things, but we were Christians, and all of those traditions were tied to false religions that should be cast away and forgotten.

Christians have their own set of traditions too. I was "saved" at the early age of "I don't remember." I was probably five or six, but I don't remember exactly. I never really had that moment where I found Jesus, or he found me. I did, however, have that moment as a child when I reviewed my resources, calculated my risks, and weighed my options to come to the conclusion that "salvation" was the best course of action for self-preservation.

But getting saved is only the first ritual for Christians. The next required big one is baptism, which happens after you get saved, when you're ready to make a public statement about being a Christian by being dunked in water so everyone can see you mean business. It's the ice bucket challenge for Christianity. I didn't get baptized until my teen years, when fitting in is the most crucial.

Growing up as a Christian, I learned how to lie and say phrases like "I appreciate the artistry and history of hula" rather than "I love it because it's beautiful and sexy." The funny thing is that there are plenty of Christians who participate in all of those non-Christian cultural traditions. Hula is actually performed in many Christian churches in Hawaii. Even the very Mormon Brigham Young University–Hawaii has classes on Polynesian dance and puts on regular hula performances.

But my turn at religious human Plinko—a game of chance—landed me in a fundamentalist Christian isolation zone, complete with a very small church and a homeschool curriculum. I sometimes describe myself as being born an extrovert and raised an introvert. Once, as a child, I told a fat joke to a large woman but interrupted myself to explain, "But it's not about you." What ever happened to that fearless child? Not that I condone fat-shaming or sexist jokes, but what ever happened to that child that wasn't afraid of anything, especially making mistakes? These days, I loathe even having to tell someone at work that their credit card is declined. I've adopted the philosophy of "maybe if I don't talk about it, it will fix itself or go away on its own." I still let my hair grow out just so I don't have to talk to the barber, and if there were an Uber-like app for getting your car fluids changed without having to interact with a single soul, I would pay extra for it.

On second thought, I actually do know what happened to that fearless child. It died—of emotional starvation. From the age of eleven to eighteen, I essentially had no friends and for all practical purposes had no real high school education either. I basically homeschooled myself from the age of twelve to eighteen because, for reasons I don't want to go into, no one else was available. Some kids have the discipline and drive to school themselves; I did not, and I learned almost nothing in those years. I'm pretty sure that the kids who felt like they didn't learn anything in real high school actually did learn something, even if it wasn't necessarily educational in nature. Even if you don't learn math or science, you're still going to learn where you fit in the world. Failure itself can be a learning experience, but, sadly, I never learned from failure either because that would first require an opportunity to accomplish something.

My friends were the television and the internet-less computer, both of which were strictly monitored and limited. That lack of human interaction in my formative years is the reason I never grew into any social groups or comfort zones and also why I never really developed the social skills to connect with people on a deeper level. During that time, I learned to talk only to myself and not to my parents. I never asked them any of life's biggest questions during those critical teenaged years, when growing up is scary, exciting, and dangerous. Why go to them when you're always wrong, they're always right, and nothing they tell you is ever helpful? The only advice they ever gave was that "mankind has a sin nature." That was the answer to all questions about sex, politics, economics, ethics, and anything else a teenager can think of.

Good Christian children don't have opinions; they're just minions. Therefore, thoughts don't matter unless they're in line with established dogma, which is why I became good at providing fake responses.

Just say yes to everything.

Do you love church? Uh-huh.

Do you believe in God? Uh-huh.

Do you want to get saved? Uh-huh.

Are you a Republican? Uh-huh.

Do you want to never have sex ever? Uh-huh.

To this day, my parents have never had "the talk" with me. As a child, my family and I read a book about how to take care of our new dog, but we stopped reading it before we reached the chapter on sexual reproduction because I wasn't old enough to understand it yet. I'm still not old enough, apparently, and neither are my brothers and sisters. In a twisted way, I saw attending Bob Jones University in 2004 as my ticket to freedom.

BJU Traditions

I already mentioned cultural practices that fundamentalism wouldn't allow me to indulge in while at home; I had the same frustrations at BJU too. Trying to find an appropriate major at BJU just reinforced how anything I liked was considered taboo by the fundamentalist culture on campus. I wanted to be a paleontologist, but evolution is bad. I wanted to be an actor, but Hollywood is evil. Artists are worldly and materialistic. BJU Christians don't dance because dancing can only ever be sexual. Fashion design? Hell, no. That's why I majored in broadcasting. Well, I majored in speech first but literally failed at that because introversion doesn't mix well with speech communications.

I discovered that I could earn good grades while hiding behind the apparatus involved in broadcasting. In hindsight, maybe I gravitated toward broadcasting because it was the most liberal thing you could do at BJU. But, then again, I was never actually raised to know what a liberal or a conservative was because that would require knowledge; knowledge leads to independent thinking; and independent thinking runs contrary to the spiritually minded mantra "He is greater than I."

Broadcasting would have to suffice as a major because BJU didn't offer any cultural studies remotely connected to the Obon festival, Chinese lions, or hula. So I poured myself into the major because it was the one thing I was reasonably good at that was actually related to a career. That was the first time I felt I was good at something useful. But it became clear that the news-gathering part of broadcasting was not for me because that required talking to people who don't want to talk to you, which is even worse than talking to people who do want your attention. So I made myself comfortable filling behind-the-scenes roles like producing and editing.

BJU: An Island of Possibilities

The surprising part about BJU that most outsiders may have difficulty understanding is how it offered the most freedom I'd had in my whole life up to that point. Up until the age of eighteen in Hawaii, I knew nothing but isolation. We lived near no one I knew, with a big fence around the edge of our property. I never had a car, phone, or access to the internet. There was nothing within walking distance, and church was a thirty- to forty-minute drive away, so I entertained myself with my own imagination.

Maybe if I had had a close friend, I might have had the motivation to run away like those children do in those inspirational coming-of-age movies. But I didn't. I remained home, an obedient and humble Christian who was "dead to self," as they say, and I learned to make a comfort zone out of isolation and taught myself to enjoy being antisocial. I had become an island literally raised on an actual island, away from culture, people, and anything I dared to desire.

But at BJU, I lived with roughly four thousand other people my age, most of whom were raised in a similarly isolating religion. We were all held together by the common bond created by our fear of anything outside of our churches and schools. We were brought up to feel like the whole world hated us because they were wrong and we were right, which made the whole world jealous and resentful of our superiority. The fact that we were weird was just proof that we were right, and any time an outsider thought we were abnormal, we interpreted it as persecution. Nothing brings people together like the illusion of being persecuted.

On campus, we could go to the library, the campus store, the snack shop; we could attend recitals, eat at the dining common, and look at the art exhibits. We could do all these things whenever we wanted to—to a degree, of course. For someone who grew up as an island on an island, it was sensory overload for my social interaction muscles. It was like tasting salty, greasy fries for the first time after a lifetime of only getting to smell them. It's no wonder that I—an introvert who'd rather eat the wrong food order at a restaurant than correct the waiter—flew 4,500 miles to the other side of the country all by myself. I was starving for some kind of human connection. I needed a sign that I was alive.

BJU is in South Carolina, which is basically a foreign country when you're from Hawaii. If you travel the distance from South Carolina all the way to California, and then do it again over the ocean, you'd arrive in the Hawaiian Islands—the fiftieth and final state. Morocco is closer to Greenville, South Carolina, than Hawaii is.

My BJU Status as a Hawaiian

The first thing I needed to learn when I arrived on campus was that being from Hawaii doesn't make you special or interesting; it only makes you different. And my introversion did not help the situation at all. In Hawaii, when people find out you're from some faraway place, you become the center of attention and everyone wants to know what you eat, what you wear, what the weather is like there, and what music you listen to. In California, when people find out you're from Hawaii, they ask if you surf and play volleyball. At BJU, they don't really ask you anything.

Let me clarify. There were many popular students at BJU from Hawaii who grew up in private Christian schools and larger churches and who had the social skills and athletic abilities to make new friends. They also had the support of their own circle of friends who came with them.

I had none of those advantages.

Very few people at BJU ever wanted to know anything about where I was from. It was strange. If I ever brought it up, people would either ignore it or immediately change the subject, and every time I was invited into someone's home for dinner, they would never be interested in Hawaii or anything about me that was not directly related to BJU. My identity only seemed to matter as long as it was tied to BJU, so they only ever wanted to talk about my major, how my classes were, or what local church I was attending.

In the rare occasion that Hawaii was ever discussed, it was always in the context of it being a "mission field" in need of the gospel. In fact, during one awkward mealtime conversation, an elderly woman informed me that she had been to Hawaii before. She thought it was a beautiful place, but she added how unfortunate it was that many "fornicators" were there. She then described the fornicators that she could see all over the streets from the windows of her car.

To be fair, the average person from Hawaii probably couldn't tell you much more about South Carolina than they could about Moscow or Morocco, but if you're from any of those places, people will want to know everything about you. It took me a while to realize that the population of the campus of BJU is not exactly representative of South Carolina, since resident students were so restricted from consuming outside media or leaving campus. And BJU was the center of Christian superiority: I was there to absorb its culture, not to share my own. In my case, I wasn't just from somewhere far away; I was also a mixed racial minority from a small conservative Christian church, a chronic introvert, and a closeted, self-hating homosexual in denial.

The Walls of BJU: A Giant Condom of Protection

I had been to the West Coast several times, but my awareness of the world and its geography beyond my front gate was pretty minimal, and it would be several years before I saw the world from a non-BJU perspective. BJU had a very restrictive policy on when a resident student was allowed to leave campus. The time of day, one's classification, and the destination off campus determined the kind of permission required. In many situations, you could only leave campus if you prepared an electronic pass in advance and had that pass approved by the staff in the dean of men's office. Your pass could be rejected for various reasons: if you were on some kind of probation, if you're going to be with the opposite sex without an approved chaperone, if it's after curfew, or if the destination is not an approved location. Because of the overwhelming restrictions, I practically never left campus, so my first few years' impression of South Carolina was limited to just BJU.

The wall that surrounds the campus is meant, figuratively and perhaps also literally, to keep both the real world out and the manufactured illusion in. Paradoxically speaking, I'm grateful that, while BJU was the site of new-experience overload for me, it still served somewhat as an insulator for me in my ignorant "innocent" days of adjustment to this new outside world. I can't imagine what kind of trouble I would have gotten into had I gone to a regular college, especially without having any prior education whatsoever regarding sex, drugs, alcohol, and breaking the law. At that time, I didn't even know it was illegal to have an open bottle of beer in your car. This was definitely not every BJU student's experience, but it was a good transitional period for me to figure things out slowly while I lived in a community where sex, drugs, alcohol, and breaking the law were egregious sins.

In a sense, you could say BJU was a giant condom to "protect" me (or keep me oblivious) from all the worldly things I didn't learn about in my teenaged years. Perhaps my parents raised me to be dependent so I had no choice but to do what they said. That kind of upbringing certainly makes it easier for places like BJU to assume that same parental role: as long as I'm ignorant on how to live in the real world, I'll fear everything outside and have no choice but to stay on campus for safety.

I still think about my safety when reminiscing about my first sexual encounter back in 2010, at two in the morning in a shady neighborhood with a complete stranger I found on Craigslist. And a year after that, I can't even believe I let a stranger do what I think was bath salts in my car just months before hearing about that Florida man who ate another man's face while on bath salts. These sound like the scary stories BJU tells you to keep you within its hedge of protection, but I would have much rather been educated about all facets of sex beforehand. Maybe then I would have actually had the sense to not put myself at risk of having my face chewed off in my own car.

But BJU's fortress walls cannot keep the world out completely, and at the top of the list of subversive ideas that somehow penetrated those walls was the idea that I never truly chose this religious path for myself. I learned that my religion is nuts because it all hinges on my illusion of choice, a choice I had to believe was mine, and since I'd never made a real decision before in my life, the illusion was strong. It's difficult to pin down exactly when this revelation occurred, since, unlike clear turning points in the movies, real life is messy. But I think what did it for me was the simple fact that I felt like a religious fraud, and somehow I realized it, but the religious zealots on campus never did. How could the religious leaders serving the Omniscient Being not notice I was a fake?

The Threat of Invasion

I became self-aware that I wasn't even trying all that hard to blend in; it felt almost effortless. In April 2007 I sat through the infamous anti-gay chapel services given by then-president Stephen Jones.[2] I found myself nodding and agreeing with all the propaganda being spewed about the evils of homosexuality. Since my entire life was tied to this religion, I ate up the rhetoric about the "homosexual agenda" when Soulforce, an American social justice and civil rights organization, made their stop at the front gate of BJU that same month in 2007.[3] BJU convinced me that the whole world hated us because we represented the truth, and that for those who are wrong, the truth hurts. The fact that the "uninvited" activist group planned to invade our safe haven was evidence that we were doing God's work: they were persecuting us.

Stephen Jones's first chapel message focused on the Genesis stories of creation, procreation, and God's intentions for establishing the institution of marriage. "God created Adam and Eve, not Adam and Steve" is a saying often heard from the conservative crowds that make up the vast majority of BJU's demographics.

On the second day, Jones covered the most common New Testament anti-gay passages so we could confidently debate anyone on this topic. The point of the chapel message was that accepting homosexuality meant accepting pedophilia and bestiality. Had those chapel services been presented as hateful propaganda, they might not have been so powerful; instead, Jones gave his messages as someone coming from a place of care and concern, not with an us-versus-them tone, but rather with a compassionate desire to bring the gays to salvation just like any other sinner. Since all humans are sinful and in need of redemption by God, and since homosexuality is no different from any other sin, homosexuals should be treated like any other human being. And I bought into that message.

I believed what BJU taught about the wickedness of homosexuals. More importantly, I thought I had come to this conclusion myself. But before you can say you truly believe something, you have to question what you know about the topic, which is ironically what I was taught in my ethics class, my Bible doctrines classes, my educational psychology class, and pretty much every graduate class I took at BJU.

That's the beauty of education, even at a place like BJU: at some point you have enough information to start putting the pieces together yourself. I began to form my own conclusions and question things. My first question was, "I've heard that certain feelings I've been having are bad. But am I truly convinced they're bad, or am I just letting someone else tell me to feel that way?"

Oddly enough, the teachers at BJU were the ones who shaped my thinking on homosexuality. Change didn't come from activists outside our fortress; it came unintentionally from faculty within our own walls. During my first year in grad school, a teacher said, "Before college you should just take education at face value, but now that you're an adult, you should question everything." I think my teacher meant we were to become stronger in our faith through all the questions, but this moment gave me permission to ask myself the most taboo question: is my homosexuality really wrong?

The Landslide of Questions

Because of BJU's fundamentalist stance, it's easy to believe that everyone there holds the same beliefs and experiences; however, bigger numbers of believers create variety, and where there's variety, there's a chance that teachers and students may harbor different perspectives they may not be allowed to fully reveal while there. I felt that my teacher's comment had given me permission to search for answers myself rather than have them handed to me.

If you never questioned your beliefs and just took them at face value, that's luck, not faith. And the truth that I could no longer deny was that no matter how much I sincerely tried to pray it away, I had feelings for the same sex. To biblically prove that homosexuality is a sin, you have to do some complex finagling, but it's easy to find scripture condemning eating too much, loving money, not helping the poor, putting nation before God, and allowing women to open their mouths in church. Yet somehow homosexuality has climbed to the top of the list of most damaging sins.

I mentioned the "Adam and Eve, not Adam and Steve" adage. Since questioning everything was my new lease on life, I began with the simple question: "If God didn't create Steve, where did Steve come from? Because Steve is undeniably real; I've seen him with my own eyes." This led me to another question: "If God created the institution of marriage to be just one man and one woman, are non-Christian weddings exempt from that rule? Are, for example, Buddhist marriages required to include the Christian standards of one man and one woman?" And what about things nowhere mentioned in the book of Genesis that we take for granted today, such as email—or sexual consent?

It's shocking now to think we weren't taught the concept of consent at BJU, likely because we were expected to practice abstinence. But when a fellow questioning student introduced me to the subject of consent, I realized the flawed rhetoric presented in the chapel messages: consent separated both homosexuality and heterosexuality from bestiality and pedophilia. Christians can't tie homosexuality to bestiality and pedophilia if they also teach consent. Once I gave myself permission to start asking, it was like an unstoppable landslide of almost two decades of ignored questions began to pour down. It was an uncomfortable intellectual journey, but it was the first time I could truly say I actually believed anything: being gay was not a sin.

Starved for Male Friendship

I still can't believe how clueless I was about the guy who lived next door to me my freshman year and who would later become a fabulous drag queen in Philadelphia. It's not like he hid his persona at all, but when you grow up in the fundamentalist Christian community, you find yourself skilled in absentmindedly making excuses for other people's queer behavior: "He's not gay; he's just a musician, an actor, celibate, from Europe, or"—fill in the blank.

Without realizing it, I even provided these excuses for myself. It's embarrassing to admit, especially because I've had these feelings forever, but I actually believed I wasn't gay until my time at BJU. Because I was so starved for male friendship growing up, I believed my feelings for other men at school were somehow tied to this need for friendship. Conversely, I interpreted not having any sexual desires for women as a sign that I was somehow free of the burden of sinful lust, which I wouldn't feel until I met the right woman and we were bound together in holy matrimony. My ability to avoid making social connections with virtually anyone on campus kept me from ever getting into trouble with men and also kept me from getting expelled, arrested, or hospitalized. But this was a hollow victory because it also kept me from living life or having meaningful romantic relationships.

For the duration of my time at BJU, my friendship with the pre–drag queen next door remained a wholesome Christian one instead of the fabulously gay one it could have been. But while on campus, I realized I had been hiding my homosexuality from myself. I was lonely and wanted *more* than just friendship. I also recognized that what I was calling "more" was beyond the boundaries of the acceptable and it already had a name: "gay." These feelings of wanting "more" intensified as I was exposed to new situations at school: dormitories, hundreds of people my own age, even the changing room at the cafeteria where I worked. What I wanted was all around me every minute, and it was constantly trying to get my attention.

While I appreciate the dangers others might have experienced by coming out at BJU, part of me is sad I never came out to anyone there because it means I didn't have a strong enough bond with anyone to confide in. I've always been a safe person with a sixth sense for staying out of trouble. I call it a "sixth sense," but perhaps it's more accurate to call it a constant paranoia. Either way, it's a blessing and a curse because it prevented potential risks, but it also kept me from having much of a social life.

What makes me sadder is hearing how some of the friends I did manage to make, despite my introversion, struggled with their own sexuality around me without my support. An example of this happened my sophomore year, when one of my few friends invited me to his house near Columbia, South Carolina, every other weekend. I enjoyed visiting him and getting away from a campus I realized no longer harbored the freedom and opportunity I thought it had the year before. He enriched my life in many ways. He introduced me to Harry Potter, which was considered actual witchcraft at BJU. He inspired me to love reading, to care how I dressed, to cook, to like photography. We ate meals together and went to plays, recitals, and church together.

But in all the time we spent, we always avoided the topic of homosexuality unless it was to say something obviously worded in a way to vindicate ourselves. We had to be careful never to implicate ourselves, even to each other, which is why he never shared his feelings of confusion and conflict after being kissed by a man for the first time. The fear of being outed at BJU was too great.

The Isolation Tactic

Being outed at BJU meant far more than public ridicule and social stigma; it meant the strong likelihood of expulsion, which may sound like a welcome sentence of freedom away from campus, but the consequences overshadowed any illusion of freedom. You could be shackled with financial aid debts and potential loan penalties, no degree after years of hard work, credits that most likely won't transfer, no refunds for all the semesters you've already paid for, the loss of friends, and rejection from your family. All of these dangers discourage gay students from reaching out, and BJU prefers it that way. When the campus structure values turning others in to boost your own standing, it's easier to divide and conquer by keeping gay students paranoid, alone, and without allies, especially when anyone on campus could be a spy.

As a result, most of us stayed under the radar and never shared our feelings with each other during those times when we needed each other the most. Years later, after walking out of the gates of BJU and into the real world, my good friend from Columbia and I have openly discussed over wine our past struggles away from the rule-enforcing minions of BJU. He understands the pressures we were all under, but I still wish I had made more of an effort, especially in a place where gay students would out each other just to save themselves from the watchful eye of the dean of men's office. I should know: it happened to me my last year of grad school.

I was called into the office to explain why a male student claimed to have "made out" with me but felt remorseful and repentant about it afterward. I didn't need my paranoid sixth-sense skills to escape that trap, since I knew my accuser likely made up the story on the spot to focus attention on someone else while under investigation himself. But this incident illustrates the isolation strategy even between gay students on campus. At BJU it's every gay for themselves: "Kill or be killed."

Ignoring the fact that the dean of men divulged private information to me about someone who was undergoing "counseling," I found it funny how easy it was to find out who was spreading rumors about me. I simply asked, and the dean told me his name. Yes, I knew the accuser, but he was completely unthreatening, so I told the dean the truth: the student probably made the story up because he was scared and confused and needed help.

Part of the reason I was so calm in that moment was that I thought I had been brought in for a much bigger matter that had been haunting me for months. Someone claiming to be a former student had found out about my "homosexual lifestyle" and had anonymously threatened me online using a fake profile on a dating app. This anonymous person knew enough personal details about me to be convincing, and when he said he would tell the dean of men about my secret life, I believed him.

I had braced myself for months and was actually losing hair over the stress of working on a degree that might be taken away from me at the last minute because of this anonymous person. If there ever was a time I needed a gay ally, those few months were it. But the campus's isolation strategy for gay students was effective, leaving me burdened with an invisible adversary only I could see, which is why I must have looked so relaxed, confident, and innocent when I found out I was brought in for some petty accusation from a current student that had nothing to do with me. My response must have been convincing because I never heard anything else about that matter again, and, to my great relief, nothing ever came of that online anonymous accusation, which remains a mystery to me to this day.

Owning My Island Identity

Much time has passed since I was called into the dean of men's office, and I no longer live in fear that the details I have provided here will expose my identity. I have nothing to hide. The only reason I have chosen to remain anonymous for now is that I plan to come out soon to a few specific individuals, but I can't come out to them yet because of a valid, private reason that has little to do with me. Out of respect for them, I prefer to have that conversation with them in a situation that I can control rather than having them find it in a book. But if they or anyone else who has a problem with me has read this chapter and figured out who I am, let me just say, "Surprise! You're the target audience. I'm glad you've taken the time to read this, and I hope you learn something."

Since I completed graduate school in 2011 and walked off campus with a diploma, I have been amazed to find so many other former students with different backgrounds from mine whose stories share similar themes. I've met people who suffered under BJU's interracial dating policy. Luckily, my time at BJU was during the years right after this policy was dropped, when the university tried to act like it had never existed. My first roommate at BJU told me I would undoubtedly be on all the university's promotional material because I was an ethnic minority. This never happened. However, I was aware of subtle forms of racism from individuals while there, but these incidents became white noise to me after a while, especially because I needed to integrate into this fundamentalist society I had sworn religious allegiance to since I was a child.

BJU may believe it has redeemed itself from its historical controversies dealing with race, but that is not the case when it comes to BJU's stance on homosexuality. When BJU teaches that homosexuality is a sin to its student body and to its network of fundamentalist churches, it perpetuates a feeling of isolation among gay kids who are taught to think we are alone in our "abominations," because as long as we're alone, we're easier to control. But we're not alone. I've enjoyed meeting many gay former BJU students who can relate to the kind of isolation I experienced while there.

At the beginning of my story, I mentioned how I felt alone because I didn't fit into any one group. That part of me hasn't changed much. I still don't fit into any groups and still struggle with loneliness. But since my departure from BJU, I've discovered that the outside world has done a better job of embracing diversity than BJU ever will. I used to think I was the only one without a clique, but the truth is that so many people in the world grew up in isolation just like I did, having some form of an "island identity," whether that be geographic, emotional, familial, or otherwise. Now I'm allowed to find those like-minded people without the fear of being voted off the proverbial or literal island. I'm also allowed to find myself. I know "finding yourself" is an overused millennial phrase, but in this case I think it actually has meaning. By finding myself, I have realized that my worth is not dependent on my ties to BJU.

Notes

1. The author of this chapter is writing under a pseudonym.
2. Jones, "The Bible and Homosexuality"; Jones, "The Bible and Homosexuality 2."
3. "Equality Riders Face Anti-Gay."

chapter 11   RACHEL OBLAK

> When I was there, a woman was expected to go on
> a first date if a man asked her. BJU's unspoken ra-
> tionale for this expectation was simple: campus was
> the place to find your future spouse. Accepting dates
> wasn't a written rule per se, but it was such a strong
> part of the culture that most women didn't refuse.
> I found myself accepting one obligatory date after
> another and then fastidiously ghosting those men
> afterward.

The Deepest Depravity

I grew up as most fundamentalist children do: going to church multiple
times a week to hear about the depravity of humanity and my need to be
"saved" in order to go to heaven. I was four the first time I remember fear-
ing for my life, thinking that I might die in my sleep and wake up in hell—
so I climbed out of bed and trotted to my dad to be led through the Sinner's Prayer, where I confessed my sins and surrendered my life to God.

Based on Romans 1:21–32, I was taught that homosexuality was one
of the worst sins, that it was a choice that revealed the deepest depravity
of the soul, and that it was a struggle only if a person had been rebelling
against God for so long that God gave up on them. While the Old Testament was interpreted as describing same-sex relations as an "abomination," this New Testament passage seemed to describe it as arising out of
a progression of ungodliness.[1] As a child, I never met a gay person. One
of the older boys in youth group came out as gay years after leaving the
church. I assumed that was proof in favor of that biblical passage and
proof that he had chosen to be gay—a choice possible because of many
prior choices where he had rejected God.

I suppose the clues that I was bisexual were all around me; I just didn't recognize them. I thought my intense longing to be around certain girls was just a desire for friendship—not the same thing as the crushes I had on boys. I told myself the butterflies I got when I saw a pretty girl were normal—that everyone could recognize beauty in the same sex. I convinced myself that I was merely able to see those girls as a guy might see them. I thought the achy feeling I got around those girls was an indication that I knew they were more beautiful than me and more what I should have been like.

I developed a somewhat twisted coping strategy throughout my adolescence by attempting to force my body to conform to the look of the girls that gave me that achy feeling. I distracted myself from my attractions to them by convincing myself that I needed to *look* like them. Unfortunately, this method only managed to turn my feelings of attraction into feelings of disgust with myself when I realized that I couldn't look like those I admired, which turned my attraction toward them into hatred because they served as a constant reminder of my "shortcomings." It was an unhealthy strategy but one that allowed me to remain safely unaware of my own desires—safe from having to question whether I was one of those utterly depraved people mentioned in Romans.

The Fulfilled Fundamentalist Woman

The culture of fundamentalism teaches women that marriage (to a man) is the ultimate goal or prize and part of God's plan for a fulfilling ministry for women. But halfway through my time in high school, I decided I didn't want to get married. I had almost sought permission from my father to date only once, but I became disillusioned with the guy's condescending treatment of me before I had even talked to my parents. Yes, I needed permission to date. I'm aware of how outdated that sounds, but that is the world of fundamentalism, a place where I was indoctrinated into thinking that my duty as a daughter—as a young woman—was to remain pure and submissive to male authority, first to my father, then, later, to my husband.

I had aspirations for my life trajectory: I wanted to travel and learn and live unencumbered, but those plans didn't correspond well with what fundamentalism had taught was my duty. I'd been groomed to be a wife and mother, but I knew that if I got married, I'd be doomed to a life as a submissive, stay-at-home mom, which sounded entirely unfulfilling.

I also felt disgusted by the ideas I'd been taught about my sexual role as a future wife. Not only was I supposed to gratify my husband and serve his every whim, but I was also taught that providing him sex whenever he wanted was the only way to keep him faithful. *My* desires didn't matter. I felt sick at the very idea of being available to my husband for both "bed and breakfast," which is how one guest speaker described the wife's role to the women of my church.

I felt certain that marriage wouldn't satisfy me. Without going into detail about how much I was repulsed by the fundamentalist picture of marriage, I told my family my intention to remain single forever, justifying my choice by pointing to examples such as the Apostle Paul and the missionary Amy Carmichael, who both had "served God" as single individuals. Even back then, I knew it was a weak justification. Most women within fundamentalism likely remained single because they couldn't find a husband, yet here I was as a young lady already saying that I didn't want one. My declaration singled me out as different; it shouldn't have surprised me that questions followed.

Not long after I began declaring my intention to remain single, my brother asked if I was a lesbian. I knew that I wasn't. I was well aware of my attraction to men: my juvenile celebrity crushes on Devon Sawa and Justin Timberlake, my guilty fantasies about being kissed, and the shame-inducing stirrings of desire as my body matured sexually. Since "no" was an accurate answer to my brother's question, I gave it with gusto, thankful that I wasn't living with "*that* sin." However, it wasn't the only time I had to field that question from him, and the thought lingered in my mind. Each time I would tell him "no," I added silently to myself, "But I probably could have been had God not saved me from it." Since I wasn't repulsed at the thought of being with a girl, I thought that *I* was also proof that homosexuality was a choice. Unlike that boy from my church, though, I comforted myself that I was different because I could keep those desires in check so long as I remained faithful to God.

When I graduated from a fundamentalist Baptist homeschooling program, I chose to go to Bob Jones University. I thought my choice was based on God's will, but looking back, I realize it was more from fear and coercion than anything. After I took the SAT, I received invitations to apply to various Ivy League schools, including Harvard, which lived in my imagination the way Hogwarts lives in the imaginations of most people of my age. I was hungry to learn, and an Ivy League education seemed like a feast of knowledge to me. A large part of me wanted to know if I could make it at such a prestigious place; however, my parents refused to offer financial support for anything other than an approved Christian college. They warned me that I would lose my faith if I attended a secular school. Losing my faith would likely mean I had never been saved in the first place, despite my prayer at the age of four, putting me at risk of damnation when I died. When college came down to a choice between heaven and hell, it wasn't hard to choose the option that the church and my parents wanted me to make.

BJU: Dating Expectations and Limited Sexual Vocabulary

Once at BJU in 2005, I held on to my intention of avoiding marriage and also tried to tack on a dating prohibition for good measure. The latter part didn't last long, not because my intention was weak, but because of the dating culture on campus. When I was there, a woman was expected to go on a first date if a man asked her. BJU's unspoken rationale for this expectation was simple: campus was the place to find your future spouse. Accepting dates wasn't a written rule per se, but it was such a strong part of the culture that most women didn't refuse. I found myself accepting one obligatory date after another and then fastidiously ghosting those men afterward.

I was lonely, though. I wanted love, but I didn't want to be tied down to someone who would take my autonomy and individuality away. I felt caught between a choice: either sacrifice myself to BJU's fundamentalist dating system so that I could belong to the community, or resist the system, maintain my freedom, but remain an outsider and miss out on social interactions. Perhaps there was another option. I began thinking about finding a friend who would also not want to get married—a woman who would join me in my celibacy and provide the emotional connection that I needed without the chains of marriage or the obligation of sex. I figured I could be quite happy to live with a female roommate for the rest of my life. Since the friendship wouldn't involve sex, I told myself it wouldn't remotely resemble a lesbian relationship—though I secretly knew I wouldn't hate one of those either. I even had someone in mind that I envisioned living with contentedly for years to come. We periodically talked about the possibility of being lifelong companions so long as neither of us found someone we wanted to marry in that time.

To this day, I'm still unsure if I was in love with that woman or just desperately lonely. Throughout this time at BJU, I was extremely ignorant about my own sexual orientation. This might seem strange to someone outside fundamentalism, but my vocabulary and understanding about sexual orientation in general were quite limited, which might have been an unexpected blessing at the time. It was bad enough to feel so disconnected from the fundamentalist roles that were supposed to make me happy and fulfilled; I don't think I could have tolerated further knowledge of my differences. Thankfully, my unconscious mind was capable of tremendous feats of denial regarding any indications that I might not be as heterosexual as I wanted to be.

My prohibition on serious dating unraveled approximately two years into my studies at BJU. I met Jacob, who quickly became my best friend, and I fell in love without realizing what was happening, long before Jacob ever asked me (and then my parents) to be more than a friend. We had a lot in common, including pretty strong homophobic views. On April 4, 2007, Soulforce, a nonprofit LGBT-affirming organization, came to town to protest BJU's homophobic stance and offered to come to campus to debate whether homosexuality truly was a sin. BJU refused them access to campus, much to Jacob's and my relief, and three of the protestors who did come on campus were arrested.[2] Jacob and I stayed safely behind the gates, discussing our mutual disgust and fear of the group that, we believed, had fallen prey to Satan's lies.

Implosions

Still, Jacob and I were both incredibly inquisitive people, and we eventually led each other into questioning the doctrines and rules of the school as well as of broader fundamentalism. These questions began with small things like whether haircuts or music could be inherently sinful, each of which had been covered in-depth in classes we had taken. Eventually, we found ourselves butting up against some of the bigger doctrines. Through this collaborative questioning process, I made a startling and welcome discovery: Jacob was probably the first man I knew who treated me like my mind and ideas were valuable and equal to his. I finally started to feel like I belonged with someone—that all of me could be present, not just the meek and submissive parts that fundamentalism trained women to promote in a relationship.

Just before the start of my senior year in the fall of 2008, we both ended up leaving BJU with uncompleted degrees: Jacob because BJU denied him reenrollment when they felt his questions provided too much fodder for "sowing discord," and me because I knew I wouldn't be allowed to have contact with him if I remained at BJU after he was asked to leave. It was a decision that took months for me to reach. Initially, I planned to return and finish up with as little trouble as possible, both to try to hide from my parents that Jacob wasn't allowed to return and also to obtain my own degree without interruption. But I knew as I packed for the fall semester that I couldn't return. I'd finally found a person who gave me companionship without trying to control me, and I simply couldn't afford to lose that.

I told my parents my doubts about returning to BJU. As I expected, everything seemed to implode. My parents' esteem for Jacob vanished—he was now the threat that was destroying both my education and my spirituality. While I had initially planned to hold off on my wedding until after I graduated, we moved our wedding date to within the year. I think my parents supported the wedding out of sheer avoidance of the shame and embarrassment of an elopement.

In the few months between when Jacob was denied reenrollment and our wedding, things became so contentious in my parents' home that I became severely suicidal and started researching concepts like emotional abuse and trauma for the first time. I think my parents expected to break me of my rebellious attitude and probably break my engagement in the process, but the worse things became, the more determined I became to leave home. Had I not still been under the impression that I needed to be married in order to leave my parents' house, I would have escaped much sooner. Ironically, after avoiding the cage of becoming a wife for so long, marriage became my escape from both home and fundamentalism and the key that would eventually lead me to question my beliefs about homosexuality and discover my own sexual orientation.

To my relief, I discovered that marriage only equaled enslavement within fundamentalism, and the further we distanced ourselves from that movement, the happier we were as a couple. During that time, however, I struggled even more with my self-image. Being around beautiful women was painful both because I felt devastated that I couldn't be them and also because I thought I was depriving my husband of something that surely he would want more than I did, especially given how badly I wanted them myself. Nevertheless, I still told myself that these feelings were only my own awareness of how men would view women and not about my own sexual attractions.

Questioning the Slippery Slope to Damnation

Questioning BJU's stance on haircuts and music was one thing; taking a closer look at sexuality was quite another. The church's position on homosexuality was tough for me to question, especially because so much ingrained fear was attached to this specific issue compared to the other doctrines we had questioned in the past: fear of hellfire as well as of the impending threat of the "gay agenda."

I don't know whether it was taught to me explicitly or not, but I had internalized the belief that if the descent into homosexuality was a result of moving away from God, then questioning that doctrine alone was putting me on that slippery slope to damnation. I couldn't imagine a Christianity that didn't take the Bible literally, and I couldn't imagine an interpretation of either Leviticus or Romans that didn't condemn same-sex relationships. The six or seven passages that are often used to support the doctrine against homosexuality seemed ironclad as far as meaning went. To question them felt nothing short of blasphemy.

My stance on this topic gradually evolved. The first crack in that armor of resistance came when we discovered a friend of ours was gay. Even in my early twenties, I had never gotten to know someone who was openly gay. It was an earth-shaking discovery for me because my friend wasn't the depraved, godless sinner I had imagined gay people were. The more I knew about him, the more I finally started to recognize that, for him, it wasn't a choice: there was just no attraction to women. Period.

I began to shift my beliefs, first from "it's a sin and a choice" to "it's not a choice but still a sin, something to be endured but not practiced." I came to the conclusion that my friend probably wasn't in sin as long as he remained celibate, which allowed me to remain friends with him while I still held on to my faith. To his credit, I am not quite sure what prompted him to maintain our friendship, especially considering my beliefs at that time, but I am certain that his patience with me during this process of questioning and learning laid the foundation for the ultimate changes in my belief system.

My position on homosexuality continued to evolve through my university education. After leaving BJU, I was determined to complete a degree. I had spent the fall 2008 semester at a community college in my hometown, where I was introduced to and fell in love with psychology as an area of study. After researching numerous university options and discovering most schools wouldn't take my unaccredited BJU credits, I finally enrolled at the University of Vermont, where I eventually completed my degree with a BA in psychology, but it would take me an additional two years of full semesters and summer classes (three years' worth of work) to do so.

My education there led me to a women's psychology class. In that class, I learned about intersexuality. When I learned how complicated gender and sex could be, I realized I couldn't tell someone that their sexual or gender orientation condemned them to celibacy, nor could I read about such complexities as androgen insensitivity syndrome and believe that God would expect people who didn't fit our gender categories to follow the dichotomous view taken from a handful of passages in the Bible. Because of these findings, I decided to dig more into the homosexuality and religion debate and to really challenge myself to consider alternative doctrines.

First, I read Mel White's autobiography of his own coming-out journey, which complemented my friend's story and fully destroyed the myth that homosexuality was a consequence of depravity or some form of choice.[3] White's description of his agony and the lengths he went to in order to change his sexual orientation left me with no doubt that "good Christians" could have natural attractions to the same sex.

From there, I finally had the courage to challenge my interpretation of the Bible by reading *The Children Are Free: Reexamining the Biblical Evidence on Same-Sex Relationships* by Jeff Miner and John Connoley.[4] Miner and Connoley didn't convince me they were right, but they didn't need to. They provided a strong enough argument to shake my certainty in the Clobber Passages. More importantly, they provided compelling evidence of potentially same-sex affirming passages, drawing on familiar stories such as that of David and Jonathan and demonstrating how one's reading of those passages often depended on preconceived expectations. I realized the Bible wasn't as self-evident as I had thought, and I was finally free to release the fear-based doctrines I'd been holding for so long.

Finally Seeing Myself

My women's psychology class helped me learn more about myself too. I first heard the term "bisexual" in that class, which piqued my interest. I wanted to ask follow-up questions, but I was too nervous. Instead, I began wondering: Could I have been bisexual if I'd had more than one partner? At that point, I knew that being gay wasn't about sexual activity but instead about internal attraction, yet I failed to apply that logic to myself. Looking back, I wonder if a large part of my resistance to claiming this identity was rooted in the day Soulforce came to BJU's campus. During our marriage, Jacob's views on the doctrine of homosexuality were changing, perhaps even faster than mine, but I couldn't shake the memory of his disgust about Soulforce. I kept imagining how exploring that part of myself would destroy our marriage.

The night I came out to myself and Jacob, we were watching the movie *The Girl Who Kicked the Hornet's Nest*. The main character started kissing another woman. Jacob became fixated on my face, which I can only imagine was riddled with conflicted emotions, and asked, "Do you like that? Would you like to kiss a girl?"

I wanted to lie. I was scared to death that I would break his heart, but I couldn't justify lying to him. Instead, I told him what I had been telling myself for some time: "I might be able to be bisexual if I weren't monogamous."

He responded with what I knew was true in my heart, telling me that it's not about my sexual activity but about who I am inside.

After a moment of silence, I responded, "I guess I'm bisexual then."

"I know," he teased. "I just wanted to hear you admit it to yourself."

It was a profound shift for us—and for me.

My marriage didn't fall apart as I (and others) had feared it would with my coming out. Honesty and self-acceptance actually enhanced my relationship rather than damaging it, bringing us closer together as I began to lose the instant loathing comparisons I usually would draw about myself around other women. I could now understand what those feelings were about.

The Cost of Leaving Fundamentalism

Though coming out improved my marriage, my journey wasn't without its costs. Living within fundamentalism and leaving fundamentalism were both traumatic for me. I've spent almost as many years in therapy as I have been outside of fundamentalism. Between leaving fundamentalist Christianity and coming out, I have lost almost every relationship I have had throughout the first twenty years of my life, including my immediate family, my church, some extended family, and my best friends. Some were losses based on others rejecting me. Perhaps more painful still were the ones where I made the decision to end the relationship for my own well-being after realizing that I could never be treated by them with decency and respect.

I may always fear rejection or hatred when I initially come out to others, but I've learned that I don't really want to hide parts of myself just to be around certain people. It's far better to build new relationships with those who will accept all of me than to tiptoe around the ones that cannot offer that acceptance.

My sense of being an outsider didn't necessarily end when I left fundamentalism. Being bisexual in a straight-presenting relationship comes with its own share of erasure and exclusion from the LGBT movement, despite the inclusion of B in the acronym. Additionally, no matter how much I distance myself from fundamentalism, it will always be a part of my background that will seem foreign to most people I meet. There's a good chance that my extreme fundamentalist upbringing will make me feel different at any social gathering, but compared to when I first arrived at BJU, I'm now better capable of dealing with my feelings of difference.

Fighting for Visibility and Inclusion

After getting over the initial existential crisis that comes with rejecting the fundamentalist worldview, I discovered that life can be a fun journey of self-exploration and expression. With a deeper connection to my own authentic self, I don't feel as lonely when I don't fit in. Publicly embracing my sexual orientation allows me to both deepen my authenticity and fight for visibility and inclusion at the same time.

These days, my personal and professional energies are spent helping others discover and accept themselves in similar ways to how I was helped. Telling my story is part of that desire to help someone else. Mel White and my first gay friend showed me that telling my own story is potentially the most powerful form of activism because it interrupts the dominant narrative and humanizes a topic that so easily remains abstract and theoretical for those within fundamentalism.

After finally finishing my undergraduate degree in 2011, I went on to obtain a master's degree in mental health counseling. I now have a private psychotherapy practice in Vermont, with a strong focus on supporting the healing journeys of those who have exited abusive or extremist groups or situations, those recovering from trauma, and those who may be struggling with understanding and accepting their own sexual orientation or gender identity. I've written and spoken at conferences about the factors that facilitate worldview change and the recovery challenges of those coming out of abusive systems and high-demand groups, drawing from my own experiences as well as the extensive reading I've done on coercive control in relationships and group systems.

Sadly, there is a dearth of literature and research about the experiences of minorities specifically within extremist and fundamentalist groups. Filling in that gap requires getting those stories out to the public. I can start with my own, and I hope one day to be instrumental in helping others tell their stories. While my private practice takes up most of my time currently, I hope someday to be involved in research efforts that raise visibility and increase the knowledge about minorities within controlling and oppressive systems like fundamentalism.

Jacob and I are still happily married, purposefully avoiding the marital rules taught at BJU and church. I made peace with Christianity but ultimately realized that it wasn't a great fit for me. I still have a vibrant spiritual life, but it's more personal and much more private. That being said, I do admire those who have managed to come out and find a home for themselves within progressive churches, and I'm glad that the reason I left church wasn't because I didn't feel I could remain Christian and bisexual. If Christianity had truly been meant to be part of my current life, I know I could reclaim that space for myself within an appropriate and affirming church. I am no longer that same woman who felt stifled and restricted during her time at BJU. With an understanding of who I am, I've found a new sense of purpose and a vitality I never thought possible when I was growing up.

Notes

1. Leviticus 18:22, 20:13.
2. "Equality Riders Face Anti-Gay."
3. White, *Stranger at the Gate.*
4. Miner and Connoley, *The Children Are Free.*

chapter 12   BLAIR DURKEE

I subconsciously absorbed this and many other narrow-minded attitudes toward gender on campus, but even more upsetting was how I internalized fundamentalism's teachings on self-worth. From the earliest age, I was taught that the self is desperately wicked, irreparably broken, and needs to be "put to death." This precept was so ingrained that I thought my gender dysphoria was just punishment for my sinful self, a thorn in my flesh. I was born male, and that was my burden to carry. To wish otherwise would be selfish and morally wrong.

The Treadmill of Fundamentalism

I didn't always know.

I'd like to say I grew up completely aware of myself and the world around me, but I didn't, and that was by design: I was born into a fundamentalist Christian household that believed righteousness was the absence of worldliness. I was sheltered for the good of my own soul. Rock music? Off-limits. Pokémon? A demonic influence.

This isolation from the world was enforced in many ways but primarily through the constant fixation on religious devotion. My childhood revolved so entirely around religion that I wouldn't have had the time to explore the world even if I had been conscious enough to want to. Christianity *was* my world—the world that had been thrust upon me, the only world I knew.

Twice on Sundays, once on Wednesdays. Once a week in elementary school. Twice a week in high school. Four times a week at Bob Jones University (except for that "special" week of Bible Conference, which had sixteen). And those were just the full-fledged sermons. Eighteen years of weekly Sunday school. Sixteen years of Christian schooling, including twenty-four semester hours of Bible class in high school and fourteen in college. Five years of Awana (children's religious club).[1] Four years of Bible quizzing. Six years of youth group. Vacation Bible School, The Wilds, Northland, and countless other Christian summer camps—year after year.[2] Mission trips. Church choir. Bible studies. Prayer groups. Revival weeks. Missionary conferences. Family devotions at home. Christian radio in the car. Christian friends. Christian family. Christian environment. Christian *everything*.

It's like awakening to find yourself on a treadmill stuck at a very high speed. There is no safe way to dismount, so you run for your life. You're so consumed by the running that you don't have time to catch your breath and ask, "Why am I running, anyway? How did I end up here? What would happen if this thing stopped?" Instead, you just run and begin to accept the treadmill as a normal part of your life. After all, you don't know any different.

Many of the fundamentalist restrictions and activities grew tiresome, particularly as I aged into high school. But for the most part, I embraced the culture I was raised in for the simple reason that indoctrination *works*. I "got saved" at four years old—too young to know what that meant, but old enough to understand social expectations. Everyone around me was waiting with bated breath for me to do it, and I saw the lavish praise others received when they did. Naturally, I wanted in on that social approval. This desire remained for many years, through high school and even college.

Fundamentalist Gender Norms

I was twenty-two years old before I was allowed to ask the question "Who am I?" because questioning in general is not a privilege afforded to those raised in fundamentalist culture. I had very little choice in the substantial aspects of my life. I was not free to choose my religion, my schooling (including college), my activities, my friends, my music, my philosophy, my politics, my lifestyle—my gender.

Perhaps that last one surprised you. Nobody gets to choose their gender, right? Yes, I suppose that's true. Mine just happened to be wrong.

One of the most basic precepts of this subculture—one reinforced by society at large—was gender norms. I was assigned a male gender at birth, and though it never meant much to me personally, I quickly learned that it was a monumental concern to those around me. Gendered behavior was drilled into my psyche through overt social cues. I don't ever recall consciously thinking, "I'm a boy; therefore, I must act this way." Instead, it was the unconscious effects of classical conditioning. Whenever I violated the norms of what a "boy" should be, I felt shame from those around me, in ways big and small. To avoid shame, I moderated my behavior to become who I needed to be in order to survive.

It's difficult to pinpoint exactly when the frustrated feeling of gender difference began, especially because running on that fundamentalist treadmill consumed my life and attention early on. Still, the feeling happened repeatedly, recognized or not.

It happened when the red-faced preachers gave their passionate diatribes on the divine appointment of strict traditional gender roles. I wasn't a particularly feminine (or masculine) boy, yet these sermons made me fume inside. Only occasionally did I wonder why none of the other boys seemed to care as much as I did.

It happened when I hit puberty. All of my peers were eager for it. My teachers told me it was normal to be proud and excited about becoming a man. I wanted to be normal, so I pretended I was.

It happened when I became aware of my sexuality around that same time. I stood in front of the mirror, crossing my legs to hide my genitals, but I had no idea what I was doing or why. It just felt right for some reason. I passively assumed every boy must feel the same way. I went on with my life.

It happened when I started high school, eager to form new friendships. I was drawn to the girls in my class. What a rude awakening to learn that young men and women couldn't have platonic relationships. I resented the heavy restrictions against co-ed mingling, but not for the same reason as the other guys.

It happened at BJU when I was forced, like all new students, to join a society—BJU's version of fraternities and sororities—and interact on a weekly basis with people of my assigned gender. I clearly did not fit in. I hated their rowdy games and their ruthless hazing antics, but it was more than the activities; it was an acute difference of mentality. Eventually, I skipped meetings and turned myself in for the demerits. "How good the girls must have it," I thought.

It happened every single day.

The feeling didn't go away, however. I knew how I should act in order to blend in, but inside, I still resented it. Often the mere sight of girls my age would evoke a piercing sadness, but I never considered what the cause might be because it never occurred to me that my feelings might be indicative of something bigger. Plus, I had no time to deal with these issues because my thoughts were often drowned out by the constantly running treadmill. I became too busy feeling guilty to conjure the desire to pray or read my Bible for a remedy.

After high school, I enrolled at BJU in the fall of 2006. This decision (if it can even be called that) was overwhelmingly the path of least resistance. My family lived in Greenville—the home of BJU's campus. My parents were both alumni of the school. My mother's job at BJU Press got me free tuition. And most importantly, my parents and my community all expected me to attend BJU. To attend college elsewhere would have been an uphill battle that I—still completely dependent on my parents—wasn't prepared for or interested in.

My four years at BJU were largely unremarkable. As a "townie"—someone who lived at home and commuted to school every day—I kept a low profile by going to classes, to my job at the university's IT help desk, and not much else. My survival tactic, as it had been long before, was to make the best of a bad situation. "Nobody likes a miserable person," I'd constantly remind myself, so I put on a smile in public. At home, I escaped from the real world by playing video games, in which I would always play as the female avatar.

Questioning the Treadmill

Spending time at college gave me opportunity to rethink my own views, especially on religion. I still championed Christianity, but I rationalized my own private interpretations of its tenets. In contrast to BJU's very legalistic teachings, I came to believe that grace superseded works and that total abdication of sin was a futile and ultimately corrosive endeavor. Curiously, this doctrine gained traction even within corners of fundamentalism during my time at BJU. The administration and faculty were keenly aware of this movement, though, and sought eagerly to quash it. Training students to pursue lives of strict holiness and ascetic discipline is BJU's raison d'être, and this doctrinal shift posed nothing less than an existential threat to BJU. I kept my thoughts to myself.

BJU was constantly fending off the influence of liberal Christianity. In 2007 an organization named Soulforce came to campus to protest the university's anti-gay policies.[3] This group simply wanted to engage in dialogue with members of the campus community. However, they were summarily threatened with trespassing by university administrators and blocked at the entrance gate by local police; three protestors were arrested when they set foot on campus. I watched the surreal scene from the inside but didn't know what to make of it. I didn't know these people, nor had I ever met an out gay or transgender person in my life. All I knew was the propaganda spread by BJU officials: the activists were sad, broken people seeking to impose their lifestyle on others in a desperate search for validation of their sinful ways. By this time, I knew enough not to accept BJU's view at face value, but I didn't know how to take that next step to decide what to make of this situation.

The longer I spent at BJU, the more I felt burdened by the oppressive atmosphere and incessant obligations. The sheer number of required events took its toll as I struggled to maintain endurance on this treadmill. Specifically, the daily chapel sermons exasperated me, one in particular: the preacher scolded us over the sin of being too academically focused at the expense of our religious devotion. It was perhaps the clearest articulation of an underlying attitude at BJU—this ostensible institution of higher learning disparaged the value of education to its own students. I almost hit my breaking point, but I was resolved to finish my degree, so that's what I did.

Meeting Myself after BJU

I graduated from BJU in 2010 on good terms with the school, which had no awareness of my inner turmoil. While it was a relief to be finished, I felt unprepared for independence. What next? Up to this time, all I had known was my family and religious community. It was time to make a clean break, so I enrolled into a graduate program at a public university and moved away from my family for the first time.

Soon after I arrived, I began to make contact with a person I had never been allowed to meet before—myself. It wasn't sudden or profound, but slow and somewhat unexpected. Some would say I began to change. Others would say I rebelled, rejected my heritage. The truth, however, is that for the first time ever in my life I began to see my own personhood through the smoke of unrelenting religious guilt and indoctrination.

The joy of my newfound physical freedom was exceeded only by the pleasure of the intellectual freedom waiting for me there. It was like I had spent years surfacing from underwater and was finally gasping for air.

The constant, daily rituals of fundamentalist Christianity had ceased for the first time in my life, and it was more liberating than I could have possibly imagined. I now had the time and the mental capacity to think for myself—and about myself. And my emotions of feeling wrong, of feeling out of place, became more apparent.

Searching for My Problem

I still didn't know the cause of this feeling, but at least I was finally ready to address it. As the feeling intensified, I sought as much knowledge as I possibly could, desperately searching for an answer, but it's difficult to search for an answer when you don't even know what the problem is. In reality, I was searching for my problem—the source of my negative emotions.

Several phenomena occurred during this time of self-discovery. For one, I felt a growing discontent with my gender. But I still didn't fully recognize this discontent for what it was, much less know how to deal with it. My upbringing had succeeded in keeping me astonishingly sheltered in most areas, including self-awareness.

Second, during this same time, I underwent a spiritual disillusionment. Up to that point, I identified as a Christian and had passionately defended Christianity. Despite having serious misgivings about Christian doctrine (notably its overt misogyny), I rationalized my way to a personal theology that felt sufficient to suppress my cognitive dissonance. But the more I discovered about reality, the more I was forced to amend my theology. Free from BJU's pervasive atmosphere of guilt and enforced conformity, I found the courage to call it the charade that it was.

Unraveling BJU's Belief System

I realized that the Christian worldview is a woeful representation of what we know about reality. In my ethics class at BJU, we were taught about a liberal agenda to destroy the God-ordained categories of male and female. An example of this was the International Olympic Committee's debate over the criteria of gender for competition purposes. This was preposterous to our Christian instructor: "God created Adam and Eve, and that's all there is! And furthermore, we can determine which is which by a simple chromosome test." But outside of the confines of the BJU campus, I read about hosts of intersex conditions that categorically disprove that claim—conditions like de la Chapelle syndrome, which results in an XX person being born phenotypically male, or androgen insensitivity syndrome, which results in an XY person being born phenotypically female.[4] The ideology presented to us at BJU seemed simplistic, even naive.

And that's just the tip of the iceberg. In the same area of sexual development, I also learned that a human fetus by default develops as female and that, to become male, hormones suppress the femaleness and develop maleness. In other words, Eve did not come from Adam. Adam is the altered form; Eve is the original. The more I understood, the more it became clear that the author of Genesis was woefully misinformed about human biology.

On the other hand, I found the use of the Bible to condemn transgender people to be a tenuous one. There were no explicit Clobber Passages for trans identity, or at least I was never presented with any. And yet this fact did not seem to temper the strident convictions of these supposed authorities. The same, of course, could be said for a variety of fundamentalist doctrines, from music to dress to alcohol consumption. With even the slightest application of critical thought, these dogmas were laid bare for the post hoc justifications they were—the invocation of ancient divine texts to dogmatically enforce a modern conservative cultural tradition.

Each time I pulled on a thread of fundamentalist belief, the entire spool began to unravel. I read books like *Fundamentalism and American Culture* by George M. Marsden, which documented the rise of this sect as an offshoot of American revivalism and a reaction to scientific enlightenment. I learned that seemingly esoteric developments—such as the decline of postmillennialist eschatology in favor of dispensational premillennialism—heralded tectonic shifts in Christian theology and its renewed emphasis on personal holiness over social beneficence (an early twentieth-century phenomenon historians have coined the "Great Reversal").[5]

I became disillusioned with what I had been taught all my life, discovering that the origin of truths I believed were passed down by God himself could actually be pegged to specific dates in history barely even one hundred years ago. Once I had learned that the totality of Christian theology had been molded and shaped by men long ago in accordance with the milieu of their time, I realized that I, too, could discard these beliefs just as easily as those who had constructed them. I had seen *behind* the man behind the curtain, and the illusion had control over me no longer.

I don't hold judgment against those who find comfort and fulfillment in religion, but I must convey my personal experience of Christianity as a brutal and suffocating tool of oppression. My adherence to it was only ever maintained through the manipulations of fear and indoctrination. Without those external forces, I found—and continue to find—no aspect of Christianity to be emotionally or intellectually compelling. And with that realization, I could now express what I knew to be true without needing to reconcile it with some unfalsifiable claim from religion. The burden of fundamentalism was lifted. Free from the identity that had been forced upon me, I could finally turn my attention to constructing a positive identity of my own.

Finding My Identity

I can't remember the first time I heard the word "transgender." Maybe it was in college, when Soulforce visited, but the closest visual I can recall is associated with sensationalist TV shows like *Jerry Springer*, which portrayed individuals as a spectacle. Meanwhile, in my religious environment, the subject was practically never mentioned, not even in the context of homosexuality. Maybe it was so unthinkable that it was beyond mentioning.

One noteworthy exception came from a guest speaker in one of my classes at BJU, an alumnus who was now out in the secular workforce. He had returned to prepare us for the big, scary, devil-filled world by telling a story about a certain coworker named Jeremy. One day, as the story went, a department meeting was called, and Jeremy was seated at the head of the table. It was announced that Jeremy was in the process of becoming Jennifer and that everyone should be respectful and supportive of her. As the speaker related the moment to our class, his face contorted slightly with disgust, as if this were the ultimate portrayal of depravity in our world.

I subconsciously absorbed this and many other narrow-minded attitudes toward gender on campus, but even more upsetting was how I internalized fundamentalism's teachings on self-worth. From the earliest age, I was taught that the self is desperately wicked, irreparably broken, and needs to be "put to death." This precept was so ingrained that I thought my gender dysphoria was just punishment for my sinful self, a thorn in my flesh. I was born male, and that was my burden to carry. To wish otherwise would be selfish and morally wrong.

I now know that teaching to be an insidious lie. There is no reason for me to be ashamed of who I am. That's not a new age platitude, as I was taught. It's just human dignity. But to refute this lie, I still needed time to educate myself about the transgender community.

I spent hours reading, thinking, researching, discussing, and pouring out my thoughts and feelings in writing. I learned about the condition of being transgender and the overwhelming amount of scientific research and evidence behind it. I learned that transgender people are just normal people, not at all like the sexualized caricatures I had seen in the media. I learned what I had always wanted to hear but what nobody had ever told me—that not every girl is born in a typical girl body and raised as a girl. And for those in that situation, transitioning to live as a girl is not only considered acceptable, but it is also deemed psychologically and medically necessary by numerous professional organizations, including the American Medical Association and American Psychological Association.[6]

Finding Security in My Gender Identity

Reading about such support from the AMA and APA was extremely gratifying, but I couldn't seem to shake that fundamentalist fear and shame to find security in my identity. I sought out the assistance of therapists and supportive individuals through the internet and at graduate school. Their words were a balm to my fundamentalist wounds. They of course couldn't tell me my identity, but what they gave me was even better—the unconditional love and acceptance I had always heard about growing up but had never experienced. And that was all I needed because, buried under the years of pretense, I knew exactly who I was. Finally, I had the self-assurance to admit that my instinctual desire was itself the answer I was looking for.

Just one year after graduating from BJU, I came out to myself as a transgender woman. What an overwhelming relief that admission was. It was as if all my life was leading to this moment, a sort of foreboding that I couldn't quite pinpoint before. Now everything made sense. My previous, desperate attempts to articulate my complex and contradictory self were now easily summarized in the statement, "I'm a girl."

And, oh, how proud I am to say it.

Being a trans woman is not primarily about changing my body—and it certainly isn't about my sexuality. I know I am a woman because every bone in my body tells me so, and the consequence of being perceived as a man by society creates enormous dissonance in my mind and heart. My gender identity is simply an extension of who I am as a person in the same way it is for non-transgender people.

Soon after coming out, I began hormone replacement therapy that would allow me to transition into living as a woman. The process of transitioning was intensely difficult and expensive, but more than worth it. There is no cost too great for authenticity.

Now having lived as a woman for many years, I hardly think about my identity anymore. My life is the same as it was before, just without the confusion, self-loathing, and misery. I have also left behind the burden of religion and live a contented, secular lifestyle. While many of my friends from BJU have adopted a more inclusive version of Christianity, my most authentic self is not religious in any way. I simply don't experience any religious impulse.

Writing this story today—nearly a decade removed—feels strange. My fundamentalist past feels distant, like a forgotten prologue to the life I now live. I harbor no strong feelings of anger or resentment toward my old community—they're simply not worth the effort. I am, however, mournful that others continue to be indoctrinated and oppressed in that environment. As for me, all I can say is that I have happily moved on.

In perhaps a stroke of poetic justice, I've chosen to dedicate my life to the cause of LGBTQ rights and acceptance. I've endeavored over the past several years to push for positive change in both my academic and professional careers. Where once I found solace in the secluded virtual worlds of video games, I now advocate for LGBTQ representation and inclusion within the video games industry itself, so that others can see and discover themselves in ways I never could growing up.

If BJU and fundamentalism have had a lasting impact on my life, it is primarily through the feeling of getting a late start. I have been robbed of countless coming-of-age experiences that most adults simply take for granted, a one-two punch of religious cultural isolation and gender mismatch. Though I do my best to fit in, I constantly struggle with gaps in my knowledge of popular culture and customs of secular society. In many ways, I'm still trying to get up to speed with my peers from non-fundamentalist backgrounds, and I probably always will be.

But some things don't change, and my conviction to make the best of a bad situation is one of them. Fundamentalism has shaped who I am for better or for worse, and I try to use that to my advantage. For one, I have an easier time empathizing with those who believe differently than I do. The astonishing arc of my life is certain proof that people can change for the better—and that acceptance and understanding are the most powerful tools against fundamentalist dogma. I hope to use my knowledge and experience to create a world where nobody will have to go through what I went through.

That world will be a much brighter, much friendlier place.

Notes

1. *Awana*.
2. *The Wilds*; *Northland*.
3. "Equality Riders Face Anti-Gay."
4. "What Does Intersex Mean?"; Dupuy et al., "De La Chapelle Syndrome," 369–72; "Androgen Insensitivity Syndrome."
5. Marsden, *Fundamentalism and American Culture*, 85–93.
6. Miller, "AMA Takes Several Actions"; "Transgender, Gender Identity."

Family, Guilt, and Shame

Children, obey your parents in the Lord: for this is
right. Honour thy father and mother; which is the
first commandment with promise.

EPHESIANS 6:1–2

If any man come to me, and hate not his father, and
mother, and wife, and children, and brethren, and
sisters, yea, and his own life also, he cannot be my
disciple.

LUKE 14:26

This first passage from Ephesians would probably be familiar to children
born into fundamentalist circles because of its importance to the family
unit and the overarching model of fundamentalist hierarchies. Both of
these verses in Ephesians would likely be required memory verses as part
of a child's curriculum at church, school, or elsewhere. The second passage from Luke may be less familiar, may not be the most-often-required
memory verse, and may seem jarring in juxtaposition with the Ephesians
6 passage. But these words, spoken by Jesus, lend insight into this book's
fourth part about family. Modern translations and interpretations of this
verse explain that Jesus is not commanding people to literally hate their
family members or themselves, but that they should be willing to put Jesus above everyone else in their life. However, these passages can serve as
a way of considering the stories from David Diachenko and Peter Crane.
Both of these stories could have fit in other parts of this book, but I believe their common topic about family is an important one to address in a
collection of stories about queer people who have lived through a fundamentalist emphasis on strict obedience to parents and God.

In the twenty-first century, it is commonplace to hear that queer people can choose their own family, which is certainly empowering, encouraging, and heart-warming. But what happens to queer individuals who
have developed a genuine relationship with their immediate, blood-
related family over the course of their childhood into early adulthood?

The coming-out process is understandably fraught for queer people who have a fear of an unknown or worst-case-scenario response from religious family members. Conversely, fundamentalist parents and family members also have to wisely choose their response to a coming-out moment as part of their separatist culture. How devout are they willing to be, in light of Luke 14:26, to prove that they love Jesus more than anyone, including themselves or their children?

Diachenko's and Crane's stories both incorporate the influence of their family in similar and contrasting ways as part of their own journeys in identity self-awareness. Consider Luke 14:26 again, especially the part about how a person is supposed to hate "his own life also." Although we know this verse is talking more about self-denial than self-loathing, it becomes difficult not to think about how growing up queer in fundamentalist circles casts a shadow over our ability to love ourselves, especially when growing up with experiences and desires that contradict our obedience to a specific belief system.

Both stories talk about a persistent cycle of feeling tortured as they navigate a spiritual minefield of responses to their gay encounters. David Diachenko notes that his early sexual experiences created a long-standing cycle of same-sex activity, followed by a period of extreme remorse and self-hatred, then more sexual activity. He describes BJU as a haven that he believed could help him change his sexual identity. Attending during the mid- to late nineties, David remained as music faculty after graduation until around the mid-2000s. Knowing that he could not be gay and a member of the BJU community, David describes how he left his job, his church, and his family on his own terms.

Some may say that guilt and shame are different sides of the same coin. But Diachenko argues that guilt pertains more to personal actions, while shame concerns personal essence: in other words, what a person does versus what a person is. Regardless of where the distinction may be drawn in theological, psychological, or developmental terms, we can appreciate how David learned to release the powerful grip of guilt about his actions, and also how to expunge an ingrained obedience to an oppressive religious system. In so doing, David had to perform an inverted form of Luke 14:26: the price he paid for his personal freedom outside of fundamentalism and religion was losing the fellowship of his family.

On the other hand, Peter Crane's story shows how his cyclical experience with shame resulted from a struggle to find a mental foothold against the Clobber Passages from the Bible. Peter recounts how the civil-union issue in Vermont prompted his father and brother to make public political statements against homosexuality, which further reinforced his need to keep his same-sex desires a secret. During his time as a student in the early to mid-2000s, the dating expectations were sexually confusing for a closeted gay student. After graduating, he worked on staff at the BJU Press in the graphic design department until 2012. With the help of his gay uncle, Peter discloses, he began to love himself as a gay man, which gave him the courage to come out to his immediate family and develop a relationship with them. Crane also honestly admits that a level of shame can return at unexpected times, making it important to remember that residual religious trauma and years of indoctrination can be difficult to fully erase. Both stories in this part illustrate the influential power BJU's fundamentalist application of the Bible can have over family dynamics and relationships.

chapter 13   DAVID DIACHENKO

> Living so close to campus, I already knew what
> school would be like there. I'd be surrounded by
> Christian people, attending chapel daily, studying
> in a Christian environment, and making new godly
> friends. I couldn't think of a better atmosphere to
> help me finally win my spiritual battle.

The Perfect Christian Family

I was born into a fundamentalist Christian home in Greenville, South
Carolina. Dad was the head of the home, but he wasn't abusive, and mom
truly enjoyed being a stay-at-home wife and mother. After me came two
more boys and a girl. Ours was as "normal" a home as one could wish for.
Sure, it was strict, but it was also a loving environment.

I became a born-again Christian when I was four years old. Nearly
every night, I would ask my parents, "Am I saved yet?" and every night
they would respond that I had to understand salvation for myself; they
couldn't do it for me. Finally, I made the connection and told my father
I needed to be saved, and on a summer night after a Wednesday prayer
service at Southside Baptist Church, I asked Jesus to save me. I truly believed in what I was asking, and isn't that exactly what the Bible talks
about: the faith of a child?

Because of our family's religious convictions, we had no television, and
my father believed computer games were a waste of time, so I developed a
love for books. I wasn't into sports or the outdoors, so when not in school
or doing chores, I could usually be found curled up in a chair with a book.
Of course, I was encouraged to make the Bible my highest priority, but I
also read other books, such as missionary biographies and Christian fiction published through Bob Jones University Press. Around age thirteen,

I discovered the classics. My mom introduced me to *The Count of Monte Cristo* by Alexandre Dumas, and I devoured it in two days. Soon, I was feasting on *The Three Musketeers*, *The Scarlet Pimpernel*, the Sherlock Holmes mysteries, and works by Dorothy Sayers, Jules Verne, Agatha Christie, C.S. Lewis, Sir Walter Scott, Mary Shelley, and Bram Stoker. From sixth grade to the end of high school, I was homeschooled, and my mother would make time after lunch each day to read to us, which is one of my favorite memories from childhood. Eventually, she came to Tolkien's *The Hobbit* and *The Lord of the Rings*, both of which captivated me like no other stories ever have.

I also discovered classical music around this time, when my aunt gave me two recordings for Christmas: Bach's Goldberg Variations and piano concertos by Schumann and Grieg. As with Tolkien's works, a new world suddenly beckoned me irresistibly. Our family purchased a piano when I was thirteen, and I started taking lessons, developing fairly quickly as a musician. This preparation would lead to my pursuing a piano performance major in college.

So that was my childhood: a quiet, normal Christian home; saved at an early age; classic books and classical and conservative sacred music; and like-minded friends who were approved by my parents. This is a story that should end with me in full-time Christian service as another reliable Christian in the fold. But I had a dirty little secret.

"The Talk"

I didn't know what homosexuality was, had never seen it in action, nor did I have a "black sheep" gay uncle that we weren't allowed to mention. But by the time I was twelve and becoming sexually aware, I consciously knew that I was attracted to men. Even earlier than that, around the age of five or six, I enjoyed, in a nonsexual way, looking through the men's clothing section of catalogs and advertisements, especially the underwear and swimsuits. When I was thirteen, I started acting on my urges with a neighbor boy who was a little older. I was not pressured from him to experiment sexually. To the contrary, I was the one who initiated contact and asked him questions. I knew that he was sexually active with a couple of his friends, a guy and a girl, so he became my sexual education. Well, both he and porn did. And lest anyone think that gay porn was what made me "choose" to be gay, my first exposure to porn consisted of *Play-*

boy and *Penthouse* magazines that I found in a dumpster near our house, but I was most drawn to the pictures with men in them. For the next three years, my neighbor friend and I met frequently at his house because his parents were at work late, and I was a homeschooled kid with afternoon free time.

One evening when I was fourteen, completely out of the blue, my father asked, "What do you know about sex?" After nearly falling off the couch, I blithely gave the response he expected: "Pretty much nothing other than the word." So we had "The Talk," which was as awkward as I'm sure it is for everyone, but it was also an exercise in acting because I couldn't tell him that I could have given him "The Talk" myself by that point in my life.

The Cycle of Guilt

All this time, I was racked with guilt. Again, I had never heard anything about homosexuality to this point, but it was drilled into us that any sexual activity outside of marriage was sinful. Nor were we to discuss sex in a casual manner. Sex only occurred in conversation whenever the parent had "The Talk," and it was understood that it would not be mentioned again until the wedding night. Even though I didn't have the vocabulary to identify myself, I did know that my attraction to guys was different from anything I could see around me, and I certainly wasn't married to the neighbor guy, so I felt like what I was doing was wrong. Consequently, I would pray, repent, and scour the Bible for passages to help me resist temptation. Every encounter with my friend would lead to this cycle: guilt, repentance, "I'll never do it again, God!"—wash, rinse, repeat.

Unlike many I know, it was not shame I was dealing with, but rather guilt, and I feel it's important to distinguish between the two. Shame is inward looking: "I feel bad about who I am." It often leads to self-loathing, and I never experienced that. Guilt is outward looking: "I feel bad about what I've done." In my mind, the struggle was not about hating who I was but about changing my behaviors.

During this time, I started messing around with another neighbor guy. By the time my parents discovered what I was doing, when I was sixteen, the burden of "being in sin" was overwhelming for a fundamentalist Christian teenager. I couldn't work up the courage to confess on my own, so I wanted to get caught. My parents had a long talk with me, but they didn't react as I had expected. I always figured, "They'll kill me!" But instead they took a very level approach, I imagine, because they thought it was just a phase and that with enough prayer, Bible reading, and counseling, I could get the "victory" over this, just like any other "sin." I thought the same thing, and I was fully vested in my redemption path.

I had a couple of counseling sessions with Mark Minnick, pastor of Mount Calvary Baptist Church, where our family was attending at the time. Like my parents, he also was very kind and loving: apparently, I was still "rescuable" at this age. Since my actions hadn't involved anyone else in the church and weren't related to any kind of abuse, he didn't advise making a public confession, which I was grateful for. At that point, no one else knew that I had been "struggling" with homosexuality. On his advice to my parents, I was tested for STDs at the public health clinic in Greenville. Counseling with a licensed professional is provided as part of that testing, but the counselor wanted to talk to me alone, without my father present. My father wouldn't hear of it, and so we left without getting the test results. In hindsight, this event reveals the control my parents weren't willing to give up and the incredible irresponsibility my father demonstrated. I often wonder, "What if I had been infected with something back then? How could he have been more concerned with ideology (his or the counselor's) over my physical well-being and the possibility that I could harm others?"

For the next six years, I had no sexual contact with anyone. However, a day or so after my confession to my parents, I was masturbating again, and doing so with images of men in my head. The pitiful cycle of action, guilt, and repentance continued. Nevertheless, I kept this to myself, because I knew the response this time would be harsher and less forgiving.

Once I finished high school, I knew Bob Jones University was the only school for me for many reasons: my parents had attended, we lived just five minutes away, I knew many of the people there, and I was familiar with the campus. Also, I earnestly believed attending BJU would help me "gain the victory" over same-sex desires. BJU's well-known recruiting slogans over the years—"The Opportunity Place," "God's Special Place for You," and "The Fortress of Fundamentalism"—reinforced my expectations. Living so close to campus, I already knew what school would be like there. I'd be surrounded by Christian people, attending chapel daily, studying in a Christian environment, and making new godly friends. I couldn't think of a better atmosphere to help me finally win my spiritual battle.

"God's Special Place for You"

I enrolled as a freshman in the fall of 1995, and I stayed at BJU for eleven years, years that I thoroughly enjoyed. I completed my undergraduate degree and master's degree in piano performance, then joined the music faculty teaching piano full time for another four years. I can honestly say I have many fond memories of my time at BJU: the music study and the academics, my teachers and friends, and my colleagues and students. During rush week, when we freshmen had to choose a literary society to join, I picked the Phi Beta Chi Bulldogs, largely because several of my friends from church were there. As far as my overall BJU experience goes, society wasn't that big a deal to me, but I did participate in Scholastic Bowl, an intersociety tournament whose finals are held each year during commencement week in front of the entire student body. We were the winning team my junior year, an achievement I was quite proud of.

There were many other facets of the school I genuinely loved: the Shakespearean productions; my piano study with David Lehman, my teacher, mentor, and friend; the wonderful friendships I developed across the years, a few of which even survived my coming out. BJU was a world I could see myself staying in for many years, and once I decided to stay and teach, I planned on doing just that. I loved teaching, investing my energy into students and seeing them develop their talents and grow as people. During my stay at BJU, I also felt like I grew as a Christian in most areas of my life.

But during all the time that I was a citizen of the campus with the best possible Christian influences all around me, the old pattern of guilt had never ended. I had no interaction sexually with anyone during my undergrad years, but I was still masturbating quite regularly (a normal activity, in hindsight), and with that activity came the cycle of feeling guilty, repenting, holding out for a while, and repeating. And unlike many like me who went through the fundamentalist system, the so-called Clobber Passages were not influential in my life. Of course, I knew about them, but I was focused on the passages in the Bible that concentrated more on guilt (my actions) than on shame (my essence), passages that talked about walking in the Spirit and resisting temptation. These were the scriptures that I prioritized when trying to combat this cycle.

In grad school I once again began occasionally meeting guys for sex, but never on campus and never with anyone connected to the school (as far as I knew). The psychology of my mind at that time is a strange thing on which to reflect, but there were several factors at play. First, my self-preservation instinct understood the dangers of getting involved with anyone at BJU. Any BJU person could potentially have a crisis of conscience during chapel or Bible Conference (BJU's version of spring break which included numerous sermons designed to manipulate students into confessing any sins) and turn me in. Second, I didn't want to get involved with anyone long term because I knew how the cycle worked: once I repented, I would quit having sex (for a while) and wouldn't want to see them again. Third, it was a dangerous time for me because I never practiced safe sex. Carrying a condom suggested premeditation, which I never did because that would be willfully sinning. Instead, my encounters would typically happen after a prolonged mental process:

a) "I'm horny."

b) "It's wrong. I can't do it again. I need to stay strong. Lord, keep me focused on you."

c) "Damn, I'm horny."

d) "No, I can't."

e) "Oh, look, the person in the stall next to me is tapping his foot."

f) "I can't hold out any longer."

Fourth, I assumed I was the only one at such a godly school who was facing this kind of temptation and struggle. Finally, as a very private person, I didn't trust the counseling system on campus to be sympathetic or to keep matters confidential. In some ways, I had become comfortable with this method of living. I was resigned to struggle like this for a long time.

Growing Doubts

What precipitated the change in my thinking was a growing frustration with BJU's rigid musical standards. I began exploring beyond strictly classical and conservative sacred music, first with contemporary Christian music, which I often found more meaningful than many traditional hymns and gospel songs. Then, I expanded to other genres of secular music and realized that the arguments BJU used against both contemporary Christian music and rock music weren't valid. Contemporary Christian music actually left me more focused on God despite what BJU described as its "worldly influences and sounds," and while the beat of rock music might get my body moving a bit, it certainly didn't cause me to want sex.

Plus, I noticed when visiting the homes of various faculty members and deans that their music collections were pretty eclectic. Logically and artistically, my mind was already entertaining doubts about BJU.

During my years on faculty, I lived off campus, which afforded me a greater measure of freedom. In early 2006, three catalysts completely altered my life journey. First, I watched the movie *Latter Days*, where I saw real love being portrayed between two men, not just lust and fun, but deep, soul-wrenching love. In all my struggles against sexual behavior, in all my "falling into sin" and having sex with men, it had never occurred to me that true, intimate love was possible. Second, that same week, on the way back from an event out of town, I stayed overnight with a guy for the first time. I had never done that before because the guilt would kick in too quickly. But this time I did, and as I lay relaxed and drowsy in his arms, I suddenly realized, "This feels right. Not just good, but absolutely and completely right." The third and most important catalyst came about a week later, through my love of film music.

I'm that nerd who looks at the liner notes of film score recordings and becomes familiar with the film conductors and orchestrators because that has always been my dream job. In January 2006, I browsed the website of one of my favorite film composers and noticed he had listed all his usual associates along with their contact info. I recognized the name of his usual orchestrator, Damon Intrabartolo, and I sent him a gushing fanboy email. Usually, I only received generic responses like "Thanks for your interest," so I was pleasantly surprised to receive a genuine note of thanks from him, along with a comment about what he was working on currently, and also a question about my email address: "What's bju.edu, besides amusing initials?"

At the same time, I found a copy of a show he created with Jon Hartsmere called *Bare*. The music itself was amazing, but the storyline changed my life: a coming-of-age story about two gay students at a Catholic high school. I researched Damon more and realized he was gay. And he had written me back and showed interest in continuing a conversation. At this point, I panicked and almost didn't write him back. But I was reaching a breaking point with both the topics of music and sexuality and had suddenly found someone who could relate to both.

Knowing how BJU monitors everything on its accounts, I switched to my Gmail and wrote back a message explaining a bit about the world of BJU and how I was getting frustrated with their music standards. In the last paragraph, as a desperate "Let's see what happens," I mentioned that

I was also struggling with my orientation. I sent the email, not knowing what to expect. Would he ridicule the world I was in? Would he never respond? Would he be understanding?

To my relief, he replied with more curiosity about my world and noted similarities between fundamentalism and the Catholicism in which he was raised. He also gave me his phone number and said it would probably be easier to talk rather than to write. Sensing that this was some sort of lifeline, I called him, and we talked that first time for three hours about music, life, sexuality, and BJU. He wisely never belittled the world I inhabited but instead just listened as I unpacked years of frustration and confusion. I'm sure I rambled and contradicted myself, but I'd never had the chance to talk to anyone sympathetic and nonjudgmental. Ever.

After we hung up, I realized how messed up my psyche was, but I could also see a glimmer of light in the darkness. After several more phone conversations and emails, I met him in New York City for a whirlwind twenty-four hours that opened my eyes to the true possibilities of a life of authenticity and freedom. Sadly, Damon died in 2013, but I will never forget how much he changed my life on such a profound and personal level. I would not be free today without him.

When I arrived back in Greenville after the twenty-four hours in New York, I knew that the remaining hinges of my internal closet had been torn off, and I started to look at my life with more objectivity. I realized that I had tried to be straight my entire life and that I had experienced growth in my Christian life in all aspects except this one, so something obviously wasn't adding up. It seemed that my attraction to men was innate, that it had always been there in spite of everything in my life being designed to ensure "normality."

Shedding the Guilt

I came to the conclusion that either God had made me/allowed me to be this way but also condemned it; God had made me this way and did not condemn it; or God did not exist and people are who they are because that's how it happens. If it was the first, then God was a monster who didn't deserve my worship and obedience, no matter how powerful He was. If it was the second, then there was a loving God I had never really been taught about and needed to get to know in a new way. If it was the third, then I would have to relearn my entire way of interacting with the world. I initially felt that the only things I really knew were that God was real and that He loved me. I couldn't logically get around Him at that point. Everything else I would need to figure out from there, but I was finally at peace with being a gay man.

I said before that my struggle wasn't about shame; it was about guilt. Once I realized who I was, I very quickly accepted it and was happy and content. And once I figured out that the urges and "temptations" were a natural part of my essential self, I determined that there was nothing to feel guilty about. The guilt disappeared. That was a huge relief, but I still needed to decide what to do about the practicalities of life—namely, my situation at BJU.

Because I knew that coming out would mean immediate termination at BJU, I decided to complete the academic year before coming out to the world in May. I feel privileged that I could come out entirely on my own terms, because it is somewhat rare to have that kind of control at BJU. On May 15, 2006, I sent a letter to my church; sent my resignation letter to the school; prepared an email for my colleagues, friends, and students so they could hear my story directly from me and not from rumors; and then I asked my family to meet me at my parents' home.

I knew that coming out would likely result in my family cutting me off, but that was no longer the most important thing to me. My job, most of my friends, and my reputation in my old life were all gone, and I was prepared to start over completely alone. But presenting my true self to my parents and siblings was the hardest thing I've ever done, not because I doubted my identity, but because there's a big difference between knowing the consequences and experiencing them.

It wasn't easy weathering their reactions, but when I walked out of their house, I took a deep breath, and for the first time truly experienced that cliché saying about having the weight of the world lifted from your shoulders. I had already shed the guilt. Now I was completely open and free. No more secrets. No more trying to be something I wasn't. No more living for other people's expectations. I could now be my authentic, complete self. Mount Calvary held a church discipline service that Wednesday evening for me, but my letter to them stated that I no longer valued their interpretation and input. My family did indeed cut me out of their lives nearly completely. Thankfully, a few friends did stick with me, making it easier to restart my life. Within a few weeks, I had a new job where I finally experienced acceptance and where no one cared if I was gay.

Over the last several years, as I've continued to examine life and faith, I have come to a place of agnosticism, bordering on atheism. The idea of God no longer makes any sense to me, certainly not the idea of an omnipotent, omniscient, benevolent being who exists in the same universe as the Holocaust, killer tsunamis, and bone cancer in infants. Life is much simpler without a faith that contradicts evidence and experience.

I'm happily married to a wonderful man, I have a job that I love, and I work with BJUnity to provide community and resources to people who are within or leaving the world I left. I return to New York City as often as I can, continuing my love affair with the city that began with that first trip to meet Damon. My chosen family is large, continues to grow, and shows me on a daily basis what unconditional love really is.

Having left the insular bubble of fundamentalist Christian life and BJU, I am gratified to be a part of a larger community where I can be myself. While Greenville, South Carolina, is certainly not the most open area of the country, I get to interact with people from all walks of life and demonstrate to them, many for the first time, that gay people are as normal and vital a part of our world as they are. I also get to experience a much wider diversity of thought and perspective. It's an amazing life, and I can't wait to see where it leads me.

chapter 14   PETER CRANE

Over the next year, as I began sharing my true self
with more and more friends, I felt lighter with each
successive revelation. I was systematically unburdening myself from the lies and the shame I had
been maintaining since adolescence. But this unburdening came with a dangerous catch: during this
time, I was still employed at BJU, so I had to be extremely selective with whom I shared this part of
myself. BJU has a strict policy against homosexuality, and my job would have been in danger even
if I had promised to remain celibate, something I
had no intention of doing. Working at such a place
caused an internal, unsustainable conflict in my life
that I would have to address soon.

Learning Shame

Ever since I was a young boy, it seemed I was destined to go to Bob Jones
University. To put it another way, I don't ever remember *not* knowing
about the school or its fundamentalist culture. I attended a small, independent fundamentalist Christian church and school called Trinity Baptist in Vermont, where both my parents were heavily involved. My father
was the head of the school board, and my mother was a French and biology teacher in the high school. BJU was infused into every part of my
early education. Not only was our pastor a BJU graduate who was well regarded in its social circles, but also most of our curriculum was produced
by BJU Press, the publishing arm of the BJU machine. If that wasn't
enough, we were frequently visited by traveling groups from the school,
which was a clever promotional campaign that touted the virtues of that
"most unusual institution."

When I was four years old, a traveling evangelist came to Trinity and preached a rather fiery message on hell and the depravity of man. I can still clearly remember the fear that sermon instilled in me. At the end of the sermon, when the usual call for repentance began, I turned to my father and asked how I could be saved from eternal damnation. I made a profession of faith that night with my father on the steps in our church lobby. In the first grade I renewed that profession and was baptized by our pastor. Later, in my teen years, I would struggle with the assurance of my salvation, due in no small part to my internal struggles with my sexual orientation. In youth group activities at church, we were told that true children of God would be given grace to overcome our sinful natures, but my desires always seemed to have more power than my faith. I would fall into temptation time and again, looking at gay pornography and even having a few sexual relationships with boys that felt good in the moment, but these only fueled the shame that threatens to haunt me even to this day.

Like many gay men, I knew I was different from other kids by around the age of five. I didn't have the vocabulary or experience to put it into words, but it was clear to me and to others that I wasn't quite like other boys. I can recall a game of dress-up with another boy taking a bad turn when I put on one of my sister's princess outfits. As I grew older, my differences became even more apparent as I became keenly aware that I needed to hide those differences from my elders, my peers, and, more importantly, from my very own family.

In the late nineties, around the same time that I was realizing my sexual attraction toward men, Vermont had entered a fierce legal debate around the subject of gay marriage and became the first state to allow civil unions for gay and lesbian couples.[1] My sexuality had been thrust into the forefront of my consciousness through frequent sermons about the evils of homosexuality from our pastor, who was very vocal in the state with his opposition to marriage equality. I was bombarded with these anti-gay messages at church, and I couldn't avoid these same messages from my own family, either, even through a public platform. I still remember seeing my own father on the evening news at our state capitol, reading a letter written by my brother—who was about seventeen at the time—about the dangers of marriage equality.

Fundamentalism trains children from an early age to espouse its views, and my brother was doing his part. Having family so involved in this debate impacted how I saw my own developing sexuality. Not only did I have to hide my secret from the world, I also had to hide it from those closest to me. What would they say or do if they found out?

Family Secrets

In a weird yet comforting twist, this public debate in Vermont led to my discovery that one of my own family members was gay. One day, as we were riding home from church in the car, my brother said something quite hateful and ignorant about gay people. My mother didn't miss a beat and told him how wrong it was to say something like that, especially because our own uncle John was gay. This blew my mind. What?! Uncle John was gay? I guess I shouldn't have been surprised at this announcement: Uncle John's "friend" David did come with him to all our family gatherings. But still, why hadn't our parents told us about this? Whatever the reason, my mother had decided in that moment to show that love and family were more important than hiding the truth from us. This revelation didn't give me enough courage to come out then, but it did plant the seed of hope that one day I could tell my family the truth about me and still be loved and accepted. That day would have to be in the future because that kind of freedom was not possible for me as a child living in a fundamentalist household.

That moment of truth about Uncle John subsided as I had to negotiate the reality of my home, school, and church environment, where I was constantly reminded how important it was to keep my shameful secret of same-sex desires hidden from everyone. As I mentioned, I was taught that a true Christian could say no to sin through the help of the Holy Spirit, but I kept finding myself trapped in a cycle of satisfying my gay desires followed by hating myself for my actions and the sin behind those actions.

Guilt became a constant companion as I began to live a double life. As a kid who grew up with computers, I could navigate the new world of the internet much more adeptly than my parents and peers, and around the age of thirteen, I discovered gay porn. A traveling evangelist came to speak on the dangers of internet pornography and unintentionally gave me lots of tips on how to cover my tracks in my quest for sexual discovery. For a while, pornography was my only outlet for my burning desires, but I eventually explored my sexuality with another boy. Our relationship was discovered, but thankfully our parents decided not to involve the church in our "discipline" because I convinced them that it was just a phase of experimentation. Even though I promised I would behave and not fall prey to that sin again, I was required to move bedrooms (losing privacy and space) as punishment. I was humiliated by this act and considered it my parents' exposure of my shame of having gay desires. I felt like a failure as a Christian. On top of all that, I felt even more shame for not having the courage to tell my parents the truth about my sexuality. The trauma from that experience has stuck with me my whole life.

Around this time, it wasn't uncommon for me to cry myself to sleep, overcome with guilt about having stumbled yet again by falling prey to the sin of lust. To protect myself, I buried that shame and constructed a facade I was sure would please my peers, my elders, and my parents. While I was genuinely that "good kid" who always volunteered first for church activities and who always helped friends and classmates with schoolwork, I also had an ulterior motive: if I could do enough good things, maybe my works would conceal my disgusting secret I was hiding from everyone.

I have to admit—I constructed a pretty good outer shell as the "good kid," too, and while I was not the most popular kid in school and endured my fair share of bullying, I survived high school relatively unscathed, or at least my outer shell did. Inwardly, I was still full of shame and self-doubt. When it came time to decide where I would go after high school, BJU was pretty much the only option on my list. It felt expected of me, and, truthfully, it was where I wanted to go. Many of my friends, including my best friend, were all going there. I had visited the school's campus multiple times for the annual Christian school fine arts competition held there, so BJU was familiar and safe. Plus, I knew I would receive a heavy discount through a work study program for Christian school faculty children. No other school was even an option.

I picked graphic design as my major, signed up for the student work program, and was soon driving down south with my brother in his little Dodge convertible. My older brother attended Clearwater Christian College in Clearwater, Florida, so I rode with him on my journey to further my goal of becoming that good Christian I had been taught to aspire to be. To achieve that goal, I would need to maintain my "good kid" persona at BJU.

BJU, Shame, and the "Good Kid" Persona

In August of 2003, I arrived at BJU a week early to prepare for my on-campus job and get settled into my dorm room. I had requested to share a room with my best friend, Tim, who had been at the school for two years already, so it didn't take me long to make friends and navigate the campus socially. Sexually, however, my time at BJU was confusing. While rules about dating were strict, we were still highly encouraged and expected to participate in the dating culture. BJU would frequently hold concerts, plays, operas, and other events for the students to attend and take dates to, and while I knew I wasn't interested in girls, I also knew that dating girls was part of what a "good kid" would do. I convinced myself that I could live as a straight man, find a wife, and check off all the other fundamentalist family-life boxes along the way. I did my part and dutifully asked girls to all the fine arts events and concerts, but there were challenging times along the way at BJU where I worried if I were strong enough to maintain this "good kid" persona.

Shortly after starting my freshman year, I had my first crush on a guy and quickly realized I had to bury those feelings deep down. It didn't help that he kept asking for back rubs in the dorm. What's a guy to do? As if that wasn't enough, I blame my first crush for directing me toward my next crush: my first crush heard me singing and encouraged me to try out for the chorus in the opera he was singing in. And who do I meet? A handsome member of the music faculty who became my personal voice teacher when, at his urging, I changed my minor to music with a vocal performance proficiency. I developed a strong connection (a.k.a. a major crush) with him over my four years at BJU.

But the eye candy didn't stop there. Before starting my freshman year, I had also applied to work for the Rodeheaver Auditorium stage crew for my work study program, and I was excited to work in the theater constructing sets and assisting on productions there. Did I mention I was surrounded by the hottest, buffest guys on campus? Let's just say I developed more than a few crushes on guys throughout my time at BJU, and through those years, I was constantly reminded from my childhood how important it was to securely live a double life. I couldn't afford to get caught again because the stakes were much higher at BJU: BJU wouldn't move me to another bedroom like my parents had done; I would be expelled instead.

But lest my initial carnal descriptions paint an incomplete picture of my priorities, let me add that I participated in a few worthwhile spiritual activities, too, because I earnestly wanted to be that "good kid" I was projecting on campus. Sometimes, though, it became difficult to keep my double lives separate. For example, the summer after my freshman year,

I spent two and half months touring Europe with fellow students as a part of the Musical Mission Team, where I developed yet another crush on one of the other boys on our team. What can I say: at least I was consistent? When I wasn't following my crush around like a puppy, we visited many churches and sang songs in many languages, including German, Lithuanian, Polish, and Russian. I'd say being on that team fed both my carnal and spiritual selves, but I was enthusiastic about participating in other college activities as well, including singing in operas, participating in student government, and throwing pottery in the ceramics department. Through it all, I made sure to stay as busy as possible to keep the shame of who I really was deeply buried.

Because I had already been familiar with the campus from my high school visits, I had anticipated the strict nature of the rules. Here are just a few of the more memorable rules for me: no alcohol, no going to the movies, no rock and roll music (or any music) with a strong beat or syncopation, no swearing, no facial hair, and absolutely no PDA or touching of any kind between the sexes—which was certainly not a problem for my gay ass. Of course, the rules back home at Trinity had been similarly strict, but they had only applied to my time at school. My parents had been much more relaxed with rules at home, so there was a small adjustment for me to live that way twenty-four seven at BJU. I continued my usual practice of being the good boy and following the rules on campus, but I did have a rebellious streak that started to poke through.

The art building became my refuge. Since it was filled with creative types, it was the only place on campus where I felt comfortable, where we could figuratively let our hair down (because men's hair length was strictly monitored) and not worry about bojoes turning us in. Bojoes, or bojes as they were more commonly called, were students who were really committed to the culture at BJU and would turn fellow students in at the drop of a hat for any infraction. Socially speaking, they weren't extremely popular because they were always the buzzkills who made life at BJU extra difficult for us small-scale rebels who had difficulty following all the rules. I wouldn't qualify myself as a large-scale rebel because I never broke too many rules, nor was I proactively defiant, but I received my fair share of recurring demerits for not passing hair check (having too much hair on my head) or not doing my daily room chores (such as making my bed or cleaning the sink or taking out the trash). BJU expects its students to keep consistent track of the minutiae of its campus life, and I did my best to keep my sanity by observing most of the rules.

During my sophomore year, I worked a few different campus jobs alongside my job at Rodeheaver, including pot-wash at the dining common and printing signage at Creative Services, but I settled into a position at the BJU Press in the book design department since it was the most relevant to my degree pursuits. I completed my four years at BJU in May of 2007 and was hired at the BJU Press to work in their marketing department doing graphic and layout design. I had worked there for three and a half years of my time as a student at BJU, so it was a natural trajectory for me.

While I enjoyed the work as a BJU staff member, I also felt stifled because my sexuality was still quite repressed; I still clung to the idea that I could make myself straight if I tried hard enough. I wanted to be that good kid. I needed to be that good kid. The alternative terrified me because I would have to face the shame of who I really was: I would have to face myself. I had dated a few ladies while in college, and even had a girlfriend toward the end of my senior year and for a short time after graduation, but there always seemed to be something missing that left me unfulfilled. I couldn't face myself yet, but I couldn't bear to force myself into something that didn't feel right, so I ended my lone attempt at a heterosexual relationship feeling just as confused as the young woman I broke up with. Under these circumstances, I didn't know how much longer I could last at BJU.

Facing the Shame, Facing Myself

After a year as a staff member, I moved home for a brief period in 2008. Something was missing from my life, but I wasn't ready to face the truth of what that was. Home seemed like a good place to collect myself and find that direction. If I could find support from family during this process, all the better. During this brief period when I was living back in Vermont, my uncle John invited me to spend time with him and his husband, David, and my cousin Becky. These visits with my uncle changed my life forever. As a child, I became aware of my shame because of my family; as an adult, I developed a way to face my shame and myself with the help of my family.

I moved back to BJU in 2009 to be in the same position as before, albeit with a little more pay, but even then, I would periodically visit my uncles' house in Provincetown, Massachusetts, or, as it's lovingly called by its residents, P-town. I would work extra hours to give myself enough time off to drive up the coast and spend time with my uncles, who refer to themselves as my "fairy godmothers." Although I realize that P-town is an unusually progressive city for the LGBT community, I noticed how happy and healthy my uncles' relationship was, a realization that led me to see all queer people differently. They were no longer the broken individuals I had been taught to see; instead, they were fellow humans wanting the same things as everyone else in this world. It hit me: I too could live openly, unashamed of who I was or who I wanted to love. I couldn't hold it in any longer. On one drive back to Vermont from P-town in June 2010, I turned to my cousin and said those two important words: "I'm gay."

It was the first time I had ever said it out loud: *I'm gay. I like dudes. I'm down for the D.* Becky just replied, "Well, it's about time." She and my uncles had assumed my secret for quite some time and were just waiting for me to realize it myself. I was a little taken aback that my efforts to hide my secret hadn't been as ironclad as I had originally thought, but I've come to learn that there are some things you just can't hide from people who know what to look for.

I couldn't help but contrast this moment in my new journey down south to BJU with my old journey down to BJU to start my freshman year. During that road trip in my brother's convertible, I had been on a journey to find the fundamentalist adult self I knew I needed to be, but that quest was unsuccessful. This time around, in June of 2010, on my way back to BJU, I embarked on a journey to find that self-accepting man. I cracked that good Christian boy outer shell and began purging myself of the shame I had harbored. It's been a messy process, but at least now things feel honest and real. I can now love myself and find love with others.

Over the next year, as I began sharing my true self with more and more friends, I felt lighter with each successive revelation. I was systematically unburdening myself from the lies and the shame I had been maintaining since adolescence. But this unburdening came with a dangerous catch: during this time, I was still employed at BJU, so I had to be extremely selective with whom I shared this part of myself. BJU has a strict policy against homosexuality, and my job would have been in danger even if I had promised to remain celibate, something I had no intention of doing. Working at such a place caused an internal, unsustainable conflict in my life that I would have to address soon.

Purging the Shame

I also couldn't ignore how my family would react when the time came. No matter how euphoric these revelations were of coming out to friends, I still faced the grave reality of talking to my parents about my sexuality. In the spring of 2012, I decided it was time to remove that barrier that had been such an integral part of my family my whole life. I had to get rid of this shame, and I needed the support of my family to do so, so I stopped at my uncles' house along the way home. My uncle John gave me a small stone to keep in my pocket and squeeze whenever I felt scared or unsure of myself, a small talisman to remind me of my fairy godmothers, who were rooting for me every step of the way.

And boy, did I need that talisman. I've had many friends who lost the support of their Christian families when they came out, and I was a little scared the same might happen to me. Now it was my turn, and I wasn't quite sure how they would react. As I told my parents my truth, I squeezed that small stone in my pocket harder than I realized. I let out a sigh of relief when they responded in a fairly supportive way. They have loved me through my process of rediscovery—even though we don't always agree on things, such as faith and politics—and I have my uncle John to thank for it. My family had gone through this coming-out experience once before with Uncle John, and because of him, they were forced to examine their beliefs about family and love. Today, we are first and foremost family, and they wish for my happiness as do I for them, but back then, my journey of self-acceptance had just begun.

The next obvious step in this coming-out process was to separate myself from BJU. If the school was obsessed with superficial minutiae in its student handbook, it would be even more adamant about the bigger issues. BJU has a zero-tolerance policy for any kind of sexual activity outside the marriage of one man and one woman: I would have been immediately fired if they had found out I was a sexually active gay man. By this time, I had begun dating men, so my departure from BJU was vital because it was becoming impossible to hide who I was. I knew I had the love of my family, but I still had to shed the shame and fear I had internalized since I was a child: I systematically cut all of my ties to the fundamentalist world of BJU. I finally left BJU Press in the spring of 2012 and haven't looked back. Since I've left, I still keep in touch with some of the friends I made there who have accepted me fully and without judgment. In fact, some of my best friends today are ones from BJU who have also had similar journeys of leaving that culture and finding their own paths.

But who was I now? During this process of purging the shame and lies, I had to decide, religiously speaking, what kind of person I was going to be. My faith had diminished over the years and, by this time, played a very small role in my life. I didn't have a strong urge or desire for a relationship with God or any divine being because my passion was now directed at learning all I could about the world around me with my new gay eyes. It was no coincidence that it became easier to shed my shame the more I let go of my belief in the scriptures. Fundamentalism had shaped my twisted idea of who I was supposed to be; now I could focus on becoming who I wanted to be.

I found solace in the philosophy of secular humanism while still holding on to many of the values I had been raised with. Despite what fundamentalists say, I didn't need Christianity or the Bible to tell me how to live my life as a good person. I also don't need to separate myself from this world, as fundamentalists want. I am a part of this world and deserve to find and make my place in it. These days, my motivation for life is love—without it, life is meaningless—and the vehicle for that love is family, whether it be the one you're born into or the one you choose. I am fortunate to have both kinds: the family I grew up with and the family of queer folk in Vermont, where I live now. I've learned to love and be loved in return for who we all really are. It's not been an easy transition, but I'm infinitely happier now than when I was that good boy with the outer shell. In fact, I don't think I'm half bad today.

As I close my story, I must admit that, even now, as I have been writing this chapter, I've noticed how this exercise in self-reflection presented challenges I had not anticipated. For example, throughout my story, I have referred to my ongoing struggle with shame. While I have made progress in letting it go, it seems that writing about this time in my life has allowed that shame to rear its ugly head again and multiply, which makes being vulnerable in sharing my story all the more difficult.

But writing this story made me realize how BJU and the wider fundamentalist community wields shame as a weapon with great skill and precision, cutting to shreds those who do not fit into the paradigm of what a good Christian person should be, according to a fundamentalist interpretation of the scriptures. My journey away from that world dominated by shame was only made possible through family and friends who helped me abandon that community I inherited as a child. But not everyone is as lucky. It is hard to find a way out when your whole world is BJU. Where do you go? Who do you rely on when things get tough? Shame is a powerful tool of manipulation, and I fear that many want to leave fundamentalism but are paralyzed to do so on their own. I hope my story can serve as that encouraging surrogate family member to those who need the support to break free from both shame and fundamentalism.

Finally, no matter when this story is published, I will always associate it with when I originally wrote my first draft: Pride month (June). I find that connection fitting because, to me, pride is all about shedding the shame that has dominated our early lives in fundamentalism. Having a sense of pride is learning to love ourselves so we can build a community around that love. When we find that love, we find the freedom to make choices not based in shame but in the love we have for ourselves and those close to our hearts.

Note

1. Goodnough, "Gay Rights Groups Celebrate."

PART FIVE

Identifying as Religious and Spiritual

> Stand fast therefore in the liberty wherewith Christ
> hath made us free, and be not entangled again with
> the yoke of bondage. But the fruit of the Spirit is
> love, joy, peace, longsuffering, gentleness, goodness,
> faith, meekness, temperance: against such there is
> no law.
>
> GALATIANS 5:1, 22, 23

Former BJU students coming out of fundamentalism and the closet can find fulfillment in the religious or spiritual sector. Five contributors in this part talk about their diverse experiences that led them away from a restrictive belief system and into a world that ranges from a more organized congregational community to a more individualized form of enlightened spirituality. Not all the contributors in this unit identify as Christian, and they may not connect completely with Galatians 5:1, but I believe all of them could appreciate the last part of the verse, which talks about leaving a "yoke of bondage." Further, I realize that, contextually speaking, the fruit of the Spirit is technically Christian-centric, but these fruits are certainly not unique to one religion but rather contain a more spiritualized dimension that is not constrained by strict Christianity. Also, as William Bagley, a former fundamentalist who is now a non-Christian spiritual person, says, "Although I do not feel Christianity has any exclusive claim to the truth, I feel Christianity can make a positive contribution to world religious culture. Not because Christianity can teach anything that is not found in other religious traditions, but because the healthier sides of Christianity have focused on a message of love and made it real in human experience."[1]

For these five contributors, this journey out of fundamentalism did not happen in a linear trajectory or within perfectly spaced increments. The path for all of these queer former BJU students can be measured in years of contemplation and adversity. First, Jeff Mullinix (the uncle of contributor Fawn Mullinix) writes how his desire to actively work in the ministry found success despite multiple setbacks, including his involvement in several conflicted romantic encounters with men at BJU, being forced to leave BJU after a short time in the late seventies, having to step down from his pastorship after a divorce, and enduring the tragic loss of his partner. After refinding his place behind the pulpit and marrying Steve Shamblin (whose story is also in this part), Jeff questions the stability of his current position in the United Methodist church. Next, Elena Kelly describes her exodus from BJU's influence of fundamentalism after developing close friendships with the Jones family and other religious faculty members when she attended BJU in the early eighties. After a successful ordination ceremony and with BJU's blessing, Elena began her ministry as a pastor in Colorado, where her desire to minister to the local queer community prompted her to sever her ties with BJU and discover where she herself fit into the queer community, which led to her awareness about her gender identity and her spiritual relationship with the divine.

The third story comes from Steve Shamblin, who began at BJU in the early eighties and spent almost twenty years at BJU as a student and then longtime staff member, working up the ranks in the business office and being groomed for an upper administrative position. While preparing his exit strategy from BJU, his marriage, and the church, Steve was physically prevented from moving his personal items from his house because of a human prayer chain of BJU men lined up in his front yard. After many years away from the church, Steve married a United Methodist minister, Jeff Mullinix, and found his desire for the ministry rekindled. Christy Haussler attended BJU in the late eighties and early nineties and graduated without any major incident because of her fundamentalist training. Her story addresses how a born-and-raised fundamentalist lacks self-awareness about sexual identity and conforming to lesbian stereotypes. After being fired from her first job as a Christian school PE teacher and coach, Christy embarked on a search for self-acceptance and a sense of belonging in the church. She credits discovering the Metropolitan Community Church as a major moment in her life and argues that she and her wife are proof that Christians can also be lesbians.

Avery Wrenne completes this part with their story about finding their place within the realm of spirituality. Born in the hospital on campus and educated at BJU their whole life, from daycare through high school, Avery studied at BJU in the early to mid-2010s. Through their account, they cover the week of chapel messages addressing homosexuality in November 2013 as well as the ramifications of the GRACE Report in 2015, a report that details allegations of abuse and mishandled counseling and leadership at BJU. After leaving BJU, Avery found personal authenticity outside of fundamentalism and identifies as genderqueer and pansexual. The five stories in this part exhibit the range of experience, emotions, and effort to deprogram the internalized fundamentalism for a more welcoming, affirming place in a religious or spiritual space.

Note

1. Bagley, "William Bagley," 190.

chapter 15   JEFF MULLINIX

I became somewhat indignant and said, "How do you know she's not right for me?" I quickly followed that comment, regrettably, with, "At least I'm dating!" At that point he grabbed me and kissed me and said, "That's why I'm not dating anyone!" Once again, I was overwhelmed with emotions. I *had* suspected something. I had even hoped. But what now?

BJU: A Chance to Be Changed

I was raised in a Southern Baptist church. Around the age of seven, I made a profession of faith and was baptized, but my conversion experience didn't really take place until I was in high school. My introduction to Bob Jones University, however, came when I was in seventh grade. My oldest brother had met Bob Jones III one summer while he was attending the Bill Rice Ranch, a fundamentalist Christian camp in Murfreesboro, Tennessee. Dr. Bob was one of the speakers that summer, and my brother was captivated by the staunch fundamentalism BJU offered, so after graduation from high school, he attended BJU.

My initial exposure to the campus came from traveling to visit my brother periodically throughout the year from our home in Ohio. I quickly learned that the university had quite a reputation: the students were expected to abide by BJU's long list of rules. Being the youngest of three boys, I looked up to my brother and sought his approval, so as the years passed and I had to make a decision for college, I was not exactly thrilled when he urged me to go to BJU.

To be honest, my heart was never fully invested in attending there because I knew I would not do well in such a rigid environment; I wanted to go to either Miami University in Oxford, Ohio, or Ohio State University.

However, the summer before my senior year in high school, my brother was persistent, even to the point of convincing my parents that BJU was the only place I should go. I relented. Since I was working a pretty decent part-time job to save money and had already registered to attend a local community college for the fall semester, I began BJU in January of 1978.

Why in the world would I go to BJU if I was gay? Honestly, I don't believe at that time in my life I had a clear understanding that I was gay. Or, if I did, it was deeply suppressed. While I recall having an attraction, perhaps as early as third grade, to boys, to male teachers, or actors on TV, I never mentioned it in my very conservative Baptist home—not when I often heard sermons of damnation about queers or my parents talking with disdain about people who were "queer" or "fags."

When I was in seventh or eighth grade, my family and I attended a Sunday evening worship service that was part of a week-long series of revival services. It was the first time I remember being hit with one of the Clobber Passages. That evening, the evangelist chose Leviticus 18:22–24 and Leviticus 20:13 as the texts. He recited, "Thou shalt not lie with mankind, as with womankind: it is abomination," and also emphasized the part of the verse that said that "they shall surely be put to death." I went home that evening quite sure I was going to hell, even though I'd never acted upon my feelings. I was living in fear and shame because I didn't want to burn in hell, nor did I want my family not to love me. While dealing with this inner struggle, I did everything I possibly could not to be gay, including consistently praying that God would change me. Though I was reluctant to attend BJU, I thought that the Christian atmosphere there might help to change me.

"It's Gonna Take Some Time" to Adjust to BJU

So there I was, an eighteen-year-old on campus almost five hundred miles away from home. I knew no one there, and beginning as a freshman at BJU was quite an adjustment. While I considered myself a Christian, I was a typical teenager of the late 1970s. I liked my own kind of music, I liked my hair longer (though I begrudgingly got my hair cut before I arrived on campus), and I didn't like to be told what to do. All of that changed very quickly.

One afternoon during one of my first weeks there, the door to my room burst open while I was studying. It was my prayer captain—the student spiritual leader of my assigned dormitory prayer group—along with the

floor monitor—the student spiritual leader of my hall. They told me I had
been reported for listening to my favorite group, the Carpenters, on a local radio station. I received twenty-five demerits for that. I was taken off-
guard that the Carpenters music "didn't check." I thought, "Are you kid-
ding me?" It made me think about another song sung by the Carpenters,
"It's Gonna Take Some Time"—and boy, did I need some time to adjust to
this new place.

One saving grace through all these difficult adjustments was that I
met other students like me who struggled with the rules. Kent was in my
prayer group, which consisted of three or four adjacent dorm rooms that
would meet most nights before lights-out to pray and share devotional
messages.[1] Kent and I quickly became friends, as we soon realized we had
similar interests in music and movies. We wound up hanging out all the
time, and I have no doubt Kent and I helped each other survive that first
year at BJU. We even decided to room together our sophomore year.

During my freshman year, I still believed attending BJU would help
me overcome my attraction to guys. I thought if I prayed hard enough—
which I did—and if I did what was pleasing to God—which I was trying
to do—I could put these desires behind me and lead a "normal" life. BJU
was supposed to be the place to help me turn "normal," but it turned out
to be the place where I became even more confused during that first year.

Unexpected Encounters with Men at BJU

As freshmen, students had an option to be assigned to "campus parents"—typically faculty and staff—to help students adjust to being away
from home and to give them some semblance of a "family life" while at
BJU. I was assigned a campus dad who was a single faculty man. As a way
of introduction, he invited his campus sons (he was a single man, so it was
appropriate that he was assigned an all-male group) to his on-campus
apartment for dinner. It was awkward: we didn't know him, and he didn't
know us. He made a nice dinner and some conversation, but there was
still an atmosphere of awkwardness.

My first impression of him was, "Hmmm, I wonder if he could possibly be gay?" I'm not quite sure why I had that impression. Perhaps it was
the way he dressed, which was stylish for a conservative. Perhaps it was
the very tasteful way he had decorated his home. Or perhaps it was my
amazement that this guy knew how to cook and set a table with class.
Whatever the reason, I got a "possibly gay" vibe from him.

Our campus dad hosted another dinner party after the first one, but only a few of us showed up. Since I started at BJU in January 1978, when I returned for the following fall semester, I was still considered freshman status and could still have that connection with my campus dad. Shortly before Christmas break, he hosted a Christmas party. Only two of us showed up. The other student left shortly after dinner, but I decided to stay and chat for a while because I was beginning to feel a level of comfort with him. As the evening progressed, so did the intensity of our conversation. At one point he touched my arm in gesturing with his hands—but his hand didn't move. Instead, he began gently rubbing my arm.

There was a part of me that wanted to run away, but a part of me felt strangely comfortable. I didn't know what to do. I became quiet. He asked, "Are you OK?" I nervously smiled and nodded my head yes. His hand then reached up behind my head and he pulled me closer. Then it happened. A kiss.

A flood of emotions bubbled up inside. "What do I do?" I thought as I fought off tears welling in my eyes. He saw that I was upset and quickly said, "I'm sorry. I should not have done that. Please forgive me." I told him it was OK, but that I should go. As I got to the door he asked me, "Jeff, please don't tell anyone about this." I told him I wouldn't.

There were no more dinners. No more contact. When we happened across each other on campus, each of us would simply look away. Even though we never talked again, my goal of losing my gay desires suffered a severe setback. At the time, I felt an array of emotions, primarily a lot of confusion and definitely some level of discomfort, but I was never angry at him. Looking back on my own journey, I totally understand his struggle through the lens of my own. My only hope is that he has finally found peace with who he is.

I was excited to return to BJU for the remainder of my sophomore year in the fall of 1979 because toward the end of my freshman year, I began to date Cathy, who was a year ahead of me.[2] I felt like I was finally beginning to put some of those gay feelings and emotions behind me. After all, I was now dating a girl! I was also looking forward to rooming with Kent. He was the one person with whom I felt the closest.

As Cathy and I continued our dating relationship, I noticed a difference in Kent. It almost appeared like jealousy. One evening after dinner, our third roommate was out, and we were alone in our dorm room. I asked Kent if everything was OK, and he responded, "Why are you dating her?" I just gave him a shrug with a curious look. He asked again, "Why are you dating her? She's not right for you." I became somewhat indignant and said, "How do you know she's not right for me?" I quickly followed that comment, regrettably, with, "At least I'm dating!" At that point he grabbed me and kissed me and said, "That's why I'm not dating anyone!" Once again, I was overwhelmed with emotions. I *had* suspected something. I had even hoped. But what now?

That was the only physical contact Kent and I ever had, but from that point on there was an unspoken understanding between us about who we both were. We never mentioned that kiss again, but it had a profound hold over me. Both the experience with my campus dad and with Kent affected me deeply. Was this who I was? What do I do now? My relationship with Cathy fizzled by the end of the first semester, and I had trouble concentrating on my studies. My grades suffered.

By the end of the semester, I was on academic probation, which was unfathomable for me because I had always been on the honor roll in high school. I struggled to focus on school when I had larger questions about myself—about my faith—that needed answers. Was I truly giving myself over to the immoral, unnatural passions the Apostle Paul speaks of in Romans 1? Once again, I felt the inner fear that had encompassed me years ago in that revival service in my home church. Once again, I found myself struggling with a choice: be true to myself or be faithful to God. Once again, I chose to suppress my feelings and make a go of being straight. So, in an effort to boost my GPA, I decided to stay on campus for summer school and move forward with my spiritual goals.

My Final Mistake at BJU

During summer school, I worked part time off campus on Saturdays doing yard work for an elderly lady in Greenville. One particular Saturday, my summer roommate asked if I would take him to meet his girlfriend off campus on my way to work. Couples were strictly forbidden from seeing each other off campus without a chaperone, and I certainly did not qualify as a chaperone, but I agreed to help him. While I knew the risk, I thought no one would know. That evening, when I returned from work, my dormitory supervisor asked me to come down to his room. My dad had been in poor health, and I thought I was being called down to be told that he had passed away, but when I went to my supervisor's room, he asked me about taking my roommate off to meet his girlfriend. We had been caught.

I was honest about what I had done. He then escorted me to the dean of men's office. My roommate was "shipped," basically expelled, and I was asked not to return in the fall. To this day, I don't understand why I wasn't officially expelled like my roommate, but I was fine with not returning because I was so tired of feeling imprisoned both physically and emotionally. I returned home to Ohio in the summer of 1980, wondering what I should do next.

I was determined to move forward with my educational plans while putting the world of BJU behind me, with the exception of Kent. We kept in touch through phone calls and letters, but I eventually met someone and became engaged. I asked Kent to be my best man when I married in 1983, but he declined. We never spoke after that. I married and had three wonderful children. While I had two years of academic credits from BJU, a harsh reality hit me when I tried to find a college that would accept my unaccredited credits. Fortunately, I discovered that Cedarville College, a nearby Baptist college in Ohio affiliated with the General Association of Regular Baptists, would accept all of them.

I received my BA in communications from Cedarville College in 1985. It was during my time at Cedarville that I began to experience another uneasiness, an uneasiness that some may identify as a "calling." I really began to have this overwhelming sense that God was leading me—"calling me"—into ministry. After struggling with this angst for a few years, I finally decided to leave my secular job and go to seminary. I received my MA in religious education from Southwestern Baptist Theological Seminary in 1995. I was serving in full-time ministry. Life was good—or so I thought.

Christian Ministry, Divorce, and Setbacks

As I grew older, I became increasingly unsettled. It felt like a storm raging within me, and I didn't know how to maneuver through it for relief. The same-sex desires I had experienced as a young adult and college student were once again emerging; perhaps they never really left. This growing conflict caused stress on my marriage, and I began to withdraw emotionally. My wife and I divorced in 1999, and a big part of me breathed a huge sigh of relief because I could now try to come to terms with who I was—but another part of me was scared to death.

My divorce brought difficult changes. It meant adapting to shared parenting of my three children with my ex-wife. It meant dealing with some financial difficulties. It meant I was single and still struggling with my sexual orientation, and it also meant I was forced to leave a vocational ministry that I loved. Before my divorce, I served in a Southern Baptist church, but I knew I could not serve in their ministry and be divorced. I was prepared for the consequences of stepping down, but I wasn't prepared for the disappointing reaction from my church. Not once was I asked, "How can we minister to you or your family?" Instead, I was matter-of-factly told what I could and could not do as a divorced man. I was done with them.

I returned to a secular career and found a part-time position serving as a music director in a United Methodist church. It was there that I not only found a place to serve in ministry, but I also found a place of healing and acceptance. As I grew to love the United Methodist church, my theology and understanding of God's love and grace for all people evolved. For the first time, I heard a message of love and acceptance. In this community of faith, I met my first gay couple. A Christian gay couple! I never knew that was a possibility. For the first time ever, I began to realize that God loves me just as I am. A gay man. I was out to myself, but I still wasn't out to many people.

During this time, I tried to reconnect with Kent, but to my extreme sorrow, I learned from his parents that Kent had died of AIDS in 1999. While this news hit me hard, I found some closure on vacation in the summer of 2001, when I visited Kent's parents. They had a wonderful lunch for me and my three children, and I had a nice heart-to-heart talk with his mother. She took me to the cemetery where Kent is buried. A serene place in the country. She allowed me time at his grave to have my time of closure, and then, before we left, she said, "I have something for you, but you'll want to read it in private." It was Kent's journal from the time we were at BJU. That night, when I read of Kent's feelings for me, I couldn't stop my tears from flowing. A part of me wondered what might have been had we known each other in a different place and time.

In the fall of 2002, I met Dan, who came from a staunch Mormon background and whose family had basically disowned him. We quickly fell in love. I had never been in a same-sex relationship, but I knew I wanted to share my life with him. We dated for a couple of years and began to talk about moving in together, but I hadn't even come out to my children yet, so we waited because we had time. Or so we thought. On March 17, 2005, my world came to a screeching halt when Dan was killed by a drunk driver. I was not welcomed to attend his funeral, so I mourned in silence. In my profound grief, I determined that this would never happen to me again. I was meant to be single.

Crossing Paths with BJU Again

I managed to move on with my life and was fortunate to serve with a pastor who encouraged me to transfer my credentials into the United Methodist church. I received my master of divinity from United Theological Seminary in 2011, and then in 2012, I became ordained as a full elder, which is terminology used in the United Methodist church to indicate an ordained clergy person. It felt so good being back in full-time pastoral ministry, and at that point in my life, I never thought I would cross paths with BJU again.

But on June 19, 2015, that's exactly what happened. A small group from the church where I served in Columbus, Ohio, decided to march for the first time in the Columbus Pride Parade. That day changed my life. On that rainy Saturday morning, we lined up on State Street next to other faith-based organizations.

I noticed the banner of the group in front of us. It read, "BJUnity: An affirming alternative for LGBT+ alumni and students of Bob Jones University." I thought, "This has got to be a joke!" I approached the group and introduced myself as someone who had attended BJU in the late 1970s. Sure enough, the group was from BJU, but definitely not endorsed by the university. I couldn't help but notice a very handsome man in the group. Our eyes met a few times. Yes, there was an attraction. I also happened to notice his name on his shirt. As I returned to my group, I quickly went to Facebook and looked up the name, Steve Shamblin. I sent him a private Facebook message, and he instantly responded. For the next two hours in the pouring rain, we messaged each other. He invited me to join the BJUnity group that evening. Of course I went.

Steve and I instantly connected and began dating over that summer. I think we both realized early on that we each had met "the one," and as our relationship became serious, I knew I would have to tell my congregation at some point. Very few there knew that I was gay, but I knew they'd eventually figure it out. And then—I became engaged! With the help of my daughter playing double-agent with both of us, Steve and I popped the question to each other at the Palace of Fine Arts in San Francisco on

March 30, 2016. I knew I couldn't hold off telling my congregation any longer.

It was easier said than done to share this wonderful news with my congregation. While many United Methodist churches are "reconciling"—open and affirming to the LGBTQ community—mine was not. Not only that, but the current stance of the United Methodist church is that "self-avowed practicing homosexuals are not to be certified as candidates, ordained as ministers, or appointed to serve in The United Methodist Church."[3] I had a decision to make: do I leave the United Methodist church, or do I stay and strive for change in our Book of Discipline? To stay as a gay married man meant that I put at risk my ordination and my ministry in the United Methodist church. I do not have the time or space here to mention the details about decisions the United Methodist church has recently made in regard to homosexuals and ordination, so I will just say that, for now, I decided to stay.

Coming Out to My Congregation

After writing a letter to both my bishop and my district superintendent, I shared in a sermon with my congregation on June 26, 2016, that it was time for me to be totally transparent as a child of God and as their pastor. I let them know that I was a gay man and that I was marrying Steve on December 17, 2016. I also told them, "Throughout my life, there are two things that have been an absolute. I did not ask for either one of them; I had no control over either of them. One was the call of God on my life, and the other was my sexual orientation." I also acknowledged the potential risk of making this announcement but said that "at this point in my life, there is absolutely no conflict with accepting who I am and following Jesus, for I know that God wants me to be healthy, authentic, whole, integrated and my truest self."

I would love to say that their response was unanimously positive. Unfortunately, that was not the case. Some in the congregation walked out, but a large number have continued to support us. As a matter of fact, our administrative council insisted that we get married in the church, and approximately seventy-five of our more than two hundred guests were church members. However, I must add that a complaint was filed with my bishop regarding our marriage. That complaint was dropped when I was reappointed to serve at another church.

United Methodist Special General Conference, 2019

The debate over same-sex marriage, the ordination of openly gay clergy persons, and the inclusion of LGBTQ persons in the life of the church has created a schism in the United Methodist church. In February 2019 a Special General Conference was held in Saint Louis, Missouri, to hear arguments and vote on a change in the United Methodist Book of Discipline. While we weren't delegates to the conference, Steve and I felt that we needed to be present. The conversations, the passionate arguments, and the voting were about us.

Several plans for the United Methodist church to move forward were presented. However, two plans made it to the voting floor. The One Church Plan would remove the harmful language regarding LGBTQ persons from the Book of Discipline, paving the way for ordination to openly gay clergy and allowing same-sex marriages in the church. The Traditional Plan would keep the wording in the Book of the Discipline the same and would also add harsher penalties to LGBTQ clergy and those who performed same-sex marriages. When the votes were tallied, the Traditional Plan had 461 votes, while the One Church Plan had 359 votes. The vote hit us like a gut punch.

While Steve and I drove back to Columbus that night, we had a very candid discussion about what our future would be. I knew that being an openly gay, married clergy person meant that I had a target on my back. We had to have a serious discussion as to whether we would stay and fight for justice in a denomination that had created so much harm, or whether we would leave and I transfer my clergy credentials to another denomination.

A New Opportunity

Shortly after the Special General Conference, a friend and colleague who serves in the Pacific Northwest Annual Conference of the United Methodist Church (PNW) mentioned that the conference was offering safe harbor to LGBTQ clergy who might be at risk of complaints in other conferences. The PNW had resolved that it would not entertain complaints against LGBTQ clergy.

Admittedly, I didn't give it much thought at the time. Moving to the Pacific Northwest was not even on my radar. A few months later, he mentioned again that we really should talk to a district superintendent who he knew. So, hesitantly, I reached out to that superintendent. Within a week I was being scheduled with a Zoom interview with a few members of the bishop's cabinet. Within the next few days, I was being scheduled to be introduced via Zoom to a small reconciling church in Bonney Lake, Washington. On May 25, 2019, we knew we would be moving to Washington by mid-July!

I would love to say that moving here changed everything. While I feel unhindered by the threat of complaint, the church is still in turmoil. We know that a schism is looming on the horizon and that the face of the United Methodist church will soon change. We hope and pray for a church that embraces the gifts of all of God's children in its life and ministry.

As for Steve and me, we wait. And we pray. And we continue on this beautiful journey together.

BJU had a profound effect on my life, obviously in the form of many negative experiences, experiences that led me to question my faith and my identity as a beloved child of God. I cannot deny that BJU was the common thread that brought Steve and me together, as we both discovered life after BJU through a community that accepts people for who they are. But I can boldly say that both Steve and I had to walk away from BJU's brand of Christianity before we could find our rightful place in the ministry.

I would like to close with a statement I wrote in seminary when we composed our spiritual biographies because I believe it encapsulates the assurance that I can clearly see and appreciate now after so many experiences have riddled me with confusion and sorrow: "I may not have gone where I intended to go, but I think I have ended up where God intended me to be." I wish I could tell my younger self what I know as a minister today, which is the same thing I want to tell my congregation: God's love is not constrained by traditional misinterpretation of scripture.

Notes

1. Pseudonym.
2. Pseudonym.
3. United Methodist church, "Homosexuality."

chapter 16   ELENA KELLY

Having been in the fundamentalist system for a
while, I knew that BJU didn't ordain women, but I
felt such a strong desire to be approved by this institution for a career as a pastor. I also knew that if
I had even talked about being female at any point in
this process, I would have been kicked out. No matter how much I tried to reassure myself that I was
on the right path—that I had the approval of God
through my successes and blessings from the upper
administration at BJU—my secret feelings of being
a girl only grew stronger.

Character Test

Dr. Bob Jones Sr., the founder and first president of Bob Jones University—then known as Bob Jones College—was noted on campus for his
chapel sayings, which were placed in large letters above the chalkboard in
classrooms for all the students to ponder. One of the first ones I remember seeing as an incoming ministerial student was "The test of your character is what it takes to stop you."[1] I was deeply moved by that saying because, according to that, I had very little true character as a girl in a male
body.

I have several memories from my preschool childhood. The two most
determinative ones had to do with my sense of God and my sense of myself. The first incident occurred when I was just three years old. My adoptive parents were fighting. The shouting and commotion scared me, so I
went back into my room and got down on my knees beside my bed, as
I had been taught. This time, however, for some reason I cannot explain,
I prayed, "Heavenly Mother, if you can hear me, please make the fighting
stop! The Heavenly Father doesn't hear me." Instantly, the house went si-

lent. No one had ever introduced me to the concept of a feminine deity, but since I was three, I have always known she was there for me.

The other memory that is imprinted forever in my brain happened at age five. Before then, my adoptive mother had allowed me to dress up in her clothes, and she even took photos of me beaming with joy as I wrapped her luxurious garments around my small frame. I admired her and felt convinced I would grow up to be beautiful just like her. But when it came time for me to begin kindergarten, she refused to let me wear her clothes anymore. I was distraught, crying, and demanding that she not make me look like a boy, but she would not hear of it. There was no doubt in my mind that I was a girl, not the boy they all mistakenly believed I was.

When I went to school, I naturally played with the girls because boys had cooties. This strategy worked in kindergarten, but when I started first grade, the teacher forbade me to play with girls, which made me cry on numerous occasions. One day she caught me playing with Sue, my best friend, and my teacher paddled me in front of the class. Sue came over to where I was crying and whispered, "I don't care what they say, I know you are a girl." That whispered message comforted me for many years. At least one person in the world really knew me. Even at the beginning of my time at BJU, I knew that something was not quite right with me, but I couldn't tell anyone. All it took for me to renounce the truth of my true gender was the implied threat of disapproval from others at a fundamentalist university.

All through my elementary and middle school years, I was harassed and bullied by boys at school. I got used to them calling me "sissy boy" and "crybaby," but I never got used to the black eyes, bloody noses, and getting punched in the solar plexus. I ran away from home three times before I was thirteen, always searching for my birth mother, convinced that she alone could explain why I was so sure I was a girl. My adoptive parents committed me to a psychiatric hospital in Denver after the last runaway episode, but I managed to run away from the hospital, too, and I lived on the streets for a few months in Denver during that summer. I spent quite a bit of that time begging in front of a McDonald's. While on the streets, I was introduced to the drug culture, and through drugs, I learned a new way to escape from the pain of my gender confusion.

Several years later, I married, had a child, and left Colorado for Northern California, specifically Chico. Within just a few weeks, two teenage girls came to our house, asking if we would let them take our four-year-old son to church on a bus. They were sweet and polite, and we relented and let him go. He loved it, and each Sunday he brought home papers he had colored and crafts he had made. Before long, my wife and I started to wonder what they were teaching him, so we went to the little Baptist church to see for ourselves. The people were very nice and welcoming, even though I had hair down to the middle of my back. Within a few months, I had made a confession of faith, had my hair cut short, and become a bus captain myself.

Conversion to BJU

A traveling group of young men came to our church from BJU in the summer of 1981. They were wonderful! I talked to one of them, named Dan, after the service. I told him I always wanted to know the original languages of the Bible so I could know exactly what they said, instead of what some nebulous translator thought they said. And secretly I wondered if total dedication to God might finally take away my belief that I was female. So I convinced our pastor that I was called to the ministry, and I enrolled at BJU. In 1981 my wife and I packed our beat-up 1963 Chevy station wagon and began a journey from Northern California to South Carolina with our sons, ages eight and two, and our first daughter, ten days old. We were starting our new life of dedication to the fundamentalist God.

The car had no air conditioning, and it was August as we crossed Nevada, then Utah and Wyoming, and finally into Colorado, where we stopped and spent time with family. No one who knew me from before could believe what a transformation had taken place. I had left home four years earlier as a hippie kid with a heavy prison sentence hanging over my head if I had made the slightest mistake, and now I was back, on my way to seminary in the Bible Belt. Plus, I spoke of the power of God to bring real change into my life, all the while hoping and praying that it would.

We drove down to Louisiana to see my adoptive mother's family and went from there to Greenville, South Carolina, and our first house was just three miles from the BJU campus. From sweltering heat in August and September, to the heaviest snowfall on record that winter, we were dirt poor, and I was working three jobs just to try to make ends meet. I worked nights at Krispy Kreme donuts, days in construction, and part time in the electrical shop in the campus maintenance department. (I had gotten my journeyman electrician license before leaving California.)

I was also taking a full load of classes. Late in my first semester, I was offered a full-time job as campus electrician and was able to quit the other two jobs.

During most of the five years at BJU, we subsisted on rice, beans, and potatoes, with occasional flour and eggs. There was a family in Greenville who we had met in Northern California, and they would bring bags of groceries to us at least once or twice a month. We had never lived in a place where heating oil was used to heat the house, and we often had no money to buy any. What we had was a king-sized waterbed, and most nights we all slept in it because it had an electric heater that kept the mattress quite cozy all night. In the mornings we awoke to find cups of water frozen solid on the kitchen counter.

I must confess that I poured myself into the BJU environment, soaking it all up and practicing what I was taught. We began nightly devotions with our children at home, became active at Hampton Park Baptist Church, went out soul-winning weekly, and were totally devoted to the school.

I threw myself into my studies, too, as I focused on ancient languages, but I also had classes in pulpit speech, counseling, and other related ministerial course work. We ministerial students were encouraged to question all of our beliefs and also to seek to find the answers for ourselves. The clear message was that if you studied properly, you would come to know that biblical fundamentalism is the only correct way to understand the divine. So I wrote many papers on topics that I knew BJU stood against, and I got A's on almost every one, in spite of their nonconforming treatments of the topic.

At a university where you were expelled if you accumulated 150 demerits, and where you received demerits for arriving one second late to class or for failing to wear a tie and jacket to dinner, I am proud to say that I went through all five of my years with zero demerits. While I am on the subject of demerits and expulsion, let me provide some context by adding that, while I was there, one of Dr. Bob Jones III's sons, Bobby IV, was kicked out of Bob Jones Academy for drinking beer. While that may sound like an amusing story decades later, the reality is that BJU was not afraid to expel anyone, even those in the immediate family.[2] I remained in the good graces of the Jones family throughout my stay at BJU.

In 1983, for our tenth wedding anniversary, my wife and I received special permission from both Drs. Bob Jr. and III to celebrate it in a unique way. On campus is a beautiful chapel called the War Memorial Chapel, which is used regularly for concerts, recitals, and weddings, but there had never been a ceremony in there for a married couple to renew their vows. Because I was the staff electrician and knew Drs. Bob Jr. and III personally, they agreed to let us do what no one had ever been allowed to do: renew our vows in the chapel. It was a beautiful ceremony, made even more special by all who attended: our children and friends, as well as many of my seminary professors and their wives, and many of the BJU staff members.

To further demonstrate just how close I was to the university president, I offer the example of my youngest son's birth. In July 1983 my youngest son, Robert Reynolds Jones Adkins, was born at the campus hospital, Barge Memorial Hospital. We named him after Dr. Bob. The morning he was born, I called Dr. Bob III, the president of the university, at home and told him there was another Bob Jones on campus that day. He immediately came to the hospital, took out his own leatherbound copy of the New Testament—the one that he carried for years in his jacket pocket and preached from often—and gave it to our son as a birth present. I will never forget Dr. Bob's act of kindness.

Upon graduation in 1986, I called together an ordination council so that I could serve a congregation as a minister. My council included a veritable who's-who of top names in the ministry at BJU: Dr. Bob Jones Jr., the chancellor; Dr. Bob Jones III, the president; Dr. Thurman Wisdom, dean of the School of Religion; Dr. David Yearick, senior pastor of Hampton Park Baptist Church, at that time the largest BJU-staffed congregation in Greenville and also where I served as lay minister for the entire five years we were at BJU; a BJU missionary who was a dear friend to me; and my pastor in Chico, California, from the church where I first had "heard the call." On paper, I couldn't have asked for a more BJU-approved council.

Looking back, I probably should've been intimidated or scared, given who was on my council, but I wasn't. In fact, I felt no fear in honestly responding to Dr. Wisdom's question on where I stood on the topic of women being ordained. He knew I would take the affirmative side because I had written a paper for his class which pointed out all the women in the Bible who were leaders, teachers, and constant followers of Jesus, unlike their male counterparts. It was an awkward moment, but the council agreed that my one "flaw" was not serious enough to deny me ordination. I was thrilled to have passed this rite of passage on my path to the ministry. I was accepted in the church planting program at BJU, and we planned to move to Aurora, Colorado, to start our own church.

I kept telling myself, "Surely God is on my side now. Surely soon those feelings of being a girl will evaporate like water in the desert." Having been in the fundamentalist system for a while, I knew that BJU didn't ordain women, but I felt such a strong desire to be approved by this institution for a career as a pastor. I also knew that if I had even talked about being female at any point in this process, I would have been kicked out. No matter how much I tried to reassure myself that I was on the right path—that I had the approval of God through my successes and blessings from the upper administration at BJU—my secret feelings of being a girl only grew stronger. It frightened me, but I couldn't tell anyone, not even those who were closest to me.

Moving Away from BJU

After graduation, in 1986, we moved back to Colorado in time for me to participate in my first two funerals as an ordained minister; the first was for my adoptive mother, who had died just two months after my graduation, and the second was for my paternal grandmother.

We moved into an apartment in Aurora, the bedroom suburb of Denver, and I started a church from scratch on East Colfax, the most impoverished area, with alcoholics, addicts, and sex workers all around. Some of them came to our church initially because we had made deals with local restaurants so we could distribute meal tickets that were good for one free meal but that had no cash value. We also had a canned-food pantry and some winter clothes we gave out to needy people who came by. We were totally self-supporting financially in about nine months, which was unheard of.

As far as my ministry there was concerned, I did many things I was taught *not* to do in church planting classes, because after leaving BJU, I started to realize that much of what I had been taught was not in accord with what I actually believed. Within the first year, the church stopped taking money from BJU because I knew the school would not be happy if it found out our church held HIV/AIDS classes on Wednesday nights instead of prayer meeting.

These classes came as a suggestion from a man at our church who was also instrumental in getting gay and lesbian people to attend our services.

When he approached me with this idea, I jumped at the opportunity. At that time, I was well aware that most fundamentalists viewed HIV/AIDS as God's curse on the gay community, and that BJU would not approve of these classes at our church because we would be bringing people in who were "sinners," people who would have been kicked out of BJU for not being holy enough. But I didn't think that way. I was proud that our congregation was the first in Aurora, and maybe all of Denver, to have classes on HIV/AIDS prevention.

But, for the sake of argument, let's say that BJU might not have minded the HIV/AIDS classes because of its redeeming community outreach; BJU would not, however, have been pleased that I had become good friends with the ministerial staff at Metropolitan Community Church of the Rockies in Denver. I even took my children there for services in the hope that they would not grow up fearful of these beautiful people known as gays and lesbians who were part of the congregation. To my delight, my children preferred MCC to our church because there was a lot more hugging and they got more attention at MCC. But there was another personal benefit for closely associating with MCC: being around gay and lesbian people was also an excuse for me to figure out if and where I might fit in with them.

For a period of time as I tried to make sense of this feeling of being a girl, I thought I was a gay effeminate man, but I soon came to realize that I could not make myself feel attracted to another man. And I couldn't be a lesbian because my plumbing wasn't right. Yet I loved the people I met there. During those years in Denver, I conducted so many funerals for the beautiful people who perished from the devastation of HIV/AIDS. I wanted to help this community more, so I became an AIDS Foundation volunteer. It was hard to explain, but I felt like I belonged in the gay community, even though I didn't really know how specifically. All I did know at that point was that it felt so much better participating in the gay community than it did pretending to be a straight man.

I had been in Denver for barely a year when I found my birth mother. She was living in Pueblo, just a two-hour drive from where I lived in Aurora. We had a magnificent reunion, full of tears and laughter, hugs and kisses, and promises never to be apart ever again. She introduced me to the entire family at my grandmother's seventy-fifth birthday and family reunion. Only my grandmother had previous knowledge that I existed. My mother and I had ten wonderful years together before she passed on in 1996.

My mother told me about my birth father, and after another year of searching, I found him in a suburb of Seattle. Once he saw some photos of me, he was convinced that I was his child and agreed to meet me just once. At that meeting he gave me the names, addresses, and phone numbers of all seven of my half siblings. I immediately set up meetings with them all.

One half sister lived in San Francisco near a couple of my half brothers, so I went there to meet them all. I instantly made a deep connection with my sister that would both complicate and inspire my quest to figure out my own identity. As a lesbian only a few months younger than me, she was like my own mirror image in many ways: how we walked, our gestures, our preferences for music, films, and even the women we were attracted to. We often joked that we were twins born of separate mothers. I couldn't tell her, but this familial connection with her made me so happy because I felt like I was one step closer in figuring out who I was. But I was uneasy still, because if I identified closely with my lesbian sister, what did that make me? I needed to find out.

The Biggest Failure of Character: A Surprise Visit from Bob Jones

My obsession in figuring out my identity through finding my birth family combined with spending time away from home with my gay friends put a strain on my marriage. And as much as I had distanced myself from the influence of BJU, I couldn't get Bob Jones Sr.'s saying out of my head: my character was being tested, but I couldn't—or wouldn't—stop. This was the beginning of the end of my marriage, and if the test of my character was what it took to stop me, then I was about to have the biggest failure of character that anyone could ever imagine.

One Sunday morning, I received a surprise, in-person visit from another Bob Jones, along with a similar feeling of failure. As I stood at the pulpit, I saw Bob Jones III and his family walk in after the service had begun and sit in the very back. I felt nervous. He shook hands with people, but because they came in late, I didn't get a chance to say anything to him. And then, after the service was over, he and his family were gone, without having said a word to me. I didn't expect that. This was the same man who had proudly given me his personal New Testament at the birth of my youngest son, but in Colorado he didn't even say goodbye.

I was left with only my assumptions about his quick departure. Maybe they were running late on their way to ski in the mountains and had to continue their trip. But I also had to wonder about his experience at my church. Maybe he had run into the guy who had suggested our HIV/AIDS outreach program and was unhappy with the trajectory of our congregation. Maybe he was taken aback by our ministry to the poor, especially by the visibly destitute woman who took care of the kids during church. Or maybe it was something as simple as a bathroom emergency that made him leave quickly. Whatever his reason was for leaving without communicating, his visit was a sign of how far I had strayed from BJU's influence. My time of acceptance by the "first family" had officially ended. My journey from being religious to being spiritual had begun.

After five years in Colorado, I resigned from the church, not necessarily because of intense spiritual conflicts, but definitely because of the threats of physical violence I received after hosting a Jewish man who had come to our church to condemn the local neo-Nazi community. After the story was published in the *Rocky Mountain News*, my family experienced various kinds of threats, and I knew it was my time to leave. I turned over the whole church to another BJU preacher boy who was living in Denver at the time, and I never looked back.

When we moved to California, we actively attended a church with a woman minister, and although we remained busy with the church, my wife and I knew that our divorce was imminent. She was going one direction in her life, and I another. Neither of us was very happy about that. We cried, hugged, and did the paperwork ourselves. It was a very amicable process, and we are still friends today.

Finally Finding Myself

I had been living in Stockton, California, for seventeen years when I received a DVD from Netflix called *Ma Vie en Rose* (My Life in Pink). As I watched the male child struggle with gender identity, I realized for the first time that I wasn't alone in these feelings. I searched the internet and learned all I could about transgender people and how they came to cope with the truth of who they are. I finally knew what I was and what I could do to reconcile my birth sex with my gender identity. I began my transition from male to female on June 6, 2008, one week to the day after seeing that DVD.

Never before in my life, with the possible exception of preschool, had I felt so alive, so authentic, and so happy to be alive each moment of every day. It's not that I didn't face huge obstacles and encounter numerous problems, but now that I knew why I was different, I could embrace that difference and live each day with confidence. One of my first thoughts was that there had to be others out there suffering needlessly. So eight months after I began my transition, I founded the Stockton Transgender Alliance and began to reach out to this community of almost three hundred thousand people. The alliance folded into the San Joaquin Pride Center in October 2011 and continues to help more than one hundred transgender people, their families, and friends as they and their loved ones go through the transition process.

In December 2010 I realized that I knew very many spiritual transgender women, and I founded a multi-faith "convent" (called the Order of Saint Hildegard) for transgender-identified women to pursue their own spiritual path and perform works of social justice. It was very well received and attracted the attention of other affirming and welcoming congregations all over Northern California. I am very proud of the positive impact our convent had on the community.

While living in California, I met a friend who had just returned from Thailand on vacation. She told me how beautiful the place was, but also how sad it was that many women and girls are taken advantage of there. I knew I wanted to see the place for myself and to help in whatever way I could. I wound up living there for six years, and in that time, I loved everything about the country. I worked with elderly people who needed help getting to doctors and the pharmacy or who needed help with rent and food. I've come a long way from begging in front of that McDonald's in Denver as a teen, but I know what it's like to be out there and hungry. During the summer of 2019, I returned briefly to live in California, but I have already made plans to return to Thailand.

I have three mothers: my birth mother, my adopted mother, and Mother Mary. All three of them still speak to me and help direct my path. I've learned that I have to follow what is right for me. If I hear something that sounds good for me, I have to take it on myself. Of course, this kind of advice is in direct contradiction to another famous chapel message by Dr. Bob Sr., titled "Do Right though the Stars Fall." Specifically, he said, "You students in Bob Jones University know what is right. We have told you over and over again that the two biggest words in the English language are the two little words, DO RIGHT. We have said over and over again, 'Do right regardless of the consequences. Do right if the stars fall.'"[3] For Bob Sr., doing right meant following BJU's placement of the authority of the Bible. But just like so many other of his chapel sayings that I have forgotten, this one has lost its power over me too. I might have needed his words back then, but I don't need them anymore. I still correlate femininity with the divine. How could I not? She has been with me since I was three. It took almost fifty years, but I have finally found myself.

Notes

1. Jones, *Chapel Sayings of Dr. Bob*, 8.

2. For more description about Bob Jones IV's expulsion, see Merritt, *Secrets of a Gay Marine*, 66–67.

3. Jones, "Do Right Though the Stars," 10.

chapter 17 STEVE SHAMBLIN

> While I moved my stuff to the porch, my friend who
> had come with me carried the stuff from the porch
> to the U-Haul. But after about twenty minutes, my
> yard started filling up with people from BJU, peo-
> ple I used to work with. Some were faculty and staff;
> others were deans. Soon it became clear they all
> were there to form a prayer chain—men standing
> side by side and praying out loud—across the yard to
> block my friend from loading things.

BJU: An Investment of Half of My Life

They say hindsight is twenty-twenty. Looking back at these last approximately twenty years since I've not been allowed on Bob Jones University's campus because I'm gay, I never thought I'd say that BJU had a positive effect on my life, but my story shows how it did.

In August 1999 I was months away from my thirty-sixth birthday. By
that point, I had spent half of my life, eighteen years, at BJU. I had graduated from BJU with a BA in art in 1985 and an MS in counseling in 1997;
plus, I had been taking additional courses toward the educational doctor-
ate program. Since 1985 I had been on BJU staff and eventually served
as the business office manager for several years while also occasionally
teaching part time as an art faculty member. Additionally, I was married
with three children. But most of all, I was gay—I am gay, and after I came
out, my years of service meant nothing to BJU.

Within days of my coming out, I had lost my job and all connection to
a set of friends I had worked with for fourteen years. My marriage dis-
integrated, and my family would never be the same. What's more, I received a letter from BJU saying that I would be arrested if I came onto
campus, and I received another letter from Morningside Baptist Church

telling me I was no longer welcome there, where I had spent years working with the children's Bible program. On top of that, the Bob Jones University Alumni Association ended my paid lifetime membership.

Church had always been a part of my life, though. I grew up in West
Virginia, and when I was in kindergarten, my mother was saved and became an active member of the church, taking us kids with her. I was in
church for Sunday school, morning worship, afternoon youth group,
Monday night Awana club, and Wednesday night prayer meeting. On Friday nights we worked on the church bulletin, and on scheduled Saturdays
we cleaned the church. We also participated in Vacation Bible School and
any special meetings or revival services.

As a kid, I made a profession of faith. However, my fear of water kept
me from being baptized until I was in late junior high school, but I finally
went through with it because only full members of the church who'd been
baptized could hold an office. When I reached high school, I played the
organ for Sunday services and was elected to be the church clerk, taking
all minutes for business meetings and handling church membership rolls.

Technically, I didn't always know that I was "gay" because I did not
have that vocabulary in my youth, but as a child, I was attracted to boys.
Junior high was rough. I hated gym class, but I loved the shower time because it allowed me to appreciate the male body. Most guys around this
time noticed girls and took them to dances, but I happily credit my fundamentalist Baptist church as my official excuse for not having a girlfriend. I wasn't allowed to go to dances or movies, so that pretty much
took care of social activities in my small West Virginia town. This pattern
of not dating girls continued in high school as I conveniently hid behind
my religion.

BJU's Convincing Promotional Strategy

BJU came on my radar my last year of high school. In February of 1981,
the brass ensemble from BJU visited our church. As part of BJU's promotional strategy, the school sends out different traveling musical and dramatic ministry teams or ensembles throughout the year to visit churches
and Christian schools around the country. BJU's strategy was very successful because those six guys looked very sharp. All of them wore collar
bars with their ties and looked very professional.

My parents and I were so impressed with them that we went to see
them in a church an hour away that next week and in other churches the

next few weeks while they were still in the area. I was convinced, so I applied to BJU and was accepted, turning down a math scholarship I had to the state university in the process. I wouldn't fully appreciate my college decision until approximately thirty years later.

My parents separated right after graduation, which made leaving home even harder, but I still was determined to go to BJU, so my mom took me to Greenville for the fall 1981 semester. In my three years on campus, I stayed in the Ernest Reveal dormitory. But my mother was hired at BJU right before the 1984 Bible Conference, so I moved out of the dorm and lived as a town student for the rest of my junior year and for all of my senior year.

During my freshman year, I met a senior girl from Bob Jones Academy who was friends with people I knew from elementary school. She had lived in a Maryland town near my little West Virginia town and attended the local Christian school with other kids from my church. I asked her out to lunch on campus in the dining common, and we wound up dating for four and a half years. (The university allowed college students to date academy students as long as there was no more than a two-year age difference.) She graduated in December 1985, and we married in February 1986.

After I graduated in August 1985, I worked on campus in the business office with the intent to stay only a few years. Instead, I kept getting promoted over the years while my wife remained as a faculty member. I began as a loan clerk, processing student loans the university offered since federal monies were not available. Within a year and a half, I was promoted to business office supervisor. After a few years in that position, I switched titles and became the university credit manager for a few years until I eventually merged the supervisor position with the credit manager position with a title of business office manager.

The Greenville Gay Resolution: BJU and County Council

In 1996 the Greenville County Council passed a resolution that announced that gays were not welcome in Greenville.[1] Before the vote on this resolution, BJU notified us of an interest meeting about the resolution that would be held in the city, so I went, not because I supported the resolution, but because I was curious to see what other gays looked like.

At the university, I had heard many times how wicked the gays were, how they lived in debauchery. As an example, the university told us about what had happened in San Francisco in 1993 to Hamilton Square Baptist

Church, whose pastor was a BJU board member. As the story goes, a mob of angry, violent gays had picketed against the church to show how much they hated religion.[2] Sermon illustrations like these held much more impact over me than any use of the Clobber Passages to show that the gays were wicked and trying to take over everything we held sacred.

These sermons always told us that gays were belligerent, anti-church, and anti-God. In fact, the year before I came to the university in 1980, Bob Jones III ruthlessly said that gays should be stoned because of their wickedness.[3] Ironically, when I went to that meeting, the belligerent people speaking were actually the ones *from* the churches. The LGBTQ members speaking would step up to the microphone and say how the ordinance discriminated against them. Their argument went back to church versus state and how the state shouldn't be creating a church with government policy. At the time, that county council had a number of BJU community members who were the ones pushing this ordinance, which should be no surprise, considering BJU's ties to the community go back to when the university was offered the land by the city. And with this long-standing tie of BJU's having the county council in its back pocket, it should be no surprise that the ordinance passed.

Contrary to what I had been taught, these gays did not appear wicked, but instead were regular people like those at the university—like me. As I left the meeting, the rainy weather had turned into a rainbow outside, and one of the nearby guys whose shirt identified him as gay noted, "That is *our* rainbow. God's promise to all of us. Someday, it will be different." I didn't tell anyone then, but I desperately wanted to believe his words.

After Dr. Bob Jr. died in November 1997, I was offered the art gallery director position, but I turned that down because it required a lot of travel: I knew myself enough to know the temptations on the road would be too great, and my suppressed sexuality would likely be discovered. Beginning in the spring of 1998, I became part of a group of younger men who were being groomed for administrative positions, meeting with Dr. Bob III every few weeks to discuss the history and mission of the school. Additionally, in the fall 1998 semester, I was asked to begin teaching a couple of art classes to freshman majors.

Trying to Find My Exit from BJU

By the spring of 1999, I wondered how much longer I could stay in the closet. For years I rose an hour before anyone in the house just to pray and read my Bible, always hoping to find some scriptural or divine break-through that would take the gay away. But I never found relief. I knew that the Apostle Paul had prayed many times to have something removed from his life, but even though he prayed, he still had it. Was that going to be my case? Was I just going to have to suppress these feelings, this part of me, for the rest of my life?

While I had loosely read about LGBT people and issues when I was out of town, I had started to use the internet to explore. I would often do this at night, after everyone was in bed. One night, as I was on a gay site, my wife snuck into the room. She asked what was going on, so I told her that I was gay. She immediately wanted me to tell the administration, but I told her that I needed time to figure out who I was.

At the same time, I had also decided to leave BJU to pursue a gradu-ate degree in education so that I could teach high school. I had already told the university of my general plan so I could train my replacement. In May 1999 I drove to Charleston, West Virginia, to check out a graduate program at a local university, which became a tedious task because my undergrad and master's degrees were unaccredited from BJU. BJU had spent years telling students that accreditation was not crucial for further-ing education or finding careers outside of Independent Fundamental Baptist circles, but I was experiencing all kinds of complications. While in West Virginia, though, I met in person some gay teachers who I had previously met online in a chat room. It was refreshing to meet people who were both gay and teachers with productive careers, which dispelled the stories told from the BJU chapel platform.

Locked Out: The Prayer Chain

In August 1999, I moved out of the house. It was not really what I had planned, but after my wife told her parents and the pastor at our church about the news, I knew it was my time to exit. My father-in-law was not happy about my plans, though. He purposely blocked my vehicle in the driveway to keep me from leaving so my wife could meet with the pastor about my leaving. When she returned, her father moved his vehicle.

I moved back to West Virginia with plans to begin graduate school, and when I told my plans to the teachers that I had met, they offered me a place to stay to get my head clear. Moving in with them marked the be-ginning of a ten-year relationship I would have with one of them.

About a month after moving out, I returned to Greenville to get the rest of my things, but when I got to the house, no one was there. My key didn't work, so I went next door and called for a locksmith. While I waited for the locksmith, two cars pulled up: a police car and then another car with my wife and her father. I showed the policeman my identification and told him the locks had been changed. He asked my wife if she had the key, and she asked if she had to let me in. The policeman said that I still owned the house as much as she did and that he'd "hate to see Mr. Shamblin have to bust out the leaded glass in the front door in order to get in." She let me in.

What followed next completely shocked me. I had parked the U-Haul along the street instead of in the driveway because of what my father-in-law had done in August. While I moved my stuff to the porch, my friend who had come with me carried the stuff from the porch to the U-Haul. But after about twenty minutes, my yard started filling up with people from BJU, people I used to work with. Some were faculty and staff; others were deans. Soon it became clear they all were there to form a prayer chain—men standing side by side and praying out loud—across the yard to block my friend from loading things. They were trying to obstruct my leaving and would not move an inch to allow passage out to the trailer. Their prayer chain was pretty hostile in both attitude and in physical placement on my property.

Fortunately, the policeman was still there. He told me that my presence had been called in as a "domestic dispute," but he now realized that wasn't the case. He also said he had called for backup because there was now "a hostile crowd in your yard." I didn't want to cause a scene. I just wanted to get out of there as quickly as possible, but having to walk around the prayer chain was slowing the process. All I needed to do, the policeman said, was to ask them to leave my yard while he was in earshot; that way, I could ask the police to remove them if they refused.

That's exactly what happened: I asked them to leave, but they continued to pray, so I asked the officers to remove them from my yard. With the officers' instructions, the people moved to the street, after which the police further dispersed them for blocking the street. I was truly thankful for the police's involvement. In all my years at BJU, I'd been aware of people leaving under negative circumstances or of couples divorcing—which was considered extremely taboo by the administration—but I had never witnessed any act of intimidation like this.

A few years later, I learned that my wife had temporarily moved onto campus with the kids shortly after I left in August because the university had convinced her I would return unannounced and commit violent acts (because gays are violent). She moved back in after I had retrieved my things that day in September. My mind went back to that county ordinance meeting: just like then, the hostile ones in this situation were the university and church people, not the gays (me, this time).

The Lasting Shadow of BJU and Fundamentalism

Even though I now lived in West Virginia, I couldn't shake the negative influence of BJU. The graduate school withdrew its initial approval because of BJU's not being accredited and the graduate school's recent change in administration, so I had to spend the next two years completing another bachelor's degree, this time in education.

During these two years, I worked in a landscape design center because a friend hired me, but I had wondered why I couldn't get other jobs until one day when one of my employers showed me the recommendation letter they had received from BJU. The university's letter gave incorrect employment dates and had a one-sentence statement about my work at BJU that said I "had good organization skills." After almost fourteen years working there—streamlining operations and procedures, training as rising administration, teaching classes—all I received was a one-sentence recommendation. That explained a lot of things. Thankfully, I successfully graduated and spent the next seventeen years teaching in the public schools of West Virginia, where I have been influenced by diversity in ways I couldn't have imagined. For example, in my Advanced Placement literature class one year, I had students representing seven different religions.

When I came out in 1999, I not only came out of the closet, but I also came out of fundamentalism and all things related to church. I figured that if the church and God didn't want me, then I didn't want them. Occasionally, I would attend a Christmas Eve service with my Catholic or Episcopal friends, or I would go to church with my kids when I was in Greenville, but that became awkward. Even more awkward, and somewhat humiliating, was when I had to acquire special permission to return to campus to attend my kids' graduations—just so I wouldn't be arrested. Above all, the most difficult part of being out was that no one really understood how much lasting influence BJU held on my life, especially as someone who now wanted nothing to do with the church but had spent my entire life up to age thirty-five connected to it.

The Gay BJU Reunion

After my ten-year relationship ended, I was in a relationship with a guy who was more familiar with church culture, which allowed for beneficial conversations. We were together for almost four years, until the fall of 2012. One night during the summer of 2011, when I couldn't sleep, I moved to the couch and googled "BJU" to catch up on the latest controversy. I came across a blog by a former faculty member who had been there while I was on staff. I was captivated by her blog because of the way she detailed how she and her husband had been treated on campus and also their eventual departure from BJU. Finally, I'd come across someone else who had experienced a similar wrath from BJU. That blog led me to a Facebook group filled with people who had gotten away from BJU as quickly as they could—or as quickly as the university had expelled them.

In that group was a gay guy who added me to a private Facebook group of about six or seven gay guys who had also been at BJU. Being added to that group was like finding long-lost brothers. The university's proclamations about the anomaly of being gay went out the window. More guys joined the group, and it felt like an online reunion. We remarked how comforting a group like this would have been when we had come out and thought we were alone. Furthermore, we discussed how many kids in fundamentalist circles have been kicked out of homes when they were found out to be gay, which prompted us to form an organization that would help people in those situations. By late winter, we had set up a board of directors and started working on bylaws for our organization.

In January 2012, we went live with our new website, LGBT-BJU, and published our coming out stories. Mine was the first to be published, and every week we tried to publish a new story, which always brought in web traffic, but we needed a name for our new organization. We floated around several suggestions, and mine fit: BJUnity, a shortened form of BJUniversity, without the "vers," since Bob Jones University in no way endorsed our organization. We drafted our mission statement and set a date for our first meeting to coincide with New York City Pride in June 2012.

With approximately fifty people, we held our own reunion there, which we called a ReConnect, and we marched as a group in the NYC Pride Parade. I will never forget the overwhelming emotions of acceptance and belonging as we marched behind our BJUnity banner down Fifth Avenue. I kept telling myself the lines from Tennyson's "Ulysses": "One equal temper of heroic hearts, / made weak by time and fate, but strong in will / to strive, to seek, to find, and not to yield."[4] We in BJUnity were doing just that—standing up against the ills of fundamentalism.

During this deeply emotional moment, I realized something startling: not all churches were the same. Church groups were scattered along the route and were passing out water to the gays marching in Pride—that was eye-opening, even shocking. Here were churches actually supporting us. They weren't sending out letters denouncing us or canceling our memberships. I was well aware of churches that BJU considered liberal and heretical, but I never imagined that these—or any—kind of churches could be open and affirming to the queer community.

Since New York City, we have annually marched at different Pride events, hoping our visibility will help those with similar backgrounds. In the first few years, people weren't sure if we were a joke, just a play on words (BJU). Hopefully as the years progress, BJUnity will be more well known.

A Life-Changing Parade

In 2015 our march in the Columbus, Ohio, Pride Parade changed my life and helped me better appreciate my time at BJU. We waited on State Street for the march to begin, and a man approached our director because he had seen our banner mention BJU. He introduced himself as the pastor of the United Methodist church group beside us and told us that he had attended BJU from 1978 to 1980. I was intrigued by this man, and as soon as he returned to his group, I asked who he was, but the card he gave our director only had the church name on it, not his. He eventually returned to our group: this time I paid attention, heard his name (Jeff Mullinix), and then immediately went to Facebook to find (stalk) him. But I couldn't find him. Thankfully, within a few minutes, I had a friend request from him. He had gone back to his group and was doing the same thing as I was. It turns out I had been misspelling his last name, while he easily knew mine because it was embroidered on my shirt.

I felt and acted like those boys I knew back in junior high: we texted until we began marching in the parade. We texted throughout the parade. We even chatted after the parade when our groups crossed paths. I wanted to get to know him better, so I invited him to attend that evening's ReConnect event. He came, and I monopolized his time that evening until he left the party early because of church services the next morning. Nevertheless, I still managed to take more of his time by texting back and forth with him until about 2 a.m.

Since Monday, June 22, 2015, we have talked on the phone every evening we were not together. We had our first date when I returned to Columbus on July Fourth weekend, and we continued our long-distance dating via phone for most of the summer. By Christmas 2015 I told my colleagues I was going to marry him, and I planned to propose to him over spring break, while we were in San Francisco visiting his daughter. On March 30, 2016, Jeff and I walked around the park at the Palace of Fine Arts, but before I could propose to him, he got down on his knee and proposed to me first—and with the exact ring that I had in my pocket for him. I was stunned, to say the least. After I said, "Yes," he stood up, and I got down on my knee and pulled out my ring for him. He was just as stunned as I was. I'm still amazed that the two of us picked out the identical ring at different jewelry stores three hours apart without any conversation between us.

Providential Return to Church Culture

My return to church culture was gradual, but it feels nice to be back. I had become a regular attendee at Jeff's church, leaving Charleston, West Virginia, on Fridays after school to be in Columbus for the weekends. During that time, I began to meet and know people in the congregation. For the most part, these were older people, which made it even more surprising that people from older, conservative generations would welcome me into the church. Each week, they would greet me before services. During the Passing of the Peace time, some wouldn't settle for a handshake and would give me a genuine hug instead. Some even invited us to join them for meals.

This was not the kind of church I had known in my previous years. Their mission wasn't to draw lines to keep people out; they were looking for ways to reach into the community, to love and help their neighbors next door, not those on some idealized mission field. Eventually, I began helping in the ministry at Jeff's church by creating altarscapes. After a year, I joined the church, which led to serving communion, leading adult Lenten studies, and even directing Vacation Bible School.

Our wedding ceremony itself serves as another example of how providential it was for us to be together and also how exceptional our congregation was toward us. When this congregation heard of our plans to get married in another church, they asked why, which was more a question about the United Methodist church's ban on same-sex weddings in the church. The administrative council then called for a vote to allow us to get married in *our* church. Not only did they make the church available to us, which was contrary to the UMC's rules, but a number of people—again older folks who I had always assumed were against the queer community—stepped up to serve at our reception.

On that icy December day, we had about two hundred guests share the day with us. Looking at the guest registry after the wedding, we saw that about seventy-five guests were church members, which for our church represented about 75 percent of the regular attendees. As Jeff and I did our row-by-row dismissal so that we could speak to everyone there without the long wait of a receiving line, there was one dear old saint who brought tears to my eyes. She was about eighty-five and had been sick at home for the past week. As we thanked her for coming and questioned her health, she told us, "There was no way I was going to miss this wedding." This was a very different kind of church that welcomed me back. It was a magical time for me.

Growing up in a fundamentalist church, the only thing I really internalized was that we were true Christians because we did everything we were supposed to. It was like a religious checklist of church behavior. Ironically, my mother's oldest sister was part of the United Methodist Women. She attended church some and was always involved with things outside of Sunday church, like doing bake sales, but she drank beer and cussed sometimes. My mother often said, "Aunt Lee, she goes to the Methodist church, but she's not Christian." Now I realize that Aunt Lee exercised her faith to others in the community in many more ways than our whole fundamentalist church did. She truly reached out in love to her neighbors; she wasn't keeping a scorecard on how they were or weren't living up to a naughty-or-nice list.

My Wilderness Experience: Erasing the Fundamentalism

I've recently been calling my sixteen-year hiatus from church my "wilderness experience"—referring to the lengthy time in the Old Testament that the children of Israel wandered in the wilderness before reaching the Promised Land. My time away from church allowed me to clear my head of the fundamentalism that had filled it for so many years. It took a while to establish my own sense of my theology, especially after my BJU education.

When I was at BJU, I had been heavily interested in the ministry: I took thirty hours of Bible classes required for the graduate school theology program, I took Greek as my foreign language, and I took the Preacher Boys class as well, which was required for ministerial students and optional for other male students. Dr. Bob Sr. had created the class to keep the ministerial students up to date about current issues in churches and fired up about evangelism.

But my interest in ministry hadn't stopped there. As an upperclassman, I drove a group of students to North Carolina and preached at nursing home services on Saturday evenings. After my undergrad, I started the graduate theology program, but I only finished half of it because, deep down, I knew that being gay disqualified me from the ministry. (That hesitancy was certainly confirmed when I was kicked out of my Baptist church when I came out.) I couldn't live with the fear that someone would discover my secret. Yet thirty years after graduating from BJU, having given up on any thought of going into the ministry, I met and married a minister. I sometimes joke that I never thought I'd be a "pastor's wife," but I wholeheartedly give thanks that the BJU connection brought Jeff and me together, even though I know that Dr. Bob Sr. would not approve of how I turned out as a former Preacher Boys student.

Complications in the United Methodist Church

As it's a fundamentalist institution, BJU's stance against gay marriage is not surprising, but being a married gay clergy in the United Methodist church presents its own set of issues, too. The rulebook of the church, the Book of Discipline, states that homosexuality is incompatible with Christian teaching. This statement was introduced into the UMC in 1972, four years after its establishment when the Methodist church and the Brethren Church united. Over the years, sexuality has become the big sticking point of the denomination. Each year, progressives have tried to change the language to be inclusive of the LGBTQ community, and each year the conservatives try to add more restrictive measures. In previous General Conferences—the once-every-four-year conference of all international delegates to create and to vote on church policy—the language has been expanded to restrict United Methodist churches from hosting same-sex weddings, to prohibit church funds from being used for LGBTQ ministry, to penalize clergy who are openly gay, and even to remove their clergy credentials with the church.

By May 2016 the UMC General Conference was at its breaking point. Many wanted to split the church. In an attempt to prevent this, the General Conference voted to have the bishops create a Commission on the Way Forward. This commission group was a representation of bishops, clergy, and laity, straight and queer, progressive and conservative. A Special General Conference happened in February 2019 to vote on the plans developed by the commission.

In February 2019, Jeff and I went to the Special General Conference as observers. We watched as three plans were presented to almost nine hundred worldwide delegates. The majority of bishops had recommended the One Church Plan, which would allow each church to decide how it would minister with or exclude the LGBTQ community. For the first time since the 2016 General Conference, many different lobby groups were making strategies to get their favored plan passed. The Traditional Plan, which increased penalties against LGBTQ clergy and churches, passed with a small majority. While the majority of the U.S. delegates favored the One Church Plan, which allowed local contextualization, many of the foreign delegates were adamantly against it, and their vote along with the U.S. minority vote passed the new measures with 56 percent.

Podcasting and Preaching Opportunities

During this conference, Jeff and I met the team from the *Crackers and Grape Juice* podcast. I had been listening to the podcast over the past couple of years on my weekly commute between West Virginia, where I was still teaching, and Columbus, Ohio, where Jeff was still pastoring. The podcast, which bills itself as "talking faith without stained glass language," has a team that includes three UMC pastors, and they had come to the special session to do daily reporting. Jeff and I were invited to be guests on one of their live broadcasts, to talk about our story and how it affects ministry.[5]

After that, we were invited to Roanoke, Virginia, in June 2019 to be featured guests again on the podcast. On the evening before the Virginia Annual Conference, *Crackers and Grape Juice* was hosting a podcast at Ballast Point Brewery, where we again shared our story and discussed how things were changing in the denomination. As we closed the podcast that evening, Jeff presided over communion, which was very special. Although we only knew the three guys from the podcast at the time, to share in communion with others in our denomination, many of whom were also working toward an inclusive church, was a very touching moment for me.[6]

Not only have I married a minister, but I have also had the opportunity to preach myself. During the month of May 2019, the bishop of the West Ohio UMC Annual Conference had asked for all churches to focus on the book of Galatians, having experienced the 2019 Special General Conference. (The Annual Conference in the UMC is a regional district made up of all of the clergy as well as elected laypersons who together do business for that district, such as budgets, resolutions, initiatives, and clergy ordinations. While the General Conference is the international elected body that has representation from every regional district, the annual conferences meet yearly to do the local business. The General Conference meets every four years to do the work—new guidelines, operations, finances—of the whole of the UMC.) In light of the Special General Conference in February 2019, where international representatives voted with a narrow majority to *increase* sanctions against LGBTQ clergy and churches that allowed same-sex weddings, the bishop had chosen the theme of the Gospel of Grace.

For the Sunday service that I preached, the text was Galatians 5— the Fruitfulness of Grace. I had asked Jeff if I could preach this specific service because the passage held great meaning for me. That morning I shared much of what I have shared here about my journey. I told the congregation:

> A couple of verses that I had memorized many years prior started popping in my head. One of them was Romans 8:1, "There is therefore now no condemnation to them who are in Christ Jesus." The other was Galatians 5:1, "Stand fast therefore in the liberty wherewith Christ hath made us free." The constant remembrance of those two verses would drive me back into studying the Bible and dusting off my Greek to re-read and study to find a theology that may be different from what I had experienced for more than thirty years.
>
> I am here because of verses that I had memorized many years before God would use them in my life: "Stand fast therefore in the liberty wherewith Christ hath made us free." That is the Grace of the Gospel.
>
> Let us pray: God of great grace and infinite love. May the Spirit of mystery and communion sweep over us this morning. Quiet the noise of life

and the world in these moments. May the words of my mouth and the meditation of all our hearts be acceptable to you. Amen.

When I preached that sermon, neither Jeff nor I understood that the spirit of mystery would soon be moving us to Washington State, a place neither of us knew, to a church where we knew no one.

Moving On

On July 10, 2019—almost twenty years after the prayer chain incident on my front lawn—the moving van was loaded for our move. On the morning of July 11, Jeff and I along with Wesley, our year-and-a-half-old black lab–boxer mix, began our westward trek in two vehicles. Five days later, we met the trustee in Bonney Lake, Washington, for the keys to our parsonage.

Even from that initial meeting, we were welcomed with food and necessities sitting on our kitchen counters. Several of the church members stopped by the house to lend a hand in the unpacking or just to get a chance to welcome us, even before our first Sunday at Foothills United Methodist Church. Again, I was overwhelmed by people who actually welcomed us into their church and lives. They worshiped with us. They fellowshiped with us. And they have allowed me the opportunity to get involved.

In September 2019 Jeff began to have some mobility issues and pain in his back and legs. From the first of September to mid-October when we met with a surgeon, Jeff could barely stand and had to walk with a cane. He couldn't drive, either. The surgeon told us that three of Jeff's neck discs were compressing his spinal cord and needed surgery. On the first Monday of November, Jeff had surgery to remove those three discs and was confined to very limited activity while he healed.

For the two Sundays that he convalesced, I preached again. This time, one sermon would be about personalizing ministry, while the other would be about prioritizing ministry. For someone who thought that preaching and ministry would never happen for me, I have been pleasantly surprised at these opportunities.

While the surgery has given Jeff back his mobility and physical therapy is increasing it, I still have been looking for a teaching position. We moved so late in the year that all vacancies were filled for the fall. This is the first time in nineteen years that I have not been in a classroom on opening day. I can't help but think that some of the delay in my finding a position was to allow me to be free to care for Jeff through this time. Though it has been very discouraging at times, "I am confident of this, that *the one* who began a *good work* among *you* will bring it to completion by the day of Jesus Christ" (Philippians 1:6, NRSV).

Since then, I've enjoyed more preaching opportunities, such as when Jeff traveled to Ohio for a family wedding in March 2020, or when he had additional surgery in October 2020. During Holy Week 2020, because of the pandemic, Jeff and I recorded daily devotionals for the congregation. The day we went to the cemetery to record an Easter sunrise devotional, Jeff said, "You know, you should really consider ministry." I had never forgotten his Christmas 2018 sermon when he asked, "What is God calling you to do?" because my answer was to pursue the ministry, but our move to Washington had made it impossible to continue those desires at the time. But his comment at the cemetery gave me a clear sign that ministry was indeed in my future.

In April I contacted the UMC district superintendent about the process of becoming a Licensed Local Pastor (LLP), sharing with her the call and journey that I had been on. While I would like to go to seminary for a master of divinity, the process of years to do full ordination as an elder would take me almost to retirement age. Instead, the LLP would allow me to be assigned to a church as a pastor. Part of that process is being recommended by the church council to become a candidate for ministry as well as being voted on by the whole congregation to proceed in that candidacy. The next steps would then be with the district and conference boards of ministry for interviews about my call and theology as well as attending the pastoral licensing school. On November 17, 2020, the Foothills UMC Leadership Council and the district superintendent met with me to interview me about recommending me as an LLP candidate to the congregation. On Sunday, November 29, at the annual church charge conference, the congregation voted to move me forward as a candidate to ministry. I can truly say that as a closeted gay preacher boy at BJU, I never thought that openly out, married me would ever become a pastor.

Telling My Story: My Accidental Ministry

While I grew up in fundamentalist churches that operated more as a selective club than as an inclusive place for all people, I have finally found churches and people who aren't like that. I never dreamed that I'd ever come out of both the closet and fundamentalism, nor did I ever imagine that the journey would lead me *back* to church.

I tell my story often because I know someone out there needs to hear it. In fact, I have never hidden my story in my classroom. In the past two high schools where I have taught, I have sponsored students who wanted to start a gay-straight alliance. As a member of the American Federation of Teachers–West Virginia and a local officer, I have stood in front of the state convention to advocate for resolutions to support state legislation that would protect the LGBTQ community in housing and employment.

In November 2017 I was interviewed by a journalist with the *Charleston Gazette-Daily Mail*. On November 6, the nearly full-page article appeared with the title, "Gay Teacher Shares Story of Journey to Truth."[7] If people in my school district and community were not sure about my orientation before, that article definitely settled the matter. I had students and colleagues stop by my room for support. I had parents thank me for my presence in the school. As a member of our district's diversity collaborative, I suggested and led the district in recognizing one week per year as Inclusive Schools Week, and I was part of the team that developed and delivered professional development sessions to educators in preparation for that. This week of observation has now become an annual part of the district's calendar of activities.

The Inclusive Schools Week initiative illustrates how passionate I am to make my classroom a safe space for everyone. I have made it a point to include social issues discussions with the literature that I teach. One of my greatest teaching joys is to hear from former students who have shared their coming-out stories and thanked me for being authentic in the classroom. What's more, it is not unusual for me to get messages on Facebook from people wanting more information about being inclusive, especially in religious circles where the LGBTQ community is renounced as sinful and, in the words of the United Methodist rules, "incompatible."

One of the most recent messages I received was from a mother in West Virginia whose son had recently come out. She had been raised in conservative, fundamentalist churches and had been taught that being gay is a sin. When her son came out, she knew there had to be something more, so she started researching how others reconciled their religion and sexual orientation. In her research, she came across the *Gazette* article about me and reached out to me, knowing that I had been through all the same religious obstacles. We had a wonderful dialogue: I found out that her son was going to the homecoming dance with his boyfriend and that she was totally supportive. She, of course, was worried about her son's safety, but I was relieved to discover that her son attended the very high school I had just left. He was in good hands in the district where I and others had worked so hard to make sure everyone was accepted. These are just a few of the examples why I continue to tell my story often.

When I preached on November 10, 2019, at our new church, Foothills United Methodist in Buckley, Washington, I shared part of my story. The focus for the month of November was on ministry. That Sunday, my sermon was "Personalizing Ministry: The Faithfulness of Stewardship." In my message I said:

> We all have stories to tell. I tell my story often. *Maybe* too often. Sometimes, I tell it in small groups where I am comfortable—sometimes, in larger groups where I am not so comfortable. One thing I have learned from experience, and I know as a literature teacher, is that stories are often the connecting points between people. It's our stories that can be used to minister to others. Telling my personal story has given me, for lack of a better term, accidental ministry: an accidental ministry of connecting with some of the marginalized youth in schools and communities. Many of these kids may never be in church, and that's ok. For this ministry, my classroom was the place of connection. And every one of us here today has a whole sphere of people and places and connections through which to minister—and you may not even know about the ministry you had, until years later. You just have to be present and share.

I wanted my words to the congregation to be just as encouraging as they would be to anyone who may read this chapter, which is why I also said in that November 10 sermon: "Nothing pushes you to deconstruct quicker than having the world you've known for thirty-five years suddenly and abruptly stop. In hindsight, that was the best thing that happened to me. It caused me to reevaluate everything that I had learned and heard in church. It gave me a new perspective." My coming-out was not just out of the closet but also out of the fundamentalist church. That dual coming-out has led me on a journey of finding myself and of finding my faith. I left behind a very limited and angry God of the fundamentalists and am happy to have experienced a God who is so much bigger and more loving.

Notes

1. Slack, "Gay Rights Movement."
2. Innes, *The Little Church of Hamilton*, 65.

3. NBCNews.com, "Bob Jones III Apologizes."
4. Tennyson, lines 68–70.
5. Marshell, "Voices of the General Conference."
6. Marshell, "Episode 213—Live Podcast."
7. Wells, "Innerviews: Gay Teacher Shares Story."

chapter 18   CHRISTY HAUSSLER

> I was still so closed off emotionally from people. Besides, the social structure of BJU made me feel awkward around guys anyway. We were not trusted to be alone with men—ever—because of BJU's fear of sexual temptation, yet the school simultaneously placed an inordinate amount of effort to desexualize any desires we might have. The mixed signals created a confusing dating atmosphere, which made me even more comfortable not having to deal with men in my life.

Portrait of a Christian Lesbian: My Fundamentalist Beginnings

My path to becoming a Christian lesbian feminist would probably be considered an unconventional one at best. Who I am today is a far cry from the girl who surrendered her heart to a life of service to God as a full-time missionary. I accepted Christ in my kindergarten Sunday school class and was baptized shortly thereafter. Growing up, I thought I would spend my life on the mission field, winning souls to Christ as my vocation. By doing so, my own sense of worthlessness and self-hatred could be overcome, especially if I wrapped myself tight enough in a Savior who I had been taught would condemn me if I revealed to anyone, including myself, who I really was. Thus began my lifelong journey of denial.

I grew up in Decatur, Alabama, in a loving Christian home. My parents had a happy marriage, and I was the middle child—I had an older sister and a younger brother. When I say that I was raised in church, I don't mean that I grew up in a family who made it a habit to attend church; I mean, I was literally raised in church. We were there as a family a minimum of three times a week, or every time the doors were open. Not only did we attend church regularly, but I also went to Christian schools throughout my childhood. My parents strongly believed in Christian education, so even the thought of going to a public school seemed completely foreign to me.

To give you an idea the type of dogma my church taught, let me briefly explain its extreme focus on all types of sin. Even though we were taught that we were born as sinners into a fallen world, we were also told that we needed to be as sinless as possible. On the occasions that we did fall into sin, repentance had to be immediate, or else the judgment of God would come upon us. From the pulpit, we were taught that all forms of sex outside of marriage were wrong. Homosexual activity was especially worthy of damnation, oftentimes presented to us as the unforgivable sin.

We were constantly reminded about our own worthlessness too: the only good we were capable of doing was because of God, not from our own capacity. God was not to be questioned, nor was our pastor or our faith. To be spiritually enriched, we had to be fully submissive to the church and its rules.

Today, I can easily recognize this kind of mind control as a form of biblical abuse, but I couldn't back then, when I was in a constant state of repentance, consumed by my long list of flaws to remedy so that I could be fully righteous in God's eyes. Today, I can identify so many inconsistencies in the theology of my youth that formed the foundation of my self-loathing because I was different from the other kids in my peer group.

It's hard enough to reconcile the social stigma of being queer without even considering the additional burdens of a religious paradigm. It is no surprise, then, that queer youth contemplate suicide at a higher rate than the general population: queer kids don't want to live with the stigma of their queerness.[1] My self-loathing as a queer kid prompted me to make every effort to deceive myself about myself. I couldn't face the alternative: rejection from my family and religious community.

I didn't know the word for it at the time, but I have since realized that Christian fundamentalism thrives on tribalism: differences and diversity were seen as rebellion, empathy for why others couldn't embrace our ideology was frowned upon, and conformity without questioning was rewarded. No wonder queer youth raised in this kind of religious subculture travel a long journey for self-acceptance as God's creation.

Early on, we were indoctrinated that Bob Jones University was a college approved by both our church and school. In addition to the BJU cur-

riculum being taught in our classrooms, we were always hosting evange-
listic teams, ensembles, and drama teams from BJU at our church, so we
constantly received the message that if you were following God's plan for
your life, you would go to BJU too. In my particular situation, discern-
ing God's will for a college was made a little easier when my father told us
that if we went to BJU, he would pay for our college education. However,
if we went anywhere else, we would have to pay for it ourselves. Not much
more needed to be said about my choice.

Necessary Obedience and the Threat of Purges at BJU

As a child brought up in fundamentalism, I was taught to obey. I wanted
to please the adults around me, so I wasn't at all resistant to going to BJU;
in fact, I looked forward to it. Here was my chance to be a part of this
godly college that always felt like the pinnacle of spirituality and Christian fun whenever BJU teams would visit. I wanted to look just as spiritual and put-together as all those college students who were paraded in
front of our church and school my whole life.

In retrospect, I went to BJU at exactly the right time in my life to have
a good experience. I began my college career there in September of 1987
and went straight through and graduated in May of 1991. As a product
of the fundamentalist system that constantly reinforced the necessity of
obedience, I had little trouble adjusting to life there. I completely bought
into its dogma and followed every rule to garner favor with those in authority and also to avoid being called out for spiritual problems.

I had not started thinking for myself yet, nor had I begun to question
God or His path for my life. Instead, I was seeking God's will the only way
I had been taught: by passively soaking up all of the teaching during my
entire college experience. Since I grew up believing that critical thinking
is akin to rebellion, I fit right in with how BJU operates. It should be no
surprise that such an obedient kid made it through college with minimal
demerits and without committing any major infractions.

In fundamentalism, obedience often is the product of fear, and my
experience with fear was no different at BJU. I was terrified of getting
"shipped" (expelled). I knew it could happen quickly to anyone who succumbed to temptation and made a bad choice. Every time there was a
"purge"—a period where many students would get shipped because of an
investigation into their infractions—it rippled through the entire campus
as a warning to others who might choose the wrong path. People could

get kicked out of BJU for what now seem like very minor things: attending a movie at a theater (even G-rated), renting an R-rated movie from Blockbuster, visiting a home off campus with a group of young men and women without an official chaperone, or committing what we would consider more serious offenses like drinking or stealing. When these purges happened, the verse "be sure your sin will find you out" always came to mind.[2]

However, as scary as those purges sounded, I was never overwhelmed by them because in my estimation, those who got shipped were the "bad" kids; they had made poor choices and broken the rules. I had no reason to fear because I was "good": compliant, obedient, submissive, and never questioning. And that is exactly what BJU wanted—absolute submission.

The Christian Lesbian Self-Deception at BJU

As I mentioned, part of my fundamentalist mentality never allowed me to dwell on the thought that I could be gay. I had to constantly deceive myself. At school and church, we were well aware of what heathen homosexuals looked and acted like to make them such an abomination to God.

I remember countless sermons preached about Romans 1:26–29. This passage mentions how God allowed a certain group of people to be given over to their depravity because they exchanged the natural for the unnatural. The reference is to gay people, as it describes men exchanging what was natural with women for what is unnatural with men. It also talks about how these unrighteous people would be punished for engaging in these unnatural passions and be doomed to live a life apart from God. I desperately did not want to fall on the wrong side of God's favor. I wanted to live a righteous life and have others perceive me as a model Christian. I earnestly loved God and wanted to serve Him in full-time Christian service. No gay person would ever do that, right? I had to find comfort in this line of thinking as I maintained my self-deception.

This self-deception was strong at BJU. I can't help but admit I was a dead ringer for a Christian lesbian. I majored in health and physical education, so I hung out in the gym all day with other sporty girls, many of whom I had crushes on. The PE department was flush with single female teachers who had worked for BJU for years but had never married, never dated, and never really ventured too far from the safe cocoon of the department. Many of these teachers looked gay to me: they were more masculine than a lot of women on campus, they didn't wear a lot of makeup, and they didn't do much to enhance their desirability to men. Most men would never consider women like these in the PE department to be attractive, and that was fine with me because I wasn't trying to attract attention from the guys, either.

But it was a delicate balance for me. I followed feminine norms and always wore makeup and never missed an opportunity to buy new lipstick. I would tweeze my eyebrows with the best of them! I still wanted to be attractive and look like every other lady. The more I could look like a "normal" person, the better I could convince myself that I was just like every other lady on campus.

At this point in my life, I didn't identify as a lesbian, but I was definitely intrigued by those around me who I felt might be. Perhaps even then, without knowing the proper terminology, I was making good use of my gaydar. Furthermore, I wasn't aware of the stereotypes associated with female PE teachers. I mean, after all, I was going to teach in a Christian school or on the mission field, so why would anyone ever think I could fit a gay stereotype? I reasoned with myself that we certainly couldn't trust male coaches in the female locker room, so of course there had to be female PE teachers, no matter how gay they might appear while dressed in culottes.

Even though dating one-on-one wasn't permitted at BJU, the school provided many social activities that were considered opportunities for "dating." For example, each society (BJU's alternative to fraternities and sororities) hosted a dating outing once a year. Members were expected to ask someone of the opposite sex to attend as our date; otherwise, we didn't even attend. Throughout my entire time as a student, I only went on two of these dating outings, both times with a guy I wasn't romantically interested in. We participated in the activities as if we were strangers, so with no real connection, there was never any follow-up contact.

Dating outings were a yearly reminder that I didn't fit in with BJU's heterosexual expectations. But there was a painful, daily reminder, too, of just how lonely I felt. The inter-dormitory note system would kick into full force every evening after sundown. Each dorm had these long wooden boxes in the lobby with designated sections in the boxes for each of the men's dormitories. If you wanted to send a note to a member of the opposite sex, you would write it during the day, putting the person's name, dorm, and room number on the envelope, and then you would drop it in the respective box. Many students would spray the crap out of their letters with cologne or perfume, so you can imagine the combined stench coming from the boxes each night. Different societies would be responsible for collecting and delivering the notes each week. Around 9–10 p.m. each night, notes would be slipped under the recipients' door and the occupants of those rooms would rejoice in their new deliveries. So many of my roommates who were dating steadily got those darn notes every night, while I, on the other hand, probably received one or two notes my entire four years of college. It was a new opportunity to feel rejection every day.

Given my need for self-deception to maintain my persona as a BJU Christian, it's probably no surprise that I was very closed off emotionally from everyone during these years. Besides, the social structure of BJU made me feel awkward around guys. We were not trusted to be alone with men—ever—because of BJU's fear of sexual temptation, yet the school simultaneously placed an inordinate amount of effort to desexualize any desires we might have. The mixed signals created a confusing dating atmosphere, which made me even more comfortable not having to deal with men in my life.

I graduated from BJU in 1991 without having had a serious boyfriend. I was acutely aware that many of my friends were dating, engaged, or getting married, while I hadn't even entered the dating field yet. I wasn't self-aware enough to feel like maybe I had missed my best opportunity to find a husband while at BJU, but I didn't have any desire to date any of the guys I did know. Instead, I felt like I was going to be single for a while, especially because I couldn't imagine having to share my life with anyone at this point.

"Homosexual Tendencies":
Making the Administration Uncomfortable as a PE Teacher

After graduation, I faced a difficult transition to the real world. Since I had only ever been in Christian schools growing up, I never really entertained the thought of getting a secular job: I was afraid of the real world and had no idea how I would fit in. I tried teaching at a Christian school, but my horrible experience there completely quashed any aspirations I had for the mission field. In my teaching efforts, I made the administration uncomfortable in ways I couldn't have predicted.

I was recruited by a well-known Christian school in the BJU network to teach girls' PE and be the women's athletic director. I moved into a tiny apartment that the church owned, which was across the street from both the church and school. Even though I was in a strange city, I was surrounded by the familiar construct of the church's school and sports teams. I felt like I could make it work.

I coached girls' volleyball and basketball, which meant that I had a different relationship with my students than the other teachers in a traditional classroom. I had to take the girls on overnight trips to play in tournaments, and I became extremely close to all the girls on my teams. I allowed some of the senior girls to hang out with me at my apartment, and we would also go out to eat together. These actions might be a rookie teacher's mistake, but the fact of the matter is that no adults in that church or school ever made an effort to befriend me, so the senior female athletes on my team became my only friends. Besides, I was only about two or three years older than them, so I felt more kindred with them than I did their parents or other older teachers in the school. But not everyone appreciated what I was doing.

I started teaching there in August. By the middle of October, I had been called in to the principal's office. In no uncertain terms, he asked me to resign because he thought I had "homosexual tendencies," but he told me to say in my official letter of resignation that I had resigned for "personal reasons." I was mortified, blindsided, and speechless. Here I was serving my best in a fundamentalist Christian school approved by BJU, but my efforts were clouded by my principal's fear of my committing an unforgivable sin.

This was the first time anyone had ever insinuated that I could be a lesbian. How could I respond? I obviously wasn't in a place to admit and embrace my queerness: I hadn't even admitted that to myself yet, but more importantly, I hadn't ever physically acted on my queer desires, and here he was accusing me of preying on high school girls. I didn't understand how I could deny his accusation either, so just like that, I resigned, packed my things, and left town within a day, as if I were running from the truth. I never told anyone what that principal said to me in private that day. Instead, I explained this crazy departure by creating a different narrative.

After this terrible experience, I was scared of doing any sort of Christian service jobs for fear of having a similar outcome, so I jumped into the secular world, determined to redeem myself, prove my worth as an employee, and put as much distance between me and the "lesbian" narrative as I could. After all, I was the only one who had heard those words from the principal, so there was no need to further examine them. It was better to just run from them. Once again, my self-deception was in high gear.

Does This Ford Explorer Make Me Look Gay?

I bounced around to a few different jobs and moved to several different cities—Memphis, Asheville, then back to Greenville—still trying to figure out where I fit in. Along the way, I stayed in church and was active in the "college and career" groups, but, honestly, none of the guys in these groups were dating material; they were socially awkward men who didn't know how to interact with anyone, much less women. I probably had only a handful of dates in the five years or so after college. Nothing ever got serious, and by that point I never even imagined myself with anyone romantically—male or female.

After settling into a steady job at a call center, I bought a house on my own in Greenville, South Carolina, and was still hanging out with a group of friends from BJU. Some of them were dating and engaged, and a few had gotten married, which is to be expected in BJU culture. But as long as I live, I will never forget a chilling incident that opened my eyes to my lack of identity self-awareness.

Around 1997 as I grew financially independent, I finally decided that I had worked hard enough to deserve a new car. I'm not really sure why, but I decided to buy a Ford Explorer. When my old roommate and friends who also went to BJU saw my car, one of them made a comment that a Ford Explorer was a "lesbian car" and that only lesbians drove Explorers. I have no idea if I had ever given off any lesbian vibes to them at this point. I also wasn't sure if the comment was just a random dig said in jest or if they were trying to get a confession from me. All I know is that I was totally blindsided by the comment, similar to how I felt when I was confronted by that principal.

After the shock of the statement wore off, the shame and denial crept in. Could it be true that I was so gay to the core that I inadvertently was drawn to the lesbian car? Did everyone who saw me in that car automatically think I was a lesbian? This probably was the first time I had ever allowed myself to even remotely entertain the thought that I could be gay. Of course, during this semi-revelatory moment, I still never said the words, not even to myself: denial was my safety net.

During the first ten years after college, I was in and out of church because I never really felt accepted there. At this stage in my life, I hadn't yet accepted myself or my trajectory, and I felt like I stood out at church because so many of my friends were getting married, having babies, and starting families. I was still single, unattached, and alone, and I was afraid to fully understand why I was this way.

There's a Church for Gay People?!

After some time passed, I met a few gay people at work and managed to form relationships with some of them while also gradually tolerating myself more. Even though I knew a few gay people at work, I didn't really fit in with what I had seen of the gay community either because let's face it: it's a really big transition from Bible-thumping BJU student to gay person while navigating the stereotypical scene of gay clubs, drag queens, and diesel dykes on a regular basis. It's just a lot to process. So while neither extreme was in my comfort zone, I began mentally letting my mind dwell on the fact that I probably was . . . gay. It was still a struggle because I didn't desire to be an abomination to God. I didn't want to have eternal damnation awaiting me in the afterlife. I had to figure out a way to reconcile the fact that God had created me with the reality that I was probably gay. I still loved God and wanted to be in Christian fellowship, but no church I knew of would tolerate me as a gay Christian.

By the time I had reached my midthirties, I had become more comfortable identifying as gay, but even though I was out at work, I had not yet dated a woman, nor had I told my family or any of my old friends from BJU. I kept it a secret from everyone I knew in my old life at BJU and its affiliated churches after I graduated. Also around this time, I was no longer attending church, but that would change the day I read an article that mentioned Metropolitan Community Church—a worldwide church started by gay people as a place for gay people to come back to the church and be fully accepted in all their gayness. My mind was blown.

I immediately found the MCC website and clicked on the "Find a Location" tab. I put in my location and almost fell out of my chair when it revealed a hit for Greenville, South Carolina. I ran over to a gay Christian coworker's desk and blurted out, "Did you know there is a gay church in Greenville?" She had never heard of it either, and for the next few weeks, I researched everything I could about the gay church. I drove by to check it out. It looked normal. I found the courage to attend a service, but I was afraid: it was the first time in my life going to a new church alone. Who or what would I find there? I was still very new to the LGBT scene and was a little bit nervous to meet people from this community who were different from me. When I attended, I noticed a diverse church population filled with diesel dykes, transgender people, and more. I was definitely out of my comfort zone.

That initial fear subsided as I expanded my circle of friends to include these new gay Christian friends at MCC Greenville. I heard story after story from them about how they had been kicked out of the church and marginalized by their families. These stories bound us together as we tried to soothe our pain and come to terms with who our creator made us to be. After all this time, I finally felt like I had found a home church doctrinally similar to my own background. It was basically an odd mixture of Southern Baptist theology with Episcopal service elements: the congregation believed in salvation, repentance, redemption, and forgiveness, and they weren't afraid to sing the old hymns I had grown up with. This experience of meeting these gay "recovering Baptists" allowed me to fully come to terms with who God created me to be and also became the origin point of my becoming the person I am today.

It took a long time to stop playing in my head those sermon tapes of condemning messages I grew up with. Instead, I studied, prayed, and had so many therapeutic conversations with other people in the same situation. I experienced enough acceptance in Christ and from other believers to know that God didn't hate me for my authentic identity. After thirty-five years of torment and questioning, I finally got to know who I really was and be okay with it. God created me the way I was, and that's as "natural" as I can get, no matter how fundamentalists interpret Romans 1:26–29.

To add to my joy, I met a woman at MCC Greenville who would later become my wife. It happened unexpectedly, but the more I got to know her, the more I realized she was the one God had planned for me all along. She was the perfect complement to me, yet we had very similar family backgrounds. We began dating and eventually moved in together. My heart was full, but a sickening feeling creeped in: I needed to let my family know about my situation.

Telling My Family

By this point, I had never come out officially to my family. I don't think they suspected anything; they just thought I was a single career woman. Because my life didn't include a lot of interaction with them, I hesitated to have that coming-out conversation with my family. Why should I have to put myself out there for their approval in such a personal matter? On paper, my fear didn't make a lot of sense: I was an independent thirty-five-year-old woman; I didn't live in the same city as any of my family; and they had no role in my day-to-day life by that point. Yet I was tremendously afraid of their potential judgment and rejection. Despite this fear, I still loved my family and needed to let them know I was moving.

I had a conversation with my sister about my move. She asked questions about my partner: Were we more than friends? Did I consider myself to be gay? I took a deep breath and replied yes to both questions. Although we exchanged no cross words during that conversation, there was a period of time where we became very distant. I knew she didn't want me or my partner around her kids, my only nieces and nephews. To be honest, I think the distance was due more to my sister's husband's wishes than her own feelings.

What's more, I think they both believed this "gay lifestyle" was somehow very far removed from the way I was raised. However, the reality was that I worked each day as a model employee and came home every night to cook dinner and to spend time with my pets and my girlfriend. We would play Christian music on the piano and guitars and sing the songs of our faith. There was no clubbing, no naked pool parties, and no drugs. My life was what anyone would want for their daughter to have with a man, only I was sharing mine with a woman. I was hoping that one day my sister and brother-in-law would understand me. Given enough time and space, they do, and today we have a good relationship.

By the time I had to make my situation known to my family, my mother had already passed away (in 1986, at the age of forty-one, of ovarian cancer) and my younger brother had also passed away (in 1999 due to some sort of drug interaction), so my father was the only other family member to break the news to. I worked up the courage to make that fateful call, and I told him the situation. To my relief, he didn't pass judgment or lecture me and only wanted to make sure that the housing and financial arrangements were "fair and equitable" since we were cohabiting. I'm not saying my dad was overwhelmingly supportive. In fact, I think he wanted the earth to swallow him up so he couldn't have this conversation with me. Even so, our relationship was never broken over this matter, and although we have never really had an in-depth conversation about it, I think he realized he had no choice but to accept the situation or I wouldn't be in his life. Over the years, my father has always had a very cordial relationship with my partner.

My wife and I have been together for almost fifteen years, and in that time, as a sign of our commitment, we hosted a holy union ceremony in 2007—since marriage was not yet legal—and then we also got married legally in April of 2015, after gay marriage became legal in Florida. We didn't make a big deal about a marriage ceremony. Instead, we just went to the courthouse where the clerk was the witness. We had not invited our families to any of our previous ceremonies, and we didn't share the news about our legal marriage, either, because we felt it would be awkward for them and for us. When it comes to these types of decisions and subject matter, we just don't share with either of our families. Honestly, I don't know that we will ever feel completely accepted by our families in that regard.

The Toleration Game

Although I believe both my wife and I have strong relationships with our families today, the best way to describe the situation is that our families tolerate us. As far as my immediate family is concerned, my sister has worked part time for my business for the last four years, and she and all my nieces and nephews—who are now grown and starting their own families—love to come visit us. (It helps that we live in the Florida Keys, a vacation destination.) When we had to evacuate from Hurricane Irma, my wife's parents allowed us and our five dogs to stay with them. None of us knew we would be evacuated for six weeks, but they were extremely gracious. It's kind of strange to describe our relationship in terms of toleration, but in our minds, people who are fully accepting also become allies as we fight for equality that anyone would want for their family members; neither of our families are at that stage yet.

Politically speaking, we know that our votes potentially cancel out theirs because we are on completely different sides of the issue, but we are thankful for the progress we have seen thus far and for the limited inclusion we experience with them today during such activities as family vacations and holiday visits. But my wife and I always practice a level of filtering when we are around them: we don't show affection to each other, we don't use any pet names, and we try to avoid anything that could remind them of the reality of our relationship.

Maybe we are more preoccupied with this filtering than they are, but because we have never verbally received their support of our relationship or heard them talk about our relationship in any way, we always feel a bit more tolerated than accepted. While we are realistic that our families will likely never fully advocate on our behalf, we are thankful for our family of choice, which is full of supporters who rally around us.

Finally Finding Acceptance in Church

Today, my wife and I live in the beautiful Florida Keys, and we still attend an MCC church, so if you are ever in the area, please come see us at the MCC in Key West. My wife plays the piano there and we continue to be very involved in many aspects of the church. Moving to the Florida Keys has been one of the best decisions we have ever made because it has exposed us to more diversity than we have ever experienced before. Also, it has allowed us to see true Christianity in action. There's no judgment in it. There's no dogma that has to be followed. There is only love and support. Even though MCC was started for gay people, our church has more straight couples than any other MCC in the world, right in the heart of gay Key West.

We are living proof that Christians can be gay. My wife and I still love and serve God and don't believe being gay gives us an excuse not to use our talents to serve. More than ever, we feel called to help bind the wounds of our gay brothers and sisters who have been hurt in the name of religion. It breaks my heart to witness how mainstream Christianity and fundamentalism have done so much damage to reaching the gay community.

I am thankful for my Christian upbringing, but I am also thankful that I am a recovering fundamentalist, which has provided me with an important perspective now that I am on the other side. Finally, I am free of its clutches and am living the life I dreamed of with the partner God created especially for me. I'll never be convinced that my marriage is not of God or somehow less than what a straight couple would feel, and I'm not the only one who feels this way, either. I have been tickled to meet a few other gay BJU graduates at our church here in Key West who share the same philosophy of being thankful for our Christian roots and also for the freedom we feel from living our authentic lives.

In many ways, my true Christian education happened after I left BJU, which thrives on rules and judgment. The God I now know lovingly accepts that we can never be perfect. No longer am I in that constant state of repentance from my childhood. The conformity of BJU's fundamentalism has no power over me. I know I can't sever my relationship with God, and I no longer view scripture in the literal context of my upbringing, so I am no longer condemned by the law in any form. I am instead enjoying God's grace.

My ultimate thrill is knowing that many gay Christians are finding their peace with their sexuality and their faith. Far too many gay people have been hurt and wounded by the church and the condemnation of their true identity. I want other gay people to know that they were created by God to be exactly who they are, that God loves them and wants a relationship with them, and, most importantly, that God does not equal fear.

We don't have to fear God anymore, nor do we have to hide. Being accused of having "homosexual tendencies" by that so-called Christian school administrator produced intense fear. Being labeled a lesbian for owning a Ford Explorer instilled self-loathing. But today, I enjoy a Christian freedom that repels any stigma based in fundamentalism. The more we can talk about how God has worked in our lives, the more we can help others understand that we are not evil and that we are not the enemy of Christianity. We have the opportunity to draw the circle of God's love ever wider, ever more inclusive.

BJU's fundamentalism may preach that salvation is free, but it practices a religion that places so many conditions on its students. My Christianity says that there are no conditions on God's love. We can't earn it. We can only be ourselves. Once we have accepted that, we can be the vessel for God's love and allow it to flow through us. It is time to love ourselves and love each other. The greatest gift we as gay Christians can offer and receive is love.[3] I can only pray that all professing Christians will believe and respect that.

Notes

1. Kann et al., "Sexual Identity," 19.
2. Numbers 32:23.
3. I Corinthians 13:13.

chapter 19   AVERY WRENNE

> Every semester, BJU holds weekly required chapel
> services from Monday through Thursday, but I
> had never witnessed BJU devote all week to this
> one topic that was so personal to me. I not-so-
> affectionately call that week "Anti-Gay Week" be-
> cause it was filled with various administrators and
> professors from such departments as biology and
> Bible who were preaching and discussing how ho-
> mosexuality is genetically and spiritually wrong.

Born into the BJU System: Biblical Counseling at the Academy

I was literally born into the Bob Jones University system. I was born
in Barge Memorial Hospital on the campus of BJU in South Carolina,
largely because both my parents were employees of the university. At age
four, I first made a profession of faith, and I was baptized soon after. I
attended BJU's daycare, preschool, elementary school, and junior high,
and I graduated with honors from the high school. Throughout middle
school and high school, I participated in mock trial. Because my parents
were employees of the university, they were given a child tuition benefit,
which meant I could attend BJU for free up to the completion of a bachelor's degree.

By my senior year of high school, however, I was facing several co-
morbid mental health issues: major depression, general anxiety, anorexia
nervosa, and self-harm. Both my parents and the school decided that I
should see their biblical counselor for these issues, as well as have occasional conversations with my youth pastor, who was a BJU graduate. This
primarily began because my parents were unsure how to handle my mental health issues, and they thought that sending me to a biblical counselor
would help stabilize me emotionally.

It began simply enough—having someone to talk to helped. However, it became more and more of a requirement because of the seriousness of my mental health issues at the time. During one conversation with my youth pastor, I informed him that I was suicidal and was formulating a plan to end my life. He told me to write a note stating that I was happy and okay, or else he would tell my parents. Not having my plan exactly finalized just yet, I did as he asked, and the issue was put to rest. But just a few weeks later, I spent several days in Barge Memorial Hospital on BJU's campus, rather than at a legitimate psychiatric ward, after beginning to carry out a suicide plan. My mock trial coach and my youth pastor both questioned me afterward regarding what had happened, and I explained it away, since by then I recognized I was not being taken seriously. My coach later told me that other students had informed him of my self-harm, but he chose not to act because he never personally saw my scars.

During my biblical counseling sessions, I was told countless times that I needed to pray more and read scripture passages about peace, truth, obedience, and thankfulness. If I did so, my mental health issues would go away. As I began to realize this method was not working, I became resistant, wishing for validation that I had real mental disorders, but I was not given an option to stop the counseling. Instead, I was continually gaslit by being told that my issues were spiritual rather than psychological or emotional. What's more, I was regularly weighed and asked about my eating and self-harm practices and patterns. Because my mental health was treated as a spiritual issue, I was expected to change my attitude and behaviors to resolve my problems.

During my senior year of high school, the morning after a particularly distressing evening when I had self-harmed, I walked into the high school office with tears on my face and requested to call a friend's mother, whom I trusted. Instead of permitting me to call her, an administrator decided to talk to me himself and have the office call my parents. During that conversation, he asked why I was so upset. Knowing that there would be more serious ramifications if I admitted to self-harm or being suicidal, I instead admitted that I wasn't sure if I believed God existed and explained my depressive angst as being related to that. He hastily threatened that if I told anyone how I felt, I would be expelled. I kept my thoughts to myself and graduated from high school on time, but that incident reinforced to me just how fiercely the BJU administration at all levels wants to quash any critical thinking, no matter how benign the intent may be.

Mental Health Issues = Sin

Having gone through BJU's counseling system from the time I was in eleventh or twelfth grade (2010), I felt very disenfranchised with BJU's version of God and Christianity. I had been told repeatedly that I was sinning against God by being depressed, having anxiety, harming myself, and not eating. This was the message I was hearing from BJU: my mental health issues were caused by my own pride and anger.

When it came time to choose a college, I really didn't consider any other schools because I knew I had a free ride waiting for me at BJU since my parents worked for the school. Besides, I was dealing with severe mental health issues and did not have the emotional or mental space to think too much about college options. When I entered college in the fall 2011 semester, I had secretly determined that I was an agnostic, but I had to play BJU's game as a professing Christian to stay enrolled.

At age seventeen, and as someone who had spent their entire life in the BJU system, I was incredibly sheltered from all things sexual and hadn't yet realized how queer I was. Because I had been in music lessons and choirs since age five, I chose music education as my major, but after that first semester, I decided it wasn't for me at that time. I changed my major to BJU's version of psychology—called "biblical counseling"—because I was personally interested in the subject matter and wanted to better understand my own issues and how to handle them; plus, I thought it would be good to help others handle these same issues. Unfortunately, for the duration of my entire twelfth grade and freshman college years, my aforementioned mental health issues made it progressively more difficult for me to function at school. As a result, I had a major mental health crisis during my second semester of college that forced me to withdraw from school before the semester finished.

Around this time, I began my journey through another internal crisis: figuring out my sexuality. The beginning of this journey was marked by unexpected darkness. During the summer of 2012, I didn't want to admit that I might be gay. I had already begun questioning my sexuality, but I wanted to make myself straight, so I tried to flirt with and date a family friend who was conventionally attractive. The result was traumatic: I was sexually assaulted and left in a state of despair, trying to make sense of and seek help for the assault, but without much success. My journey had not started as I had imagined, but during this traumatic time, I tried to figure out how my sexuality factored into my spiritual identity.

How Do I Fit into Christianity?

I spent the next several months continuing to ask myself questions about who I was, trying to navigate my internalized homophobia. Living entirely within BJU's fundamentalism, I hadn't been taught much about sexuality, except to hear homosexuality disparaged in those long Clobber Passages in the Bible. Gay people were gross perverts, according to them. Conversely, we were told that a "good Christian woman" accepts traditional gender and sexual roles. Up until that point, the big services I'd attended on campus had mostly avoided discussion of homosexuality. But that would change.

I took the 2012–2013 year off from school to work, to get a better handle on my mental health through counseling and spending time with friends and family who understood my struggles, and to also figure out how I could reconcile my faith with my sexuality. My parents supported me through this time because they understood that I was not ready to go back to school until I was more stable.

During my time off from school, I read Wesley Hill's book *Washed and Waiting*, which argues that Christians can be gay as long as they are celibate.[1] This was the first book I read that did not argue against individuals coming out, even though it did argue for celibacy rather than equal same-sex marriages. I felt validated by Hill's argument that it was okay for Christians to be openly gay, even if he did stipulate that they not participate in same-sex sexual activity. Even though I was not sure exactly what my sexual orientation was, Hill's book helped me realize it was okay that I wasn't straight.

I started coming out as bisexual to close friends and my parents. Coming out to my parents was tough. They cried, and my mother later expressed her worries that I would not be able to work with children if I publicly came out. I had done a lot of babysitting and working in a daycare, and I enjoyed that work; I was even considering education as a career at that point, so learning this concern bothered me. Meanwhile, I continued to study what the scriptures said about sexuality because I deeply longed to reconcile the love I felt for someone with my understanding of my Christian faith.

As part of this coming-out journey, I realized that I had fallen in love with my best friend in high school, which was why my relationship with her meant so much. I was working at Red Lobster at the time, and my friends from work accepted my identity completely. But my friends from

BJU reacted differently. They accepted my identity but firmly believed I must either choose to marry a man or be celibate in order to honor God; others incorrectly believed I was questioning my sexuality because of the sexual assault. I embraced the term "bisexual" at the time because I had experienced romantic attractions to both men and women, but only sexual attraction to women. Without much vocabulary or understanding of the nuances of romance, sex, and relationships, calling myself bisexual seemed to fit. Around this same time, a close friend from Bob Jones Academy came out as gay. Much of the BJU community ostracized them, but I was encouraged by their announcement, and I confided in them with my own struggles to figure out my identity.

A Return to BJU: Facing "Anti-Gay Week"

I returned to BJU in the fall of 2013, motivated both by the tuition benefit and by the astounding debt I would have incurred by going to another school. As a student this time, I had to keep both my faith and sexuality a secret. My beliefs had gravitated back to Christianity, but in a more liberal form that would not be welcomed on campus, and I reluctantly supported BJU's stance on sexuality—one man and one woman, married for life— because I did not yet have the logical resources to prove what my heart already believed did not *feel* true about BJU's policy. I attended BJU for the following two years, majoring in music, and finished up most of my coursework for my music degree.

It felt like the topic of sexuality was coming up on campus in different ways when I returned. First, I reconnected with my high school best friend and came out to her, explaining my feelings for her during high school. Our friendship had ended badly during my first year of college, and I wanted reconciliation. I knew there was danger in telling her, but I felt like I owed it to her to tell her my truth. She responded that she never felt the same way, but we reconciled and became close classmates again, though my coming out to her left some residual tension. That tension, and my eventual relationship with a woman, led to our growing apart for good.

Next, during this same semester, in November 2013, BJU held a special week of chapel services focusing on one theme: issues of sexuality and marriage. Every semester, BJU holds weekly required chapel services from Monday through Thursday, but I had never witnessed BJU devote all week to this one topic that was so personal to me. I not-so-affectionately call that week "Anti-Gay Week" because it was filled with various administrators and professors from such departments as biology and Bible who were preaching and discussing how homosexuality is genetically and spiritually wrong.[2] The previous year, when I had taken a break from BJU, I had come out to one of the music professors and his wife. (I knew it was dangerous to be vulnerable at BJU, but I only came out to a few people there, either because I really trusted them or because I knew they would also have something to lose if they told.) During that "Anti-Gay Week," I went into his office and screamed into some of the pillows on his couch out of frustration and feeling alone, knowing that, while he didn't agree with me, he still had compassion for me. I knew him well enough to know he would not turn me in just because I had recognized my sexual orientation; he would not snitch on me. As frustrated as I was, this "Anti-Gay Week" had unintentionally inspired me to speak out and connect with faculty and students about this issue. Future conversations on campus about this chapel week proved very interesting.

During the summer of 2014, I decided to take individual voice lessons on campus. During one of those sessions, another music professor asked about students' feelings about BJU because he genuinely wanted to connect better with students and be approachable. I was afraid of getting myself into trouble, so I said that I was speaking for "friends" who were part of the LGBTQ2IA+ community at BJU; I told the professor what those friends felt about BJU in general, but also specifically how they felt about the "Anti-Gay Week." The professor was willing to hear my concerns but did not question my own sexual orientation or gender identity, likely because I was read as a cisgender straight woman. After that discussion with the music professor, my accompanist for those music lessons became one of my best friends that summer. While venting our frustrations over a mutual contact's homophobic comments on social media, we felt safe enough around each other to come out: they came out to me as gay, and I came out to them as bisexual.

My Final Year at BJU: The GRACE Report Era

I was still coming to terms with my sexuality during the 2014–2015 school year at BJU, my final year there. I joined one of BJU's choirs and noticed a pretty young lady, S, who sometimes came to choir with a tear-stained face. I wanted to ask her what was wrong, but I never had the courage to do so: she sat on the other side of the room, which made things inconvenient to chat with her, and I didn't want to attract the wrong kind of attention from my peers and the administration. Rumors could be very dangerous on campus.

I found myself the subject of rumors with a young lady in one of my classes anyway. At the end of the fall 2014 semester, I befriended this young lady and discovered she was dealing with serious mental health issues like my own. We kept in touch over the break, and the following January, she came out to me as bisexual, at which time I also came out to her as bisexual. I was happy to know someone else who was bisexual, but she had tremendous guilt over her sexuality. She had a mental health crisis—a buildup of several significant factors—at the beginning of the term and left school. My involvement with taking her to the hospital and staying at the hospital with her, as well as visiting her in the psychiatric ward and keeping a close relationship with her afterward, sparked rumors that we were in a romantic relationship. These rumors started because just before she left school, she had come out as bisexual to a few mutual classmates, who, even though they did not know my sexual orientation, assumed that my close relationship with her was something more than just a friendship. I was lucky those rumors did not escalate into something more against me.

During that spring 2015 semester, most of campus was talking about the GRACE Report, an in-depth document detailing concerns from a private third-party organization about both alleged sexual abuse and assault on BJU's campus and also how BJU administrators and counselors responded to students who had been victims of assault outside of campus. The report stated clearly that two administrators—specifically Bob Jones III and Jim Berg—should be censured for their failure to administer or counsel properly. BJU refused to follow this recommendation and still sold Jim Berg's counseling materials at the campus bookstore.[3] I was mortified at BJU's response, especially because I was just beginning to see a licensed sexual assault trauma counselor in the area in March 2015. My family supported my decision to seek professional help, and I found out about the counseling organization, which specializes in sexual trauma counseling, through a friend. Even though I had not personally contributed to the GRACE Report, BJU's lack of real change signified to me that BJU was not a safe place to discuss what had happened to me.

During the fall semester of my final year at BJU, I received counseling through my parents' church, Suber Road Baptist Church. I was still struggling to reconcile my sexuality with the Bible, so I sought advice, which turned into counseling sessions with a couple who were leaders of the collegiate group in the church. Neither of them were licensed counselors or psychologists, but they seemed to care about me, so I trusted them, even though their advice was contrary to my own ideas about the reconciliation of my faith and sexuality. They advised me not to come out publicly or pursue any romantic relationships with women. Furthermore, this couple, along with the church, set up what was essentially conversion counseling through a local Christian counseling center, Greenville Counseling Associates. My parents supported my going to the counseling sessions but did not have much knowledge of its content. After a few sessions with that counselor, I was frustrated enough not to return, and I continued doing my own research on how sexuality fits with the Bible.

Finding Myself away from BJU

My answer finally came. Matthew Vines's book *God and the Gay Christian* had recently come out, and that book helped me finally realize that I could indeed positively resolve my sexuality with God and with the Bible.[4] Vines's book points out the historical and contextual issues of interpreting "homosexuality" as it is found in many English translations of the Bible today. His new approach, which is contextually more valid than traditional church methods, celebrates LGBTQ2IA+ people in their sacred experiences of gender identity and sexual orientation. Around this time, I received advice from an older gay friend who taught me that love is the greatest commandment and matters most. The timing couldn't have been more perfect. Both Vines's book and the advice from my friend gave me the encouragement I needed to finally leave BJU's grip.

After the spring 2015 term ended, I transferred to Converse College, where I finished my bachelor's degree in music. I chose Converse initially for its music therapy program, although I eventually changed my major to a general music degree because I realized I had a different career goal in mind. I also knew that my views of marriage and sexuality would be welcome at Converse because it is a private women's college in Spartanburg, South Carolina. While I was still concerned about the financial burden of attending Converse, I received a significant scholarship, and I was able to keep my student loans low because I worked part time during school. It only took me three semesters and a January term to finish my degree because about 70 percent of my credits from BJU transferred to Converse. Because of that, I graduated at the end of January 2017 and marched in Converse's graduation in May 2017.

The summer after I left BJU, I briefly attended a Southern Baptist church in the Greenville area. My parents supported my need to branch out to different churches than what I was used to, and because the over-all theology of the Southern Baptist Convention is not terribly different from their own, they were not concerned. During that time, I dated a guy, which made me believe for years that a) I could not make marriage to a man work, and b) that guy was not good enough for me. (I contin-ued questioning my attractions to men and eventually began dating men again.) As it turns out, S, the young lady from my choir, helped me dump that guy. I started getting to know her that summer via social media be-cause she "came out" about her eating disorder, so we first connected over that and how to deal with it at BJU. Soon, we realized we had feelings for each other, but because she was still attending BJU, we had to date secretly.

Here's a synopsis of my time with S: we secretly dated for several months while she was still at BJU. She was interrogated, stalked, ma-nipulated, and lied to by the BJU administration. Eventually, she was ex-pelled based on suspicions of our relationship—for which they never had any real facts—and when we came out in early April 2016, we were both banned from BJU's campus. Because it's a private university, we were both sent letters stating that we could be arrested if we set foot back onto the campus. We both lost a lot of friends, both inside and outside of BJU. If it hadn't been for First Baptist Greenville of Greenville, South Carolina, the faith family we had settled with in the beginning of our relationship, we would have been homeless, but the generosity and hospitality of many members, specifically Judy Snyder and her husband, John, kept us afloat and helped us find stable ground again.

Neither of our immediate families attended our wedding in August 2016, but my grandfather and great-uncle celebrated with us, and my grandfather walked me down the aisle. My parents chose what probably felt like middle ground for them: although they did not feel they could attend our wedding, partially because they were both still employees of BJU, they had a rather awkward but kindly attempted breakfast with us on the morning of our special day. My accompanist-turned-best-friend (who uses they/them pronouns) from my summer music lesson accom-panied our wedding, with their nails painted, makeup perfectly done, and adorable wedge booties. They performed beautifully. I wore a light pink dress, and S wore a lavender dress. We wrote our own vows, we combined pink and purple sand, we proceeded down the aisle to "Walking on Sunshine" by Katrina and the Waves, and then we had an ice cream bar and danced our hearts out. It was a small wedding, with about sixty people who truly love and support us, and it was perfect.

Queerly Avery

My life changed dramatically after coming out of BJU and conservative Christian fundamentalism. After we got married, S and I moved across the country and up to British Columbia, where she was raised. I attended theological school in Vancouver but had a rude awakening: just because an ecumenical Christian theological school has an inclusion policy does not mean all its administration or faculty actually believe in welcoming or affirming LGBTQ2IA+ people to their school. I experienced discrimination and educational bias at that school because I dared to name their inclusion policy as being seriously inadequate and dysfunctionally applied. However, while at this theological school, I found the means to massively deconstruct my fundamentalist and post-fundamentalist theology. As a result of that deconstruction, I felt spiritually lost for a few months before finding my spiritual home as a universalist.

In August 2019 S and I decided to open our relationship, and we started practicing ethical non-monogamy. It was around this time that we met a recently separated ex-evangelical figure for whom I developed feelings. That situation made me reexamine my understanding of my sexuality, and I started dating men again. I maintain that I am gay AF[5] and I absolutely bring queer energy to my relationships with men, realizing that this is because my gender is also queer.

Then, in early October 2019, S decided to end our marriage after only three years. She informed me that, over time, she had begun to relate to me differently and was no longer in love with me. She blamed my ongoing mental health challenges as a significant contributing factor to her shifting feelings. Although I did not want my relationship with S to end, particularly because of the significance that marriage equality holds for me, I can see now, almost two years later, that it really was the best thing for both of us. It was not easy. Her leaving me was incredibly painful, and parts of the way she did it still feel very raw to this day. But it's what she needed to do for her. And I will always wish the best for her. We filed a joint uncontested divorce in October 2020.

In the first month after S left me, I began to reexamine my gender identity. For quite some time, although I had not done specific gender exploration, the identifier "woman" had felt confining and frustrating to me. With the support of friends and chosen family, I came out as nonbinary in November 2019, although today I prefer the label genderqueer. I use they/them pronouns. "Nonbinary" is an umbrella term for folks who do not identify with strict gender binaries of man or woman, and "genderqueer" is a term for folks who do not subscribe to conventional Western gender roles.

I also started playing with my name. I had never felt like my birth name suited me, and with the end of my marriage, it felt like the perfect time to start thinking seriously about changing it. First, I changed my last name to Wrenne. Wrens are songbirds, and the state bird of South Carolina is a wren. I changed the spelling to give it more flair, because what are gays without our flair? I tried using my first initial as my name for a while, but that still didn't fit. I found the name Avery and something inside me instantly said, "That's it!" There is something incredibly empowering about choosing your own name. Now, whenever someone tells me they like my name, I gleefully thank them and tell them I chose it myself.

Today, I identify both my sexual orientation and gender identity as "queer" because I like the fluidity, ambiguity, and color of the term. I also use the terms "pansexual" and "bisexual" because I understand my sexual orientation as being free-spirited and fluid. "Bisexual" is a term for people who are attracted to more than one gender, and "pansexual" is a term for folks who are attracted to people of all genders or regardless of gender. I am attracted to people both because of and regardless of their gender identity and expression. When I put all these identifiers together, I am a non-monogamous genderqueer pansexual humxn.[6] Religiously or spiritually speaking, I now identify as an agnostic universalist rather than identifying with a specific religious or spiritual tradition. Specifically, I find significant value in earth-based spirituality. I no longer attend religious services on a regular basis, but I still engage in religious and spiritual conversations with friends and partners on a regular basis. I believe in a higher power, but I am not exactly sure Who or What that is. I know that I am loved by God(dess) wholly and unconditionally—queerness, quirkiness, and all. And I am open to adding religious and spiritual rituals to my repertoire as I see fit. Why not have the best of all worlds?

As someone literally born into the BJU community, I experienced an unspeakable liberation in letting go of the Christian label and partaking in other spiritual practices. This openness has helped remove any inherent, residual guilt from fundamentalism. I no longer feel the fundamentalist pressure to label my relationship with a church, or even to have a formal relationship with organized religion. I recently completed a second bachelor's degree, this one in social work, from the University of British Columbia, a degree that lets me help other people in a holistic way and recognizes the value of healing and wholeness in all people. My goal now is to work with queer people from a trauma-informed social work approach.

But as much as I would like to paint this journey away from BJU as successful, it is not without painful consequences. My time at BJU still impacts me as I continue to deal with strained relationships with friends and former professors and mourn for lost friendships. And because of difficult family circumstances which clarified the incredibly dysfunctional boundaries and priorities of my family of origin and siblings-in-law, I unfortunately am no longer able to have any contact with them. I took the pain from my time at BJU into my experience at theological school and unexpectedly felt more hurt at the end of my time there: the discrimination I faced because of my queerness and courage to speak up about injustices felt eerily familiar to my experience at BJU.

But the pain that is part of this process should not discourage anyone. Coming out to yourself and deeply letting go of internalized homoantagonism and transantagonism is long and exhausting, but it is a journey worth taking. Trauma therapy is really helping with this. I am happy, hopeful, and feeling the most alive I've ever felt because I'm getting to know myself and celebrate who I am made to be in the world. Yes, letting go of my religious roots takes its toll mentally, emotionally, and spiritually, but now I can do real, guilt-free reconstruction and practice my spirituality in the way that fits me best. I couldn't have undergone this makeover without finding a community that would help me with the different phases: the deconstruction, sitting in limbo, letting go of guilt, and starting my reconstruction. The new, chosen family I have made throughout this process gives me hope that I am on the right path.

Notes

1. Hill, *Washed and Waiting.*
2. Jones, "Bible Say about Homosexuality? Part 1"; Jones, "Bible Say about Homosexuality? Part 2"; Daulton, "Transformation through Christ"; Ormiston, "Relating to Those Who Struggle."

3. Riddle, "Bob Jones University Issues Response."

4. Vines, *God and the Gay Christian*.

5. Gay AF, or "gay as fuck," meaning super queer in the broad sense of the word.

6. I'm using this spelling of "humxn" to convey a more gender-neutral meaning, as well as taking the patriarchal power away.

conclusion　　Queer Times at BJU

> And the angel which I saw stand upon the sea and
> upon the earth lifted up his hand to heaven, And
> sware by him that liveth for ever and ever, who cre-
> ated heaven, and the things that therein are, and the
> earth, and the things that therein are, and the sea,
> and the things which are therein, that there should
> be time no longer.
>
> REVELATION 10:5–6

What Time Is It?

Time. Temporality. At BJU, we were constantly reminded that time was
finite. Most of us contributors who began our religious education as children learned about eschatology—the study of the end times—through
such terms as "the Second Coming," "the Rapture," "the Tribulation," "the
Millennium," and other fun concepts interpreted from the book of Revelation and other places in the New Testament. For children, these terms
were supposed to inspire joy because they meant that our struggles were
temporary, but our reward in Jesus was forever. Our job was to mature
in our Christian walk, revel in the inscrutable puzzle of infinity, and keep
our eyes toward eternity.

Time can serve so many roles in our life. It can teach patience. It can
antagonize. It can deescalate tensions. It can orchestrate serendipity. It
can catalog our impatience. It can expose our insecurities. It can warm us
with nostalgia. It can become weaponized. It can erase unpleasant truths.
It can exacerbate jealousy for other people's productivity. It can soften
pain. It can discombobulate. It can cultivate perspective. It can weaken
the gravitational pull of internalized ideologies. It can numb.

It can also behave in such a queer, unpredictable fashion. Time in the era of COVID-19 has managed to warp our senses like a funhouse mirror, forcing us to scrutinize the function, worth, and effects of time and how we use it.

Time is all we have. Until it's gone.

Time is queer.

The Queer Timing of This Book

This book has a queer relationship with time too. Its very existence can be credited in part to the voices from the past who provided personal and professional encouragement to create and curate *BJU and Me*. The first voice came in October 2011 from a person I met in an online community of people like me: former BJU students who had left—or were in the process of leaving—fundamentalism primarily because of their queer identities. Rich Merritt suggested that we in this community should compile our true stories of our time at BJU. I was excited at this chance to express myself but fearful because I hadn't yet officially come out. Because of my trepidation, I approached this venture under a pseudonym.

But time can change circumstances quickly. By 2012 I had begun my new trajectory as an out gay man and had even marched in my first Pride parade with many of my friends from this online community. I also found myself overseeing this book project when Rich had to step down to work on other projects.

During the research and composition process, I discovered anthologies of first-person accounts from queer people or from former fundamentalists, which revealed the richness of voices from the past.[1] *BJU and Me* follows in the tradition of those collections because many of their editors openly admit how long it took them to publish their respective books. Translator John Borneman says Jürgen Lemke worked on his project for "seven uncertain years" and "was still doubtful that it would be allowed to come to fruition."[2] Edward T. Babinski notes he spent six or seven years "collecting testimonies" for his book.[3] And Reta Ugena Whitlock says her "collection has been almost 4 years in the making."[4] Sometimes, time moves glacially, like a taunting enemy, reminding us of all the labor we've put into a still-unpublished project. It makes us curl our empty hands into fists because we have nothing concrete to show for the invested years. But time, with all its queerness, can make the waiting worthwhile when it finally produces a meaningful product.

For scholar Jack Halberstam, "queer temporality" rejects the traditional timeline of entering adulthood with a spouse and family.[5] Many queer BJU students wrestle with this internalized view of time: investing their energies at school to find a spouse as a means of eschewing their queer desires and conforming to traditional expectations of finding a mate, procreating, and raising their family in a fundamentalist church. *BJU and Me* highlights this struggle surrounding the functions of time, revealing BJU's strategies of erasing queer identities from its fold and its past. This book purposefully provides a present space for our queer voices to recount our past experiences against religious heteronormativity. Halberstam goes on to say that "queer time and space are useful frameworks for assessing political and cultural change in the late twentieth and early twenty-first centuries (both what has changed and what must change)."[6] That last part about what "has changed and what must change" is critical to both distinguish and underscore when we consider the historical and current practices of BJU because it has created its own kind of "queer space," not as a nurturing place for queer BJU students in the way Halberstam intends, but as a separated college campus that surveils and eradicates non-normative elements.

BJU and Me takes special interest in highlighting voices that testify about what happened to them in the past on campus so that readers can understand the kind of critical change still needed for BJU's future. In so doing, I want to catalog significant changes made by the school that seem to destabilize its traditionalist past. In some ways, BJU's current trajectory appears very queer (strange) in the sense that its separatist brand has become unrecognizable to students from the past. BJU's motto in 1997, which claims to improve its future through significant change, is a good place to start this analysis.

Still Standing, but Not Standing Still: Changing with the Times

When I was a student at BJU during the school's seventieth anniversary in 1997, the PR department designed an attractive new BJU logo with the slogan, "Still Standing, but Not Standing Still." It was a clever turn of phrase. It implied the school's devotion to its fundamentalist Christian foundation while simultaneously projecting the school's forward momentum for the future. But what would that momentum look like?

For some reason, every time I walked by that logo on front campus, I would concentrate on the words "Not Standing Still" and imagine the university's focus on physical expansion, technological innovation, and spiritual renovation. Change. Perhaps that was idealistic of me, but now, approximately twenty-five years later, as I am part of the older generation of BJU alumni, I wonder about the ways BJU has fulfilled that slogan from 1997. Has BJU remained the same in looking queer (strange) to the outside world as a means of evangelism through its fundamentalist separation? Conversely, has BJU successfully maintained a forward momentum through change? And how successfully has it tried to balance its emphasis on strict religious tradition with its need for maintaining its relevancy in higher education? Since I have come out of the fundamentalist closet and identify as queer in the twenty-first century, my questions about BJU's 1997 slogan can also include concern about the status of queer students at BJU too. I can echo a question I presented in the introduction when I asked if there is a place for queer students at BJU: How will the queer student on BJU campus in the twenty-first century factor into or be affected by the school's forward momentum? All the questions in this paragraph funnel into the bottom line: How queer is BJU's future?

To be fair, students and alumni at any kind of school, no matter its affiliation, expect a fair amount of constant change about elements like technological advancement and convenience. For example, the generation at BJU before me had to share phones placed in the dormitory halls, whereas my generation had a phone in each dorm room. And I don't need to explain how contemporary cell phones have revolutionized communication for today's BJU students. Certain aspects of generational differences and comparisons will never cease to either benignly amaze or possibly scandalize any alumni.

For this book, revisiting BJU culture to gauge certain changes has instilled conflicting feelings for me as an out-of-touch old timer, especially about major institutional changes toward topics that were at one time considered by the administration to be a matter of strident religious conviction. What's more, it's daunting trying to keep up with BJU's institutional policy changes in the twenty-first century because it feels like these changes happen with much more frequency in the past few years. Some of that overwhelming feeling may just be a matter of my age and perspective. Thankfully, I am not expected to tally an exhaustive list of BJU's changes for this project; instead, I close this book by highlighting a few ways that BJU is "Still Standing, but Not Standing Still," connecting these ways back to the contributor stories in this book, and then thinking about the ramifications for the next generation of queer BJU students as we recognize

BJU's institutional pattern of manipulating, erasing, and revising elements of its own past to maintain a pious, fundamentalist persona in the present.

Times Have Changed: Dress Codes, Accreditation, Tax-Exempt Status, and More

In the past twenty years, BJU has made significant changes with its policies and public image. These days, anyone can access BJU's current student handbook online to make a more-informed decision about attending the school. This was not the case in Bill Ballantyne's story when he unknowingly broke a serious rule before he registered for classes. At that time, BJU did not distribute its handbook until students arrived on campus. This kind of recent access suggests a modicum of transparency, but only a modicum.

In other ways, BJU has taken strides to improve its relationship with public sentiment from the outside world. The *Chronicle of Higher Education* reported in 2002 that BJU was creating scholarships for minority students. In 2017 BJU celebrated its first "MLK Holiday on campus," which is a far cry from the school's response to the news of his assassination in 1968, and in October 2020 it created a "new student-led organization to empower minority students." Plus, BJU implemented its first-ever spring break in 2016, and Steve Pettit recently announced that "Labor Day will become an institutional holiday and [that] a four-day fall break will be scheduled in mid-October" beginning in 2020.[7] These advances help the school's public image and raise student morale. Many of us from the past remember a separated lifestyle on campus that meant *not* participating in secular college culture, which included *not* enjoying a spring and fall break and *not* having Labor Day off from classes.

Also, students are now expected to attend a BJU-approved church off campus on Sunday mornings instead of attending services on campus, which was an issue for Micah J. Smith's family. Additionally, BJU now allows students to wear headphones, unlike during Sandra Merzib's time.[8] And as Curt Allison, Andrew Bolden, David Diachenko, and Rachel Oblak note in their stories, BJU still spiritualizes music as either inherently good or bad, but it has significantly extended the handbook's section on music between the 2018–2019 and 2019–2020 editions and mentions how classroom instruction about music will give students "a working knowledge of a broad range of genres, some of which we as an institution choose to exclude from our worship and recreational contexts."[9] My first reaction to this news was wondering if students will now be allowed to learn about jazz in music appreciation class, which I wasn't allowed to do in the late nineties. This change in music access might be a nuanced alteration, but it speaks volumes to alumni. Sometimes "Not Standing Still" appears more like religious contradiction than loosening administrative control, and sometimes those changes fall somewhere in-between.

But the changes don't stop there. The next three are quite revolutionary. First, BJU has considerably changed its public image with sports. Since 1933 BJU students of the twentieth and early twenty-first century participated solely in intramural activities because of the way sports culture was believed to have impeded the spiritual emphasis of the school. However, in 2012, BJU "reinstated intercollegiate athletics" and in 2020 was approved by the NCAA for provisional membership in Division III sports. Moreover, BJU noticeably altered its dress code, allowing women to wear dress pants to classes and shorts when participating in athletic events.[10] Second, in 2018, after approximately ninety years as an academic institution, it was announced that college students at BJU would soon enjoy having locks on their dormitory room doors,[11] a need addressed in quite a few contributor stories, including Fawn Mullinix's. Third, BJU has added a price tag to disciplinary infractions. Depending on the severity of the behavior, students can be fined $25, $50, $75, or $100 for their actions, with a corresponding $25 fine per "each 25 demerits that the student accumulates each semester."[12]

These three changes make me pause because BJU's brand of biblical fundamentalism has always been intricately linked to how its student community functions as separate from the outside world. I will be the first to acknowledge the historical double standard regarding women and dress codes on campus. Men will never understand the thrill of replacing countless pairs of worn-out pantyhose or the joys of enduring another "dress check," so men should support any advancement like this for women. That said, BJU's overall stringent and conservative dress code signified how its students proudly appeared markedly different from mainstream society. How does this change in wardrobe influence the way BJU spiritualizes dress codes and modesty? Second, I'm happy for the semblance of more privacy and security that the dormitory room locks will give students. But if the lack of locks symbolized how a Christian campus could operate on a biblically mandated honor system, what does this change suggest about the growing independence of the student body? And will this action limit administrative surveillance?

But I am probably the most speechless about the third revolutionary change: the addition of a price tag to the demerit system. What kind of school would do such a thing? According to anecdotal evidence, at least one other religious school has done something similar. The former pastor at my parents' church was around my age and had graduated around the same time from Hyles-Anderson College, a Bible college with a significantly different fundamentalist brand from BJU. He had mentioned that students in the past could allegedly work off their demerits at Hyles-Anderson through physical labor, which scandalized me because of its resemblance to Catholic indulgences that we fundamentalists believed were heretical. Another church member, a 2014 Hyles-Anderson graduate, informed me that the college had phased out demerits and had implemented fines by the time he arrived there in 2010, so it seems that Hyles-Anderson's disciplinary policies have evolved, and perhaps student conduct fines are more commonplace in religious schools than I had realized. And now BJU has monetized sins with no opportunity for redemption. Instead, BJU students literally pay for their own sins. I couldn't help but ask myself: Which is the worse heretical practice, paying off your own sins through physical labor, or paying them off financially? I'm sure the BJU administration believes that college students pay more attention when monetary penalties factor into the rules, but when a school's entire sociological infrastructure is modeled on biblical principles, policies like this one are tainted by the theological implications.

Arguably the biggest institutional change for BJU came in 2017, when BJU received regional accreditation, regained tax-exempt status, and restructured itself into two units: a nonprofit called BJU, Inc. and a for-profit called Bob Jones Education Group, Inc.[13] Similarly, the university announced in November 2019 that its nursing program has been approved for accreditation by the Commission on Collegiate Nursing Education.[14] These recent advancements with accreditation have certainly helped BJU through the financially perilous COVID-19 pandemic because the school received more than $2 million from the U.S. Department of Education in 2020 through the Coronavirus Aid, Relief, and Economic Security (CARES) Act.[15] It is hard to imagine a twentieth-century version of BJU where its students could receive federal financial aid, but these institutional changes reveal how BJU has been busy constructing its forward momentum as a means of self-preservation. But are all these changes progressive, superficial, or detrimental? That's a tough call. As BJU tries to find its footing in a regionally accredited world, it might find itself polarizing its own fundamentalist demographics with some of these changes, especially changes viewed as contradictory to its own separatist brand. Despite institutional changes that may suggest a progressive environment, BJU's standards indicate that it remains committed to controlling its students.

Times Haven't Changed:
Still Controlling Students through Accountability

For the most part, BJU's fundamentalist policies have not changed the control it wants to keep over its student population. Today, students are still not allowed to marry during the semester, which corroborates Marshall's story from the eighties. Men and women are still not allowed to be "alone together in a classroom" without a third party or chaperone because that physical proximity still classifies as a date. As Peter Crane remarks in his story, students' rooms are still checked every weekday to make sure they've been cleaned, and BJU still sends out ensembles and traveling ministry teams to advertise for the school and procure more students, as Steve Shamblin, Elena Kelly, and many other contributors describe.[16]

Also, students are still required to attend chapel and Artist Series, as many contributors, like Blair Durkee, note. Nightly prayer groups in the dorm still exist but with a modified schedule and terminology, which is still mainly consistent from my story. And students are still not allowed to withdraw from the university to avoid "disciplinary action," with the handbook noting its rationale through that same decree I pointed out in the introduction: "Attendance at BJU is a privilege, not a right."[17] Overall, the university's expectation for students is the same as always: students ought to participate in the campus community with a "filter of gratitude"[18]—a phrase that translates to a contented submission to the university administration.

One significant method of BJU's control is through spiritual euphemisms. For example, in the seventy-five pages of the 2020–2021 student handbook, the words "accountable" and "accountability" appear twenty-one times to reinforce BJU's need to surveil its students—declaring specifically that "accountability is intended to be a form of encouragement and support to obedience. Faculty and staff are involved in students' lives, and students are involved in each other's lives. The campus community pledges to help each other grow and hold each other accountable with the goal of encouraging the spiritual success of every individual on campus."[19]

In fundamentalist circles, "accountability" can be used in different contexts. For children, the term "age of accountability" concerns the time period when children become responsible for their own soul and recognize their need for salvation through faith in Christ. Fundamentalist adults can utilize "accountability partners" as a support system to refrain from sinning while remaining obedient to biblical and church doctrine. The general principle behind both of these contexts is the same: each promotes an obedient submission to a religious system. For BJU, this same principle implies an intimidation into obedience to the school. As the handbook quotation illustrates, "accountability" explains why faculty, staff, and other students can insert themselves into any student's life: it's all in the name of "concern" for a student's spiritual well-being and campus-wide harmony. Megan Milliken's story is an excellent example of this kind of concern expressed by both her friends and the administration, while Jeff Mullinix's story reveals how any student can be turned in to the administration by an anonymous voice. With the fear of anyone becoming privy to their personal business, the average BJU student will be motivated to remain at least superficially obedient to the rules because any manifested "concern," no matter how benign, feeds the culture of surveillance.

This accountability as surveillance especially comes in handy against students who deviate from cisgender/heterosexual expectations. These students can experience intense scrutiny from all sides. Stories in this book from contributors like Andrew Bolden, Christy Haussler, and Reid all testify about the extent to which they were held accountable by administration and other students who became involved in their lives while at BJU or at BJU-network schools.

This theme of accountability for queer students continues with BJU's spiritual "concern" both in the "Anti-Gay Chapel Week" from 2013 that Avery Wrenne refers to in their story and also in the 2019 Connect Renew Equip (CoRE) Conference on campus sponsored by the BJU Seminary. According to an article in the *Greenville News* by Mike Ellis, Sam Horn, dean of the seminary school, remarked that the "annual event is aimed at seminary students" and deals with "an issue pastors are facing today."[20] On its website, the BJU Seminary lists online archives for five conferences. The 2015 conference, "In the World, but Not of It," covered the topic of biblical separation; the 2016 conference discussed how to deal with suffering; the 2018 conference was about "Biblical Counseling, Psychology, and Mental Illness"; and the 2019 conference theme, "Gender, Sexuality and the Church," offered three workshop tracks, one for men, one for women, and a general one called "Helping Those Struggling with Homosexuality and Gender Confusion."[21]

Jim Berg, the former dean of students at BJU, said in Ellis's article that "his approach [to queer people who may attend their churches] would be a welcoming one." (Remember that Berg is referenced by contributors to this book, like Sandra Merzib, for his inappropriate, ineffectual, or insensitive approach to counseling queer students.) Berg is also quoted as saying, "'We ought to be willing to minister to anyone who comes across our path.'"[22] The terms "welcoming" and "to minister" here seem to be just as euphemistic as "accountability" in the BJU lexicon. The contributor stories in this book show how BJU approaches students accused of acting on, "struggling with," conforming to, lobbying for, or questioning their queer identities: at best with a cynical spirit eager to punish through probation and counseling, and at worst with a dismissive spirit, ready to expel. There is nothing welcoming or ministering about punitive scrutiny or being cast out.[23]

There was also nothing welcoming about BJU's response to conference attendees who no longer support its fundamentalism. Sharon Hambrick, a former BJU student and current BJUnity board member, had registered to attend the conference, only to be denied attendance and refunded her registration fee. What was the reason? The administration interpreted BJUnity's online statement about "confront[ing] fallacies with facts" as a "threat to a safe environment for the conference."[24] In other words, BJU couldn't muster accountability for its own content. This silencing of Hambrick reminds me of Blair Durkee's story in this collection. She writes about the misinformation on sex and gender disseminated in BJU classrooms and also about silently questioning BJU's portrayal of the Soulforce protestors as depraved individuals. In the next section, I discuss BJU's difficulty assuming accountability with those both inside and outside the gates of its campus.

Facing the Past, but Resolved to Stand Still: 2020 CoRE and the GRACE Report

Time has an interesting way of intertwining past, present, and concurrent actions to remind us of BJU's familiar pattern of fighting for control and influence over students and the local community. Steve Shamblin's story mentions his attendance at a 1996 Greenville County Council interest meeting about a resolution condemning "the gay community" from being welcome in the county. The resolution was highly contentious and reactionary "against the International Olympic Committee's support for gay rights" since the torch for the Atlanta Olympics was scheduled to go through Greenville County.[25] To no one's surprise, Bob Jones III was quoted supporting this anti-gay resolution: "'Since when has an Olympic torch flaming briefly through the streets of Greenville been more important to the people of Greenville than moral sanity and the sacredness of family and those Bible values that so clearly condemn acts of homosexuality?'"[26] The resolution passed 9–3 and was then buried in time, mostly forgotten, until it resurfaced in early 2020.

From January to March 2020, the controversy about the 1996 resolution reignited in the local media, leading to a series of county council meetings, disagreements on a course of action, and failed votes to quash the twenty-four-year-old resolution. Finally, on March 11 the county council approved a compromise 7–5 that would "sunset" any "non-binding resolutions" that were more than four years old, which avoided taking a new stand on the queer community while expiring the old one.[27] Two of the council members who dissented, Bob Taylor and Sid Cates, are "conservative Republicans with strong ties to Bob Jones University."[28] While neither Taylor nor Cates were on the council in 1996, their presence on it in 2020 is consistent with Shamblin's comments in his story about BJU's community influence.

The months of controversy leading to this March 11, 2020, vote may seem like a setback for BJU's public image and influence, causing the administration to reconsider its past decisions about the queer community, as it did with its segregationist views. But this very same week—on March 9–10, 2020—BJU hosted its 2020 CoRE Conference with the theme "New Life: Hope and Help for an Addicted World," which featured several panels on sex, sexual sins, or sexuality.[29] One of John D. Street's breakout sessions on sexuality, "Distortions of God-Designed Sexuality," incorporated several of the Clobber Passages when discussing both "Homosexuality/ Sodomy" and "Transvestitism and Transsexualism," at one point suggesting that "bisexuality and homosexuality are often by-products of transvestism and transsexualism."[30] Street's presentation shows that BJU's views on the queer community have not changed and that its network of local churches and alumni remains formidable. After all, the county anti-gay resolution was finally removed, but only after great effort and through the path of least resistance—without censure.

But Street's presentation was not the most troubling part of this conference. Rather, Jim Berg's continued presence on BJU's campus indicates the school's inability to substantially address accountability for its past actions. Ellis's article about the 2019 CoRE conference also mentions the GRACE Report, which is a three-hundred-page document published in December 2014 by an independent organization at the request of BJU. This report details how university administrators failed to handle sexual assault cases provided by students, and it largely places blame on Bob Jones III and Jim Berg. The report recommends that Jim Berg should refrain "from both counseling and teaching counseling and that the school [should] no longer use or sell his books or DVDs."[31] In their story, Avery Wrenne notes their disappointment in discovering that BJU disregarded the report's recommendation. Berg continues his counseling lectures on campus, having spoken once at the 2019 CoRE Conference and four times at the 2020 CoRE conference.[32] Jim Berg's continued visible status on BJU's campus contradicts any credible attempt by the university for accountability, change, or trust with its students and the local affirming community. Furthermore, the CoRE presentations by Street and Berg that incorporate the Clobber Passages and pathologizing language about the queer community illustrate how BJU is standing still on its separatist, fundamentalist roots.

Time to Refute BJU's Clobber Passages

Just as those outside the administration are still questioning BJU's accountability about Jim Berg's position on campus, so are others, former insiders, calling for more accountability in how BJU and other fundamentalists treat queer students. As the introductory chapter mentioned, BJU's use of the Clobber Passages against LGBT students has not changed and can be found in appendix B of the *2020–2021 Student Handbook*.

Three queer BJU graduates—L. Robert Arthur, Jeff Miner, and Virginia Ramey Mollenkott[33]—have published or cowritten refutations of the fundamentalist interpretation of these Clobber Passages. Below, I briefly list their refutations to provide models for current and future queer BJU students to resist what Curt Allison refers to in his story as a "filtered fundamentalist" lifestyle.

GENESIS 19: SODOM

One way Miner (and coauthor Connoley) and Arthur refute the Sodom story in Genesis 19 is to point out that verse 4 describes the presence of men but also "all the people from every quarter," which would include women.[34] Arthur adds that the "word for 'people' ('am), is a word specifically chosen to indicate men and women."[35] Accordingly, this no longer becomes a message about gay people. Mollenkott (with coauthor Scanzoni) uses the content of Ezekiel chapter 16 to argue that the sin of Sodom was inhospitality, not homosexuality.[36]

LEVITICUS 18:22 AND 20:13: ABOMINATION

All three scholars note that the Leviticus 18:22 and 20:13 passages refer to ways that the Israelites of the Old Testament were not supposed to engage in homosexual actions because the pagan people around them did these acts in their temples. All three reason that the overall rule was meant for the Israelites to refrain from idolatry, which does not apply to us in the twenty-first century.[37]

ROMANS 1:26–27: UNNATURAL

Idolatry and temple sex practices are also the explanation for the message of Romans 1:26–27, which all three scholars argue were mentioned by Paul in a certain context for New Testament times.[38]

I CORINTHIANS 6:9–10: MALAKOI

The next three refutations address the flawed reliance on the literal interpretation of KJV verses without considering historical and linguistic context. All three scholars note the same problem of translating the Greek word malakoi*—which literally means "soft" in I Corinthians 6:9—into the word "effeminate" and how both* malakoi *and "effeminate" referred to specific character qualities of the time, not to contemporary notions of homosexuality.[39]*

I CORINTHIANS 6:9–10 AND I TIMOTHY 1:10: *ARSENOKOITAI*

Even more controversial is the translated phrase "them that defile them-selves with mankind" from the word arsenokoitai *in I Corinthians 6:9 and I Timothy 1:10, which is a difficult word to translate because it seems that Paul was the first person to write it down. All three scholars believe the word refers to male prostitutes.*[40]

JUDE 7: STRANGE FLESH

Finally, all three scholars interpret Jude 7's reference to "going after strange flesh" in Sodom to mean angels instead of homosexuality.[41]

But none of these passages address or refute transgender identities. Mol-lenkott's book, *Omnigender*, however, makes a biblically affirming case for transgender identity by refuting the complementarian view tradition-ally interpreted by fundamentalists: that the creation account in Genesis naturally divides the gender binary into males and females. Instead, Mol-lenkott argues against the notion that "our current male-female polariza-tion is based on the image of God. It isn't. God is not literally male and female and neither is the human race. People's experience, biology, and psychology have alerted us to the facts of human gender diversity, and the creation accounts of Genesis 1 and 2 do nothing to undercut or refute those facts."[42] In other words, Mollenkott's comments about Genesis 1 re-fute BJU's current statement about gender identity in the student hand-book's appendix B by addressing the most relevant of the three passages mentioned.[43] Her commentary would also support what Rachel Oblak and Blair Durkee mention in their stories about people with intersex and other genetic conditions whose bodies do not conform to a strictly binary view of sex.

This brief section about refuting fundamentalist interpretations of scripture should equip queer students at BJU with substantive, prelimi-nary ideas on how better to see themselves (mis)represented in the Bible. It could also help them better define and defend their authenticity against the immersive fundamentalist curriculum on campus to make the school more accountable in their ministry. But I do not recommend a direct, vo-cal approach by students to defend their authenticity or to demand ac-countability from the school unless they are willing to risk their student status or privileges. The stories in this collection show that BJU expects complete conformity and does not welcome theological or administrative scrutiny. In the next section, I briefly share a more recent student example that confirms this.

What Does BJU's Future Look Like?
Dependency and Potential Change

At the beginning of this chapter, I asked about the queer potential of BJU's future, specifically in the way it might remain queer (separate, strange) to the outside world as well as what that future might mean for closeted queer (non-normative) BJU students. But how can I assume there will be queer students at BJU in the future?

Given the separatist nature of fundamentalism that causes children and adolescents to become psychologically, financially, and emotionally dependent upon their parents or guardians, my prediction is that queer students will continue to find themselves at BJU for reasons similar to those given by the contributors to this collection. David Diachenko's story comes to mind as an example of this kind of fundamentalist family dynamic. Even at age sixteen, David was heavily dependent on his father, who, in one part of the narrative, would not allow David to be counseled at the clinic alone outside the authoritarian presence of his father. A similar kind of student reliance on fundamentalist parents is evident in the *2020–2021 Student Handbook*, which requires students to receive their parents' approval when selecting the "right" local church to attend.[44] BJU has always embodied the *in loco parentis* principle by sharing parental power with fundamentalist parents over its students, so this church selection policy is just another example of how college students heavily depend on authority figures both at home and school.

So, what will BJU look like at one hundred years old, in 2027? Given its financial troubles and faculty layoffs in 2018 and more furloughing of employees in 2020 because of the COVID-19 pandemic, a cynical observer might ask, "Will BJU make it to one hundred years?"[45] I am not invoking schadenfreude here. Instead, I want to consider how the stories represented in this collection can expose the unsafe status of the conscientious, queer Christian who might find themselves on BJU's campus at a future date. We absolutely acknowledge that BJU is a private institution that can govern at its own discretion. But we in this book can publicize those policies to educate potential queer students that the campus environment is not a healthy one—at least for now.

Perhaps change can be brought about in mysterious ways on campus.

I briefly described in the introduction how BJU made major institutional changes about regional accreditation and interracial dating. These examples reveal how BJU established policies based on scriptural principles, then lost control of that authority through outside pressures. In both cases, BJU conveniently "re-aligned," at least in part, its doctrinal foundations to accept a twenty-first-century mindset, revealing inconsistencies of administrative practices to the casual outsider and severe biblical contradictions to the fundamentalist insider: if the Bible is inerrant and infallible, why has BJU allowed such major policy changes that were based on biblical principles? Since the Bible verses have not changed, is it more the interpretation and application of those verses by the first three presidents of BJU? And if that is the case, will this show the next generation that even the president of BJU can be fallible? And who is to say whether BJU's biblical worldview on other topics, such as sexual orientation and gender identity, might be modified in the future?

I must admit: the fact that Avery Wrenne notes in their story that they could recently come out to one of their professors without fear of being turned in is quite radical to me as a student from the twentieth century. Their story gives me hope that change is possible . . . at some point. But while a queer-affirming campus at BJU may exist outside the realm of possibility for the foreseeable future, the voices included in this book can serve as the catalyst for some kind of change, not unlike the changes BJU has already implemented in other matters, such as with regional accreditation and interracial dating.

Rhyming History: The Equality Act and REAP

If it is more correct to say that history rhymes rather than repeats itself, let us consider a developing case that may invoke similarly recurring sounds and statements from BJU's past. On March 17, 2021, BJU President Steve Pettit announced his concern for the troubles that the current Equality Act could cause for the school. The Equality Act, which was passed by the U.S. House of Representatives and has yet to be discussed in the Senate, "would add gender identity and sexuality to the groups protected under the Civil Rights Act, while significantly weakening exemptions for religious groups and people."[46] Pettit worries that this will drastically affect the school's religious liberty in many ways, including how the government could "potentially deny federal financial aid to students at faith-based colleges and universities unless those schools abandon policies and practices reflecting their sincerely held beliefs about marriage and sexuality."[47]

In the introduction, I briefly plotted BJU's previous run-in with the Civil Rights Act and resistance to racial integration, showing how BJU's tax-exempt status was still at risk in the seventies after admitting Black students with interracial dating restrictions. In 2021 history is not repeating itself; it's more like a rhyming amalgamation of BJU's twentieth-century separatist stance on religious liberty against government sanctioned integration and regional accreditation. BJU's fear of losing is the same, but the stakes of what could be lost has compounded to include not just tax-exempt status but also its financial aid for students and its accreditation status.

Less than two weeks after Pettit's announcement, another potential legal challenge surfaced. On March 29, 2021, the Religious Exemption Accountability Project (REAP), which is sponsored by the national non-profit, Soulforce, filed a class-action lawsuit—*Elizabeth Hunter et al. v. U.S. Department of Education*—with thirty-three plaintiffs who attended religious colleges in the United States. Paul Carlos Southwick, the director of REAP and an attorney representing the plaintiffs, commented that religious schools should not be receiving government funding and be allowed to invoke Title IX religious exemptions that discriminate against sexual orientation and gender identity.[48] In the class-action complaint, each plaintiff briefly tells their story of discrimination based on their school's policies against the queer community. Elizabeth Hunter, whose name is first on the suit, graduated from BJU in 2019.

From what Hunter has shared in the lawsuit, newspaper articles, and on REAP's website and social media, her story resembles various ones in this collection. For her first three years, she was in good standing with the school, but she was ambushed with a surprise three-hour meeting with university officials about her social media posts, such as tweeting "Happy Pride" and reading and writing literature featuring lesbian characters. When pressured to confess that she was gay, Hunter admitted that she was "not straight" but suggested she might be asexual, like the Apostle Paul. She also refused to denounce the queer community. According to Hunter, BJU punished her by taking away her campus job, putting her on disciplinary probation, making her take counseling sessions with the dean of women, and fining her seventy-five dollars.[49]

Hunter's story is a sobering example of how BJU is "Still Standing, but Not Standing Still" by illustrating old and new manipulative and punitive tactics. Just as Megan Millikin described, Hunter was ambushed into a traditional meeting designed to evoke a confession, but with the help of new technology, the administration used printouts of Hunter's social media against her. Just as Sandra Merzib and Andrew Bolden were, Hunter was required to attend counseling sessions, but unlike the contributors in this book, Hunter was additionally punished in a new way that is consistent with my discussion earlier in this chapter: a monetary fine for her sins. Hunter was forced to pay seventy-five dollars for her sins. Let me repeat that for the readers in the back: Elizabeth Hunter was required by BJU to literally pay for her own sins.

In the previous section, I repeated the question about the consistent presence of queer students at BJU. Hunter herself represents a major demographic attracted to places like BJU: in the words of Southwick, "A lot of 17-year-olds don't have the agency to choose their school." He adds that "many are committed to their faith" and may be looking for a way to be free from their struggles. Elsewhere in that same article, he critiques the popular question I mentioned in the introduction—"Why would queer people go to BJU?"—by suggesting that the question itself is a form of "gaslighting, because the assumption is they don't belong there." Southwick argues that queer students will always attend Christian colleges because queer people will always be "in those Christian communities."[50] *BJU and Me* confirms his assertion through its stories from students across the decades who represent that queer population Southwick is referencing. In their stories from decades past, they mention how BJU's religious liberty took aim at issues like interracial dating and regional accreditation. In 2021, the Equality Act and the REAP lawsuit mark BJU's latest controversy with religious liberty and the government, and this time the controversy is officially against the queer community.

Petimus Credimus: Time for Change

The long-standing motto of BJU has been *Petimus Credimus*, which means "we seek, we trust." As BJU explains in its promotional materials about its motto, it wants students to seek knowledge and to trust "the Bible as the inspired Word of God."[51] I invoked *Petimus Credimus* on this book's dedication page to several different families I belong to, not out of irreverence, but out of celebration. The motto's literal translation has a flexibility to connote different meanings for different communities. For example, what I "seek" from my extended family may differ from what I "seek" from my chosen family or from the general public. In a broader scope, the writers of this book want to queer BJU's version of *Petimus Credimus*.

When trying to articulate this queering, I wanted to write something clever by adding some kind of twist to the motto, such as *Petimus Credimus Queerimus*. But that doesn't work linguistically, and it seems forced. The more I think about it, the more I realize I don't have to alter the literal words of the motto. Instead, I can appropriate the translated meaning behind it. In this case, we *seek* affirmation and we *trust* that our stories will create an open-minded conversation so that queer students who may find themselves at BJU in the future can be valued for *who* they are, not *in spite of* who they are.

It has often been suggested that a successful way of changing someone's mind about a topic is to humanize it by attaching a face, or name, or story to that topic. Several contributors to this collection noted their preconceived notions about queer people based on what they had been told from the pulpit or the fundamentalist classroom, only to discover that they had been misinformed once they met queer people. Our book of stories can have a similar kind of impact by humanizing queer people for those from resistant religious or other kinds of conservative communities.

In a queer twist, it seems that even Jim Berg believes in the humanizing power of queer stories. Allegedly. According to Ellis's article, this is what Berg had to say about the 2019 CoRE Conference: "Hearing personal stories from people with same-sex attraction helps to ease the 'hard edge' that some Christians have demonstrated toward the LGBT Community." He encouraged the hundreds of students and conference attendees to listen to people from different backgrounds and different lifestyles.[52] Despite the fact that Berg uses terms like "same-sex attraction" and "lifestyles," which reinforce the school's inability to think beyond the fundamentalist construct of pathological sexual identities, and despite the fact that he doesn't take any ownership for his own "hard edge" practices with former students like Sandra Merzib, I say we should take his statement as an invitation. He needs to hear our stories about the dangers of fundamentalism and a controlling institution that lacks accountability. He needs to appreciate our experiential resistance against an oppressive ideology. He needs to listen. Change is possible when people listen. *Really* listen. Perhaps because of what he said, other Christians will begin to listen to his admonition, despite Berg's own history of insensitive actions.

The literary precedent for this kind of humanizing change has already been suggested in the BJUniverse from Rich Merritt's memoir, *Secrets of a Gay Marine Porn Star*. In Merritt's story, he mentions his friendship (and rivalry) with classmate Bob Jones IV during their time in school. Years later, as adults, Merritt reconnects with Jones IV and is pleasantly surprised that Jones IV maintains his friendship with Merritt, in spite of Merritt's renegade status with the school. Though Jones IV, according to Merritt, says he does not affirm Merritt's queerness, Jones IV does believe in the importance of Christians having queer friends.[53] It is not a stretch to interpret Jones IV's positive attitude toward Merritt as a result of his personal connection and history with him. In light of Berg's recent charge for Christians to listen to queer stories, we can take Merritt's story about Bob Jones IV as a hopeful sign that perhaps someday there will be an affirming place for queer students at the world's most Christian university. Through such openness BJU could truly show the world that it is "Still Standing, but Not Standing Still." That is why I tend to gravitate partially toward the sentiments of Southwick, who says the lawsuit is not trying to close religious schools. Instead, he argues that "the aim is to apply pressure, from within and without, to get them to change."[54] We need to continue telling our stories to make that change happen. Who knows? Maybe in time, in the queer future, the impossible will be possible: a new queer BJU.

From a New Heaven and a New Earth to a New Future

In the introduction, I briefly defined the word "queer" and applied it to four concrete meanings. As I close this chapter, I want to think about "queer" as a state of being so we can focus on the future, an optimistic future, a new future. Scholar José Esteban Muñoz notes that "queerness is a longing that propels us onward, beyond romances of the negative and toiling in the present. Queerness is that thing that lets us feel that this world is not enough, that indeed something is missing."[55] We former fundamentalists can relate to his sentiment; we were trained to believe that this world is missing something because it has been irreparably broken by sin, and because of that sin, someday this world and time will end. But until then, we remain in this imperfect world, working toward a perfect life after this one.

But now that we recognize ourselves as members of the queer community, we think about the future in a different way. It may still be as life beyond the present, beyond this imperfect world, but now, outside of fundamentalism, our perspective has changed about what we think makes a better future, *a new future*. As Muñoz says, "Queerness is essentially about the rejection of a here and now and an insistence on potentiality or concrete possibility for another world."[56] This rejection he mentions reminds me how we now recognize our past indoctrination about our fundamentalist future. His comments here elicit comparisons between a "concrete possibility" and fundamentalist thoughts about the terrestrial and the celestial, the earth and the world beyond the earth that we as fundamentalists believed we had been promised according to the Bible: a "new heaven and a new earth," as it says in Revelation 21:1. But now, I instead want to think of a new future that openly acknowledges and values the lives, desires, and experiences of our past that BJU tried to erase, a past it tried to deny when preaching against or casting out queer students. This kind of queer future looks beyond this present world as a way of resisting its current practice of reducing identities to an abomination. It is a future fundamentalists are scared to envision, but it has been a past that former queer BJU students have been afraid to relive.

When describing how queer students feel at BJU, Elizabeth Hunter says, "We all live in fear of being caught, of being outed, of being expelled, of facing discipline for just existing."[57] I have not yet met Elizabeth Hunter, but her compelling words deftly paint the colors of anxiety at the forefront of the queer student's mind. Every day on campus counts as a potential opportunity for a surprise interrogation. *BJU and Me* embodies the time that we both lost and found in our collective lives and experiences while living in and leaving fundamentalism. As Reid points out in his chapter, BJU uses isolation as a tactic to shame queer students into remaining silent inside the void of the past. But not anymore. This book uses voices from the past to call for a new future, exposing BJU's futile attempt to erase our truth and keep its "institutional closet" without blemish.[58]

In David Levithan's novel *Two Boys Kissing*, the narrator is a chorus of dead voices of gay men who died of AIDS. At one point, the chorus describes how empowering our future can be: "What a powerful word, *future*. Of all the abstractions we can articulate to ourselves, of all the concepts we have that other animals do not, how extraordinary the ability to consider a time that's never been experienced. And how tragic not to consider it."[59] It is invigorating to think about the potential for BJU's new future as well as the future for the queer students who may attend the school. I can picture Pride flags hoisted up all the poles that used to stand across the Bridge of Nations on front campus, emblazoned with affirming possibilities. That would really make BJU "the Opportunity Place" it once marketed itself to be. As the chorus in Levithan's book suggests, it would be tragic not to think about all future possibilities, including how BJU's queer future could look once it began to listen, aspire for accountability, and change—truly change.

The voices in this book say the best time to change is now.

Notes

1. Adair and Adair, *Word Is Out*; Babinski, *Leaving the Fold*; Curtis, *Revelations*; Dann, *Leaving Fundamentalism*; Lemke, *Gay Voices from East Germany*; Morris, *Southern Perspectives on the Queer Movement*; Whitlock, *Queer South Rising*.

2. Lemke, *Gay Voices from East Germany*, 1.

3. Babinski, *Leaving the Fold*, 13.

4. Whitlock, *Queer South Rising*, xix.

5. Halberstam, *In a Queer Time and Place*, 1. Halberstam says, "Queer uses of time and space develop, at least in part, in opposition to the institutions of family, heterosexuality, and reproduction." See Halberstam, *In a Queer Time and Place*, 6 and 152–53 for more about queer time.

6. Halberstam, *In a Queer Time and Place*, 4.

7. Flores, "Image Polishing"; Bob Jones University, "Bob Jones University 2016–2017 Annual Report," 14; *BJU Today*, "Minority Students Lead New Student Organization"; Associated Press, "Bob Jones University Schedules"; BJU Today, "BJU's Academic Year."

8. *Bob Jones University Student Handbook, 2020–2021*, 14, 31.

9. *Bob Jones University Student Handbook, 2019–2020*, 28.

10. *Bob Jones University Student Handbook, 2020–2021*, 6; Turner, *Standing without Apology*, 40–41; Cooper, "Bob Jones University Becomes"; *Bob Jones University Student Handbook, 2020–2021*, 35–36.

11. Quigley, "Locks Coming to Campus"; "NAPCO Security Technologies Announces."

12. *Bob Jones University Student Handbook, 2020–2021*, 49–50.

13. "BJU Granted Regional Accreditation"; Cary, "Bob Jones University Regains."

14. BJU PR, "BJU Nursing Program."

15. Nicholson, "SC Colleges"; Bob Jones University, "Higher Education Emergency Relief."

16. *Bob Jones University Student Handbook, 2020–2021*, 43, 26, 44.

17. *Bob Jones University Student Handbook, 2020–2021*, 23–24, 13, 54.

18. *Bob Jones University Student Handbook, 2018–2019*, 2.

19. *Bob Jones University Student Handbook, 2020–2021*, 8.

20. Ellis, "Why Bob Jones University Hosted."

21. Bob Jones University Seminary, "CoRE Conference 2015"; Bob Jones University Seminary, "CoRE Conference 2016"; Bob Jones University Seminary, "CoRE Conference 2018"; Bob Jones University Seminary, "CoRE Conference 2019." It is unclear why the year 2017 is missing.

22. Quoted in Ellis, "Why Bob Jones University Hosted."

23. The words of Jesus in John 6:37 are especially poignant here: "All that the Father giveth me shall come to me; and him that cometh to me I will in no wise cast out."

24. Ellis, "Why Bob Jones University Hosted"; BJUnity, "Statement on BJU's CoRE Conference for 2019."

25. Mitchell, "'Get This Off the Books.'"

26. Wyman, "1996 Archive Story."

27. Connor, "Greenville County Anti-gay Resolution."

28. Mitchell and Walters, "Greenville County Council Race"; Mitchell, "Measure That Would Have Rescinded." Incidentally, the county council voted on this same issue on March 4, 2020. On this day, in a committee meeting that met two hours before the regular meeting, Bob Taylor and Joe Dill had voted to cancel the 1996 resolution. However, they changed their votes in the regular meeting after hearing opposing community members use scripture as part of their argument.

29. Bob Jones University Seminary, "CoRE Conference 2020."

30. Street, "Distortions of God "; Street, "Distortions of God—PPT Slides"; Street, "Distortions of God—Notes."

31. Riddle, "Bob Jones University Issues Response"; Grace, "GRACE: The Final Report."

32. Berg, "Ministering to Those"; Berg, "Unmasking Addiction."

33. Mollenkott, "About Virginia Ramey Mollenkott." Virginia Ramey Mollenkott passed away on September 25, 2020. We owe her a tremendous amount of gratitude for her scholarship and energies she put into providing biblical encouragement for the next generation of queer students.

34. Miner and Connoley, *The Children Are Free*, 3; Arthur, *The Sex Texts*, 61.

35. Arthur, *The Sex Texts*, 61.

36. Scanzoni and Mollenkott, *Is the Homosexual My Neighbor?*, 60.

37. Arthur, *The Sex Texts*, 63–64; Miner and Connoley, *The Children Are Free*, 10–12; Scanzoni and Mollenkott, *Is the Homosexual My Neighbor?*, 63–66.

38. Arthur, *The Sex Texts*, 68–69; Miner and Connoley, *The Children Are Free*, 12–16; Scanzoni and Mollenkott, *Is the Homosexual My Neighbor?*, 66–74.

39. Arthur, *The Sex Texts*, 67; Miner and Connoley, *The Children Are Free*, 16–18; Scanzoni and Mollenkott, *Is the Homosexual My Neighbor?*, 78.

40. Arthur, *The Sex Texts*, 67; Miner and Connoley, *The Children Are Free*, 16–22; Scanzoni and Mollenkott, *Is the Homosexual My Neighbor?*, 76.

41. Arthur, *The Sex Texts*, 61; Miner and Connoley, *The Children Are Free*, 6–7; Scanzoni and Mollenkott, *Is the Homosexual My Neighbor?*, 61–62.

42. Mollenkott, *Omnigender*, 92–93; See also, Mollenkott and Sheridan, *Transgender Journeys*, 48–52.

43. *Bob Jones University Student Handbook, 2020-2021*, 68.

44. Ibid., 13–14.

45. Daprile, "A SC University Cuts 50 Jobs"; Wilkie, "Bob Jones University Will Begin."

46. Boorstein, "Dozens of LGBTQ Students."

47. BJU president, e-mail message to author, March 17, 2021; Pettit, "From the President: Equality Act."

48. Gilreath, "Bob Jones University Graduate"; *Elizabeth Hunter et al.*, 10–12.

49. "Elizabeth Hunter"; "Elizabeth Hunter Shares Her Story"; Boorstein, "Dozens of LGBTQ Students"; *Elizabeth Hunter et al.*, 10–12.

50. Avery, "LGBTQ Students at Christian Colleges."

51. *Bob Jones University Undergraduate Catalog, 2018-2019*, 11.

52. Ellis, "Why Bob Jones University Hosted."

53. Merritt, *Secrets of a Gay Marine*, 305.

54. Avery, "LGBTQ Students at Christian Colleges." My partial leaning towards Southwick's perspective is my own opinion and not representative of the contributors to this

book. I have a feeling many contributors and the larger BJUnity community would be divided on this topic.

55. Muñoz, *Cruising Utopia*, 1.
56. Ibid.
57. Gilreath, "Bob Jones University Graduate."
58. Turner, *Standing without Apology*, vii; Ephesians 5:27.
59. Levithan, *Two Boys Kissing*, 155.

glossary of BJU terms

This glossary should help the reader better understand the queerness of BJU's separatist culture, but it is not meant to be an exhaustive list. Instead, these terms—which were used, practiced, or implemented at one time by the student body or the administration during BJU's history—are listed because they are mentioned by the contributors in their stories. For reader convenience, I have listed after each term the names of the contributors who use it, in the order their stories appear in the book. As the nature of language and terminology is fluid, some of these terms may not still be in use at BJU, but preserving the terms here helps to reflect the times of respective contributors. I have not attempted to pinpoint the exact time period when each term was used, but in certain cases, I have added details from my personal experience.

Artist Series: Required formal events on campus—such as dramatic productions, operas, and concerts—designed to culturally enrich and socially engage students. Intended as dating opportunities. Mentioned by Lance Weldy, Andrew Bolden, and Micah J. Smith.

Assistant Prayer Captain (APC): Every dorm room is assigned a spiritual leader, either an assistant prayer captain or prayer captain. An APC is the lowest member of the spiritual leader hierarchy in the dorms. Primary responsibilities include leading devotions when prayer group meets in the APC's room and spiritually evaluating roommates at the end of the year for potential spiritual leadership advancement. Mentioned by Lance Weldy, Andrew Bolden, Micah J. Smith, and Sandra Merzib.

Barge Memorial Hospital: The hospital on BJU campus that served as its primary medical facility. At one point during BJU's history, students were only allowed to miss classes due to illness if they checked into Barge. Mentioned by Elena Kelly and Avery Wrenne.

Bible Conference: A week-long series of multiple church services and sermons per day that substituted for a spring break during the spring semester. Mentioned by Lance Weldy, Fawn Mullinix, Marshall, Blair Durkee, David Diachenko, and Steve Shamblin.

Boj/Boje/Bojo: Slang for students who take the rules seriously and are not afraid to turn in rule-breakers of any kind to the spiritual authorities. Mostly a derogatory term. Mentioned by Micah J. Smith and Peter Crane.

Call Slip: Formal summons to meet with an administrator or spiritual superior. Mentioned by Andrew Bolden.

Campus Parents: Faculty and staff who act as surrogate parents to help students acclimate to campus and adjust to living away from home. Mentioned by Jeff Mullinix.

Campused: Prohibited from leaving campus. Disciplinary action resulting from accruing too many demerits in a given semester. On page 19, the *Bob Jones University Student Handbook, 1997–1998*, lists this punishment for when a student reaches one hundred demerits. Mentioned by Curt Allison.

Chapel: Mandatory service for undergraduates at 11 a.m., typically four times a week, forty-five minutes long, and including singing, announcements, and some form of sermon or admonition. Mentioned by Bill Ballantyne, Andrew Bolden, Megan Milliken, Curt Allison, Micah J. Smith, Reid, Blair Durkee, David Diachenko, Steve Shamblin, and Avery Wrenne.

Chaperone: Members of the BJU campus with trusted university status to oversee social interactions between undergraduate men and women students in a variety of contexts on and off campus. Typically graduate assistants, faculty, and staff. Mentioned by Lance Weldy, Andrew Bolden, Fawn Mullinix, Reid, Jeff Mullinix, and Christy Haussler.

Check, Doesn't Check; Checkable, Uncheckable: Colloquially ascribed status to materials and behaviors that are or are not sanctioned by the listed or unlisted rules and expectations of BJU. *Used in a sentence:* I walked by a friend's dorm room and politely warned him not to play music by the new age artist Enya because her music doesn't check. Mentioned by Andrew Bolden, Curt Allison, Sandra Merzib, and Jeff Mullinix.

Choir Tour: Part of the overarching promotional campaign of the university in which students from a specific university choir tour a specific part of the country for approximately a week during the semester, visiting and singing for Christian schools and churches in the BJU network. Mentioned by Andrew Bolden.

Dating Outings: Social events hosted once a year by individual literary societies, formal or casual, and either on or off campus. Traditionally, casual dating outings were one of the few events when hand-holding during games between men and women could be allowed. Mentioned by Lance Weldy, Fawn Mullinix, and Christy Haussler.

Dating: Technically, any instance where a man and woman undergraduate student may find themselves in the same space relatively alone—no matter if the two individuals know each other or not. Requires a chaperone or third party to prevent the appearance of impropriety or the temptation for improper physical interaction. Mentioned by Lance Weldy, Bill Ballantyne, Andrew Bolden, Sandra Merzib, Rachel Oblak, Peter Crane, Jeff Mullinix, Steve Shamblin, and Christy Haussler.

Dean of Men and Dean of Women: University officials who specifically deal with a variety of matters, including disciplinary ones, pertaining to the male or female population of the student body. Mentioned by Lance Weldy, Andrew Bolden, Fawn Mullinix, Micah J. Smith, Marshall, Reid, and Jeff Mullinix.

Demerits: Unit of measurement for negative behavior. Accruing specific amounts in a given semester leads to ever-increasing negative consequences and restrictions. Throughout most of BJU history, accumulating 150 demerits in one semester meant expulsion. Mentioned by Lance Weldy, Andrew Bolden, Curt Allison, Micah J. Smith, Sandra Merzib, Blair Durkee, Peter Crane, Jeff Mullinix, Elena Kelly, and Christy Haussler.

Dorm Counselor: Second-highest spiritual leader in every dormitory building. Typically a graduate student who is studying for the ministry or who has a respected spiritual reputation. Duties may include problem-solving minor disputes and providing biblical counseling to undergraduate dorm students. Mentioned by Lance Weldy and Sandra Merzib.

Dormitory Supervisor: Highest spiritual leader in every dormitory building. Usually significantly older than the undergraduate students. Duties may include administering demerits for infractions and determining what student-submitted materials can be allowed in the dorms. Mentioned by Andrew Bolden, Fawn Mullinix, Micah J. Smith, Marshall, Sandra Merzib, and Jeff Mullinix.

Ensembles: Traveling student groups that represent the university through music or dramatic ministries, often for a few months over the course of a semester or a summer. Also called "ministry teams." Mentioned by Andrew Bolden, Curt Allison, Marshall, Steve Shamblin, and Christy Haussler.

Extension: Any form of community service with an implicit or explicit element of ministry attached. Examples include singing at nursing homes, providing Sunday morning special music at local or out-of-town churches, passing out religious tracts, and witnessing to passersby on nearby Clemson University's campus. Mentioned by Lance Weldy, Bill Ballantyne, and Andrew Bolden.

Hair Check: A grooming rule regulating the length of hair on men's heads. Given without warning, this is a visual test applied by hall leaders to undergraduate male students, typically as they walk to their chapel seats. Mentioned by Peter Crane.

Hall Leader: BJU's equivalent of a resident assistant. The highest undergraduate spiritual leader on every dormitory hall. Also serves as the prayer captain in his or her respective room and prayer group. Duties include problem-solving student conflicts, inspecting dorm rooms, and administering demerits for various room- or behavior-related infractions. Also called "floor monitor" or "hall monitor." Mentioned by Lance Weldy, Bill Ballantyne, Andrew Bolden, Fawn Mullinix, Megan Milliken, Sandra Merzib, and Jeff Mullinix.

Lights-Out: The time of night when students must be in their dorm rooms. At one time, most students were required to be in bed, sleeping, with lights out at 11 p.m. Mentioned by Lance Weldy, Fawn Mullinix, and Jeff Mullinix.

Prayer Captain (PC): The spiritual leader over an individual dorm room as well as over two or three nearby dorm rooms with assistant prayer captains. Primary responsibilities include leading spiritual devotions when prayer group meets in the PC's room and spiritually evaluating roommates and APCs within the PC's prayer group at the end of the year for potential spiritual leadership advancement. Mentioned by Lance Weldy, Sandra Merzib, and Jeff Mullinix.

Prayer Group: A group of individuals from three or four dorm rooms in proximity that meets in one room from 10:30 to 10:45 p.m. for a time of spiritual enrichment typically led by either the APC or PC. The location rotates weekly among the group's dorm rooms. At one time, this group met every night except Sunday and Wednesday, when each room would conduct its own prayer group session colloquially called "room group." Mentioned by Lance Weldy, Andrew Bolden, Fawn Mullinix, Sandra Merzib, Blair Durkee, and Jeff Mullinix.

Purge: Colloquial term for moments in BJU's history when significant numbers of students (or faculty) disappear from campus simultaneously as a result of being expelled for any number of reasons, including committing serious infractions and naming other involved people as part of a confession. Mentioned by Bill Ballantyne and Christy Haussler.

Rising Bell: The time when students must have both feet out of their beds and on the floor. At one time in BJU's history, dorm students were required to have both feet on the ground for rising bell at 6:55 a.m. until after the hall leader checked the room. Then the students could go back to bed. Mentioned by Lance Weldy and Fawn Mullinix.

Shipped: Expelled. Disciplinary action as a result of accruing 150 demerits. Usually includes a variation of the phrase "withdrew at request of the administration" on transcripts. Traditionally, being shipped means a student is not allowed to return for a year, but this sentence is subjective and can be longer. Mentioned by Lance Weldy, Bill Ballantyne, Fawn Mullinix, Megan Milliken, Sandra Merzib, Rachel Oblak, Peter Crane, Jeff Mullinix, Elena Kelly, Christy Haussler, and Avery Wrenne.

Social Parlor: Colloquially called the "dating parlor." A university-designated space on front campus designed for co-ed interaction at allotted times. At one time, the space provided equipment to play ping-pong, foosball, and a host of board and card games (but not face cards). Before the advent of cell phones, this was also a space where couples could use a shared phone to talk to their parents. Mentioned by Lance Weldy.

Socialed: Prohibited from dating. Disciplinary action resulting from accruing seventy-five demerits in a given semester as noted on page 19 of the *Bob Jones University Student Handbook, 1997–1998*. Mentioned by Micah J. Smith.

Society: Formally known as literary societies. BJU's version of the Greek fraternity and sorority system, with mandatory membership for most undergraduate students. At one time, societies would meet once a week, usually on Fridays, during the time allotted for chapel. Mentioned by Lance Weldy, Curt Allison, Micah J. Smith, Blair Durkee, David Diachenko, and Christy Haussler.

Spiritual Probation: A period of time when an undergraduate student must work on spiritual or character shortcomings as deemed by the university through some form of periodic meetings with spiritual leadership. Mentioned by Andrew Bolden and Marshall.

Vespers Programs: Required events, usually devotional dramatic or musical productions, produced periodically on Sunday afternoons. Mentioned by Fawn Mullinix.

bibliography

Adair, Nancy, and Casey Adair. *Word Is Out: Stories of Some of Our Lives*. San Francisco: New Glide Publications, 1978.

Adams, Tony E., Stacy Holman Jones, and Carolyn Ellis. *Autoethnography*. New York: Oxford University Press, 2015.

"Androgen Insensitivity Syndrome." *U.S. National Library of Medicine*. Accessed May 5, 2017. https://medlineplus.gov/ency/article/001180.htm.

Arthur, L. Robert. *The Sex Texts: Sexuality, Gender, and Relationships in the Bible*. Pittsburgh: Dorrance Publishing, 2013.

Associated Press. "Bob Jones University Schedules 1st-Ever Spring Break." April 8, 2015.

Avery, Dan. "LGBTQ Students at Christian Colleges Face More Harassment, Survey Finds." *NBC News*, March 22, 2021. Accessed March 30, 2021. https://www.nbcnews.com/feature/nbc-out/lgbtq-students-christian-colleges-face-more-harassment-survey-finds-n1261752.

AWANA. AWANA Clubs International. Accessed May 1, 2017. https://www.awana.org.

Babinski, Edward T., ed. *Leaving the Fold: Testimonies of Former Fundamentalists*. Amherst, N.Y.: Prometheus Books, 1995.

Bagley, William. "William Bagley: Reflections on a Christian Experience." In *Leaving the Fold: Testimonies of Former Fundamentalists*, edited by Edward T. Babinski, 185–192. Amherst, N.Y.: Prometheus Books, 1995.

Barker, Meg-John, and Julia Scheele. *Queer: A Graphic History*. London: Icon Books, 2016.

Beale, David O. *In Pursuit of Purity: American Fundamentalism since 1850*. Greenville, S.C.: Unusual Publications, 1986.

Beale, David O. *S.B.C. House on the Sand? Critical Issues for Southern Baptists*. Greenville, S.C.: Unusual Publications, 1985.

Beasley, Myron M. "'Tribute to the Ancestors': Ritual Performance and Same-Gender-Loving Men of African Descent." *Text and Performance Quarterly* 28, no. 4 (2008): 433–57.

Berg, Jim. "Ministering to Those That Are Struggling with Same-Sex Attraction—Jim Berg, CoRE 2019." BJU Seminary, February 19, 2019. YouTube.

https://www.youtube.com/watch?v=A2FSCp6aRj4&list=PLwwHdT2Vrw
Kz3ExawQm5SEAU71H_H8i94&index=8.

Berg, Jim. "Unmasking Addiction—Jim Berg." BJU Seminary, April 3, 2020.
YouTube. https://www.youtube.com/watch?v=NeYw_Mh3k_Q.

"BJU Granted Regional Accreditation." Bob Jones University. Accessed June 15,
2017. http://www.bju.edu/news/2017-06-accreditation.php.

BJUnity. "About." Accessed January 25, 2022. https://bjunity.org/about/.

BJUnity. "Statement on BJU's CoRE Conference for 2019." January 15, 2019.
https://bjunity.org/confronting-hatred/6873/.

BJU PR. "BJU Nursing Program Earns CCNE Accreditation." Bob Jones University, November 4, 2019. https://today.bju.edu/news/bju-nursing-program
-earns-ccne-accreditation/.

BJU PR. "BJU Presents *Titanic: The Musical.*" *BJU Today*, March 5, 2019.
https://today.bju.edu/news/bju-presents-south-carolina-premiere-of
-titanic-the-musical/.

BJU Today. "BJU's Academic Year to Start Earlier in 2020." President's Newsletter, December 2019. Accessed January 5, 2020. https://today.bju.edu
/president/presidents-newsletter-december-2019/?fbclid=IwAR2QqvJoMCA
asrYEv1bSPnjyqV1FoEoZ3aazmd_Bv7WJQHDMS3Z_W8hh7Lo#section10.

BJU Today. "Minority Students Lead New Student Organization." President's
Newsletter, November 2020. Accessed December 1, 2020. https://today
.bju.edu/president/presidents-newsletter-november-2020/?utm_source
=bju&utm_medium=email&utm_campaign=presidents-newsletter&utm
_content=2020-11&utm_term=btn-cta#section6.

Bob Jones University. "Bob Jones University 2016–2017 Annual Report." Bob
Jones University Alumni. Accessed June 15, 2021. https://bjualumni.com
/site/user/files/1/2017-Annual-Report—-printable.pdf.

Bob Jones University. "Higher Education Emergency Relief Fund Reporting."
Last modified June 30, 2021. Accessed July 12, 2021. https://www.bju.edu
/coronavirus/reporting.php.

Bob Jones University. "September Chapel Messages." Accessed June 1, 2021.
https://web.archive.org/web/19990422201127/http://www.bju.edu
/whatsnew/chapel/chap9609.html.

Bob Jones University. "Statement about Race." Accessed June 1, 2016. http://
www.bju.edu/about/what-we-believe/race-statement.php.

Bob Jones University. "*Titanic: The Musical.*" Accessed October 8, 2019. https://
www.bju.edu/events/fine-arts/concert-opera-drama/archive/titanic/.

Bob Jones University. "Undergraduate Admissions Process." Accessed April 8,
2021. https://www.bju.edu/admission/apply/admission-process.php.

Bob Jones University Announcements, 1947–1948. Greenville, S.C.: Bob Jones
University Press, 1947.

Bob Jones University Brand Communications. "History of the BJU Brand."

Accessed June 17, 2021. https://brand.bju.edu/about-our-brand/history-of
-the-bju-brand/.

Bob Jones University Seminary. "CoRE Conference 2015: In the World, but Not
of It." Accessed January 12, 2020. https://seminary.bju.edu/core-archives
/2015-resources/.

Bob Jones University Seminary. "CoRE Conference 2016: Beyond Suffering."
Accessed January 12, 2020. https://seminary.bju.edu/core-archives/2016
-resources/.

Bob Jones University Seminary. "CoRE Conference 2018: Biblical Counseling,
Psychology, and Mental Illness." Accessed January 12, 2020. https://
seminary.bju.edu/core-archives/2018-resources/.

Bob Jones University Seminary. "CoRE Conference 2019: Gender, Sexuality and
the Church." Accessed June 12, 2021. https://seminary.bju.edu/core-archives
/2019-resources/.

Bob Jones University Seminary. "CoRE Conference 2020: New Life; Hope and
Help for an Addicted World." Accessed July 4, 2021. https://seminary.bju.edu
/core-archives/2020-resources/.

Bob Jones University Student Handbook, 1970–71. Greenville, S.C.: Bob Jones
University Press, 1970.

Bob Jones University Student Handbook, 1997–1998. Greenville, S.C.: Bob Jones
University Press, 1997.

Bob Jones University Student Handbook, 2018–2019. Greenville, S.C.: Bob Jones
University Press, 2018.

Bob Jones University Student Handbook, 2019–2020. Greenville, S.C.: Bob Jones
University Press, 2019.

Bob Jones University Student Handbook, 2020–2021. Greenville, S.C.: Bob Jones
University Press, 2020.

Bob Jones University Undergraduate Bulletin, 1993–1994. Greenville, S.C.: Bob
Jones University Press, 1993.

Bob Jones University Undergraduate Catalog, 2018–2019. Greenville, S.C.: Bob
Jones University Press, 2018.

The Bomb and Its Fallout: Bob Jones University v. United States. Greenville,
S.C.: Bob Jones University Press, 1983.

Boorstein, Michelle. "Dozens of LGBTQ Students at Christian Colleges Sue the
U.S. Education Dept., Hoping to Pressure Equality Act Negotiations." *Washington Post*, March 30, 2021. Accessed May 1, 2021. https://www.washington
post.com/religion/christian-colleges-lawsuit-lgbtq-equality-act/2021/03/29
/39343620-90af-11eb-9668-89be11273c09_story.html.

Boym, Svetlana. *The Future of Nostalgia.* New York: Basic Books, 2001.

Brown, M. Christopher, II, and T. Elon Dancy II. "Predominantly White Institutions." In *Encyclopedia of African American Education*, vol. 1, edited by Kofi
Lomotey, 523–26. Los Angeles: SAGE, 2010.

"The Call for Papers Website." University of Pennsylvania Department of English. Accessed June 15, 2021. https://call-for-papers.sas.upenn.edu/.

Cary, Nathaniel. "Bob Jones University Regains Nonprofit Status 17 Years after It Dropped Discriminatory Policy." *Greenville News*, February 18, 2017. https://www.thestate.com/news/state/south-carolina/article133654684.html.

Cheng, Patrick S. *Radical Love: An Introduction to Queer Theology*. New York: Seabury Books, 2011.

Connor, Eric. "Greenville County Anti-gay Resolution a Relic of History after Council Vote." *Greenville News*, March 11, 2020. Accessed June 5, 2020. https://www.greenvilleonline.com/story/news/2020/03/11/greenville-county-anti-gay-resolution-no-longer-applies-after-council-vote/5019899002/.

Cooper, Alex. "Bob Jones University Becomes Provisional Member of NCAA." *Greenville Journal*, June 24, 2020. Accessed November 25, 2020. https://greenvillejournal.com/sports/bob-jones-university-becomes-provisional-member-ncaa/.

Curtis, Wayne, ed. *Revelations: A Collection of Gay Male Coming Out Stories*. Boston: Alyson, 1988.

Dalhouse, Mark Taylor. *An Island in the Lake of Fire: Bob Jones University, Fundamentalism and the Separatist Movement*. Athens: University of Georgia Press, 1996.

Dann, G. Elijah, ed. *Leaving Fundamentalism: Personal Stories*. Waterloo, Ontario: Wilfrid Laurier University Press, 2008.

Daprile, Lucas. "A SC University Cuts 50 Jobs after Coming up $4.5 Million Short." *The State*, August 27, 2018. http://amp.thestate.com/news/local/education/article217396790.html.

Daulton, Jon. "Transformation through Christ." *Sermon Audio*. November 13, 2013. https://www.sermonaudio.com/sermoninfo.asp?SID=1118131045578.

Denshire, Sally. "Autoethnography." *Sociopedia.isa*, 2013: 1–12. doi: 10.1177/205684601351.

Dollar, George W. *A History of Fundamentalism in America*. Greenville, S.C.: Bob Jones University Press, 1973.

"Dr. Todd Couch." Francis Marion University. Accessed June 15, 2019. https://www.fmarion.edu/directory/couch-todd/.

Du Bois, W. E. B. *The Souls of Black Folk*. 1903. Reprint, New York: Dover Publications, 1994.

Duckworth, Angela. *Grit: The Power of Passion and Perseverance*. New York: Scribner, 2016.

Dupuy, O., M. Palou, H. Mayaudon, D. Sarret, L. Bordier, J. M. Garcin, and B. Bauduceau. "De La Chapelle Syndrome." *La Presse Médicale* 30, no. 8 (March 3, 2001): 369–72. https://www.ncbi.nlm.nih.gov/pubmed/11268892.

"Elizabeth Hunter." Religious Exemption Accountability Project. Accessed June 11, 2021. https://www.thereap.org/plaintiffs/elizabeth-hunter-.

Elizabeth Hunter, et al. vs. U.S. Department of Education. March 29, 2021. Accessed May 5, 2021. https://593f573b-1436-46c6-85bf-bd1475656bfe.filesusr
.com/ugd/0ae2d2_5609ca44db164a36aa04b0d706c2a106.pdf.

"Elizabeth Hunter Shares Her Story of Anti-LGBTQ Discrimination with Dept. of Education." Religious Exemption Accountability Project (Facebook page), June 18, 2021. Accessed June 20, 2021. https://fb.watch/6E9DyxDYy9/.

Ellis, Mike. "Why Bob Jones University Hosted a Gender and Sexuality Conference." *Greenville News*, February 15, 2019. Accessed June 5, 2021. https://
www.greenvilleonline.com/story/news/2019/02/15/why-greenville-bob
-jones-university-hosted-gender-and-sexuality-conference/2874781002/.

Engber, Daniel. "Is 'Grit' Really the Key to Success?" *Slate*, May 8, 2016. Accessed June 5, 2021. http://www.slate.com/articles/health_and_science
/cover_story/2016/05/angela_duckworth_says_grit_is_the_key_to_success
_in_work_and_life_is_this.html.

"Equality Riders Face Anti-Gay Protesters Outside Bob Jones University." *Soulforce.* Accessed May 1, 2016. https://web.archive.org/web/20190518111644/
http://www.archives.soulforce.org/2007/04/04/equality-riders-face-anti
-gay-protesters-outside-bob-jones-university/.

Flores, Christopher. "Image Polishing." *Chronicle of Higher Education*, April 5, 2002.

Gilreath, Ariel. "Bob Jones University Graduate One of Dozens of LGBTQ Students Suing U.S. Department of Education." *Greenville News*, March 31, 2021. Accessed April 5, 2021. https://www.greenvilleonline.com/story/news
/education/2021/03/30/bob-jones-university-graduate-lawsuit-us
-department-education-lgbtq-students-title-ix/4808380001/.

The Glory and the Power: Fundamentalisms Observed. Vol. 1, *Fighting Back.* Produced by William Jersey for WETA-TV. Washington, D.C.: PBS Video, 1992.

"Good Luck! Bob Jones University Looks to Recruit Black Students." *Journal of Blacks in Higher Education* 35 (Spring 2002): 65–66.

Goodnough, Abby. "Gay Rights Groups Celebrate Victories in Marriage Push." *New York Times*, April 7, 2009. https://www.nytimes.com/2009/04/08/us
/08vermont.html.

GRACE. "GRACE: The Final Report; For the Investigatory Review of Sexual Abuse Disclosures and Institutional Responses at Bob Jones University." December 11, 2014. https://static1.squarespace.com/static/5b0a335c
45776ee022efd309/t/5bb72a12a4222fafof8bd4da/1538730518938/Bob
%2BJones%2BU%2BFinal%2BReport.pdf.

Green, Deven. "Betty Bowers Explains Traditional Marriage to Everyone Else." YouTube. Filmed June 2, 2009. Posted June 2, 2009. https://www.youtube
.com/watch?v=OFkeKKszXTw.

Halberstam, Jack (as Judith Halberstam). *In a Queer Time and Place: Transgender Bodies, Subcultural Lives.* New York: New York University Press, 2005.

Henderson, Bruce. *Queer Studies: Beyond Binaries*. New York: Harrington Park Press, 2019.

Hill, Wesley. *Washed and Waiting: Reflections on Christian Faithfulness and Homosexuality*. Grand Rapids, Mich.: Zondervan, 2010.

Holland, Sharon P. "Foreword: 'Home' Is a Four-Letter Word." In *Black Queer Studies: A Critical Anthology*, edited by E. Patrick Johnson and Mae G. Henderson, ix–xiii. Durham, N.C.: Duke University Press, 2005.

Honan, William H. "Bob Jones Jr., 86, Leader of Fundamentalist College, Dies." *New York Times*, November 13, 1997. https://www.nytimes.com/1997/11/13/us/bob-jones-jr-86-leader-of-fundamentalist-college-dies.html.

Innes, David C., ed. *The Little Church of Hamilton Square: A Grand History of 120 Years*. 2nd ed. Anaheim: Pace Publication Art, 2003. http://hamilton square.net/site/user/files/1/HSBC_Book.pdf.

Johnson, E. Patrick. "'Quare' Studies, or (Almost) Everything I Know about Queer Studies I Learned from My Grandmother." In *The Routledge Queer Studies Reader*, edited by Donald E. Hall and Annamarie Jagose, with Andrea Bebell and Susan Potter, 96–118. New York: Routledge, 2013.

Jones, Bob, Sr. *Chapel Sayings of Dr. Bob Jones Sr., Founder of Bob Jones University*. Greenville, S.C.: Bob Jones University Press, 1990.

Jones, Bob, Sr. "Do Right though the Stars Fall (Chapel Address on February 1, 1957)." In *"Do Right!": Great Messages by the Eminent Evangelist and Founder of Bob Jones University*, 9–22. Murfreesboro, Tenn.: Sword of the Lord Publishers, 1971.

Jones, Bob, Sr. *Is Segregation Scriptural?* Greenville, S.C.: Bob Jones University Press, 1960. Available at https://drive.google.com/file/d/0B6A7PtfmRgT7 RjhGanZ2NF9tN2M/view. Via Camille Kaminski Lewis, *A Time to Laugh: He Has Made All Things Beautiful in His Time* (blog). http://www.drslewis .org/camille.

Jones, Bob, Sr. *The Perils of America*. Chicago: Chicago Gospel Tabernacle, 1934.

Jones, Bob, III. "Dr. Bob Jones III Discusses the Controversy Swirling around Bob Jones University." Interview by Larry King. *Larry King Live*, March 3, 2000. http://cnn.com/TRANSCRIPTS/0003/03/lkl.00.html.

Jones, Bob, III. *Taking the Higher Ground: The Accreditation Issue from the Bible Point of View*. Greenville, S.C.: Bob Jones University Press, n.d.

Jones, Stephen. "The Bible and Homosexuality." *Sermon Audio*. April 9, 2007. https://www.sermonaudio.com/sermoninfo.asp?SID=41007143356.

Jones, Stephen. "The Bible and Homosexuality 2." *Sermon Audio*. April 10, 2007. https://www.sermonaudio.com/sermoninfo.asp?SID=41007143517.

Jones, Stephen. "What Does the Bible Say about Homosexuality? Part 1." *Sermon Audio*. November 11, 2013. https://www.sermonaudio.com/sermoninfo .asp?SID=1118131039560.

Jones, Stephen. "What Does the Bible Say about Homosexuality? Part 2." *Ser-*

mon Audio. November 12, 2013. https://www.sermonaudio.com/sermoninfo
.asp?SID=1118131042244.

Kann, Laura, Emily O'Malley Olsen, Tim McManus, William A. Harris, Shari L.
Shanklin, Katherine H. Flint, Barbara Queen, Richard Lowry, David Chyen,
Lisa Whittle, Jemekia Thornton, Connie Lim, Yoshimi Yamakawa, Nancy
Brener, and Stephanie Zaza. "Sexual Identity, Sex of Sexual Contacts, and
Health-Related Behaviors among Students in Grades 9–12—United States
and Selected Sites, 2015." *Morbidity and Mortality Weekly Report Surveil-
lance Summaries* 65, no. 3 (August 12, 2016): 1–202. https://www.cdc.gov
/mmwr/volumes/65/ss/pdfs/ss6509.pdf.

Kim, Grace Ji-Sun, and Susan M. Shaw. *Intersectional Theology: An Introductory Guide.* Minneapolis: Fortress Press, 2018.

Lemke, Jürgen. *Gay Voices from East Germany.* Translated by John Borneman.
Bloomington: Indiana University Press, 1991.

Levithan, David. *Two Boys Kissing.* New York: Random House, 2013.

Lewis, Camille Kaminski. "A Is for Archive: The Politics of Research in the
Southern Archive." *Carolinas Communication Annual* 31 (2015): 15–18.

Lewis, Camille Kaminski. *Romancing the Difference: Kenneth Burke, Bob Jones
University, and the Rhetoric of Religious Fundamentalism.* Waco, Tex.: Bay-
lor University Press, 2007.

MacDonald, Dennis Ronald. "Dennis Ronald MacDonald: From Faith to Faith."
In *Leaving the Fold: Testimonies of Former Fundamentalists,* edited by Edward T. Babinski, 109–16. Amherst, N.Y.: Prometheus Books, 1995.

Mallan, Kerry. "Queer." In *Keywords for Children's Literature,* 2nd ed., edited by
Philip Nel, Lissa Paul, and Nina Christensen, 161–63. New York: New York
University Press, 2021.

Marsden, George M. *Fundamentalism and American Culture.* 2nd ed. New
York: Oxford University Press, 2006.

Marsden, George M. *Understanding Fundamentalism and Evangelicalism,*
Grand Rapids, Mich.: William B. Eerdmans Publishing, 1991.

Marshell, Tommie. "Episode 213—Live Podcast: Jeff and Steve Mullinix:
B.J.Unity." *Crackers and Grape Juice Podcast.* June 28, 2019. https://crackers
andgrapejuice.com/episode-213-live-podcast-jeff-steve-mullinix-b-j-unity/.

Marshell, Tommie. "Voices of the General Conference—Jeff Mullinix and Steve
Shamblin-Mullinix: You Are a Beloved Child of God." *Crackers and Grape
Juice Podcast.* February 25, 2019. https://crackersandgrapejuice.com/voices
-of-the-general-conference-jeff-mullinix-and-steve-shamblin-mullinix-you
-are-a-beloved-child-of-god/.

Martin, Michelle and Rachelle D. Washington. "Kitchens and Edges: The Politics of Hair in African American Children's Picture Books." In *The Embodied Child: Readings in Children's Literature and Culture,* edited by Roxanne
Harde and Lydia Kokkola, 83–94. New York: Routledge, 2018.

Marty, Martin E., and R. Scott Appleby. *The Glory and the Power: The Fundamentalist Challenge to the Modern World*. Boston: Beacon Press, 1992.

Matos, Angel Daniel, and Jon Michael Wargo. "Editors' Introduction: Queer Futurities in Youth Literature, Media, and Culture." *Research on Diversity in Youth Literature* 2, no. 1 (2019): 1–17. Accessed October 7, 2020. http://sophia.stkate.edu/rdyl/vol2/iss1/1.

Ma Vie en Rose (My Life in Pink). Directed by Alain Berliner. Blue Light Distribution, 1997.

Merritt, Rich. *Secrets of a Gay Marine Porn Star*. New York: Kensington, 2005.

Miller, Robert Nagler. "AMA Takes Several Actions Supporting Transgender Patients." *AMA Wire*, June 12, 2017. https://wire.ama-assn.org/ama-news/ama-takes-several-actions-supporting-transgender-patients.

Miner, Jeff, and John Tyler Connoley. *The Children Are Free: Reexamining the Biblical Evidence on Same-sex Relationships*. Indianapolis: LifeJourney Press, 2011.

Misztal, Barbara A. *The Challenges of Vulnerability: In Search of Strategies for a Less Vulnerable Social Life*. New York: Palgrave Macmillan, 2011.

Mitchell, Anna B. "'Get This Off the Books': Local Group Calls on County to Rescind 1996 Anti-gay Resolution." *Greenville News*, February 4, 2020. Accessed June 5, 2021. https://www.greenvilleonline.com/story/news/local/2020/01/20/local-group-calls-greenville-county-rescind-anti-gay-resolution/4493071002/.

Mitchell, Anna B. "Measure That Would Have Rescinded Anti-gay Resolution in Greenville County Fails by 1 Vote." *Greenville News*, March 4, 2020. Accessed June 5, 2020. https://amp.greenvilleonline.com/amp/4942689002.

Mitchell, Anna B., and Haley Walters. "Greenville County Council Race Is Split by a Single Vote and too Close to Call." *Greenville News*, June 10, 2020. Accessed June 5, 2021, https://www.greenvilleonline.com/story/news/politics/elections/2020/06/09/greenville-county-council-race-split-single-vote-too-close-call/5330840002/.

Mollenkott, Virginia Ramey. "About Virginia Ramey Mollenkott." Accessed April 5, 2021. https://www.virginiamollenkott.com/about.html.

Mollenkott, Virginia Ramey. *Omnigender: A Trans-religious Approach*. Cleveland, Ohio: Pilgrim Press, 2001.

Mollenkott, Virginia Ramey, and Vanessa Sheridan. *Transgender Journeys*. Eugene, Oregon: Resource Publications, 2003.

Morris, Joe E. *Revival of the Gnostic Heresy: Fundamentalism*. New York: Palgrave Macmillan, 2008.

Morris, Sheila R., ed. *Southern Perspectives on the Queer Movement: Committed to Home*. Columbia: University of South Carolina Press, 2018.

Muñoz, José Esteban. *Cruising Utopia: The Then and There of Queer Futurity*. New York: New York University Press, 2009.

"NAPCO Security Technologies Announces Large School Security Project at Bob Jones University in South Carolina." *PR Newswire*, June 18, 2018. https://www.prnewswire.com/news-releases/napco-security-technologies -announces-large-school-security-project-at-bob-jones-university-in-south -carolina-300667111.html.

NBCNews.com. "Bob Jones III Apologizes for 35-Year-Old Call to Kill Gays." March 22, 2015. https://www.nbcnews.com/news/us-news/bob-jones-iii -apologizes-35-year-old-call-kill-gays-n328281.

Nicholson, Zoe. "SC Colleges, Universities to Receive Millions of Dollars from Coronavirus Stimulus Bill." *Greenville News*, April 10, 2020. Accessed June 10, 2020. https://www.greenvilleonline.com/story/news/local/2020/04/10 /coronavirus-sc-universities-receive-millions-dollars-cares-act/5126092002/.

Northland. Northland Camp and Conference Center. Accessed May 3, 2017. https://www.northlandcamp.org.

Oral Roberts University. "General Information about ORU." Accessed June 1, 2021. https://oru.edu/news/oru-general-info-media-kit.php.

Ormiston, Jason. "Relating to Those Who Struggle with Homosexuality." *Sermon Audio*. November 14, 2013. https://www.sermonaudio.com/sermoninfo .asp?SID=1118131047190.

Pensacola Christian College. "History of PCC." Accessed June 1, 2021. https://www.pcci.edu/about/history.aspx.

Pensacola Christian College Undergraduate Graduate Catalog, 1991–1992. 1991.

Pensacola Christian College Undergraduate Graduate Catalog, 1993–1994. 1993.

Pettit, Steve. "From the President: Equality Act Hits Religious Liberty." *BJU Today*. March 17, 2021. Accessed May 5, 2021, https://today.bju.edu/president /from-the-president-equality-act-hits-religious-liberty/.

Players Guild Theatre. "*Titanic: The Musical*, May 17–June 2, 2019." Accessed October 15, 2019. https://www.playersguildtheatre.com/titanic.

Quigley, Daniel. "BJU Presents Broadway Musical *Titanic*." *The Collegian*, March 7, 2019. https://www.collegianonline.com/2019/03/07/bju-presents -broadway-musical-titanic/.

Quigley, Daniel. "Locks Coming to Campus, but What Kind?" *The Collegian*, April 20, 2018. http://collegian.wp.bju.edu/files/2018/04/Volume31Issue2 4color.pdf.

REAP. Religious Exemption Accountability Project. Accessed June 4, 2021. https://www.thereap.org/.

Religious Freedom Imperiled: The IRS and BJU. Greenville, S.C.: Bob Jones University Press, 1982.

Riddle, Lyn. "Bob Jones University Issues Response to GRACE Report." *Greenville News*, March 11, 2015. http://www.greenvilleonline.com/story/news /education/2015/03/10/bob-jones-university-issues-response-to-grace -report/24697779.

Rose, Stephanie Firebaugh, and Michael W. Firmin. "Racism in Interracial Dating: A Case Study in Southern Culture and Fundamentalism." *Christian Higher Education* 15, no. 3 (2016): 140–52.

Ruthven, Malise. *Fundamentalism: A Very Short Introduction*. New York: Oxford University Press, 2007.

Savage, Dan. "Episode 592: Teen Sexting = Big Trouble." *Savage Love*. February 27, 2018. https://www.savagelovecast.com/episodes/592#.W_sevTFRfIU.

Scanzoni, Letha Dawson, and Virginia Ramey Mollenkott. *Is the Homosexual My Neighbor? A Positive Christian Response*. New York: HarperSanFrancisco, 1994.

Slack, Kevin. "Gay Rights Movement Meets Big Resistance in S. Carolina." *New York Times*, July 7, 1998. https://www.nytimes.com/1998/07/07/us/gay-rights-movement-meets-big-resistance-in-s-carolina.html.

Somerville, Siobhan B. "Queer." In *Keywords for American Cultural Studies*. 2nd ed. Edited by Bruce Burgett and Glenn Hendler, 203–207. New York: New York University Press, 2014. https://keywords.nyupress.org/american-cultural-studies/essay/queer/.

Strauss, Valerie. "Breaking Up with Your Favorite Racist Childhood Classic Books." *Washington Post*, May 16, 2021. Accessed June 1, 2021. https://www.washingtonpost.com/education/2021/05/16/breaking-up-with-racist-childrens-books/.

Street, John D. "Distortions of God-Designed Sexuality—John Street." BJU Seminary, April 3, 2020. YouTube. https://www.youtube.com/watch?v=wFpcaagyl5U.

Street, John D. "Distortions of God-Designed Sexuality—John D. Street Notes." Bob Jones University Seminary. Accessed June 5, 2021. https://seminary.bju.edu/files/2020/03/Street-Breakout-2-Distortions-of-God-Designed-Sexuality.pdf.

Street, John D. "Distortions of God-Designed Sexuality—Dr. John D. Street PPT Slides." Bob Jones University Seminary. Accessed June 5, 2021. https://seminary.bju.edu/files/2020/03/PowerPoint-Street-Breakout-2-Distortions-of-God-Designed-Sexuality.pdf.

Tennyson, Alfred. "Ulysses." *Poetry Foundation*. Accessed June 24, 2021. https://www.poetryfoundation.org/poems/45392/ulysses.

Thomas, Quincy. "Performing White and Fine: The Ruin of a Racial Identity at Bob Jones University." *International Review of Qualitative Research* 12, no. 2 (2019): 165–78.

"Transgender, Gender Identity, and Gender Expression Non-Discrimination." *American Psychological Association*. Accessed May 5, 2017. http://www.apa.org/about/policy/transgender.aspx.

Turner, Daniel L. *Standing without Apology: The History of Bob Jones University*. 75th anniversary ed. Greenville, S.C.: Bob Jones University Press, 2001.

United Methodist Church. "Homosexuality: Full Book of Discipline Statements." United Methodist Communications. Accessed May 1, 2017. http://www.umc .org/what-we-believe/homosexuality-full-book-of-discipline-statements.

University of Guelph. "LGBTQ2IA+ Students." Student Experience. Accessed June 15, 2021. https://www.uoguelph.ca/studentexperience/LGBTQ2IA.

Vines, Matthew. *God and the Gay Christian: The Biblical Case in Support of Same-Sex Relationships*. New York: Convergent Press, 2014.

Walsh, Brent. "Fearless Authenticity." YouTube. Accessed October 8, 2019. https://www.youtube.com/watch?v=pW-_WjIMemk.

Walsh, Brent. "Full Frontal Faith." *LifeJourney Church*, July 25, 2010. http:// lifejourneychurch.cc/audio/2010/JesusMCC-2010-07-25.mp3.

Warner, Michael. "Introduction." In *Fear of a Queer Planet: Queer Politics and Social Theory*, edited by Michael Warner, vii–xxxi. Minneapolis: University of Minnesota Press, 1993.

Weldy, Lance. "Graphically/Ubiquitously Separate: The Sanctified Littering of Jack T. Chick's Fundy-Queer Comics." In *Graphic Novels for Children and Young Adults: A Collection of Critical Essays*, edited by Michelle Ann Abate and Gwen Athene Tarbox, 263–77. Jackson: University Press of Mississippi, 2017.

Weldy, Lance. "Part 1: Wounded Children?" *BJUnity*. Accessed May 1, 2018. http://bjunity.org/who-we-are/lance-weldy-part-one.

Weldy, Lance. "Queer Life at Bob Jones: A Lecture by Lance Weldy." CLAGS: The Center for LGBTQ Studies, February 19, 2014. YouTube. https://www .youtube.com/watch?v=mQScDiAl5lQ.

Weldy, Lance. "Religious Cognitive Dissonance and the Christian Fundamentalist Teen in Aaron Hartzler's *Rapture Practice*." *ALAN Review* 46, no. 3 (Summer 2019): 35–46.

Wells, Sandy. "Innerviews: Gay Teacher Shares Story of Journey to Truth." *Charleston Gazette-Daily Mail*, November 6, 2017. https://www.wvgazett email.com/news/columnists/sandy_wells/innerviews-gay-teacher-shares -story-of-journey-to-truth/article_953ce1b8-98bc-5e8b-960c-af593dfeaoff .html.

"What Does Intersex Mean?" *American Psychological Association*. Accessed May 4, 2017. http://www.apa.org/topics/lgbt/intersex.aspx.

White, Mel. *Stranger at the Gate: To Be Gay and Christian in America*. New York: Simon and Schuster, 1994.

Whitlock, Reta Ugena, ed. *Queer South Rising: Voices of a Contested Place*. Charlotte, N.C.: Information Age Publishing, 2013.

The Wilds. The Wilds Christian Association. Accessed May 2, 2017. http://wilds .org.

Wilkie, Ella. "Bob Jones University Will Begin Furloughing Staff as Coronavirus Pandemic Continues." *Fox Carolina*, April 7, 2020. Accessed June 1, 2020.

https://www.foxcarolina.com/coronavirus/bob-jones-university-will-begin
-furloughing-staff-as-coronavirus-pandemic-continues/article_9a363ea8
-7906-11ea-bbf1-d78f9abeb5a3.html.

Winell, Marlene. "Understanding Religious Trauma Syndrome: It's Time to Recognize it." *British Association for Behavioural and Cognitive Psychotherapies.*
Accessed November 6, 2019. https://www.babcp.com/Review/RTS-Its-Time
-to-Recognize-it.aspx.

"World's Most Unusual." *TIME Magazine*, June 16, 1952.

Wright, Melton. *Fortress of Faith: The Story of Bob Jones University.* Grand
Rapids, Mich.: William B. Eerdmans Publishing, 1960.

Wyman, Scott. "1996 Archive Story: County Council Votes 9–3 against Gay Lifestyles." *Greenville News*, January 20, 2020. Accessed June 5, 2020. https://
www.greenvilleonline.com/story/news/local/2020/01/20/1996-archive-story
-county-council-votes-9-3-against-gay-lifestyles/4498709002/.

about the contributors

Curt Allison (he/him) was born in Greensboro, North Carolina, and grew up in Hickory, North Carolina. He now lives in Vancouver, British Columbia, where he owns a recruiting firm and is an ordained United Church of Canada minister, serving on pastoral staff at a downtown Vancouver church. He attended BJU for three semesters from 1983 to 1984 and then transferred to Appalachian State University, where he completed his piano performance degree in 1987. He graduated from the Oral Roberts University Seminary in 1989 with a Master of Arts degree in church music. He has served through music leadership at the Naramata Centre's summer programs, the EVOLVE British Columbia youth conference, and the Imagine LGBT weekend, all United Church of Canada events. Curt and his partner live with their two Dachshunds, Jim and Bob.

Bill Ballantyne (he/him) was born in Baltimore, Maryland, and grew up in its blue-collar suburbs. He attended BJU from 1981 to 1985, receiving a Bachelor of Science degree in mathematics education. Bill taught in a Christian school for two years before pursuing a career in information technology, including becoming a certified instructor for both Microsoft's and IBM's authorized training programs. He is an amateur photographer whose photos have been used by the *Washington Post*, *Los Angeles Times*, and the National Park Service. Bill married his longtime boyfriend in July 2016, and they live in Spartanburg, South Carolina, where they both enjoy supporting the local arts scene and roller derby teams.

Andrew Bolden (he/him) is a giant ginger who prefers bow ties and bright colors, adores giraffes, and is always looking for his light. His love of period costume dramas is second only to singing in a good choir. He graduated from BJU in 1999, holds master's degrees from Converse College and Emory University, and was named a 2016 New America Fellow to support his work composing a new musical based on the Edward Snowden revelations. He resides in Massillon, Ohio, where he conducts the choir at St. Timothy's Episcopal Church and maintains a private voice studio.

Peter Crane (he/him) was born and raised near Burlington, Vermont, where he now lives and works at a microprocessor manufacturer called Global Foundries. He attended Bob Jones University from 2003 to 2007 and received his Bachelor of Science in graphic design. If Peter isn't smothering his niece and nephew with attention, you can find him knitting and cooking delicious meals with his uncles and cousin in White River Junction, Vermont. He has maintained a passion for art in many forms and can be found sketching or snapping photos around the beautiful state of Vermont with his little pup, Cujo.

David Diachenko (he/him) was born and raised in Greenville, South Carolina. He attended BJU from 1995 to 2002, completing undergraduate and master's degrees in piano performance. He also taught piano as a member of the music faculty from 2000 to 2006. David is currently a store manager with Starbucks and a board member of BJUnity. In his meager free time, he enjoys classical music, film scores, and symphonic metal, British comedy panel shows, and reading, particularly comedic fantasy. He lives in Greenville with his husband.

Blair Durkee (she/her) was born and raised in Greenville, South Carolina—the hometown of BJU. She attended BJU from 2006 to 2010, earning a degree in computer science. After college, she pursued graduate education from Clemson University in Clemson, South Carolina, where she continues to reside. Now living a happily secular life, Blair devotes herself to progressive causes in politics, media, and LGBTQ acceptance. She currently works as a consultant for GLAAD.

Christy Haussler (she/her) was born and raised in Decatur, Alabama. She attended BJU from 1987 to 1991 and received a BS in health and physical education. Christy currently lives with her wife and five dogs just outside of Key West, where they enjoy fishing, swimming, and kayaking in the crystal clear waters of the Florida Keys. Christy and her wife are active in their church in Key West, where they participate in the music program and provide technical and website services. Christy and Allison work together in their business, which helps brands and businesses connect with their audiences through technology.

Elena Kelly (she/her) was born in a Salvation Army hospital, adopted, and raised on the eastern Colorado prairie. She dropped out of high school at sixteen, and at age seventeen, she volunteered in the U.S. Navy during the Vietnam War. After she was honorably discharged, she worked as a journeyman electrician. From 1981 to 1986, she attended BJU and completed her degree in Bible. After spending time in Colorado, she moved to California and has six grown children and five grandchildren. In 2014 she retired to Thailand and assists nongovernment organizations that work to end human trafficking. She attended the local Episcopal congregation, the Devi Mandir Hindu temple, and many of the amazing and beautiful Buddhist temples in Chiang Mai. She returned to California in 2019 with plans to return to Thailand and live in Paradise.

Marshall (they/them) grew up in the western United States and graduated with high school honors in the mid-eighties. They attended Bob Jones immediately following high school and studied education. After being denied reenrollment, Marshall settled in a large midwestern city where they found their partner. Since that time, Marshall has moved to a southern state, has the same partner, a grandchild, and three rowdy dogs. Active in their local Episcopal church, Marshall has also finally been able to enroll in a university to study business and earn their degree.

Sandra Merzib (she/her) was born in Calgary, Alberta, where she still lives and works as a speech-language pathologist. She attended BJU from 1997 to 2000 and from 2002 to 2003. She completed her Master of Science degree in speech-language pathology at Nova Southeastern University in 2013. Sandra is an avid reader and music lover and has amassed a sizable collection of books and vinyl records which takes up an entire room in the home she shares with her adoring wife, Kaitlyn. Her hobbies include attending concerts and playing fetch with her fur son, Henry. On January 20, 2019, Sandra finally met Lady Gaga, and it was one of the most amazing experiences of her life. She is grateful for the opportunity to hug Gaga and thank her in person for changing her life.

Megan Milliken (she/her) graduated with a BA in history from BJU in 2006. She graduated from law school in 2009 and now owns her own law firm in Wilmington, North Carolina. She is engaged to her long-term partner, McCall, who graduated from the BJU nursing program in 2005. They live with a menagerie of animals, including two dogs and two cats, and enjoy going to the beach and spending time with their nieces.

Fawn Mullinix (she/her) was born in Nashville, Tennessee, and grew up in Pennsylvania, where she now lives. She has a successful career with the federal government and has recently started an online business called MooseGear Brand. She attended BJU from fall of 1997 to January 1999 and completed her bachelor's in psychology at Clearwater Christian College in 2002. Fawn's interests include CrossFit, bowling, documentaries of all types, and sipping good whiskey with friends.

Jeff Mullinix (he/him) was born and raised in Dayton, Ohio. He is currently a pastor in the United Methodist church, where he serves at Foothills United Methodist Church in Bonney Lake, Washington. He attended BJU from 1978 to 1980 and then transferred to Cedarville College, where he received his BA in communication arts in 1985. He also received an MA in religious education from Southwestern Baptist Theological Seminary in 1995 and an MDiv from United Theological Seminary in 2011. Jeff has a passion for social justice issues, especially regarding the LGBTQ community and the church. He has been married to his husband, Steve Shamblin, since December 2016.

Rachel Oblak (she/her) was born and raised in Chesapeake, Virginia. She attended BJU from 2005 to 2008 and transferred to the University of Vermont, where she obtained a BA in psychology in 2011. She obtained a master's in clinical mental health counseling in 2017 from Antioch University. She now lives with her partner in Vermont, where she has a private psychotherapy practice specializing in working with trauma, survivors of toxic and controlling systems, and LGBT individuals. She has been published in the *International Journal of Cultic Studies* and has spoken at conferences about factors influencing worldview change and wellness within counselor education.

Reid (he/him) was born and raised on the far edge of Honolulu County in Hawaii before traveling to South Carolina in 2004 to study broadcasting at BJU where he received a bachelor's in 2009 and a master's in 2011. He worked a few years in local television news, where he discovered his interest in news media is a hobby, but not a career. He resides in Greenville, South Carolina, where he enjoys the growing arts, culture, and food scene and studying the Japanese language with the small Japanese community in the area.

Steve Shamblin (he/him) came out while a faculty/staff member at BJU in 1999 and is one of the founding members of BJUnity. He is married to Jeff Mullinix, a United Methodist minister, and is an activist for LGBTQ+ inclusion in the UMC. He holds a BA in art and an MS in counseling from BJU, and he has a BS in education from West Virginia State University. From 2002 to 2019, Steve was a high school English and art teacher in West Virginia, a four-year member of the district's Diversity Collaborative, and three-year president of the district's Professional Staff Development Council. From 2004 to 2019, he held executive officer positions in AFT–Kanawha Local 444, a local in the American Federation of Teachers union, and a state executive board member for AFT–West Virginia. Since 2020 he has worked as a middle school English Language Arts and Advancement Via Individual Determination teacher with Tacoma (Washington) Public Schools.

Micah J. Smith (he/him) was born in Denver, Colorado, and grew up in Maryland, where he now lives. He attended BJU from 2002 to 2003, then transferred to Pensacola Christian College, where he was later forced to withdraw. He passionately volunteers at various nonprofit organizations in his community and has been an active member of a local nondenominational church since 2008. Other interests of his include music, gardening, and interior decorating. Micah currently resides in Bel Air, Maryland, with his partner, Mike, Mike's two daughters, and their Chiweenie named Baxter.

Lance Weldy (he/him) received his BA in creative writing from BJU in 1998. Later, he earned his MA in English at the University of Illinois–Springfield and his PhD in English at Texas A&M University–Commerce. During the 2006–2007 academic year, he was a Fulbright Fellow junior lecturer in Germany. He is professor of English at Francis Marion University in Florence, South Carolina, where he specializes in teaching children's and young adult literature.

Avery Wrenne (they/them) was born in Greenville, South Carolina, and attended Bob Jones University's primary and secondary schools. From 2011 to 2012 and 2013 to 2015, they attended BJU before transferring to Converse College, where they completed their degree in music in 2017. Avery now lives in Vancouver, British Columbia, where they are a social worker. They are passionate about music, practicing yoga, and spirituality, and love taking walks around Vancouver and enjoying the beautiful natural scenery. Their goal is to work from a queer-centered, trauma-informed social work approach with LGBTQ2IA+ populations and eventually teach social work or gender studies.